The Culture of Enterprise
in Neoliberalism

Routledge Advances in Sociology

For a full list of titles in this series please visit www.routlege.com

The Culture of Enterprise in Neoliberalism

Specters of Entrepreneurship

Tomas Marttila

Routledge
Taylor & Francis Group
NEW YORK   LONDON

First published 2013
by Routledge
711 Third Avenue, New York, NY 10017

Simultaneously published in the UK
by Routledge
2 Park Square, Milton Park, Abingdon, Oxon OX14 4RN

Routledge is an imprint of the Taylor & Francis Group,
an informa business

Library of Congress Cataloging-in-Publication Data
Marttila, Tomas.
    The culture of enterprise in neoliberalism : specters of entrepreneurship
/ by Tomas Marttila.
        p. cm. — (Routledge advances in sociology ; 87)
    Includes bibliographical references and index.
    1. Entrepreneurship. 2. Neoliberalism. I. Title.
    HB615.M3722 2013
    338'.04—dc23
    2012029044

ISBN: 978-0-415-63403-8 (hbk)
ISBN: 978-0-203-09469-3 (ebk)

Typeset in Sabon
by IBT Global.

Printed and bound in the United States of America on sustainably sourced
paper by IBT Global.

For Susanne and Rosa with love

In memory of my grandparents Aimo and Kaija

Contents

Tables

Foreword

Derrida rejected the meaningfulness of anything like a foreword. He claimed that before the foreword, there had been writing and words that would be disregarded and forgotten by any artificially set starting point. Before this foreword came into being, a considerable amount of writing was done. Before that writing, there were numerous persons without whom this book would have never been written in the first place. I would like to take the opportunity to express my gratitude to all those people and organizations that made this book possible.

First of all, my sincere thanks go to Richard Münch, the supervisor of my PhD thesis. For a young social scientist, it is all-important to be able to rely on a patient and optimistic supervisor who gives ideas—no matter how oblique—time to develop. It is due to the never-ending optimism and patience of Richard Münch that this book could mature over a period of seven years (2005–2012). I would also like to thank Richard Münch for the possibility to subdivide the original (some 500-page) manuscript into two separate books, of which this is the first, more empirical one. Writing a PhD thesis under Richard Münch's supervision appears anachronistic in a world in which social research becomes ever faster. My fellow PhD students and I at the Department of Sociology II in Bamberg found ourselves in a scientific sanctuary where we had time to immerse in theoretical if not even metaphysical discussions, become creative in the truest sense of the word, and address questions that hardly accelerated the pace of our PhD projects. In my eyes, Richard Münch is the true embodiment of a sociologist in the most positive sense; it has been immensely rewarding to work with him as a supervisor and discussion partner for so many years.

I would also like to thank Bob Jessop for offering me the opportunity to come to Lancaster and spend some four months in an intellectually pulsating environment at the Department of Sociology. I am grateful to Bob for the comments on earlier drafts of book chapters and his instructions about the usage of Occam's razor in scientific work, even though I might not quite have got it right. Bob's research on Cultural Political Economy (CPE) has been crucial for understanding the macro-economic transformations that have been going on in Sweden for quite some time. The visit to

Lancaster also made it possible for me to meet many inspiring young scientists, including Kim Kullman, Katharina Manderscheid, Ali Riza-Taskale, and Graham M. Smith. I would like to thank Ali, in particular, for having etched the four types of nihilism into my mind forever. Oliver Marchart, professor of sociology at the University of Lucerne and second supervisor of my PhD thesis, has offered a wealth of valuable comments on theoretical ideas about discourse theory. Oliver Marchart's texts on post-foundational social theory and the concept of the political have been the biggest intellectual source of influence for this book. My thanks also go to Martin Nonhoff, Rainer Diaz-Bone, and Reiner Keller for their instructions on methodological questions related to discourse analysis.

The years spent at the University of Bamberg offered me the opportunity to meet fellow PhD students participating in the doctoral program "Markets and Social Systems in Europe." First of all, I cannot praise enough Christian Schmidt-Wellenburg as a friend, colleague, and reliable critic of last resort. I would also like to thank Christian's family for the memorable time in Bamberg and the shared football fanaticism. Henrik Schillinger, Monika Radek, Monika Sander, and Dominik Heller were some jolly bunch of PhD students with whom it was a pleasure to work and spend our leisure time. Thank you for shared sporting activities, late evenings, and even having been merciless enough to beat me in your game of Skat over and over again. The three-year scholarship from the German Research Foundation allowed me to work on my PhD thesis under convenient circumstances and to take part in the doctoral program at the University of Bamberg. In 2005, a six-month grant from the Swedish Institute (www.si.se) and the German Academic Exchange Service (www.daad.de) made cultural integration in Germany a lot easier. It allowed me to cut down on my work as banquet waiter in Berlin and start making some serious plans for a PhD thesis instead.

My wife Susanne is the person without whom I would have neither written this book nor become a social scientist, not to mention having become a resident of Germany for almost a decade now. To paraphrase a great artist: life takes place while you are busy making other plans. There is no doubt that without Susanne, I would not have left my native country Sweden for Germany, started learning German, taken up a PhD thesis, ended up in Bamberg at some point, a provincial town in Upper Franconia of which I had never heard before, and finally become the proud father of our daughter Rosa. There are no words to describe how thankful I am for having met you. The last ten years have been the absolutely thrilling adventure of two Erasmus students who once met in Dublin's fair city. The birth of our daughter Rosa has accompanied the final work on this manuscript and helped to set things into the right order of relevance and replace even the slightest striving for perfectionism with more down-to-earth pragmatism.

Much to my own surprise, Routledge actually accepted the initial proposal for a book manuscript. It is a courageous decision made by the editorial team of Max Novick to publish a no-name scientist from Sweden working in Germany on a theme that hardly anything new seems to be said about. Max Novick and his colleagues at Routledge have made publishing this book a smooth and enjoyable process. Thank you also to the two anonymous peer reviewers whose critique of the initial manuscript made a substantial contribution to the final draft. Brigitte Münzel—my personal linguistic watchdog at the Department of Sociology II in Bamberg—did, as usual, an excellent job in proofreading the final draft. Brigitte has in general done a lot to improve my writing in English. Nils Ebert and Vincent Gengnagel have invested loads of time to adapting the manuscript to the Chicago manual style. Last but not least, I would like to thank my parents and my sister Ida for their untiring support.

This book was submitted as PhD thesis in 2010 at the University of Bamberg.

1 Specters of Entrepreneurship

Marx and Engels' "The Manifesto of the Communist Party" begins in the following famous manner: "A spectre is haunting Europe—the spectre of communism. All the powers of old Europe have united in the holy alliance to exorcise this spectre. The Pope and the Czar, Metternich, and Quizot, the radicals of France, and the police-spies of Germany" (2003: 125). It is no accident that communism should be called a specter. After all, what the opponents of communism exorcise are the presumed expressions and manifestations of communism in the form of opposition parties and the adversaries of power. Recently, another, this time celebrated, "spectre of entrepreneur" has appeared in Europe. Governments informed by the neoliberal principles of rolling back of the state, marketization of the public sector, transfer of responsibilities from political authorities to communities, and individual subjects have considered the entrepreneur a partner that sustains the re-orientation of the government.

Characteristic of the entrepreneurial government is how earlier collective objectives of economic growth, social security, and employment are outsourced from political institutions to enterprises and individual subjects, trusted to possess endemic entrepreneurial capacities (cf. Rose 1996: 165). Also, markets have gained an unforeseen importance following certain convictions that they enhance competition—and thus productivity—between different enterprising entities and increase the efficiency in resource utilization and allocation (Du Gay 1996: 183; Osborne and Gaebler 1993). The entrepreneurial government is also accompanied by the so-called "capability approach," which replaces, at least partly, the collective responsibility for individual social security and employment by the individualization of that responsibility (cf. Lessenich 2003a; Salais 2003; Schmid 2004; Trubek and Mosher 2003). The emphasis on the individuals' capability to be active in the government of their own social security draws on the neoliberal notion of the endemic capacity and interest of individual subjects to realize their personal life projects. However, it remains a collective responsibility to teach and advise individual subjects how they should conduct themselves so as to make the most use of their personal freedom. It is in this context that we encounter the unprecedented importance of the entrepreneur. In the framework of the entrepreneurial government, entrepreneur has become one of the projected role models and scripts of subjectivity in the form of which individuals are asked to make both a contribution to political government and to engage in active self-management of their own social welfare and employment (Bröckling 2007; Burchell 1993; Rose 1996b).

A curious aspect of the unprecedented importance of entrepreneur is how the earlier, very distinctive characteristics defined by economic theories begin to dissolve. Contrary to Schumpeter's (1961, 1928), von Mises' (1980a, 1980b), and Kirzner's (1973) notions of the entrepreneur as founder or innovator of an enterprise, the entrepreneur has turned into a metaphor that now refers to a vast number of entrepreneur-like social practices. Within the context of the entrepreneurial government, for instance, entrepreneur has become a general role model for the way social subjects should conduct themselves in order to maximize their own social security and employability. Entrepreneur has become a concept with considerable contentual variations because it could relate equally well to business founders as to "school superintendents," "principals," "airport managers," "welfare commissioners," or "labour secretaries" (Osborne and Gaebler 1993). The entrepreneur has become a specter[1] because instead of referring to a particular and distinctive social practice (founding enterprises, initiating economic innovations), it has turned into a general dictum or ethos for the way in which a number of different social practices should be carried out. As Bröckling (2007) notices, the transformation of the entrepreneur into a general role model of social subjectivity basically transforms all subjects into "entrepreneurs of themselves." A general construction of the entrepreneur involves rather complex processes of metaphoric construction, or sprectralization, which opens for projecting it on a number of unprecedented activities, projects, institutions, and social roles.

The contemporary spectral being of the entrepreneur can be illustrated by describing a passage/scene in Shakespeare's *Hamlet: Prince of Denmark* (2008), in which the "ghost" of Hamlet's father, the dead king, re-appears to first the guards and then his son (and thus the audience as well) in current time. Not recognizing the ghost at first, one of the guards wonders:

> What art thou that usurp'st this time of night,
> Together with the fair and warlike form
> In which the majesty of buried Denmark did sometimes march?
> By heaven I charge thee speak. (Shakespeare 2008: 89)

Explaining itself, the ghost advises Hamlet, "I am thy father's spirit," defining its purpose in manifesting itself to Hamlet as:

> Doomed for a certain term to walk the night,
> And for the day confined to fast in fires,
> Till the foul crimes done in my days of nature
> Are burnt and purged away (Shakespeare 2008: 117f)

The condition of the ghost is one of conceptual indeterminacy. Agamben (2007: 91) describes that it is essential for the being of a ghost to "appear threateningly . . . as an unstable signifier *par excellence*, which can assume to the diachronic signified of a perpetual wandering." In the case of Hamlet, the appearance of the ghost leads to the distortion of the existing, presupposedly natural, and normal order of the state as it becomes haunted by the suppressed past. Specters generate disorder in the social edifice since their sudden appearance puts the continuity of the present social order in question (Agamben 2007: 91, 95). What the ghost of Hamlet's father symbolizes are the past socio-historic conditions on which the present state of Denmark is founded. The ghost of Hamlet's father casts the social order into turmoil by refusing its own historical death and confinement to the past as separated from the present exercise of rule by Hamlet's uncle. Haunting now the subjects of the new social order, the dead king manifests the unsound historical origins of the present reign. In general terms, the present-day entrepreneur and the ghost of Hamlet's father have a number of similarities. First of all, both the ghost of the dead king and the entrepreneur manifest the conceptual openness of both terms. How could it otherwise be possible to comprehend that the meaning of the dead king and of the entrepreneur can change from one moment to the next? For Derrida, the spectral being of the objects of cognition, that is their conceptual indeterminacy, is possible only against the backdrop of the ontological indeterminacy of significations (Derrida 1981: 292). In terms of Althusser (1971), both the emergence of the ghost of the dead king and the projection of the entrepreneur to a number of unprecedented social activities and functions manifests a process of *overdetermination* through which new meanings are transferred to an existing object.[2]

Overdetermination is not a unilinear but rather a bidirectional process of transference of meaning involving both the concept, which is being transferred, and the objects affected by the transference. In the context of the entrepreneurial government, an entrepreneur is no longer the founder or innovator of a business but a general idea of how enterprises and individual subjects should get things done. In Hamlet, the dead king of Denmark is no longer the retired "king" but the victim of a terrible crime. The objects affected by the transference of the meaning appear in a different light when associated with the entrepreneur and the dead king, respectively. In the context of the entrepreneurial government, for instance, the unemployed are no longer involuntary victims of the market economy entitled to social welfare, but subjects who should discover their intrinsic entrepreneurial spirits in order to make themselves employable. Observed against the backdrop of the ghost of the dead king, the existing rule of the state of Denmark appears as something rotten. However, Just like the ghost of the dead king became readable and understood after it had declared—"I am thy father's spirit"—so does it become possible to associate entrepreneurship to a new set of social practices only when we have learned that "[t]he true meaning of the word [of the entrepreneur] is broader . . . than was known before" (Osborne and Gaebler 1993: xix). These kinds of re-significations are by no means innocent and without normative and ethical implications. After all, the new meanings of the entrepreneur and the dead king open up for new kinds of social agency. Just as the ghost of Hamlet's father follows a dictum—"[r]evenge his foul and most unnatural murder" (Shakespeare 2008: 118)—the social subjects associated with entrepreneurial capacities are expected to have an almost "magical effect on economics" (Greene et al. 2008: 3) or to carry out public sector reforms (Osborne and Gaebler 1993: 115).

Against the backdrop of the initial discussion, the specter of entrepreneur can be described to consist of the following elements. First, even though the entrepreneur already had a particular meaning—as defined above all in the economic theories—the neoliberal entrepreneurial government changed the meaning of entrepreneur through its promotion to a general role model for the social subjects' conduct of themselves. Second, there was a change in the meaning of things described as entrepreneurial characteristics, properties, and objectives. In both regards, we encounter a bidirectional process of *opening* of meaning and anew *closure*, or fixation, of meaning. My argument that entrepreneur is a specter denotes this process of continuous and subsequent stages of re-definition of what an entrepreneur might be exactly and what kinds of things might be possible to attribute entrepreneurial characteristics. However, the spectral being of the entrepreneur not only refers to this considerable process of re-conceptualization but also to the ontological possibility of re-conceptualization as such. Against the backdrop of the deconstructivist and post-foundational ontology of meaning, as presented further in Chapter 3, the fascinating thing about the recent construction of the entrepreneur is not the fact that its meaning and range of social applications has changed, but rather that the more extended and general meaning of the entrepreneur as a role model of social subjectivity has become a normal way of thinking about the entrepreneur. The specter of entrepreneur refers therefore to three different processes of opening, closure, and retention of meaning. However, yet another aspect must be taken into account. Contrary to Jones and Spicer's (2009: 37) argument that the entrepreneur does not have any clearly definable meaning nowadays, recent research on entrepreneurship observes a considerable enrichment of the ideas related to entrepreneurship (see Chapter 2). It appears therefore reasonable to argue that an extension of the meaning constitutes the fourth aspect in the spectral being of the entrepreneur. Furthermore, it is this extension of the meaning of entrepreneur that has made it possible to relate to a number of unprecedented social practices, institutions, and social roles of a remarkably recent date (Hodenius 1997; Marquand 1992; Reckwitz 2006). In particular, the so-called Foucauldian "governmentality studies" (Bröckling 2007; du Gay 1996; Opitz 2007) have retraced the historical origins of the recent idealization of the entrepreneur to the increasing predominance of the neoliberal rationality of political government. In other words, the historical development of the entrepreneur toward a general role model of social subjectivity reflects another, more pervasive and fundamental process of neoliberalization of the political rationality.

There is nothing new about the cultural hegemony of neoliberalism and how its ideological edifice has come to guide the thoughts and strategies of political agents worldwide. However, the mechanisms, logics, and historical stages underlying the increasing hegemony of neoliberalism have been analyzed to a lesser extent. The primary objective of this study is to detect in empirical terms how the entrepreneur as the neoliberal role model of social subjectivity has not only been established as an objective fact, but also how it has been disseminated across different social sectors, in which it has become the dominant way of thinking of how things should get done. Of course, this aspiration is ambitious. Its realization needs either a rather high degree of abstraction, to account for the dissemination of neoliberalism over space and time, or an empirical case study in a particular spatiotemporal context, in which these particular case-transgressing logics and processes of cultural dissemination become observable. The focus of the following study is constrained to Swedish political discourse since the latter is a case in point of the spectral logic of being of the entrepreneur. Moreover, considering the rapid increase in the influence of neoliberalism on political rationalities and strategies (e.g., Anderson 2005; Blomqvist & Rothstein 2000; Svensson 2001) and against the backdrop of its history as a social democratic welfare state, Sweden represents a rather counterintuitive and even surprising context for the dissemination of the ideas of entrepreneurship. Moreover, not only has the entrepreneur been the object of rather rapidly increasing appreciation, but the meaning of entrepreneurship has changed and become disseminated beyond the private business and economic system. A typical statement of entrepreneur in the mid-1990s argued that "a good climate for enterprises and entrepreneurs will strengthen Sweden's long-term competitive ability" (Government Bill 1995/1996: 207, p.11). Less than a decade later, entrepreneur had become a rather general role model for how to get things done. Indeed, more or less every person across different social spheres was considered a possible site of materialization of the entrepreneurial specter. A policy paper published in 2003 by NUTEK, the agency for regional and economic growth, voiced suspicions that:

> Entrepreneurs can be found everywhere in society. To deal with problems actively and find solutions, to turn ideas into actions or to be entrepreneurial in general–these are some characteristic traits of an entrepreneur. *One who just does!* It can be at school, on construction sites, in health care, at university or anywhere else. Some start businesses. Others mobilize their entrepreneurial potential at work as employees. Others develop ideas on improvements and

innovations. They all contribute to welfare and growth. (NUTEK 2003: 6; italics added)[3]

According to this statement, everybody who "just does" and avoids satis-faction with existing conditions fulfills the characteristics required to make oneself an entrepreneur. However, a closer look at the text reveals that becoming an entrepreneur is not without ethical implications. After all, one should not become an entrepreneur for the sake of individual satisfaction, but because entrepreneurs "contribute to welfare and growth." In other words, what seems to be a statement free from any subjection and moral-ization actually performs a considerable disciplinary function because it not only appreciates active subjects, but it also postulates that activation of oneself on behalf of the collective objectives of welfare and growth is best achieved when subjects conduct themselves in the manner of entrepreneurs. In other words, the above statement defines the societal importance of the entrepreneur by means of opposing entrepreneurs to non-entrepreneurs and activity to passivity. This asymmetrical order of distinctions is founded and justified by the reference to welfare and growth. Derrida's deconstructive approach suggests that these kinds of distinctions are constitutive of all meanings. Regarded in this way, the transformation of the entrepreneur from an economic agent with a rather limited economical function to a general, more or less society-wide role model of social subjectivity must be understood as a result of numerous moments of revision and re-significa-tion of the actual meanings, utilities, and functions of entrepreneurs.

The following study departs from the deconstructive difference-theo-retical perspective on the social construction of the entrepreneur and as a genealogical analysis discovers both different historical stages in the social construction of the entrepreneur and different moments of change that paved the way for the subsequent new meaning. Each of these his-torical sequences contained its particular *specter* (i.e., a vision) of the true meaning of the entrepreneur as based on a set of beliefs about necessities, rationalities, consequences, and promises associated with entrepreneurial behavior. The indeterminacy of the concept of entrepreneur described by the difference-theoretical perspective opens an indissoluble gap between the actual and potential meanings of entrepreneur along with the possibility to wonder whether the entrepreneur might actually be something else than has been assumed so far. Opitz (2007: 104) has argued that entrepreneur might actually function—in terms of Deleuze and Guattari (2003)—as a "chiffré," that is, a point of projection and condensation of various mean-ings. In this regard, it would be the immanent conceptual openness of the chiffré of entrepreneur, which explains both the considerable diachronic variation of the meaning of the entrepreneur and the possibility of its estab-lishment as a widely appreciated role model of social subjectivity. Now this deconstructive point of view is certainly helpful for understanding the conceptual openness of the entrepreneur, and yet it explains nothing about the equally numerous attempts at not only anew pinpointing, but actually also at stabilizing and reproducing a particular definition of entrepreneur. The following study will therefore have to analyze both the openings and closures in the genealogy of the entrepreneur and interpret the development of the entrepreneur toward a general role model of subjectivity while looking back on the overall process of historical transformation.

The focus of the study is confined to one case (Sweden), one particular social domain (political government), and a historical period of time covering 1991–2004. Despite these restrictions of the analysis, the achieved empirical results are believed to be of such general and generalizable nature that the present case study can be well compared to similar developments in, for instance, the Thatcherite culture of enterprise in the 1980s (e.g., du Gay 1991; Heelas & Morris 1992; Rose 1996) and the consequences of the recent German labor market reforms (e.g., Bröckling 2003; Pühl 2003). In general, the Swedish case is believed to reflect a more universal, nonlinear, and hybrid pervasion of neoliberalism. However, an answer to the question of whether this is the case must be left to further case studies. Chapter 2 starts with an overview of the recent research of entrepreneurship and postulates the necessity to adapt a social constructionist point of view on the social functions, utilities, and practices associated with the entrepreneur. Thereafter, the focus moves along a short culturalist conception that interprets different meanings of the entrepreneur resulting from various mutually distinctive cultural systems and locates the recent idealization of the entrepreneur in the particular ethos of the neoliberal culture of enterprise. The concluding part of the chapter supplies a number of different social forms of interaction involved in the social construction of the entrepreneur and thereafter revisits the research questions and the overall structure of the book.

2 The Culture of Enterprise

Over the last few decades, different scientific disciplines have established a remarkable number of accounts to elucidate the terms of entrepreneurs, entrepreneurship, and entrepreneurialism (e.g., Blum and Leibbrand 2001; Heelas and Morris 1992: 16; Henrekson and Roine 2007; Smyth 2004: 440). Despite this prolific record, Jones and Spicer (2009) have noticed, among others, that entrepreneurship literature has tried somewhat in vain to determine what entrepreneur might be exactly. Even Casson, who elaborated one of the few cohesive economic theories on entrepreneurship (Casson 1982), has noted in a review of entrepreneurship literature that this "literature is extremely diffuse" (Casson 1990: XIII; cf. Henrekson and Roine 2007: 65). Similar observations of the conceptual ambiguity of the entrepreneur have been made by Blum and Leibbrand (2001), Henrekson (2005), Mahieu (2006), Greene et al. (2008), Lavoie and Chamlee-Wright (2000) and Pongratz (2008). Due to the obfuscating language encountered when trying to define entrepreneurship, it does not appear possible to pinpoint the essence of the literature. Neither does a historical review of the literature on entrepreneur and entrepreneurship embracing prominent social and economic scientists like Richard Cantillon, Karl Marx, Joseph Schumpeter, Frank Knight, or Mark Casson seem helpful due to broad conceptual and theoretical discrepancies. Indeed, the most interesting dimension of entrepreneurship literature does not reside in substantial theories, but in the recent proliferation of the scientific interest in how entrepreneurship is performed and how it supports achievement of political goals.[1] Blum and Leibbrand (2001: 16) notice that the semantic element of "entrepreneur" marks a point of exceptional interest to social researchers active within different disciplinary contexts, whether they be sociology, psychology, business administration, political science, or economics. The variety of perspectives, theories, and frames involved is observable through the variety of definitions of the entrepreneur. Against the backdrop of the prolific and obviously heterogeneous literature on entrepreneurs, the initial section of this chapter will not try to define exactly what an entrepreneur is, but instead make use of recent accounts to point out the meaningfulness of a social constructionist and culturalist analysis of how entrepreneurs are defined across different times and spaces.

RESEARCH ON ENTREPRENEURSHIP: AN OVERVIEW

In classical economic theory, the term "entrepreneur" was related to a person who performs innovative activities within the sphere of the market. In *The Theory of Economic Development* (1961: chapter 2), Schumpeter emphasized the creative character of the "wild spirits" of entrepreneurs and defined the entrepreneur as somebody who creates a "new" or "innovative" combination of present resources. An entrepreneurial subject attains an economic break-even due to its inherent capacity, willingness, and pursuit of achievement. As Swedberg (2000: 15f) points out, an entrepreneur was not regarded as a permanent social status or role but rather as the outcome of socio-economic activities; as such, entrepreneurs are observable with regard to the economic activities pursued. Moreover, the entrepreneur performed its particular function within the economic processes only (von Mises 1980; cf. Bröckling 2003). The origins of entrepreneurship are, according to Schumpeter (1961), to be sought in the inner incentives of a person, the motivation toward achievement, and the sensation of pleasure provided by innovation. As von Schmidtchen (1995: 607) explains, the possibility of ascribing entrepreneurs a more decisive role for economic processes and general economic performance is congruent with conceptions that attribute to them the capacity of agents who intensify competition. The economic importance of the entrepreneur derives from their conception as economic actors who, due to their composition and mindset, exercise considerable influence on the development of markets. The reciprocal relation between individual characteristics and development of markets is nothing new: after all, Weber (2006) observed already how the ethical maxims of Protestantism supported the development of the capitalist economy. Moreover, Weber characterized the entrepreneur as an individual with a rather distinctive ethical stance and lifestyle, whose endemic inventory and spirits generated the cultural expansion of the new spirit of capitalism (Weber 2006: 58f).

Whereas earlier accounts of entrepreneurship located the functions, utilities, and practices of entrepreneurs into private business and economic system, du Gay (1991: 49) has observed that since the emergence of the "New Wave Management Theory," at least entrepreneurial subjects have become essential assets for business strategies and, therefore, "excellent companies seek to cultivate enterprising subjects—autonomous, self-regulating, productive individuals." Also, and Pongratz and Voß (2003, 2000) have noticed a recent reconceptualization of employees as "entrepreneurs." In other words, the entrepreneur has successively lost its earlier definition as an economic inventor. What is new about the recent focus on entrepreneurs is not that much the interest as such, but far more the extension of the validity of entrepreneurial values, utilities, and functions from economy to further social arenas. As Perkin (1992: 36) notes, there is nothing new to the economic importance of entrepreneurs and entrepreneurship. The recent thematization of entrepreneurs expresses a "resurgence" of 19th-century civic culture ideals in contemporary social awareness. Similarly, Hode-nius (1997) speaks about a recent social "mythification" and revival of the well-known historical character of entrepreneur. In the same manner, Marquand (1992) describes, above all, the British debates on enterprise culture as an echo and revival of an earlier 19th-century entrepreneurial ideal of petty capitalism. Also Farrell (2001) argues that what is unprecedented in the resurgence of the present "entrepreneurial age" is not its themes, concepts, and ideas; after all, entrepreneurs and "entrepreneurial basics haven't changed for the past thousand years" (Farrell 2001: xviii). The novelty, according to Farrell (2001), resides in the articulated necessity of the general society-wide awakening of the entrepreneurial spirits (cf. Lavoie and Chamlee-Wright 2000; Steyert and Katz 2004).

Some commentators interpret concerns to disseminate entrepreneur-like conduct beyond the economic realm as reflecting the socio-cultural demands caused by the transition from a Fordist to a post-Fordist economy (Amin and Malmberg 1994; Jessop 1993, 1994). Amin and Malmberg (1994: 229) argue that the resurgence of the culture of enterprise symbolizes "a general shift in emphasis at national policy level, from the philosophy of interventionism to entrepreneurialism." In a similar tone, Jessop (1994: 267) has observed that within the post-Fordist economy, economic innovations are believed to originate from the general "liberation of the animal spirits of entrepreneurs." An especially significant feature of this notion is that entrepreneur is located within a wider socio-economic imaginary connecting economy, state regulation, and functions of individuals as subjects of society. Harvey (1989) has also identified a general shift of government from "managerial" centrist governing, which endeavored to achieve a modernization of economy and infrastructure in the framework of the Keynesian state, toward an entrepreneurial government, which tries to reach the political goals by trusting the innovative capacities of entrepreneurial subjects. In this regard, rational political government means "to develop entrepreneurial potential as the mainstay of urban and regional growth rather than the redistribution policies of central government" (Amin and Malmberg 1994: 240; cf. Jessop 2002: 189). Within the wider imaginary of the emerging or developed age of post-Fordism, entrepreneurship is also one of the factors determining the levels of international competitiveness of national economies. The idea of "systemic competitiveness" elaborated by Messner (1996: 48, 1997) accentuates the importance of exo-economic soft factors like the origin of the economic success of enterprises and, as such, of the systemic competitiveness of the entire economy. Even so, Lavoie and Chamlee-Wright (2000) argue that culture (in the sense of societal norms, values, attitudes, and perceptions of business life) constitutes a comparative advantage and that entrepreneurial values are more likely to generate economic success than other values (Lavoie and Chamlee-Wright 2000: 53).

In the late 1980s, the Thatcherite government in Great Britain and the Reagan government in the United States regarded the commencement of an "entrepreneurial age" to be inevitable in order to achieve a new era of economic growth (see Rose 1996b). In both cases, the entrepreneur appeared as a general social ideal of how subjects should conduct themselves so as to improve the overall national economic performance. At the same time, the entrepreneur turned from an economic innovator—as had been the case in the classical theories of entrepreneurship—to a collective heroic figure. It also become considerably more ambiguous and indeterminate to highlight all the functions and utilities associated with entrepreneurs (cf. Hodenius 1997: 123; Marquand 1992). Recent documents and reports from the Organisation for Economic Co-operation and Development (OECD) and the European Union (EU) (e.g., OECD 1989, 2001; European Commission 2003) bear witness of a considerable metaphorization of the entrepreneur. For instance, the OECD (1989) report *Towards an "Enterprising" Culture* contains both a narrow and broad definition of what being "enterprising" means. In a narrow sense, it refers to "business entrepreneurialism" that "enables young people to learn, usually on an experiential basis, about business start-up and management" (OECD 1989: 6f). In the broader sense, enterprising means "having the ability to be creative and exercise initiative and responsibility and to be able to solve problems" (OECD 1989:. 5; cf. Mahieu 2006; Smyth 2004: 36ff). The narrow definition is based on a functional differentiation of societal sectors and the different activities that take place within the economic sphere. The broader definition, in contrast, falls short of such a differentiation.

The apparent conceptual ambiguity and the obvious spatiotemporal variations in the definition of the entrepreneur have paved the way for a cultural turn in entrepreneurship research. Instead of a functional analysis of the mechanisms that "produce entrepreneurship" (Jones and Spicer 2009: 11) or hermeneutic research on the life-worlds of entrepreneurship—focusing on interpretative analyses on "how entrepreneurship comes about in day-to-day fashion" (Jones and Spicer 2009: 12)—the cultural research analysis shows "the context dependent nature of entrepreneurship" and reconstructs cultural systems responsible for the various values and utilities associated with entrepreneurs (Hjorth et al 2008: 81). Peters (1992: 2) has observed that the so-called "enterprise culture" "designed for a post-industrial society of the 1990s" has become "*meta-narrative* a totalizing and unifying story about the prospect of economic growth and development based on the triumvirate of science, technology and education" (italics added). Such meta-narratives are powerful instruments of social and cultural control because they make objects possible to be known, imagined, calculated, and controlled (cf. Jessop 2002: 6f). Culture of enterprise is also closely related to a form of meta-governance, which Kooiman (2003: 185) describes as "governing principles of governing" derived from particular governmental epistemologies. Meta-governance of entrepreneurialism is by no means value-free, but presents certain limitations concerning the possible/impossible, rational/irrational, and functional/dysfunctional forms of governance.

The notion of the culture of enterprise as a kind of meta-governance is supported by recent research accounts that discovered a number of themes having been associated with entrepreneurship. For example, welfare state institutions have been observed to diminish the incentives to entrepreneurship (e.g., du Gay 1991; Heelas and Morris 1992; Henrekson 2005). The inclusion of entrepreneurialism in the context of post-Fordist economies provides general historical coordinates for the conjuncture of the "roll-back" of established welfare regimes and the "roll-out" of new regimes, rhetoric, and routines (cf. Jessop and Peck 1998: 2f; Torfing 1999: 371). Entrepreneurship has been observed to make a positive contribution to the solution of a range of actual problems related to employment or the lack thereof (cf. Audretsch 2000: 107). In Sweden and the UK, entrepreneur has been regarded as a social role whose adaptation considerably facilitates social inclusion, regional development, and an increase of employment (de Gay 1991; Mahieu 2006). In the recent German discussion on the global economic competitiveness of German industry (*Standortdebatte*), the absence of "entrepreneurship" was claimed to be one of the reasons for insufficient economic development (Audretsch 2000: 107; von Schmidtchen 1995: 607). In the German government's strategy for employment and economic growth, a great deal of interest was devoted to support the "spirit of entrepreneurship" (Audretsch 2000: 107). Similarly, Amin and Malmberg (1994: 241) observe that the EU regional policy intends "to turn localities into self-promoting islands of entrepreneurship." De (2000: 88) observes an increasing amount of attention to the competitive environment of small and medium sized enterprises (SMEs) in the EU at the turn of the 1990s. Both national governments and the EU and the OECD devoted particular interest to improving the "spirit of entrepreneurship" (Schmid and Kull 2004).[2]

However, at the same time as entrepreneurs have been observed to have made almost miraculous contributions to economy, employment, and cultural integration, it has become increasingly difficult to pinpoint what exactly might characterize the entrepreneur (Bögenhold and Schmidt 1999: 10; Smyth 2004: 437). In this regard, Steyert and Katz (2004: 182) argue that "[e]ntrepreneurship [has become] a model for introducing innovative thinking, reorganizing the established and crafting the new across a broad range of settings and spaces and for a range of goals such as social change and transformation beyond those of simple commerce and economic drive." This definition of entrepreneur as a general societal role is supported by research accounts that define innovativeness, self-reliance, risk taking, decision making, and the introduction of new ideas or activities as typical entrepreneurial characteristics (cf. Blum and Leibbrand 2001; Bröckling 2003). For instance, Gemünden and Konrad (2005: 21) define the entrepreneur in terms of a mentality characterized by activities such as "risk taking," "innovation," and "proactivity." This makes it necessary to understand entrepreneur in broader terms than functionally differentiated roles, activities, and performance within the economic system. Recent management literature has described entrepreneurship as the mode of activity required for the efficient management of organizations (cf. du Gay 1991, 1996). Different disciplines in social sciences attribute intra- and entrepreneurship, entrepreneurial culture, and business start-ups to a specific personal stance (Frick 1999: 13f). This stance is composed of, among other things, values and norms such as "achievement motives," "creativity," "self-reliance," "willingness to take risks," and "innovativeness" (Frick 1999: 13f). At the same time as entrepreneurship has become related to a set of individual characteristics that can be learned and trained, social institutions have become increasingly keen on teaching their populace the entrepreneurial mentalities and skills (cf. Bröckling 2003, 2007a; Pühl 2003; Rose 1999: 20). Bröckling's (2007a) analysis of the diffusion of ideas of personal self-management and ideas of the "entrepreneurial self" indicate how the entrepreneur has appeared as an unprecedented and general mode of societalization in contexts of management and work, but also civic society, education, and private life. Rational conduct of political government has been increasingly observed to rely on the entrepreneurial subjects' conduct of themselves (cf. Jessop and Sum 2006: 252). Efficient conduct of political government requires the presence of "a certain 'enterprising spirit', a set of values, attitudes, aspirations, and orientations in the culture, as it does upon any so-called objective and material conditions" (Lavoie and Chamlee-Wright 2000: 11).

To this point, no conclusive definition of the entrepreneur could be provided. Yet, from the short literature review, two insights emerge. First, there has been a diachronic development of meanings and significations attributed to notions of "entrepreneur" and "entrepreneurship." Second, more recent accounts have not restricted the concept of entrepreneur to an innovative economic agent, as the classical theories of entrepreneurship did, but instead related it to a general mode of social subjectivity. Pongratz (2008) describes this second trend in terms of the universalization of the social function of the entrepreneur. The crucial insight in Pongratz's remark is its placing of "entrepreneur" within a wider evolutionary process of cultural development, the full-scale realization of which would lead to a "society of entrepreneurs" (*Unternehmergesellschaft*). In a society of entrepreneurs, every individual faces the demand to assume the role of the entrepreneur. Also governmentality research has observed the progressive character of the culture of enterprise and described how the universalization of the entrepreneur correlates with the "progressive enlargement of the territory of economic theory by series of re-definitions of its object" (Gordon 1991: 45). In contrast to a teleological perspective, however, neither governmentality studies nor the cultural analysis of Williams (1977) or Reckwitz (2006) locate any underlying necessity as to why the culture of enterprise should develop into a hegemonic culture that dominates over others. Moreover, instead of arguing that the exceptional society-wide relevance of the entrepreneur would immediately reflect the transition from a Fordist to a post-Fordist economy, Reckwitz, just like recent social constructionist research on entrepreneurship, accentuates the importance of contextually particular processes, logics, and mechanisms as the cause for the increasing importance of entrepreneurs.

In his impressive analysis of the different subject cultures of the past three centuries, Reckwitz (2006) regards different subject cultures (e.g., the civic culture of the 18th and 19th centuries, the employee culture of 1920–1970 and the creative-consuming culture from the 1970s to the present) to be internally heterogeneous, to enact interchanges with parallelly existing cultures, and to adapt elements from previously predominant cultural formations. In other words, every cultural formation, and hence also the culture of enterprise, must be regarded to constitute hybrid cultural forms (cf. Reckwitz 2006: 84f). Reckwitz's deconstructive perspective on subject cultures accentuates their indeterminate, progressive, and diachronically open character. Reckwitz's notion that cultures are subjugated to permanent re-making is also an instructive meta-perspective to understand the spectral appearance of the entrepreneur. The historically open and contextually constructed conceptualization of the entrepreneur leaves us but the alternative to empirically analyze how entrepreneurs are associated with systems of meanings, values, and functions; how these cultural formations give way for changes; and how, as a result of the accumulated historical change, entrepreneur finally turns to a society-wide role model of subjectivity. The objective of the following section is to elucidate the different dimensions of the culture of enterprise and provide a conceptual operationalization that allows for a genealogical analysis of the social construction of the entrepreneur in Swedish political discourse.

THE ETHOS OF ENTERPRISE

So what is culture in general and culture of enterprise in particular? These questions are not easy to answer. After all, culture is most likely one of the most elusive buzz-words in social science. One possible point of departure is to distinguish between realist and relativist cultural theories. Realist theories tend to reduce culture to a supplement of material and objective structures, such as economy and the systems of production, and they regard cultural systems of symbols and meanings as rhetorical and argumentative resources mobilized to back up objective interests and needs (see Chapter 3).[3] In contrast, relativist cultural theories avoid any objectively determined function or structure of cultures and argue that culture has the reality constituting function. In this function, culture is the pre-condition for any meaningful access to social reality. Social subjects become aware of themselves and their social reality by means of the intermediating function of cultural systems. As Grossberg (2006: 19) puts it, this culture constitutes the reality as observed and known by social actors. In this regard, culture is the universal condition of human existence "without which he [the human subject] would be condemned to live in a chaotic reality" (Grossberg et al. 1998: 21; cf. Fuchs 2001: 6; Grossberg 2006: 14). Culture constitutes the framework within which social objects and entities become knowable (e.g., Miller and Rose 1990: 3). Cultural analysis, again, is focused on those social practices that consistently structure their own pre-conditions of being. In this regard, and as Agamben (2007: 84) argues, "human societies appear . . . as a single system traversed by two opposing tendencies, the one operating to transform diachrony into synchrony and the other impelled towards the contrary." From this perspective, we must reject the pre-determined trajectory of cultural development (e.g., Grossberg 2007; Grossberg et al. 1998). Reality becomes both knowable and controllable through cultural frames accessible at certain times. Hence, culture is closely connected to the exercise of power since different cultural frames also select reasonable and meaningful social practices.

It is the culture-specific knowledge about society itself, within which different forms of conduct of government appear conceivable, intelligible, and reasonable. As Fuchs (2001) stated, first order observations of reality are "cultured" in the sense that observations of certain objects, subjects, processes, and activities proceed habitually through the enactment of the distinctions specific for the identified and internalized culture. In order to identify the rationality and meaningfulness of particular types of observations, such as that of the entrepreneur, we must ascend to "second level observations" and look at social subjects embedding cultural systems of observation that made their "first level observations" possible. Reckwitz (2002: 246) observes the commonality in different cultural theories in their conception of social order as: "embedded in collective, cognitive and symbolic structures, in 'shared knowledge' which enables a socially shared way of ascribing meaning to the world." What distinguishes different types of cultural theory are the smallest ontological units of observation, whether one of "mind" (*cultural mentalism*), "discourse" (*cultural textualism*), "interactions" (*cultural intersubjectivism*), or "practice" (*cultural practice theory*) (Reckwitz 2002: 245). What these different post-structural cultural positions have in common is their refusal of cultural transcendentalism. We must exclude both intentionality and transcendence as origins of culture since it is always enacted and exerted within the limits of social space and results from "the way in which human intellectual, political and moral authorities, in certain places and contexts, thought about, and acted upon their collective experience" (Rose 1996: 329).

Recent constructionist research has deconstructed the objective existence of the entities such as (welfare) state (Hall 1993; Lessenich 2003b; Seeleib-Kaiser 1999), social problems such as unemployment (Baxandall 2004), and political rationalities (Anderson 2005; Clarke 2004; Cox 2001; Jessop 2000; Lindvall 2005; Nullmeier and Rüb 1993). A typical recent example of the cultural turn is the research on the cultural political economy (CPE) established, above all, by Jessop (*passim*), which regards objects, subjectivities, institutions, policies, and even the state as outcomes of spatiotemporally particular cultural processes. The welfare state, as Jessop (1999: 352) argues, should not be understood as a rational response to objectively existing social problems. Instead, "we should see welfare state regimes as constitutive of their objects of governance and not just as responses to pre-given economic and social problems." However, after the cultural turn, the state does not disappear as a meaningful object for social analysis. In contrast, our heuristic access to objects of analysis changes: instead of assuming the objective being of the objects of analysis, we must now grasp their historical and cultural conditions of existence, too (cf. Grossberg 2007: 25; Jessop and Sum 2006: 97).

As with any cultural formation, there are no a priori determined limitations to the culture of enterprise. This means that it is not necessarily confined to a particular sector of society such as market or civic society, but it may also develop "a pervasive style of conduct, diffusing the enterprise-form throughout the social fabric" (Gordon 1991: 42). The "ethos of the enterprise" essential for the culture of enterprise may come to determine an increasing number of social activities and roles (du Gay 1996: 180). The relative dominance of the culture of enterprise reflects "its capacity to disseminate itself across the society and to become the imperative for all forms of conduct" (Burchell 1993). Determined from the perspective of the culture of enterprise, the society is entirely "structured as the pursuit of a range of different enterprises: a person's relation to his or her self, his or her professional activity, family, personal property, environment, etc." (Gordon 1991: 42). The culture of enterprise is by no means a neutral re-depiction of social relations but also promotes "the politico-ethical objectives of neoliberal government" (du Gay 1996: 65). However, the culture of enterprise not only defines the objectives of political government, but also those of individual subjects. In accordance with Foucault, it can be argued that culture of enterprise is one among many other possible cultural formations through which "human beings are made subjects" (Foucault 1984: 7). The entire human history is characterized by different conceptions of the self. Even the supposedly most liberal era of modernity has demanded the subject to accept its personal individuality and to sustain and even improve its individual logic of being. In other words, individuality has turned to a cultural dictum and an inevitable fact that defines what individual subjects are and how they should conduct themselves. Individuality is in itself a result of socially disseminated and predominant cultural conceptions of the human "being" (Bröckling 2007a: 7). In other words, the presupposed natural individuality of the personal self is nothing but one of many cultural forms that have determined the adequate and natural mode of "being with the other" and being with oneself (Bauman 1991: 73f).

However, the culture of enterprise not only defines the objectives of political government and the objectives for one's conduct of oneself, but it also determines the interface between political government and the individual persons' government of themselves. As du Gay (1996: 54) argues, all governmental rationalities—"attempts to invent and exercise different types of rule—are closely linked to conceptions and attributes of those to be governed." The culture of enterprise provides a particular epistemology that dictates to political government and individual subjects their respective functions, mutual roles, and responsibilities. In short, the culture of enterprise provides an epistemology of governmental rationality as well as the conjunctures and points of coalescence, for conceptions of the social, the rationality of government within the social space, and the personal conceptions of the self. In accordance with Rose (1996c), the epistemology of the culture of enterprise can be analyzed along its political, institutional, and ethical dimensions. In the political regard, the culture of enterprise constitutes a particular system of knowledge about political institutions and their societal functions and objectives. The culture of enterprise provides an entire system of objectives, outcomes, functional strategies, and institutions of government (Miller and Rose 1990: 8). The abandoning of bureaucratic and hierarchical modes of governance on behalf of the government "through the 'enterprising' activities, and choices of autonomous entities" (Miller and Rose 1990: 8) is typical of the political rationality informed by the culture of enterprise. The institutional dimension of the culture of enterprise denotes the knowledge about strategic "complex of notions, calculations, strategies, and tactics" (Rose 1996c: 153). New techniques and measures of cost-benefit calculation, instruments for activating entrepreneurial subjects, forms of self-reflection and self-evaluation, as well as particular social roles providing consultancy on self-management and optimization are some of the typical techniques of entrepreneurial government (Bröckling 2007a). As regards the ethical side, the culture of enterprise assigns both governments and individual subjects a number of valuable and desirable goals, which these should achieve (Rose 1996c: 153). As the combined result of the political, institutional, and ethical changes instituted by the culture of enterprise, the entire society is subjugated to a general "economization of the social" (Bührmann 2005: 1). Society is getting more and more similar to "[a]n economy structured in the forms of relations of exchange between discrete economic units pursuing their undertakings with boldness and energy, ever seeking the new endeavor and the path to advantage" (Rose 1996a: 226). In this context, individuals increasingly adopt mentalities, conceptions of the self, practices, and ethical goals similar to those of the Schumpeterian entrepreneur and, as a result, become *entrepreneurs of themselves* (Rose 1996a: 226).

Even though the culture of enterprise displays similarities with the classical liberalism, governmentality research is keen on emphasizing that the culture of enterprise is attuned more strongly to a neoliberal paradigm. There are a number of differences between liberalism and neoliberalism, which confirm the neoliberal essence of the recent wave of celebration of the entrepreneurial subject. As regards the political rationality of liberalism, rational conduct of government derived from the conviction of the positive contribution that individual freedom had in Adam Smith's terms on the social prosperity (cf. Burchell 1993: 269; Dean, 1999: 103–106; Foucault 1991a: 95, 2006). Liberalism embraced a negative and skeptical point of view of the governmental capacity of political institutions based on the assumption that political regulations would distort the self-regulating capacities of the economy and civic society. However, liberalism did not require complete governmental passivity, but advanced specific knowledge of the modes of conduct through which the government could support and advance the capacity to self-regulate the economy and civil society (Miller and Rose 1990: 2). Even though the subjects were believed to be naturally free and autonomous agents, liberalism bound the freedom of social subjects to a specific subset of ethical and moral principles. The role of the government was accordingly to capacitate individuals to "exercise their freedom in the right way" and, above all, to adapt the liberal ethics of fidelity, responsibility, and self-improvement (Burchell 1993: 271).

Where liberalism departed from the "natural" autonomy and the capacity of individuals to identify and fulfill their individual interests, neoliberalism conceives of interests as something that individuals must be taught to identify, revise, and reconsider continuously. Liberalism drew a line of difference between government on the one hand and the economy and civil society on the other hand. This boundary between the political and the social was transgressed by the neoliberal government, which was assigned the role to actively introduce, sustain, and even strengthen the logics of economic market within the society. Neoliberal government has to actively support the replacement of social relations and interchanges of solidarity, trust, and empathy with the logics of economic contract, competition, and investment. As a result, the model of economic market occupies the entire society (Foucault 2006: 207ff). Being subjugated to the iron laws of market, social subjects are not only expected to conduct themselves according to the model of *Homo Oeconomicus*, but are actively taught and instructed how to apply economic calculations in all of their social roles and functions. Liberalism was geared to secure the "laissez-faire" of the economy and, afterward, to leave it to its own self-regulation. In contrast to this, neoliberalism assigns the political a far more active role in the maintenance of the intensity of economic competition.

Neoliberalism justifies political intervention into markets on the premise of a vitalization and stimulation of competition. This idea has been most clearly expressed in the "Vitalpolitik" of the German Ordoliberal economists (cf. Foucault 2006; Gordon 1991). According to Eucken, one of the most prominent Ordoliberal economists, the government should intervene into the natural course of the economy in order to decrease production costs through the intensification of competition and counteract the decrease of profits caused by the natural market tendency toward equilibrium by means of an active investment into the improvement of productivity (Foucault 2006: 198). In the American context, the vitalizing neoliberal government should also try to re-model social practices, institutions, and processes in accordance with the economic enterprise. Enterprise was by no means just a particular kind of organization form, but instead a more general logic, or even norm and ethos of organization. As Rose (1990: 145) argues, the enterprise "provides an image of a mode of activity to be encouraged in a multitude of arenas of life—the school, the university, the hospital, the GP's surgery, the factory and business organization, the family, and the apparatus of social welfare." The enterprise form of social practice is not confined to activities of economic production and investment, but functions as a rule: a measurement and standard of evaluation of social activities and organizations that "designates an array of rules for the conduct," whether those of political government, economic institutions, or private life-forms and family (Rose 1996b: 155).

If the enterprise reflects the supposedly most natural, effective, and productive way of organizing economic and social life, the entrepreneur refers to how those participating in enterprises should conduct themselves. The congruence between the enterprise—as the organizational logic—and the entrepreneur—as the model of the organizational populace—is guaranteed by the shared ethical edifice. The entrepreneur is an enterprise that has become a subject: a subject that conducts itself as an enterprise, supported by an ethos of the self as an "entrepreneur of itself" (Foucault 2006: 313). The ethos of entrepreneur is not less regulated by a range of principles and dictates than the enterprise. Just like the enterprise should invest in itself to maximize the economic yield of its capital, so do entrepreneurs. Being an entrepreneur means that one should regard oneself as another enterprise and strive "for fulfillment, excellence and achievement" (Rose 1996b: 154). In order to better oneself, the entrepreneur is guided by a number of maxims originating from the area of human and business management (Schmidt-Wellenburg 2009). Again, the guidelines for the appropriate conducts have been derived from the neoliberal theories of enterprise, which attributes the entrepreneur characteristics "such as self-reliance, personal responsibility, boldness and willingness to take risks in the pursuit of goals" (du Gay 1996: 56).

Just like enterprises should choose strategies and calculations of how to achieve excellence, so does an entrepreneur have to "calculate[s] *about* itself and . . . act[s] *upon* itself in order to better itself" (Rose 1996b: 154). When the culture of enterprise becomes increasingly dominant not only in the economy and the private business, but all over the social, and a number of activities are interpreted in terms of enterprises, the entrepreneur turns to a society-wide role model of subjectivity (cf. Foucault

2006: 314, 321). The ethos of enterprise transported and disseminated by the culture of enterprise not only idealizes the enterprise and the entrepreneur, but also installs them as standards against which the rationality of social organizations and practices can be measured, criticized, and, in the end, changed. The culture of enterprise enables a whole range of previously inaccessible problematizations of the passivity, inactivity, and modesty, which deviate from the neoliberal ethos of continuous striving for improvement. The political government with a neoliberal epistemological perspective regards the entrepreneurs as a governmental resource trusted "to be active in their own government" and, due to their capacity, to introduce innovations, increase economic competitiveness, and actively deal with risks and problems to make regulative government obsolete (Rose 1996a: 330). Rational neoliberal political government means therefore that insofar as subjects harness the role of an entrepreneur; they must be given the freedom of self-government.

The above discussion manifested that entrepreneur is not an a priori determined nominal object but rather an outcome of cultural production of meaning. Even though the Foucauldian perspective on the culture of enterprise applied so far provides valuable insights into the meanings, functions, and ethics associated with the entrepreneur, the suggested perspective on cultural hybridity limits the spatiotemporal validity of this general picture. Instead of assuming that entrepreneur has one and the same meaning across all social contexts, cultural hybridity gives reason for more rigorous empirical investigations into the historical and contextual processes that generate different ideas about the entrepreneur (cf. Grossberg 2007: 14; Reckwitz 2006, 2007). In other words, the following investigation into the social construction of the entrepreneur in Swedish political discourse must assume a genealogical perspective, which, following suit of Bröckling (2007b: 124), does not "ask what the subject is, but what knowledge was responsible for the emergence of the particular subject as a problem . . . and which procedures were taken into account in order to form it accordingly." Following Bröckling's research strategy of the genealogy of subjectivity, the following analysis has two objectives: first, to analyze the lines of diachronic cultural development responsible for the later establishment of entrepreneur as a general society-wide role model of the social subject; and second, to highlight the points of cultural variation that paved the way for the subsequent notion of the entrepreneur. The objective of this study is, accordingly, closely associated with Fuchs' (2001: 29) research on the "sociology of culture" as an analysis that scrutinizes the historical genesis of the entrepreneur as a set of "social and historical events that might have developed differently, or that might not have happened at all." Before moving toward the definition of the theoretical and analytical framework applied in the empirical analysis, it seems advisable to delineate first of all some general phenomenological dimensions involved in the social construction of the entrepreneur.

THE SOCIAL CONSTRUCTION OF THE ENTREPRENEUR

Even though this study assumes a relativist cultural perspective on the entrepreneur, and regards it as the result of particular historical and contextual processes, it appears still meaningful to elaborate a general heuristics that makes it possible to distinguish different phenomenological dimensions involved in the cultural construction of social subjectivity. Following the heuristic framework of Foucault (cf. 2002b) that has been widely adapted in cultural research, all social subjectivities can be decoded as resulting from two interwoven processes of objectification and subjectification. Entrepreneur is hence regarded as the result of these two closely entangled social processes. Objectification refers to the construction of a subject's knowledge achieved through "a process of division either within himself or from others" (Foucault 2002b: 327). In this regard, subjectivity results from the exterior construction of the particular knowledge associated with a particular subject—such as that of the entrepreneur.

Becoming a subject is a process that involves both external influence by cultural authorities and individual efforts as individuals discover their presupposedly essential being in accordance with the cultural frames, modes, and scripts (Bröckling 2007b: 121). Objectification can be further divided into two different aspects. First, the cultural systems provide structures of meaning in which subjects are associated with specific social roles, practices, functions, rationalities, and objectives. Cultural systems grant the political government access to a particular knowledge about the entrepreneur as being distinguished and separate from other subjects. Objectification not only selects particular types of subjects as meaningful objects of knowledge, but also defines their meaning. Second, the first form of objectification provides the political government with a number of possible observations of the entrepreneur, which can be further set into relation with political strategies, programs, plans, and institutions. Whereas the first level of objectification constructs the entrepreneur as a distinguishable and separable object of knowledge, the second level teaches us how the entrepreneur is interlinked with the conduct of the political government. Governmentality studies and systems theory point out that all social institutions cognize only a subset of the range of possible subjectivities as relevant objects of observation. Entrepreneur becomes a relevant and meaningful object of observation (i.e., the matter of objectification) within particular cultural systems of observation (cf. Reckwitz 2006: 52ff). Cultural systems of knowledge, symbols, and codes constitute the system of observation, within which entrepreneur becomes connected with the conduct of the political government.

The general interest of this study is to reconstruct those cultural systems of meaning, which allowed social agents involved in Swedish political discourse to observe the importance of the entrepreneur and interpret and understand it in such a manner that it appeared of essential importance to the conduct of the political government. In this regard, this study aims to provide an "observation of an observer's observation of the world" (Fuchs 2001: 24f). The general argument claiming that cultural frames function as systems of observation to know and interpret social reality does not tell us how these systems are structured. In order to understand how social agents make observations of the world, it becomes first of all necessary to elucidate how these observations are made possible. Observations, as Luhmann (1993) argues, are always specific for the observing system in which the observers locate themselves. An analysis of the social observations, and that is also to say constructions of the entrepreneur, observe the first order observations made by the social agents in terms of the assumed nature of the systemic properties, logics, and structures of their systems of observations, whether these be ideologies (Althusser), cultures (Reckwitz, Grossberg), discourses (Foucault, Bröckling), or functionally differentiated social systems (Luhmann). As Chapter 3 describes further, the analysis of the social construction of the entrepreneur cannot be a hermeneutic reading of these constructions in accordance with the sociology of knowledge of Berger and Luckmann (1991), but instead proceeds in terms of the theoretically derived epistemology of these constructions.

The assumed theoretical perspective notwithstanding, the perceived importance of entrepreneurs can be supposed to originate from objectifications enacted in various social contexts involving theoretical propositions made by social scientists, statements made by social experts, ontologization of the subject by psychiatrists, advisors, pedagogues, and the like. The assumed perspective of cultural hybridity emphasizes the inter-discursive nature and logic involved in the construction of social subjectivities (cf. Link 1988). The meaning that entrepreneur holds within the political discourse results from knowledge originating from various social contexts now coalescing into the predominant cultural system that structures and guides the observations made by the political agents. Values, meanings, and functions observed by the political government and associated with the entrepreneur turn the entrepreneur into an inclusion figure (i.e., a role in which individuals interact with the political institutions). In more general and abstract terms of the systems theory, an inclusion figure is a social role in which individual persons gain access to system specific communications (e.g., Lessenich 2003a; Stichweh 2005: 64). Inclusion figures define the terms of membership and access to the operations of different social institutions (Stichweh 2005: 67). Simmel (1992) also refers to the role of inclusion figures, which is designed to enhance interactive, inter-subjective, and social communications. The social category of the poor, for instance, consists of a system of characteristics and classifications, which political institutions apply to sort individual persons into sub-groups. When individual persons fulfill the criteria associated with the poor, they can be addressed by societal institutions of the poor relief (Simmel 1992). Of course, depending on the definition of the poor, whether being defined in emphatic or stigmatizing terms, social institutions and the poor are inter-related, or institutionally coupled, in rather different terms.

Inclusion figures do not exist independent of those cultural systems that sort out particular social roles as especially relevant and attribute to these roles their values, utilities, and characteristics. In this manner, the culture of enterprise offers a particular and distinctive set of ideas about the entrepreneur. At the same time, it also standardizes and normalizes the social role of the entrepreneur by distinguishing between relevant and irrelevant ideas about the entrepreneur. When political institutions observe individual persons in terms of entrepreneurs, they not only sort the population in accordance with this role, but also perform a standardizing and normalizing function in the sense of reproducing a particular perspective of the social role (to be) played by the entrepreneur. However, a conception of the entrepreneur conceived as normal at one time gives way to novel conceptions when the cultural system of observation changes and opens new knowledge about the presupposedly true and essential being of the entrepreneur. To conclude, objectification is a process of cultural construction of meaning that brings to the fore both objects and social roles as possible and meaningful objects of observations by singling them out and differentiating them from other objects of observation. Depending on the actually predominating cultural system of meaning, political agents possess rather different conceptions of the entrepreneur, its functions, values, and utilities, and how it is related to the conduct of political government.

As the above introduction into the culture of enterprise indicated, social subjectivities are by no means value-neutral and objective sets of meaning, but involve also particular ethical principles, prescripts, and guidelines for one's conduct of oneself. The process of subjectification refers to this active making-up of individual persons as social subjects. According to Foucault (2002: 328), subjectification denotes the way in which "a human being turns him- or herself into a subject." In other words, social subjectivity, such as that of the entrepreneur, is a means of how social institutions guide the conducts of individual persons by setting them attune to those subject roles assigned to them (Burchell 1993: 267ff; Gordon 1991). When political institutions assign subjects the subject role of the entrepreneur, they are expected to perform these functions associated with this role: starting up an enterprise, hiring labor force, providing oneself employment, acting creatively, generating innovations, etc. (cf. Bröckling 2003; O'Malley 2000). Besides the active pointing-out of appropriate social roles, subjectification also means the active making-up of individual subjects—their subjection—into these roles. Governmentality studies have observed the active deployment of "programs, strategies and tactics, through which people are transformed into subjects, and make themselves into subjects" (Bröckling 2007b: 121). In other words, the political government not only observes synergies between political institutions and different social subjectivities, but also enforces and reproduces these synergies actively through a range of measures, strategies, and programs that guarantee the beneficial conduct of individual subjects. This means that an efficacious conduct of government depends on the capacity to enforce the observed synergies that individual subjects' particular conduct of themselves has for the political government (Foucault 2006: 349; Gordon 1991: 3).

Cultural theories in general, and the governmentality studies in particular, argue that—contrary to Vico's claim that "government must conform to the nature of the men governed"—the interface between the government and the individuals is negotiated and determined within historically and contextually particular systems of knowledge (i.e., "governmentalities") (Rose 1996b: 119). Regulative forms of government discredited by the neoliberal culture of enterprise implicated that "the relation between government and the governed passes, to a perhaps ever-increasing extent, through the manner in which governed individuals are willing to exist as subjects" (Gordon 1991: 48). Foucault's conception of the general logic of (any kind of) government as "conduct of conduct" manifests how the capacity of government to reach its endeavored objectives depends on the preparedness, willingness, and capacity of individuals to adopt, perform, and retain definite social roles. It is therefore anything but surprising that political institutions should be actively involved in "attempt[s] to simultaneously maximize certain capacities of individuals and constrain others in accordance with particular knowledge (media, psychology, pedagogic) towards particular ends (responsibility, discipline, diligence)" (Rose 1996b: 153). For governmentality studies, the operations of political institutions and individual subjects are connected within heterogeneous systems of knowledge—the governmentalities—that embrace for each governmentality particular ontologies of objects of observation, knowledge about technical, strategic, and institutional possibilities, conceptions of the meaningful and valuable ends of government, and convictions about the essential nature, capacities, affinities, and interests of social subjects (Burchell 1993: 267; Dean 1996, 1999; Gordon 1991: 3; Marttila 2012).

From the point of view of governmentality studies, the recent idealization of the entrepreneur must be interpreted and understood against the system of governmentality enabled by the knowledge, to which the culture of enterprise gives access. Also, the systems theory argues that the possibility to observe the relevance of social subjects' particular conduct of themselves is the result of the observational possibilities of the system of observation. As Hutter and Teubner (1994) argue, all social institutions reduce the social complexity by means of figuring out standardized "actor fictions" about social subjects, which enables these institutions to operate in accordance with routinized expectations about the likely conducts of social subjects. In this regard, as Luhmann (1988) argues, institutions operate by means of coupling their own operations with the operations of psychic systems of individuals. In terms of Teubner (2006: 519), the construction of actor fictions implicates that every institution (here: subsystem) "attributes actions, responsibilities, rights and duties to its persons in a different way, and equips its actors with capital, interests, intentions, goals and preferences." This means that actor fictions are actually actively and deliberately imposed on the individuals (Hutter and Teubner 1994: 118).

It is enlightening to learn of both the governmentality studies and the systems theory that they describe the political institutions that observe the functions, values, and utilities of entrepreneurs, and the entrepreneurs' observations of themselves and their social roles, to be located within the same cultural system of meaning. In this regard, the culture of enterprise provides, in terms of Grossberg et al (1998: 21), a "space of mediation" among governmental objectives, conceptions of possible and functional forms of government, and individuals' conceptions of themselves. This is exactly the point made earlier about the cultural construction of reality: cultural systems provide the point of conjuncture between two previously independent social agents by setting them into the same culturally constructed world view, which again enables the transmission and reception of inter-subjectively intelligible messages. The message passed on between the sender and the recipient is intelligible insofar as it is set in a perspective that embraces the world view and conception of the self on both sides of the communication exchange. The other, the individual observed and addressed as an entrepreneur, must either already reside within the horizon of intelligibility of the culture of enterprise or be subjected to do so. However, as Brown (2004: 384) argues, communicative connectivity facilitated by cultural systems is not only inclusive but also exclusive and repressive, since retention of communication requires "silencing of alternatives and removing information such that what is transmitted is only what is already known in advance." The possibility to address individual persons as entrepreneur depends on the exclusion of the disturbing "noise" of alternative possibilities, for example, that entrepreneurial capacity might not be endemic potential of individuals at all, or that entrepreneurship might not generate the expected outcomes of more employment and growth.

However, noise remains the steady accompaniment of communication and appears as "the lurking possibility that the gap within a communication cannot be bridged" (Stäheli 2003a: 246). These communicative dissonances would prohibit both the governmental convictions of the trust in the uttermost value of entrepreneurs and individuals' capacity to conduct themselves in accordance with the subjective role model of the entrepreneur. The culture is, in two different regards, founded on the "parasite logic" described by Serres (1982). First, before the culture of enterprise became the predominant cultural system to understand the rationalities, functions, objectives, and means of governments and the social roles that individual persons should assume vis-à-vis the entrepreneurial government, their respective roles were defined in a considerably different manner. By addressing a person as an entrepreneur, government enters as a "parasite" the existing space of communications and thus either replaces existing communication flows or establishes synergies with prevailing communications. In this regard, the culture of enterprise has colonized and parasitized the existing cultural system by installing its own cultural codes. Second, considering the lurking possibility that another non-neoliberal cultural system would similarly parasitize the existing culture of enterprise and subvert its cultural codes, the culture of enterprise is subjected to the permanent possibility of its change. Both processes of cultural parasitism accompanied by the earlier described cultural hybridity express the inherent dynamic logic of cultural systems.

The processes of objectification and subjectification borrowed from the Foucauldian governmentality studies denote that the culture of enterprise not only fosters interactions between the entrepreneurial government and the entrepreneurial subjects, but also assigns both of them their respective roles. However, the Foucauldian perspective has certain difficulties to grasp the process of cultural dissemination—how cultural codes of the culture of enterprise become possible to use and understand in unprecedented situations and social contexts (cf. Reckwitz 2006). The spectral being of the entrepreneur, as manifested by its conceptual indeterminacy, is possible to decode as the result of a remarkable dissemination of the culture of enterprise into unforeseen social practices and situations such as universities (Grit 1997; Jessop 2008), political governments (Considine 2001), schools (Mahieu 2006), the civic society (Farrell 2001; Henton, Walesh, and Melville 1997), and working life (Boreham 2006; Florida 2002). Pongratz (2008) has described how this universalization of the entrepreneur to a more or less society-wide role model of subjectivity actually also implicates a considerable transformation of the concept of entrepreneur. Jones and Spicer (2009: 37) go even as far as to argue that entrepreneur is at the present impossible to define clearly because "it is essentially indefinable, vacuous and empty." However, against the backdrop of earlier theories of entrepreneurship by Schumpeter (1928, 1961), Casson (1982, 1990) and von Mises (1980b), with their distinctive definitions about the social roles, functions, and values of the entrepreneur, the increasing phenomenological indeterminacy of the entrepreneur must be conceived to result from a particular historical development. The argument that entrepreneur has nowadays lost its distinctive meaning fails to notice the considerable enrichment of the associations that there are today to entrepreneurs and entrepreneurship. Governmentality studies have observed how the establishment of the entrepreneur as the general role model of subjectivity proceeds in a manner of diffusion of "the game of enterprise as a pervasive style of conduct, diffusing the enterprise-form throughout the social fabric as its generalized principle of functioning" (Gordon 1991: 42). Conceptual over-determination of existing social practices, institutions, and subjectivities by the culture of enterprise transforms the entire society by the ethos of enterprise (Gordon 1991: 42).

The transitional model of cultural change promoted by governmentality studies potentially fails to register that dissemination of the culture of enterprise is not a process of full-scale replacement of one cultural formation by another, but also involves considerable over-layering and hybridization of cultural codes (cf. Reckwitz 2006). In other words, instead of merely accepting and observing the universalization of the entrepreneur to a general role model of social subjectivity—that "it can be [now] found in different life worlds, where it is dominant"—it must also be more closely looked on what kinds of conceptions of the entrepreneur this process of cultural dissemination creates, how earlier meanings of the entrepreneur are transported into new and unforeseen contexts, and what kinds of hybrid forms of the culture of enterprise these result in (Bührmann 2005: 4). O'Malley et al. (1997: 501; cf. Clarke 2004; Marttila 2012; Reckwitz 2006) have argued that governmentality studies provide a view of "government programmes as univocal and as overly coherent and systematic." Even though governmentality studies have made a great contribution to the deconstruction of the increasing hegemonic status of the neoliberal culture of enterprise, they have, at the same time, fallen short of recognizing the considerable temporal and spatial variety of different cultures of enterprise, and as such they also how the essence of the entrepreneur changes from time to time, from context to context.

The theoretical and analytical vigor of a difference-theoretical approach, as used among others by Reckwitz (2006) and Stäheli (1997, 2003b, 2007a, 2007c), resides in its notion of cultural systems as symbolic systems of differences. The value of each of the cultural subjectivities, symbols, and practices depends on its relational position to other cultural elements (see further in Chapter 3). The structural-semiotic approach to analyzing organizational change used in recent organization research has illustrated how the transmission of new organizational concepts creates hybrid configurations between the transported concept and the context of its reception (e.g., Andriessen and Gubbins 2009; Cornelissen 2004; Tsoukas 1993). When an organization is described in terms of a theatre, the existing notion of the organization does not disappear. Instead, "the conjunction of the tenor [organization] and the vehicle [theatre] brings forth a particular selection of each constituent's semantic aspects and reorganizes them" (Cornelissen 2004: 709). The result is a hybrid of two cultures: the cultural system of theatre and the cultural system of the organization. In accordance with this example, the dissemination of the culture of enterprise would proceed through continuous re-negotiation of the conjuncture between the constituent parts of the culture of enterprise and the cultural system in the context of its reception (welfare state, political government, universities, public administration, etc.).

This difference-theoretical approach can help us to further understand the social logics involved in the observed spectral appearance of the entrepreneur. First, entrepreneur remains notoriously indeterminate for the very reason that its actual meaning is continuously re-negotiated in the context of its articulation. Moreover, these contexts are themselves indeterminate and variable for the very reason that the dissemination of the culture of enterprise does not fully replace existing cultural systems, but leads instead to unforeseen emergent structures. Second, the use of the entrepreneur as the role model of social subjectivity in the context of universities, work, and public administration does not mean that entrepreneur should have lost its essential meaning (cf. Pongratz 2008) or that it has no determinate meaning whatsoever (Jones and Spicer 2009). The truth lies somewhere in the middle: when the entrepreneur becomes the ideal for subjects' conduct of themselves at work, for instance, some characteristics (e.g., risk-taking, will to succeed), functions (e.g., innovations; creativity), and ethical principles (e.g., self-reliance, independence) associated with the entrepreneur already earlier will be connected with existing cultural codes (e.g., hierarchical organization, rule-following) and create a newly emerging cultural system (e.g., flat organization, employees and entrepreneurs, team- and project-based work, etc.).

The still abstract ideas about the social construction of the entrepreneur underline the relevance of two research questions. First, instead of taking the increasing dominance of the culture of enterprise for granted and assuming its homological being independent of the respective spatiotemporal context, the notion of cultural dissemination as a process of inter-cultural hybridization points out that the meaning of entrepreneur is continuously re-addressed and re-negotiated. The first objective for the following study is, therefore, to analyze how different meanings, values, utilities, practices, and functions of the entrepreneur became possible to observe, and how these observations were enabled by the changes in the cultural system of observations, which dominated Swedish political discourse at a given point of time. This first research objective deals with the process of objectification: how different ideas about the entrepreneur are established in Swedish political discourse and how they are replaced by new ones. Second, if the meaning of the entrepreneur remains notoriously open for variations, it always remains unclear who is to take up the role of the entrepreneur and how these roles are performed. This second research interest focusses on the changes in the population, which political discourse considers the potential group of entrepreneurs, and the ways in which the subjects of this population should perform entrepreneurship. Chapter 9 summarizes three subsequent stages in the social construction of the entrepreneur in Swedish political discourse described as "guardian of the market economy," "active subject of society," and "creative subject," The special feature of these three sequences with their particular specters of entrepreneur is the consistent extension of the institutional contexts and social practices, in which entrepreneur became the role model for how social subjects should conduct themselves. This overall process can be described either in terms of the universalization or hegemonization of the entrepreneur. As the universalization of the entrepreneur continues, ideas about entrepreneur derived from the culture of enterprise "colonize" an extending range of individuals, institutions, and social contexts (e.g., Jameson 1990).

In terms of Foucault, the overall aim of the following study can be well described as genealogical research, which searches for the past "substitutions, displacements, disguised conquests, and systemic reversals" as the conditions of possible later political rationalities, institutional forms, and social subjectivities (Foucault 1977: 151; cf. Dreyfus and Rabinow 1982: 143). The genealogical interest implicates that it does not suffice to re-construct different social constructions of the entrepreneur in Swedish political discourse, but also point out what displacements, substitutions, and revisions of the existing ones opened up the possibility for a new and unprecedented notion of the entrepreneur. If the observations of the entrepreneur are made in accordance with the perspective opened by the cultural frame of the existing cultural system, both social constructions and re-conceptualizations of the entrepreneur must be understood and analyzed in terms of that system.

Taking the difference-theoretical perspective on cultural systems as the theoretical point of departure, Chapter 3 elucidates that accessible "objects of knowledge," such as the entrepreneur, are always the results of articulations made on behalf of a discursive system of differences. Chapter 4 translates the difference-theoretical conception of discourse into a heuristic framework that makes it possible to reconstruct different social constructs of the entrepreneur in Swedish political discourse. This chapter elucidates the "political logic" involved in the construction of the entrepreneur and different "discursive relations," "levels of discourse," and different types of diachronic discursive changes involved in the construction of different notions of the entrepreneur. Chapter 5 methodologizes the heuristic model of discourse in accordance with the methodology of the "interpretative analytics" and describes the analysis of the semantic structure as the method that makes it possible to re-construct the structural coordinates and discursive logics involved in the construction of the entrepreneur in Swedish political discourse. Chapters 6, 7, and 8 provide an empirical genealogical analysis of the social construction of the entrepreneur in Swedish political discourse. Each of the chapters includes a particular historical sequence in the overall process of universalization of the entrepreneur. This empirical study covers the period from 1991 to 2004. It starts from the initial problematizations of the lacking number of entrepreneurs in 1991 and concludes with arguments made about the universal validity of the entrepreneur as a role model of social subjectivity in 2004. Chapter 9 provides an overview of the identified genealogy of the entrepreneur and summarizes the constituent lines of difference among the three historical sequences in the construction of the entrepreneur as well as the points of substitutions and displacement among them.

3   Discourse, Difference, Meaning[1]

The value of a particular theoretical model on social reality can be judged in terms of its objectivity, coherence, or, in pragmatic sense, as a means to reduce social complexity. What absolute value post-structural discourse theory may have to offer in elucidating the social construction of entrepreneur, and whether it ought to be preferred to other models of reality, must remain beyond the scope of possible discussion in this chapter. Post-structural discourse theory is applied as a heuristic means to understand a complex social reality, and social subjects make sense of themselves and their own reality. In accordance with the ontological position of relativism, the researchers' empirical observations are limited by the epistemological limitations of the applied theoretical framework (Fuchs 2001; Marttila 2010b). One possible way of dealing with the epistemic relativism of scientific inquiry is to adapt the methodological position of reflexive methodology and explicate the theoretical bias of research itself and, therewith, facilitate its critical reading. However, in order to achieve this inter-subjective transparency, research must start with defining its ontological and theoretical point of departure and thereafter "produce, out of its own interiority, both its object and its method" (Derrida 2004: 36). The post-structural discourse theory "enables us . . . to analyze social relations and processes, while remaining faithful to our ontological commitments" (Glynos and Howarth 2007: 111). For this reason, the discourse-theoretical conception of reality must be interpreted in a manner that grants re-observation of theoretical concepts in observed empirical objects (cf. Diaz-Bone 2006b, 2007: 34). Instruments of observation must be developed from theory, and empirical objects observed must be re-traced and re-located within the theoretically defined and limited realm of knowledge. In such a manner, empirical research implicates constant "reflexive realization" of social theory in empirical analysis (Diaz-Bone 2006b: 243ff; 2007: 39).

Consistent with the post-structural discourse theory, meaning is both relative and relational. The meaningfulness of our reality derives from the relational positions of objects of perception, and these relations, in their turn, are determined within discursive formations. This argument follows Saussure's (1966) observation that the meaning attached to an object must be considered to result from the structure (of language) to which it belongs (cf. Moebius and Reckwitz 2008: 11). This indicates that the meaning of entrepreneur is the emergent outcome of a discourse about the entrepreneur. In other words, there is no such thing as an entrepreneur, only various attempts at defining its being. Following Heidegger's (2008) distinction between the physical and material existence and their social signification, every signification is separate from the object signified. Post-structural discourse theory is an effort to define how the social being—the *Dasein*—becomes established. The relation between the subject and an object of observation is always intermediated by discursive formations, which not only provide access to knowledge but also regulate and limit the possible knowledge (cf. Deleuze 1988: 70ff). This also means that knowledge is always entangled with relations of power, which control the production of knowledge. The knowledge of reality is an effect of relations of power, and power, in its turn, is exerted by means of the control and production of knowledge.

RELATIVIST ONTOLOGY OF KNOWLEDGE

There are a number of different, more or less relativist post-structural approaches to meaning that defy natural, functional, and objective determinations of the society.[2] What can be argued to unify the different post-structural discourse theories, with the exception of realist (post-)Marxist critical discourse theory (cf. Fairclough 1992), is their assumption of the immediate reciprocal relation between discourse and knowledge. A far-reaching comparison between different theories of knowledge as well as different post-structural theories of discourse must be excluded from this work. A striking contrast that nevertheless illustrates the argument under review is the distinction between "realist" and "relativist" theories of meaning. In general, the realist perspective cognizes the central role that processes of signification play for subjects' ideas about themselves and the surrounding social world. However, where realism pre-supposes the presence of a pre-discursive social reality and the possibility that it can be more or less adequately signified, the relativist perspective postulates the impossibility of any objective, while the material reality reflects significations more or less well. In this regard, discourse does "not merely mirror the world, but [it is] . . . instead partially constitutive of it" (Norval 2000: 314). In other words, social practices of signification make up the meanings about the world and not the other way around (cf. Fuchs 2001: 5ff; Glynos and Howarth 2007).

The realist perspective reduces language to a more or less transparent medium that provides symbolization for the independently existing social reality (Stäheli 1995: 363). Realist theory of language and rhetorics has been adopted, among others, by different strands of "symbolic politics"

(Edelman 1971; Majone 1989; Schmidt 2003), "ideational theories" (Blyth 2001; Hay 2002; Hay and Smith 2005), and "critical discourse analysis" (e.g., Fairclough 1992). Without intending to delve too much into their mutual differences, it is fair to say that they all pre-suppose the possibility of a "mismatch" between language and reality. Finlayson (2004: 536) epitomizes the essence of this position well when arguing that "[a] concept, such as globalization, when employed by political actors, is a political tool of use in persuading others of the virtue of necessity of a particular course of action." By means of manipulating the representations of reality, political activities can thus instrumentalize language to achieve adherence and legitimacy. In other words, the realist suggests that social objects, mechanisms, and processes exist that are possible to know, describe, and define objectively. Objects of knowledge have intrinsic properties independent of our knowledge about them. This means that there is always something to objects, "which is there and which has a structure of its own" (Laclau and Bhaskar 1998: 10) or, as Fuchs (2001: 3) puts it, "Things are what they are because that is their nature, essence or definition." The realist perspective also implicates a relation of isomorphy between objects of observation and our experience of them. Take, for instance, the meaning of a sign: isomorphy would mean that there was some kind of "literality" in this sign, which would also be possible to perceive and locate independent of the context in which the sign appears (Laclau 1993: 432).

Relativist theories on knowledge by Michel Foucault, Jacques Derrida, Ernesto Laclau, Clifford Geertz, and others deny the intransitive natural and normal being of objects beyond the pertinent social context. Even the intransitivity itself, as Laclau (Laclau and Bhaskar 1998) argues, is a theoretical construct, that is, the result of a transitive statement (cf. Deleuze and Guattari 2003: 49f). The "intransitivity of objects which is supposed to be behind all experience as the ground of all the regularities in experience is simply one more discourse which cannot be conceded to be different in quality from the discourses which are seen as transitive. . . . [T]he intransitivity of the object is in itself transitivity" (Laclau and Bhaskar 1998: 10). The being of the objects of knowledge is therefore relative to the ontological perspective assumed by the observer. Accordingly, the meaning of a material object, or of the entrepreneurial subject, depends on the epistemological perspective that allows us to interpret and understand social phenomena. Each such epistemological system "provides a mechanism for rendering reality amenable to certain kinds of action" (Miller and Rose 1990: 7). Before even being able to cognize an object, the observation is structured by the accessible knowledge preceding the act of observation (Bachelard 1978b: 9). These kinds of "epistemological hindrances," which Bachelard used to describe the limits of observation, are equally present in our everyday lives and in scientific investigations. For Bachelard, scientific inquiries do not observe objects as they are, but instead as they are assumed to be (Bachelard 1978a: 13, 164; 1988: 141). Therefore, every empirical scientific "experience is the moment of the theoretical thought" (Bachelard 1978b: 164). This also means that in order to understand the meaning associated with an object, we must first re-construct the epistemological boundaries within which this meaning was rendered possible (Bachelard 1978b: 64; Marttila 2010b).

If meanings always reflect these meanings,enabling epistemological systems of knowledge, and these again are exterior to the objects to which meanings are attached, we encounter a dynamic understanding of knowledge (cf. Bachelard 1978a: 53). However, the dynamic nature of knowledge does not result from the continuously changing relation between the observer and the observed object, but instead from the transformation of the systems of knowledge, in which objects are located. It is the heterogeneous nature of meaning that engenders the diachronic variation of meaning associated with an object. Every particular meaning has the heterogeneous structure of a concept, which consists of "an ordering of its components by zones of neighborhood. It is ordinal, an intension present in a state of survey in relation to its components, endlessly traversing them according to *an order without distance*" (Deleuze and Guattari 2003: 20; italics added). The "order without distance" refers to the fact that every act of cognition is a social practice that mobilizes a network of relations between objects in order to make sense of them. In other words, perceptions cannot be deemed more or less adjacent to the nature and essence of objects. Instead, perceptions can be more or less conscious of their own epistemological limitations. These insights from the relativist ontology of knowledge are highly crucial for the following study because we must accept that the perceptual "march on the object is never from the very first beginning objective. We must accept a real break between the cognitive and scientific discovery" (Bachelard 1978a: 345).

The question is how post-structural discourse theory should comport itself toward its own discursive, that is, contingent, nature. Reflexive methodology as it has been introduced in the works of Bachelard and Canguilhem and further elaborated by Foucault and Bourdieu is a way to internalize the relativist nature of knowledge in the research informed by the post-structural discourse theory (cf. Marttila 2010b). Reflexive methodology denies the presence of immediate cognitions of reality, and in the same spirit, it also refuses the possibility of an immediate hermeneutic analysis of reality. The capacity to observe reality depends on the way in which observations are made. As Dreyfus and Rabinow (1982: 107) put this idea, "When viewed from the right distance and with right vision, there is profound visibility to everything." In place of hermeneutic understanding of social subjects' understandings of their own reality, reflexive methodology promotes "second-order realism," which accepts that scientific analyses do not provide objective knowledge, but knowledge that reflects the epistemological limitations of the scientist. Scientific knowledge is accordingly always a combined result of the cross-section between theoretical reason and empirical observations (Bachelard 1988: 11, 16). Following Bourdieu (2008), theoretical concepts and frameworks play a crucial role in research informed by reflexive methodology because they facilitate the objectivation of an observer's observations of the world. Objectivity does not mean that observations could be brought more or less in line with the essence of the things observed, but instead that observations can more or less consciously reflect the epistemological limitations of observation provided by the theoretical framework used. In order to make such objectivation of the observations of the observer possible, the scientist has to find ways to translate the theoretical framework used into corresponding methods, instruments of observation, and empirical interpretations (Bachelard 1978a: 343ff; Diaz-Bone 2007: 10, 39).

The function of theoretical insights, concepts, and frameworks can be more closely defined against the backdrop of "epistemological break" and "holistic methodology"—the two most central ideas of reflexive methodology (cf. Marttila 2010b). Epistemological break urges the observer to maintain a consciously controlled distance to objects of observations. Such a distance is possible only once we have abandoned everyday experiences, tacit pre-suppositions, and social conventions in favor of consciously reflected theoretical concepts and models (Diaz-Bone 2007: 10). If empirical perceptions are never structured and determined by the objects observed, but must instead be regarded as results of epistemological limits of observation, it becomes essential to know how we observe our reality in order not to essentialize our objects of observation. Epistemological break is made possible by the holistic methodology, which basically means that empirical research interests, applied methods of analysis, material used, and heuristic framework of interpretation are motivated by the consciously chosen epistemological model of reality. Holistic methodology is an essential means to secure the conformity among the a priori assumptions about the being of the objects of observations, how we observe these objects, and what empirical observations we achieve in the end (cf. Bachelard 1988: 141, 148, 170).

An anything-goes kind of pragmatist research, which confirms the relative nature of knowledge without yet acknowledging its own epistemological possibilities of observation, would be unable to bring into line the limits of perceptions and actual empirical perception (Marttila 2010b; cf. Foucault 1980b: 36). Discrepancy between the more or less reflected (theoretical) ideas about the being of objects and their empirically observed being would be highly problematic for empirical research informed by the post-structural discourse theory. Against the background of its own argument that knowledge is made available by discourse, post-structural discourse theory must accept that it is itself another discourse structured, organized, and limited by its own epistemic system of knowledge. If everything that can be known reflects the cognitive possibilities provided by some discourse, the post-structural discourse theory is itself another discourse. Therefore, an empirical discourse analysis is a re-duplication of the epistemological possibilities opened up by the discourse theory (Foucault 1980a; cf. Foucault 1984b: 48). The analysis of the social construction of entrepreneur must depart from the elucidation of the scientific theory that allows us to understand, interpret, and describe the social processes, logics, and mechanisms involved. In a way, and this might sound rather counter-intuitive, the following study must start from its own construction of the social construction of entrepreneur. The axiomatic point of departure is that all meanings are produced by some discourse. In other words, statements about the entrepreneur reflect possibilities installed by discursive limits to say something about the values, utilities, and functions associated with the entrepreneur.

What counts as a truthful statement about the entrepreneur reflects discursive rules about the true being of the entrepreneur reaching beyond that particular statement. In this regard, every statement actualizes underlying discursive rules of truth. As Foucault (1981: 61) puts it, "[o]ne is 'in true' only by obeying the rules of a discursive 'policing' which one has to reactivate in each of one's discourses." No matter whether the object of analysis concerns doctors of medicine or the imprisoned, social subjects, their societal reception, signification and practices, or attitudes and meanings associated with them, it reflects their embeddedness into underlying discursive possibilities (Foucault 2004: 875; 1994a: 676). Of course, the argument that all ideas associated with the entrepreneur originate from the discourse on the entrepreneur becomes meaningful only when we abandon other material, functional, and rationalistic explanations. The meaningfulness of the discourse as the origin of different meanings of entrepreneur derives from the a priori assumption that it is not any objective necessities but "[d]iscourses themselves [that] exercise their own control" over significations (Foucault 1981: 56; cf. 1998: 93). The truth about the entrepreneur is therefore inseparably linked with the particular discourse that establishes and opens up the possibility of this truth. Whereas the epistemological break urges us to abandon any conventional ideas about the entrepreneur and its ideational denomination by social actors, the adaption of the perspective of post-structural discourse theory and its use in accordance with the holistic methodology indicate that every particular social construction of the entrepreneur equals the specific way in which the entrepreneur is "put into discourse" (Foucault 1998: 11).

While a nominal and descriptive analysis of the social construction would focus on the meanings associated with the entrepreneur, the post-structural discourse analysis focuses instead on the discursive conditions of possibility of these meanings (Foucault 2002a: 198). Instead of analyzing what is said to be the essence of the entrepreneur, discourse analysis tries to re-construct the discourse-specific conditions of possibility of that statement. Before a particular statement about the entrepreneur becomes available and is conceived as intelligible, there must be corresponding relations of power that allow this statement to be made, allow a particular social subject to utter that statement, etc. If the particular meaning of the entrepreneur reflects certain discursive conditions of possibility to observe and utter that statement in the first place, the empirical analysis must correspondingly go beyond the nominal meanings of entrepreneur—that is, the meaning that entrepreneur has in a particular spatiotemporal context—and instead re-construct the discursive conditions of these meanings. The concept of discourse introduces a phenomenon that goes beyond the knowledge and consciousness of social subjects and introduces an epistemological break from their world views. In a way, the discourse analysis begins in the theoretically founded construction of discourse as the empirical object of analysis. The objective ahead is to define the concept of discourse by departing first from a Foucauldian theory of discourse, which, thereafter, is extended toward a post-Foucauldian, post-structural theory of discourse in line with the works of Ernesto Laclau, Chantal Mouffe, Urs Stäheli, and Niklas Luhmann.

FOUCAULT AND BEYOND

Foucault defines discourse in terms of a temporarily relative stable and spatially relatively distinctive system of knowledge that generates the meanings of both objects of knowledge as well as those of social roles and identities (Diaz-Bone 2007: 3, 65). Foucault emphasized the plurality of coexistent social discourses and observed the differentiation of society into individual discourses such as medicine, psychiatry, biology, and economics (Foucault 1991b: 53f; 2005: 27). However, such discursive formations are by no means exclusive and separate from each other. Foucault emphasized instead the interactions and interrelations between different discourses (Foucault 1984a: 54; 2005: 47). Moreover, Foucault was also keen on pointing out that discourses are neither based on constitutive oppositions or principles. He described them far more as being heterogeneous and heterodox "systems of dispersion" effectuated and reproduced in individual statements. Discourse is consequently inseparable from the social practices of statement-making (*énoncé*), in which social subjects put various themes, objects, concepts, theories, etc. in relation to each other so as to produce a particular order of knowledge. However, the concept of discourse does not refer to the meanings, but to the structural order of the knowledge produced in statements (cf. Dumézil 1989: 71; Link 1997: 15).

Foucault deconstructed the distinction between discourse—as a social structure—and the statement—as a subjective practice—and pointed out that discourse is the structural effect of statements and that statements, in their turn, are structured by their discursive embeddedness (Foucault 2002a: 58, 187). Following Deleuze (1999: 66), singular statements can be called discursive that actualize and reproduce a discursive order of knowledge. The shared discursive belonging of a set of statements is manifested in their homogenous way of inter-relating theories, themes, concepts, objects, etc. Discourse can be related to a way of thinking, inter-relating, and connecting things to each other that is actualized by means of social subjects' adaption of discourse-specific world views. To some extent, discourse is a way of thinking and speaking about the world, which is structured and incorporated by a number of social subjects, but which is going to determine social reality insofar as it is activated and continuously actualized by social subjects in events of statement-making.[3] Whenever the statements disciplining and relating power of discourse produce the homogeneity between particular statements, these statements are social practices where discourse reaches its actual "limit and where the limit defines [the social] being" (Foucault 1980b: 36).

If the relative spatiotemporal permanence of meaning is the effect of the discourse, which a group of social subjects continuously activate and reproduce in their statements, the obvious question is how it becomes possible that a set of statements can display such an evident homogeneity. Foucault rejected a number of possible reasons for the shared structurality of individual statements. First of all, discourse cannot be regarded to be secondary to any kind of material or functional necessity. Instead, discourse is itself the cause and origin of knowledge (Foucault 1981: 56). Furthermore, discourses are not arranged along any constitutive lines of difference and distinction that install transparent and cohesive distinctions between true/untrue and valid/invalid statements (Foucault 2005: 260; 1998: 100; Gehring 2004: 277). Furthermore, there is no marked and symbolized discursive limit that would enable social subjects to distinguish statements belonging to the domain of the truth from the domain of the non-truth. Instead, what remains beyond the possibility of a truthful statement does not need to be described in terms of wrong, unjust, etc. The non-articulated exterior of statements "is not a fixed limit but a moving matter animated by peristaltic movement" (Deleuze 1999: 80). However, the absence of marked discursive limits does not mean that there are no limits whatsoever. Instead, discursive limits appear retrospectively as those statements that have not been possible to make (cf. Foucault 1981: 60). Foucault observed that the homology of singular statements reflected a set of underlying discursive rules and means of "rarefaction" of possible statements. Moreover, it is the presence of these structuring devices that enables the regulation of social practices of statement-making.

Any shared regularity between statements bears witness of the discursive power that obstructs subjects from making invalid and inadmissible statements about their social reality (Foucault 2002a, 1981: 68; Dreyfus and Rabinow 1982: 143). Re-activation of the discursive rules pre-supposes their activation and incorporation by social subjects in their social practices. Whatever subjects conceive of being valid, true, and meaningful reflects their discursive subjectivation (Foucault 2004: 883). Subjectivation is manifested in two different kinds of social relations: first, an intra-subjective relation to themselves, which implicates that subjects control their own conducts in accordance with the discursive conception of their being; and second, an inter-subjective relation to other social subjects, which means that they perform a certain social role toward other social subjects (Foucault 2004: 888). Foucault assumed a post-Cartesian perspective on social subjects and denies that subjects would reach complete consciousness about their subjectivation through discourse (cf. Foucault 1970: xiv). However, this does not deny the possibility of rational and intentional social conduct, but merely implicates that subjects can act strategically within strategic possibilities structured by their discursive subjectivation (Foucault 1998; 2005: 244). Nonetheless, Foucault notices that even though the possible conducts of social subjects are structured by their discursive subjectivation, the indeterminacy of discursive rules sustains the possibility for continuous subversion and transgression of the existing discursive limits. However, as Foucault (1980b: 35) argues, transgression cannot be understood as conscious and intentional reversal of the discursive power. The transgression of discursive limits is generated by the indeterminate and incomplete discursive rules that make it "possible that one might speak the truth in the space of wild exteriority" (Foucault 1981: 61). Indeed, Foucault describes discontinuity to be the natural condition of any discourse (Foucault 2002b; 1998: 94f, 99f). However, even though discourse is regarded as a dynamic and continuously alternating system of knowledge, a relative regularity of discourse still prevails.

In *The Order of Discourse* (1981), Foucault relates relative regularity to a number of mechanisms of rarefaction of statements, which discipline subjects to reproduce the prevailing discursive order. First, there is the mechanism of "commentary" that refers to "the hierarchy between primary and secondary texts" and basically means that statements are always motivated by existing statements (Foucault 1981: 57). Second, there is the "author function" that requires the subjects to bear the responsibility for "what he writes and what he does not write" (Foucault 1981: 59). Third, Foucault observed a historical differentiation of distinctive areas of knowledge and scientific "disciplines," each of which set up their particular limits of the truth against which they could discriminate between true and non-true statements. These disciplines, such as biology, economics, psychology, and the like, consist of "a corpus of propositions considered to be true; a play of rules and definitions, of techniques and instruments," which constitute "a sort of anonymous system at the disposal of anyone who wants to or is able to use it" (Foucault 1981: 59). Fourth, Foucault observed discourses to denominate both institutional positions for subjects with their respective authorities and possibilities of social agency, as well as criteria, classification, and competences, which social subjects had to hold in order to inhabit these positions. In this manner every discourse performs its particular mode of rarefaction "of the speaking subjects" (Foucault 1981: 60f).

The common feature of these means of rarefaction is that they are not symbolized and represented by statements. In other words, in contrast to texts produced by statements, rarefactions do not have any textual form. Means of rarefaction are, in terms of Bourdieu, habitualized and incorporated by social subjects without them possessing the knowledge about the presence of such a regulative instance. Howarth (2002) has noticed that Foucault's concept of discourse pre-supposes valid knowledge to be either of transcendental origin or to result from subjects intrinsically aware of the limits of the true knowledge. In either case, discourse is located in a derivative relation beyond discourse-located functional necessities, rules, or objective social conventions. In other words, discourse as an order of knowledge reproduced by statements is controlled and regulated by something that is itself not discourse. Brenner (1994) and Jessop (2006) have similarly observed that discursive structures and discursive changes seem to reflect the exo-discursive influence of historical episteme, material pre-requisites, and functional demands, which all place discursive systems of knowledge into a relation of isomorphy to social conditions and circumstances exterior to discursive systems of knowledge. In this light, the relative regularity and stability of discourse is not reproduced by statements, which Foucault indicated, but by non-discursive circumstances.[4] Of course, such functional or material determination of discourse is certainly justifiable. However, against the initially assumed hybrid conception of culture, but also for the sake of more conceptual clarity about the concept of discourse, it seems meaningful to move beyond Foucault and adapt a post-Foucaul-dian theory of discourse. In contrast to Foucault's definition of discourse as the outcome of non-discursive mechanisms of rarefaction, post-structural discourse theory is a coherent and strictly discursive account capable of explaining the discursive production of meaning as a discursive operation. Post-structural discourse theory offers a theoretical model that describes how the systemic character of discourse originates from discursive operations within and on behalf of a discourse. The objective now is to define the characteristics and logics constitutive of discourse as described by the post-structural discourse theory.

POST-STRUCTURAL DISCOURSE THEORY

The post-structural theoretical approach to discourse, as established by the so-called Essex school in discourse theory, dissolves the distinction between the discursive and non-discursive social realms and recognizes that all social meanings are produced by and within some discourse. Whether a stone, a building, or a word, each and every socially meaningful entity is the result of its positioning within differential relations between mutually signifying elements (Laclau and Mouffe 2001: 107f). In contrast to the alleged fallacies of the Foucauldian theory of discourse, the post-structural discourse theory rejects any material or functional determination of discourse. In line with Saussure's (1966) structural theory of language, post-structural discourse theory assumes that discourse, like language, only consists of "differences." If all meanings originate from discourse, and if discourse is defined as a system of differential relations, all meanings are the result of differential relations organized within a discourse (Diaz-Bone 2006b: 248). The meaning content of an object or a word is the result of its relation to other objects (cf. Laclau and Mouffe 2001: 106, 112f). As Saussure (1966: 114) argued, the meaning of an object is not immanent to the object itself "but by what exists outside of it"—that is, other objects (or words). Even though Saussure assumed a differential theory of meaning, his structural theory of language sustained an isomorphic determination of meaning. The meaning content, which a word had, for instance, reflected objective cultural conventions and traditions connected with the usage of that word. As Jakobson (1990: 118) describes, Saussure thought language use—and as such the potential meaning of the words—to reflect "preconceived possibilities." As soon as subjects used language to denote things, they were subjected to "a collection of necessary conventions that have been adopted by a social body to permit individuals to exercise the faculty of language" (Jakobson 1990: 88).

Even though the post-structural discourse theory draws on the works of Saussure, it has abandoned the isomorphic determination of the meaning and emphasized the performative nature of language use. Rejection of functional, material, and cultural determination of meaning at the same time emphasizes that meanings are produced in singular acts of language use. As Laclau and Mouffe (1990: 102) argue, the meaning of an "object is constituted in the context of an action." If every meaning is the result of differential relations, then the formal relation of difference figures as the ontological prerequisite of meaning.[5] As Derrida (2004: 155) argues, "difference . . . [is] the condition of presence of essence," and therefore the social cannot be anything else than yet another system of differences (cf. Derrida 1981a: 28). Against the backdrop of the difference-theoretical notion of meaning, the stability of a particular meaning depends on the retention of the particular network of differential relations in which a meaning was produced initially. Diachronic variation of the differential structure of relations causes a corresponding variation of the meaning produced. As Derrida (1981b: 292) notices, such variation (here: play) is "disruption of presence. The presence of an element is always a signifying and substitutive reference inscribed in a system of differences and the movement of a chain." When the chain of differences moves over time, each movement produces unprecedented meanings, and therefore movement of the chain disrupts the previous meaning. Moreover, the erased possibility of functional, material, or transcendental anchorage of meaning "extends the [possible] domain of the play of signification infinitely" (Derrida 1981b: 112; cf. Derrida

1977: 12). If the retention of the differential chain is the pre-condition for the meaning, this also implicates that retention of the differential chain is the possibility to re-iterate and sustain earlier meanings. Post-structural discourse theory defines the concept of discourse as the temporarily relatively stable system of difference that is differentiated spatially from other chains of difference. Discourse refers accordingly to the particular order of differences distinguishable from other discourses. Laclau and Mouffe (1990: 105) describe the concept of discourse also in more general terms as the ontological condition of possibility of the essence of objects: "If the being—as distinct from existence—of any object is constituted within a discourse, it is not possible to differentiate the discursive, in terms of being, from any other area of reality. The discursive is not, therefore, an object among other objects . . . but rather a theoretical *horizon*."

The ontological possibility of discourse as the origin of meaning is located in the differential logic of signification. It is because meanings "do not arise from a necessity external to the system structuring them" that they "can only therefore be conceived as [results of] discursive articulations" (Laclau and Mouffe 2001: 107). Therefore, "every object is constituted as an object of discourse" (Laclau and Mouffe 2001: 107). Signified—the meaning content of a signifier—is the result of the immediate relation between signifiers. These relations between signifiers are outcomes of the discursively regulated social practices of articulation (Torfing 2005: 12f). Retention of significations depends on the subjugation of the articulations and, as such, also the subjects of articulations, to the conceived discursive system of differences. The systemic character of discourse is correspondingly the result of the discursive power to subjugate diachronic variance of significations, which installs a systemic order that regulates future articulations (Dyrberg 2004: 248). As Dyrberg (2004: 245) notices, the power of discourse is manifested in the mutual retention of a set of signifiers at a later point in time. Therefore, the "realization" of a particular articulation and the "blockage" of potential articulations bear the trace of discursive power. Every actualized meaning "realizes and blocks the potential because actualization, as the becoming of the potential through decisions, is an actualization of specific possibilities, and hence an elimination of others" (Dryberg 2004: 245). Reproduction of a certain meaning is accordingly a systemic effect of discourse, and yet discourse is itself reproduced "by binding the free variation of differences" in articulations (Dryberg 2004: 248).

Post-structural discourse theory comes across a familiar problem from Luhmann's theory on social systems: the problem concerning the way in which social systems regulate and control social practices (i.e., communication) so as to stabilize and reproduce their own systematicity. Luhmann (1984: 10, 61; 1997: 45) observed how social systems reproduce their distinction to other systems and sustain their systemic order over time by means of re-copying their earlier self-referential observations. A system observes its own antedating observations in a manner of second-order observations and therewith re-copies anterior distinctions between the system and its exterior environment. Laclau and Mouffe (2001: 143f) argue in a rather identical manner that reproduction of antedating significations requires the need to impose limits on the potential variation of future articulations. Against the backdrop of the differential logic of meaning, social objectivity is produced by "relational ensembles that do not obey any inner logic other than their factually being together" (Laclau 2006: 672). Reproduction of a social objectivity requires correspondingly that articulations not only produce such "relational ensembles" so as to generate significations, but also re-iterate the characteristic distinction of the particular discourse between the valid and the invalid meaning. In this regard, articulations maintain the systemic character of the discourse by means of actualizing its characteristic limits of meaning (cf. Stäheli 2000: 57).

Similar to Luhmann's (1997, 1984) theory of social systems, the concept of discourse also refers to two different systemic characteristics of the chains of difference.[6] First, discourse refers to the unity of discourse, and second, to the totality of the parts contained in discourse. In a manner similar to Luhmann, post-structural discourse theory also observes the unity of discourse to result from a distinction between *a* discourse and the environment; that is, what remains beyond its limits. In terms of Luhmann (1997: 45), this systematicity of the system constituting a "distinction between the system and the environment occurs in two different forms: as a difference *produced through* the system and as a difference *observed within* the system." This means that there is no systematicity of system without a distinction of a difference to that which does not belong to the system (cf. Knudsen 2006: 77). A system constructs its identity through a difference from the environment, which appears as a negative correlate (*Negativkorrelat*) in succeeding operations of the system and allows the reproduction of the introduced distinction between the system and the environment. However, taking into consideration that the system exists only as the result of the distinction to something that exists beyond it, namely, the environment, systems remain inter-dependent on the retention of the initial system/environment distinction.

As Luhmann (1997: 63) clearly argues, "the system and the environment are distinguished as two sides of the same form none of which can prevail without the other." Moreover, the distinction constituting the system prevails only as long as it is reproduced in systemic communications, since the system exists only as the result of "an operation within the system" (Luhmann 1997: 64). Similar to social systems, a particular discourse exists only as long as the once introduced distinction between a system of differences and its environment remains reproduced as a "re-entry" of the distinction difference between discourse and non-discourse (cf. Åkerstrøm Andersen 2005; Stäheli 2000). Laclau (1990b) refers this kind of maintenance of the systemic form of discourse to a process of "spatialization," which, while retaining the difference between discourse/non-discourse, at the same time reproduces the already actualized meaning and distinguishes it from thus far non-articulated yet perpetually potential and possible meaning.[7] Similar to Luhmann and Derrida, every actualized and present meaning depends on the equal exclusion of potential meaning. The domain of the meaningful is, accordingly, always the outcome of a process of suppression and exclusion. In this manner, the positive meaning—that is, the meaning that has become socially articulated and received—contains the trace of a past "difference between the actual and the possible" (Luhmann 1997: 50).

However, where Luhmann pre-supposed that systematicity of social systems does not have to become articulated itself, post-structural discourse theory insists that discursive boundaries must by marked and symbolized in articulations. In other words, discursive limits only possess the variability of a function constraining articulations, if what exists beyond a discourse is represented as something negative and incommensurable with the discourse (Laclau 2004: 320; Laclau and Mouffe 2001: 143f; Stäheli 2004). Luhmann considered the retention of meaning to derive from the self-referential repetition, or re-entry, of the previous distinction between the actual and the potential meaning. In accordance with the self-referential logic of communication, this repeatedly re-actualized "re-entry" of the previous distinction "becomes an autopoietic medium for the continuous selection of the decided form" (Luhmann 1997: 58). This autopoietic and self-referential reproduction of meaning is possible without signification's excluded side being necessarily marked and symbolized. Self-referential articulations are possible to repeat and reproduce even in the absence of any marked limits of articulations.

Post-structural discourse theory radicalizes the concept of discursive limits and argues that instead of unmarked discursive limits, such as the system-theoretical system/environment distinction, discursive limits must be based on an antagonistic logic. Laclau and Mouffe (2001: 143f) argue that

> A formation manages to *signify itself* (that is, to constitute itself as such) only by transforming the *limits into frontiers*, by constituting a chain of equivalences which constructs that which is beyond the limits as that which it is *not*. It is only through negativity, division and antagonism that a formation constitutes itself as a totalizing horizon. (italics added)

The notion that "limits" must be transformed into "frontiers" denotes that a discourse attains the status of a diachronically reproducible and spatially separable order of knowledge only if there are clear limits about what can be articulated in the name of a discourse. Discourse achieves a systematic character only in the presence of limits, and these "limits only exist insofar as a systematic ensemble of differences can be cut out as a *totality* with regard to something else *beyond* them" (Laclau and Mouffe 2001: 143). The distinction between the "totality" of possible and admissible and the

"beyond" of non-allowed differences requires the presence of an antagonistic boundary. As Laclau (1996b: 52) put it, an antagonistic boundary is
necessary because "[w]ithout limits through which a (non-dialectical) negativity is constructed, we would have an indefinite dispersion of differences
whose absence of systemic limits would make any differential identity possible." According to Laclau (1996b: 38), the "systematicity of the system is
a direct result of the exclusionary limit, [and] it is only that exclusion that
grounds the system as such."

The system's self-enclosed identity always depends on the projection
of its own negativity on the other—"the positivity of 'our' position consists only in the positivization of our negative relation to the other, to the
antagonistic adversary" (Žižek 1990: 253). Considering that all identities
are the result of chains of difference, discursive limits cannot constitute
another difference. In order to diverge from its outside, a discourse needs
limits that defy the logic of difference, and subsequently, the beyond of the
system cannot exist as a further field of differences (Marchart 1998: 8f).
In that case, any further difference added would be perfectly compatible
with the discourse (Laclau 1996b: 37). In order to guarantee the incompatibility of the environment, a discourse must symbolize its environment
within the discourse in terms of radical otherness. The environment must
be present as something that "poses a threat to (that is negates) all the differences within the context [of the discourse]—or better, that the context
constitutes itself as such through the act of exclusion of something alien,
of *radical otherness*" (Laclau 1996b: 52; italics added). Stäheli (2004) has
aptly questioned whether discursive limits must be founded on an antagonistic logic or whether antagonism is just one among several different logics
to demarcate a discourse.

Stäheli (2004: 236) has proposed to distinguish the ontological division
between a discourse and its environment, which is realized in an ontical, yet
not necessarily overtly uttered negativity toward the exterior of discourse.
Antagonism should be understood as one possible way of how a discourse
distinguishes itself from its environment. Regarded in this way, it would
depend "on the particular system whether it constructs its relation to the
environment not only in negative, but also in antagonistic terms" (Stäheli
2004: 235). Stäheli does not question the necessity of excluding potential
differential relations as a pre-condition of any stable meanings derived from
the differential logic of meaning. Even though exclusion is ineluctable for
constructing social identities, it does not have to be expressed in terms
of antagonistic adversaries such as just/unjust, democratic/undemocratic,
friend/enemy, etc. It would be even reasonable to argue that the antagonistic logic of exclusion becomes particularly relevant during the moments of
severe social turmoil that not only question the meaningfulness of particular identities but the entire discursive systems. If discursive limits reflect the
"impossible pure self-reference" of meaning caused by the differential logic
of meaning, an insurmountable undecidability about the valid significations

will prevail indeed (Stäheli 2004: 238; cf. Derrida 1999: 281). As Laclau (1990b: 18) argues, the ever-present meanings generating and stabilizing difference from an excluded and negated other makes social objectivity impossible. This implicates that all identities remain undecidable, indeterminate, and open for revision and contestation at all times. In terms of Žižek (1990: 252), the ontological undecidability of meaning is the society dealt with by means of externalization of an inner impossibility of social objectivity to a social adversary responsible for incomplete and instable identities. Denomination of a social adversary is a way to deal with the general impossibility of social objectivity. As Žižek (1990: 252) argues, "Every identity is already in itself blocked, marked by an impossibility, and the external enemy is simply the small piece, the rest of reality upon which we 'project' or 'externalize', this intrinsic, immanent impossibility." However, as Stäheli's (2000, 2004) treatise of the discursive limits has illustrated, the ontological negativity can be dealt with in rather different ways, of which antagonism is but one possibility. The distinction to the environment necessary for the constitution of relatively stable and coherent discourses can be dealt with either by means of symbolizing the environment in antagonistic terms as radical otherness, or it can have the status of an unmarked environment, as for example Luhmann's theory of social systems suggests.

Besides the discursive limits, post-structural discourse theory also observes the systematicity of the discourse symbolizing "empty signifiers" to play a crucial role for the installment and reproduction of discourse. An empty signifier "takes upon itself the task of representing the whole" of the discourse (Miller 2004: 220). In this manner, empty signifier represents the common identity of particular discursive entities and, therewith, makes it possible to perceive the principle of their mutual commonality. As such the empty signifier does not merely represent the superordinate principle or reason that different symbols, objects, or words belong to a discourse, but it also makes it possible to observe why these particular constituents of a discourse belong together. The systematizing or totalizing impact, which the empty signifier exerts toward signifiers, originates from two mutually inseparable functions of *differentiation* and *representation*. "Differentiation" indicates how empty signifiers introduce a partial distinction, the actual scope of the discursive system only, which like Luhmann's distinction between the inner and outer side of a social system introduces what Nonhoff (2007) describes as a "binary division of the discursive space" (*Zweiteilung des diskursiven Raumes*). "Representation" refers to how an empty signifier provides a positive symbolic image of the discourse and, at the same time, installs a common identity for the particular discursive entities. However, a representation also refers to the positivization of the distinction toward the discursive environment made in the name of the empty signifier. This symbolization of the distinction to the discursive other makes it possible to distinguish and separate the system of particular discursive entities as a whole from the entities located beyond the discursive limit. Operations of differentiation and representation enabled by the empty signifier unify the discursive system of differences as a differentiable and distinguishable "totality" (Laclau 1996b: 85).

It is the combined effect of the demarcation of a system of differences by means of discursive limits and the representation of the common identity of these differences that particular discursive elements become possible to relate to each other. The systematicity of the discourse is a combined outcome of discursive limits and empty signifiers. Discursive limits are set up and justified in name of an empty signifier, and the system of differences represented by an empty signifier is demarcated by means of the discursive limits. The particular contribution made by the empty signifier to the systematicity of discourse is its providing a "totalizing horizon" that makes it possible to conceive of the co-existence of singular discursive entities as a pre-supposedly pre-given social fact (Laclau and Mouffe 2001: 144). The systemic and systematizing impact of empty signifiers becomes tangible with regard to the terms of discursive "moments," "elements," and "floating signifiers." In the absence of their discursive structuration, signifiers assume the status of floating signifiers. This means basically that their combination with other signifiers remains more or less open so that their meaning can change from one articulation to another. The conceptual indeterminacy of floating signifiers is the immediate effect of their incapability "of being wholly articulated to a discursive chain" (Laclau and Mouffe 2001: 113). Elements suffer from a similar kind of conceptual indeterminacy as the floating signifiers do. However, where the indeterminacy and conceptual variation of floating signifiers results from their different use in different discourses, elements belong to the reservoir of the "infinitude of the field of discursivity" that has not been subjugated by any particular discourse (Laclau and Mouffe 2001: 112). Due to their indeterminate (floating signifiers) and absent (elements) discursive position, floating signifiers can be used in numerous different ways and therefore receive different meanings varying from time to time. The discursive status of moments is rather different. Moments refer to those signifiers that have been assigned a rather determinate position in a discursive system of difference. This determined position means that signifiers having the status of moments are "subsumed . . . under the principle of repetition" retained from one articulation to another (Laclau and Mouffe 2001: 108). In terms of systems theory, the determined discursive position of moments makes the re-entry of their discursive form possible in consecutive acts of articulation (cf. Åkerstrøm Andersen 2003: 67).

Post-structural discourse theory described the situation of a relatively stable systematicity of discourse that is reproduced by means of discursive limits and empty signifiers as *hegemony*. In the widest and most general understanding of the concept of hegemony, it can be referred to describe any "partial fixing of the relation between signifier and signified" derived from the presence of discursive limits and representation provided by empty signifiers (Laclau 1993: 435). Every particular case of hegemony is the subsequent outcome of the general process of hegemonization, which refers to "discursive struggle about the ways fixing the meaning of a signifier" (Laclau 1993: 435). However, there are a number of reasons that discursive systems can never reach complete stability. One such reason is the indissoluble nature of the empty signifier. First, there is no a priori reason that a certain signifier should have the function of an empty signifier. The discursive place of the empty signifier is equally open for any signifier. As Laclau (1996b: 72) argues, the place for the empty signifier is "autonomous vis-à-vis any particular order in so far as it is the name of an absent fullness that no concrete social order can achieve." Second, any chain of differences can be represented by the one and the same empty signifier. The emptiness of the empty signifier denotes its absent conceptual content. It is because the empty signifier represents a chain of differences, without itself taking any particular differential relation, that it remains without an identity of its own. Empty signifier remains therefore "a signifier without signified" (Laclau 1996b: 68). The conceptual emptiness of the empty signifier means that decisions about the chain of differences, which is represented by the empty signifier, cannot be derived from the essence of the empty signifier. After all, there is no pre-determined meaning to empty signifiers. As a consequence, the discursive order established by means of the denomination of empty signifiers remains notoriously open for future contestation. These two structural insufficiencies connected with empty signifiers obstruct the establishment of any fully closed and diachronically reproducible discursive orders. As Dyrberg (1998: 32) argues, no discourse can attain complete and "infinite linearity" (*Unendlichkeit der Linearität*) and remains instead in the condition of "constitutively failing circularity" (*konstitutiv beschädigte Zirkularität*), which basically means that the reproduction of prevailing discursive order proceeds in a manner of infinite supplements made in articulations (cf. Laclau 1990: 17; 1996b: 53; Torfing 1999a: 124).

THE SPECTERS OF ENTREPRENEURSHIP REVISITED

The general aim of this chapter was to supply a short introduction to the concept of discourse in post-structural discourse analysis. In post-structural discourse theory, the concept of discourse not only refers to the actual system of differences, but it also denotes the acts of differentiation that reproduce the systemic form of discourse over time. Discourse is not any natural form of social organization. Instead, it emerges as the way to constrain the diachronic interplay of differences and, therewith, to control the production of meaning. In accordance to Nonhoff (2007: 175), it is now possible to discern between three different meanings of discourse. First, discourse refers to the inherent structural order contained in singular articulations. Second, discourse refers to the diachronical process of re-arrangement of relations between signifiers so as to determine their respective meanings (i.e., signifieds). This means that each and every act of articulation is involved in the diachronic installment, retention, or transformation of discourses. Every particular act of articulation is conducted on behalf of or in opposition to a discourse. Moreover, as Foucault (2002a: 38, 42, 227) says, statements must be made in accordance with the existing "rules of formation." Against the backdrop of the post-structural discourse theory, this would mean that articulations must reproduce and re-actualize the validity of characteristic empty signifiers, discourse/environment distinction, and the inner system of differences. Third, discourse describes spatial differentiation of the social into mutually distinctive discursive systems of differences sustained by means of subsequent acts of articulation (cf. Nonhoff 2007: 175; Stavrakakis 1997: 264).

The post-structural discourse theory tells us that the meaning of the entrepreneur is always produced and determined within a discourse-specific system of differences. Moreover, post-structural discourse theory also gives reason to understand the actual meaning of the entrepreneur to be an outcome of a particular bundle, or chain, of differences in which the entrepreneur receives its meaning content. In this regard, the signifier of "entrepreneur" is nothing but an empty word, which within a discourse of the entrepreneur functions as a *chiffré* connecting a number of other signifiers conceived to represent something essential about the entrepreneur (Deleuze and Guattari 2003: 20). The spectral emergence of the entrepreneur as a subject without any evident social function or value refers to its status as a floating signifier, when a number of different and mutually dissonant discourses try to define its true meaning, or to its status as an element, in the absence of any discursive attempt to determine the social meaning of the entrepreneur. Every transformation into the social meanings, functions, practices, or utilities of the entrepreneur reflect the dissolution and change of the previous discourse on entrepreneur. As a matter of discursive transformation, it becomes possible to understand entrepreneurs in unprecedented terms. However, it is only the subsequent supplement in the form of a new bundle of signifiers associated with the entrepreneur that—in terms of Derrida (1977: 5)—causes "modification of presence in representation." The genealogy of the entrepreneur must therefore be regarded as a diachronic process of discursive openings and closures through which the entrepreneur received its later social function. The permanence of the idea of entrepreneur as a Schumpeterian economic agent depends on the retention of this particular discursive system in subsequent acts of articulation. This particular historical sequence or stage in the social construction of the entrepreneur is replaced by another idea of the entrepreneur when the prevailing discursive system is replaced by another one. In terms of the relativist ontology of the post-structural discourse theory, there is no historical path or teleological course of development underlying the discursive changes of the entrepreneur: we are left with the possibility of empirical analysis of all those stages, discursive transformations, supplements, and anew hegemonies responsible for the actual social status of the entrepreneur. The objective of the following chapter is to operationalize the post-structural discourse theory described so far in rather abstract and general terms and accommodate it to a heuristic framework that allows an empirical discourse analysis of the genealogy of the entrepreneur in Swedish political discourse.

4   Political Discourse

Chapter 3 elucidated discourse to be a differential system of differences with a certain diachronic and spatial distinctiveness. What is surprising about the presence of any discourse is that it implicates the control and regulation of the interplay of differences, as described by Derrida. In this chapter, attention is re-oriented from the general order of discourse to those social practices, in which different discourses are established, reproduced, re-negotiated, and replaced. The previous abstract and general discussion of the concept of discourse is obviously difficult to operationalize to any kind of empirical discourse analysis. For this reason, the objective of this chapter is to provide an analytical heuristic framework that makes it possible to analyze the discursive construction of the entrepreneur in Swedish political discourse, characterize the discursive structures in which different spectres of entrepreneur appeared, as well as describe the discursive changes and displacements that paved the way for an unprecedented notion of the entrepreneur. The first part of this chapter emphasizes the "political" logic involved in the discursive construction of reality and sets the stage for the classification of different types and magnitudes of discursive change. Thereafter, the discussion moves on to various forms of relations contained in different discourses and different substantial discursive levels. The concluding part describes different types of changes of discourse, distinguishes two different kinds of defensive and offensive articulations, and identifies two general types of institutional and popular discourse.

POLITICAL LOGIC OF DISCOURSE

The difference-theoretical notion of discourse described in the preceding chapter emphasizes the incessant historical contingency of significations. In place of an absolute relativism, which suggests that there are no limits for possible significations whatsoever, the post-structural discourse theory now argues that significations are contextually motivated. In terms of Marchart (2007, 2010), the post-structural discourse theory adapts a post-foundational perspective on discourse, which basically means that there is no justification, foundation, or reason for a signification beyond the discursive context in which that signification is articulated. However, the incessant contextual contingency of significations is only one side of the coin. The other side is, as Marchart (2010) argues, that the absence of transcendental and objective ground (i.e., nomos, reason, or motivation) for a signification generates the need for contextual foundations (see Marttila forthcoming). The absent natural (e.g., historical evolution), material (e.g., economic relations), transcendental (e.g., divine power), or biological and psychological (e.g., human rationality) motivation of significations opens the possibility for the presence of a plurality of equally willed, particular, and therefore contestable justifications of signification (cf. Glynos 2001: 192f; Laclau and Bhaskar 1998; Marchart 2007).[1]

Without delving too much into the philosophical foundations of post-structural discourse theory, which has been described clearly in Critchley and Marchart (2004) and Marchart (2007, 2010), the irreplaceable historical contingency of signification and the resulting openness of significations for subsequent contestation and critique denotes the political logic of discourse. Political is by no means comparable to the mainstream political science notion of the political as a particular social subfield of institutions (government, parliament) or social processes (voting, legislation, democratic participation). Instead, political refers to the irreplaceable existential condition of uncertainty and indeterminacy that counts for all social institutions, identities, and practices. In terms of Critchley (1999: 275), "the political can be defined as the taking of a decision without any determinate transcendental guarantee." Expressed in general terms, each and every attempt to define and describe things is an act of decision because significations cannot become commensurable with the objects they signify. As Joseph (2001: 110) argues, the distance between knowledge and the object of this knowledge remains impossible to bridge because "all our knowledge is necessarily socially and historically conditioned and . . . there is [therefore] no guaranteed correspondence between this knowledge and that to which it refers."

So how about the discursive systems then: why are discourses not capable of offering long-lasting and socially widely accepted knowledge? As the previous chapter described, discourses are perfectly well capable of offering relatively stable and coherent formations of knowledge. However, even though discourses and, above all, discursive limits and empty signifiers located therein provide contextual justifications of particular significations, discourses remain captured in their own historical contingency. In a way, a discourse of the entrepreneur reproduces the indeterminate meaning of the entrepreneur by an indeterminate discourse on the entrepreneur. No matter how objectivated, sedimented, and socially accepted a discourse of the entrepreneur is, there is no discourse that could permanently erase the historical contingency by social necessity. Even discourses are the results of historical conditions. However far we may have to go—we would still find a contingent foundation of the discourse. Or, as Derrida (1979: 146f) put this: "[h]owever far one goes back toward the limit of the first need, there is always writing, a relation, already. No first text, not even a virgin surface for its inscription." Even though Mouffe (2005: 9) relates the political logic of discourse to the social struggles and contestations between competing interests and perspectives, the political logic goes much deeper to the (absence of) ontological foundation of significations that enables these kinds of adversaries in the first place. In other words, we must conceive of the political as an ontological and existential dimension underneath significations that, on the one side, makes any objective significations impossible and that, on the other side, makes an unlimited number of significations possible. Rasch (1997) also relates the political to two constructive and deconstructive logics immanent in every discourse. It is due to its political nature that every discourse vacillates between the two extremes of relative stability and instability. It is against the backdrop of the immanent contestability of any kind of meaningful social existence that post-structural discourse theory tries to figure out how societalization remains still possible and what kinds of discursive practices are required to install any relatively objective social existence (cf. Laclau 1996b: 59f; Marchart 2007: 14; Mouffe 2005: 4).

If the fundament on which different forms of social organizations are based is absent, which the political logic of discourse indicates, societalization is an impossible operation. The impossibility of the society does not mean that there would not be any relatively stable and collectively consented forms of social coexistence. Rather, what Laclau (1990a: 91), for instance, describes as the impossible object of society is that every particular attempt to "domesticate infinitude [of meaning], to embrace it within the finitude of an order" will necessarily fail. Following Lefort (1988), whose political philosophy has played a crucial role in the post-structural political thought in general (cf. Marchart 2007), the failure of societalization results from the absence of transcendental, objective, or natural principles that would determine the principles constituting society independently of any particular social interests, perspectives, and the like. Following Lefort (1988: 17), the place occupied by a social order, such as democracy or socialism, is "an empty place" for the very reason that there is no essence to society independent of particular attempts of essentialization. As Lefort (1998: 19) further argues, the absence of an objective and transcendental anchoring of a particular social order means that social orders remain subjected to "dissolution of the markers of certainty." However, the underlying political logic of society also has a productive and constructive dimension since it opens the possibility for a number of different attempts "to act over that 'social', to *hegemonize* it" (Laclau 1990a: 90f; italics added).

Against the backdrop of what has been said so far, each and every hegemonic attempt at hegemonizing society remains captured in its historically contingent nature. After all, the ideas defining social order originate from a social location within the social. A question that post-structural discourse theory tries to answer is how particular attempts at denominating the valid being of the social succeed in externalizing their own narrow, willed, and subjective character. In order to attain social relations structuring and determining authority, discourses have to posit their own presuppositions and do so as if they epitomized some kind of historical, cultural, material, or other necessity. In terms of Žižek (1993: 150), the positing of the pre-suppositions is the general logic of how a discourse may achieve the "passage from contingency into necessity" (cf. Lefort 1988: 218f; Žižek 1997: 21). The social authority of a discourse depends on its capacity to represent its particular occupation of the empty place of the social from an external and objective position. As Lefort and Gauchet (1990: 100) argue, the stability of any particular social order is the result of the imagined pre-supposedness of that order independent of discursive practices that introduced it. In a way, we can therefore understand discursive power to result from a triple movement, which first selects and determines "the principles that generate society" (Lefort 1988: 217); second presents the pre-supposedness of these principles in the course of history, essence of culture, ontology of man, and so on; and third defines the social institutions, relations, identities, and practices that are believed to belong to the essence of these principles.

If the political is the ontological foundation allowing for discursive constructions of the social, politics refers to all those practices of signification involved in establishment, reproduction, and transformation of the discursive constructs of the social. Following Dyrberg (2004: 241), "the *political* refers to the [ontological] terrain in which articulations take place, and *politics* refers to the structuring of articulations" (italics added). Politics has a transformative function because it is involved in the transsubstantiation of the absent social order to determine a particular order. Lefort (1988: 11) argues that politics obscures the absence of any transcendental and objective necessity of a social order, and, at the same time, it is the "mode of institution" through which images of the society are made to appear. The imagined presence of a social order is the outcome of discursive representations of an order. These images of the social are characterized by their instigation of a totalizing vision that unifies and orders social institutions, identities, and practices within one and the same imaginary horizon. Politics refer to an ensemble of practices that either generates society totalizing "vision[s] of a center" or try to enumerate the social forms and organizations of such visions (Lefort 1986: 219; cf. Stavrakakis 1999: 73). Politics is, accordingly, not only a struggle of words and visions but is also about the denomination of social institutions and identities that materialize and reproduce political discourses (Lefort and Gauchet 1990: 113, 117). Politics would be a meaningless practice if it did not succeed in determining and structuring the social. In order to have this real impact on the social, political discourses must hold the "ideological grip"[2] that makes discursive representations of the social appear as something self-evident. Of course, self-evidentiality is nothing that exists independent of the social receptions of and identifications with a discursive representation of the social. As Glynos and Howarth (2007: 117) argue, the power of a discourse depends on the extent to which it is capable of making social subjects forget their "political origins." Even though social identities are indeed "the products of social and political identifications with the roles and subject positions made available by historically available discourses," identifications are possible only when subjects misrecognize, or disregard, the political nature of social identities (Griggs and Howarth 2002: 46).³ In other words, misrecognition is essential if "the radical contingency of social reality—and the political dimension of practice more specifically—[is to] remain[s] in the background" (Glynos & Howard 2007: 145).

The *first* misrecognition consists of the unbridgeable difference of the political and politics. Politics, as the ensemble of social practices involved in the constitution of the social, comes—in terms of Žižek (1995: 39)—"without any support of *the real*" (cf. Lacan 1991: 61). The notion real refers to the absent transcendental and objective necessities that would make it possible to discriminate between valid and invalid significations. The social efficacy of a political discourse depends on its capacity to insinuate its presence as something self-evidential. The self-evidential appearance of a discourse, as Žižek (1995: 33) argues, depends on whether it is capable of engendering "the illusion that it was already there, i.e., that it was not placed there by us." The misrecognition of the lacking self-evidentiality of discourse is, accordingly, the precondition for the capacity of a discourse to act on the social (cf. Laclau 2000c: 185; Laclau and Zac 1994: 31; Žižek 1991: 195; 1994b: 4).The *second* misrecognition brings us back to the discursive undecidability described in Chapter 3. The principles that establish the imaginary horizon to think about society as a unified and coherent order remain open to numerous different interpretations. Principles that generate social organizations must have a universal character and symbolize the entire society. As Torfing (1999a: 177) argues, a discourse that aims at speaking "in the name of the impossible object of society . . . must turn the particular content of its demands into an embodiment of the signifier of an empty universality." A signifier that represents the "empty universality" of the society must have the character of an empty signifier. We encountered the concept of empty signifier in the previous chapter and know that empty signifiers are ineluctable for the representation of the shared commonality of a chain of signifiers. The particular and historically contingent signifiers are transcended to a universal principle that represents the essential being of society when they are made into signifiers that establish an imaginary and totalizing horizon, within which institutions, identities, practices, processes and so on receive their particular position. An empty signifier is the general name for "a particular element [that] assumes the impossible task of a universal representation" (Laclau 1996b: 59).

It is against the backdrop of the pre-supposed universal character of an empty signifier that it becomes possible to conceive of the shared commonality of particular institutions, practices, and social identities and to regard them to be "parts of one and the same historicity, which equally counts for each and every of them" (Lefort and Gauchet 1990: 101). Whereas the first misrecognition concerned the collective beliefs that there is some objective necessity explaining why one particular principle represents the essential being of the society, the second misrecognition refers to beliefs that these principles are, by necessity, aligned to a particular content of that order. However, if any society generating principle has the function of an empty signifier, it remains basically open to any kind of substantiation. As Laclau and Zac (1994: 15) argue, the empty signifier "is indifferent to the content of the filling" (cf. Laclau 1996a: 59; Torfing 1999b: 101). It is rather paradoxical to notice that even though an empty signifier has the function of a synecdoche that "takes upon itself the task of representing the whole" field of heterogeneous social entities, roles, practices, and identities, the constituents of this field cannot be derived from the empty signifier itself (Miller 2004: 220). In other words, the association of an empty signifier with a particular social content derives from the misrecognition of the unbridgeable gap between society generating principles and the particular social forms associated with them. Altogether, the notoriously indeterminate, open logic of discourse that is vulnerable to contestation and critique reproduces the possibility of politics being the set of social practices that arrange and rearrange the relations between signifiers. Moreover, we can discern between two different types of discursive undecidability—the undecidability about the (empty) signifiers that represent the discourse, and the discursive order associated with them. Correspondingly, we encounter two different levels of politics based on the distinction of whether decisions are made "*within* a structure" or "*about* the structure" (Howarth 2004: 265; cf. Moebius 2005: 137; Stäheli 2000: 244).

TYPOLOGY OF DISCURSIVE RELATIONS

We know at this point that discourse is a relational ensemble or bundle of signifiers that is represented by empty signifiers and delineated from the environment. However, even though it might seem of lesser theoretical importance to the overall structure of discourse, it still remains unclear what kinds of relational logics and particular relations a discourse consists of. In order to answer these questions, it is useful to draw on Nonhoff's (2007) seminal and so far unsurpassed taxonomy of discursive relations. The importance of Nonhoff's idea does not refer to the clear and accessible overview of the discourse, but far more to its value as an analytical heuristic framework that makes it possible to detect, describe, and compare different discourses empirically and explicate their diachronic transformations

Before moving on to describe different types of discursive relations, it is indispensable to ask what kinds of entities are connected by discursive relations. Having previously described the constituent entities of discourse as signifiers, Laclau (2005a ; 2005b: 72) has argued later on that not a signifier but demand constitutes the smallest ontological entity of discourse. Also, Nonhoff (2006: 304) has argued that "political discourses are essentially about negotiation of the future organization of the society, whereby demands play a very crucial part" (cf. Nonhoff 2007: 182). Even though I am highly sympathetic to Nonhoff's attempt at analyzing different kinds of demands involved in discursive constitution of the society, there are a number of reasons to stick to the notion of the signifier as the smallest ontological entity of discourse. First, demands are anything but obvious and analytically accessible without rigorous empirical analysis (cf. Angermüller 2007). It is reasonable to suggest that observation of demands can be the analytical outcome of empirical discourse analysis but not its point of departure. Second, as I describe in more detail elsewhere (Marttila forthcoming, chapter 7), the focus on demands narrows the analytical applicability of the post-structural discourse analysis to particular political situations, conflicts, and crises, while we have lost sight of the everyday arrangements and negotiations of significations. The association of discourse with political ideology that has been predominant so far has limited the range of social phenomena that is open to post-structural discourse analysis. Instead of focusing on political hegemonies trying to represent the fullness of being of the entire society, post-structural discourse should be capable of analyzing the fixation of the relations between signifiers at any social level and in any social context.[4] It is because demand refers to rather particular kinds of political interactions, such as political mobilization of protests or revolutions, that I prefer sticking to the signifier as the smallest ontological entity of discourse. Moreover, since signifier can relate to any artefact, object, sign, or symbol (cf. Laclau 1993: 432), it seems necessary to point out that in this book signifier is understood as a written semantic sign (e.g., entrepreneur) or a combination of signs (e.g., entrepreneur of oneself) whose respective meaning contents are determined in relation to the bundle of other signs, with which they are connected in articulations. In this regard, signifier is closely related to the notion of concept, which meaning content derives from its relations to it surrounding further signs.

Articulatory practices actualize particular meaning contents of signifiers by setting them in relation with other signifiers. The signified—the conceived meaning-content of a signifier—is not something that exists independently of the signifier, but that—with this associated meaning—derives from the total contexts of signifiers contained in the articulation. If the discursive structure is responsible for the totality of signifieds produced by an articulation, it becomes essential to analyze how these discursive contexts are organized, what relations they involve, and how their retention is made possible. In order to elucidate the discursive construction of the entrepreneur, post-structural discourse analysis must reconstruct the discursive arrangements and structures, within which the entrepreneur receives its particular social value. The heuristic value of Nonhoff's (2007) typology of discursive relations resides in its nominal elucidation of different possible relational logics and particular discursive relations involved in articulations. Moreover, this heuristic framework makes it possible to identify and describe the points of commonalities and similarities between singular articulations and, therewith, to explicate their reproduction of one and the same discursive order.

As the differential logic of discourse suggests, *difference* is the most essential discursive relation. Every identity results from a "positional relational identity" (Žižek 1989: 98). Relation of difference pre-supposes the presence of at least two mutually distinguishable signifiers. According to Culler (1986), the relation of difference is not only a distinction of the difference between two separate entities but involves also their combination. A signifier is something that promises a meaning, and this meaning, again, is located in another signifier. For instance, when we look up the meaning of a word in a dictionary, we "find, of course, another word, which we can also look up" (Culler 1986: 143). However, relation of difference has no natural boundaries, and, as such, the actual relations of difference can change from one articulation to another. After all, all differential relations are equally commensurable. In order to justify and motivate a particular combination of signifiers, it becomes necessary to give reasons and explicate the grounds for a combination. Representation of the mutual commensurability of a bundle of signifiers overrules the relation of difference with the relation of equivalence. In place of the mutual distinctiveness of signifiers (i.e., difference), discursive entities appear as mutually equivalent now. If discursive constituents were located in relation of pure difference, the combination would not be possible to ground. In other words, every discursive system is dominated by two logics of discursive relations: *combination* and *substitution*. Whereas the logic of combination is expressed in terms of X is different to Y, the logic of substitution is expressed by the relation X stands for Y (Nonhoff 2007: 178). However, two elements cannot be mutually substitutable without making reference to a third element that symbolizes, or grounds, the substitution. Indeed, we can locate two different sources of substitution: the relation of antagonism and the relation of representation.

Antagonism does not refer to absolute incommensurability of discursive entities; that is, that they have nothing do with each other whatsoever. Instead, antagonism expresses a relation of radical negativity, which means that the presence and existence of an element A is obstructed and endangered by an element Z. Relation of antagonism introduces the possibility of substitution since it establishes a division of particular signifiers into two opposing bundles. In this manner, the elements A, B, and C are mutually substitutable in their shared opposition to the element Z. Antagonism facilitates the exclusion of an element and "*vis-à-vis* the excluded element, all other differences are equivalent to each other" (Laclau 2005b: 70). Following Nonhoff (2007: 177), the discursive relation achieved by means of the logic of antagonism can be described as contrariety. Logic of representation provides another possible source of substitution. The systemic identity of the discourse symbolizing empty signifier represents the principle of mutual commonality between various particular elements. A number of signifiers are mutually substitutable due to their belonging to the same discourse.

When welfare state (D) functions as an empty signifier, it represents the point of commonality between signifiers of full employment (A), social security (B), and solidarity (C). Each of these particular signifiers is mutually substitutable as a constituent of the welfare state. A, B, and C are mutually equivalent and substitutable with regard to D. On the other side, finance market speculation (Q), market liberalization (R), and labor market flexibilization (S) could possibly be articulated as mutually equivalent with regard to their belonging to the workfare state (P) that constitutes the antagonistic other of the welfare state. In this regard, both the discourse of welfare state and the discourse of the antagonistic other of workfare state consists of a bundle of relations of difference (B, C, D and Q, R, S), empty signifiers that symbolize the shared identity and the principle of mutual equivalence (e.g., B, C, D are mutually equal with regard to A), and an antagonistic relation of contrariety between two empty signifiers of welfare state and workfare state and their respective discursive constituents. Logics of difference and equivalence do not constitute two possible ways of establishing a discourse. Instead, as Laclau (2005b: 70) argues, the "tension between the differential and equivalential logics" is something that characterizes every discourse. Taking into consideration that empty signifiers are indispensable for any discourse, signifiers are always substitutable and equivalent with the regard to their shared identity representing empty signifier. Whether the logic of equivalence is also supported by the relation of contrariety to an antagonistic other varies from case to case and from time to time. In the presence of an antagonistic other, relations of equivalence not only operate within the discourse represented by the empty signifier, the exterior of the discourse is also subverted by the logic of equivalence. In this regard, the discursive space of representation is structured around a binary division between two mutually antagonistic empty signifiers (A ≠ P), two bundles of mutually contrary and incommensurable signifiers represented by A and P, respectively (B, C, D ≠ Q, R, S). The discursive space of representation is simplified and reduced to "two antagonistic camps" (Laclau 2005a: 148).

It should be noticed that the antagonistic other is always articulated from the point of view of the socio-political force that identifies a principle, idea, norm as the idealized state of social being, which again the antagonistic other is conceived to endanger. Empty signifier occupies "an empty place [that] becomes the signifier of fullness, of systematicity as such, as that which is lacking" (Laclau 2000b: 232f). In this regard, the welfare state as an empty signifier would epitomize the conceived ideal condition of the social being. The question I discuss more at length elsewhere (Marttila forthcoming) concerns the necessity that empty signifiers represent principles, ideals, and norms that count for the entire society. For instance, Norval (2000: 222) argues that empty signifiers are essentially representations of the unity that generate visions and imaginaries of *a* society. Also Laclau (2000b: 185) argues that empty signifiers are representations of the "absent fullness" of the social. On the other side, however, post-structural discourse theory has pointed out the "impossibility" of any cohesive and coherent representations of the society (cf. Laclau 1990b) and even emphasized the "plurality of the social" (Laclau and Mouffe 2001: 187). There are hardly any good reasons to argue that the discursive construction of reality must necessarily be involved in the construction of representations of the entire society. Moreover, there is no reason to exclude the possibility that each and every discourse is actually structured around a number of different empty signifiers, and furthermore that these empty signifiers might have rather different discursive extents. In accordance with our earlier example, the welfare state might easily have the function of an empty signifier. However, whether this is the case cannot be derived from any a priori assumption: it remains a strictly analytical question to be answered by empirical discourse analysis. Whether the welfare state functions as a single empty signifier or in combination with other empty signifiers, such as full-employment, growth, knowledge society, or something else, must be answered by empirical discourse analysis.

It might also be possible that each of these empty signifiers unifies a set of different, less general nodal points, which have the same function representing discursive systematicity, yet with a considerably lesser number of signifiers represented.[5] The idea that one and the same discourse is organized around a plurality of empty signifiers and that empty signifiers represent lower level nodal points is a pragmatic decision. However, Laclau and Mouffe's (2001) argument about the plurality of the social is hardly compatible with a picture of a homogenous discursive structure. In this regard, Keller (2008) and Angermüller (2007) have observed a rather grievous contradiction between the ontological assumption of the heterogeneous social order and the theoretical proposition of a homogenous and coherent discursive organization. Consider, for example, a social democratic discourse on the welfare state. In place of a coherent and homogenous discourse, we would be dealing with a system of empty signifiers that represent the conceived ideal social condition of being (e.g., welfare state, economic growth, full employment), contextual nodal points that symbolize and substantiate these overall discursive principles in a particular institutional setting (e.g., *labour market*: activation; *economy*: human capital mobilization; *working place*: life-long learning; etc.). These contextually particular nodal points translate the overall social ideals as represented by empty signifiers into corresponding contextually delineated social institutions, social practices, and identities.

It appears useful, therefore, to distinguish between the "empty signifier" as a symbol of the imagined fullness of society, such as social welfare, and partial contextually and institutionally particular nodal points that represent and epitomize this universal vision within different institutional contexts. There is no doubt that both empty signifiers and nodal points assume the same quilting function as they arrange signifiers into chains of signifiers whose identity they represent. However, what distinguishes empty signifiers from nodal points is the relative extent of signifiers they unify. Moreover, empty signifiers also unify nodal points into chains of signifiers. Accordingly, we are dealing with a much more complex, heterogeneous, and multi-level topography of discourse than has been recognized so far by the post-structural discourse analysts. The topography of the discourse is similar to Freeden's (1994: 157) description of the ideological structure as a centric order of core concepts that epitomize the differentia specifica of an ideology, the core concepts substantiating adjacent and more peripheral concepts (cf. Stavrakakis 1997: 265f).

The social plurality considered by Nonhoff (2007) introduces yet another discursive relation of "hyper-difference" (*Superdifferenz*). For Nonhoff, hyper-difference is an articulatory means to demarcate mutually commensurable issues, themes, and questions from incommensurable and irrelevant ones. According to Nonhoff, hyper-difference is expressed in manner of negation of any connection between different issues. For example, it would be possible to argue that gender inequality has nothing in common with social welfare. In this case, gender inequality does not constitute an antagonistic other of social welfare since the presence of gender inequality does not symbolize something that impedes the attainment of social welfare. After all, it is considered a totally irrelevant issue for social welfare. Even though social welfare and gender inequality constitute two mutually distinguishable and, as such, differential signifiers, they are impossible to interrelate to each other positively because there is a discursive space of representation missing within which they could be interrelated. Beside antagonism, hyper-difference is a further possibility to control the general field of discursivity and sustain the relative stability of the discourse.

Tables 4.1 and 4.2 summarize the previous discussion about discursive relations. Following Nonhoff's[6] seminal work, the discursive relations can be ordered into two general types of discursive relations: combination and substitution. The general formula for the discursive relations of combination is "A is different from B." There are altogether four particular relations of combination: difference, equivalence, contrariety, and hyper-difference.

The standard logic of the relations of substitution is: "A stands for B." There are two particular relations of substitution: empty signifiers and nodal points. Despite their representation of the discursive identity of empty signifiers, nodal points have a different discursive width, and therefore their separation appears meaningful. Nodal points represent local points of condensation of hegemonic discourses on the social, whereas empty signifiers represent the imaginary limits of social reality.

Table 4.1 Register of Combination

Relation	Definition
Difference	The most fundamental relation between discursive elements. Relation of difference is expressed in terms: *X is different to Y*
Equivalence	Equivalence overdetermines relations of difference as it replaces the relation of difference between elements by their mutual substitutability. Equivalence does not replace the relation of difference but instead indicates that *A is different than B, but is equivalent with regard to C*
Contrariety	Relation of contrariety expresses the incommensurability between two or more discursive elements. Discursive elements are set into relation of contrariety with regard to a shared point of reference, which represents the reason for their incompatibility. Relation of contrariety is expressed as follows: *A and B stand in a relation of contrariety with relation to C*
Hyper-Difference	Hyper-difference is one possible way of demarcating discursive systems. Hyper-difference is expressed in terms *A is different than B, but with respect to C, they have no common ground of representation*

Table 4.2 Register of Substitution

Relation	Definition
Empty Signifier	Empty signifier represents the shared point of reference and the common identity of a bundle of discursive elements. Empty signifiers allow both the articulation and the observation of the mutual commonality of signifiers, as well as the exclusion of signifiers as constituents of the antagonistic other. In this latter function, empty signifier names the antagonistic other. Empty signifier is expressed in terms– *A represents the common identity of the discourse*
Nodal Point	Nodal points share with empty signifiers the same discursive identity representing function. However, nodal points play this role on a less universal level. Nodal points function as contextual or sectorial stand-ins for the entire discourse representing empty signifiers. Nodal points can be expressed in the following terms– *A represents B, the common identity of the discourse*

LEVELS OF DISCOURSE

The previous section helped to understand every discourse to consist of a rhizomatic network-like structure covering sets of signifiers and different kinds of discursive relations that connect them. In place of a homogenous and cohesively structured discursive order, the emerging picture of the discourse refers rather well to Foucault's (2005: 28) notion of a discourse as a "space of dispersion" (*Raum der Zerstreuung*). Every discourse contains a space of dispersion that embraces the total domain of signifiers, including the marked or antagonized exterior, the relations that connect signifiers with each other and the singular signifiers, which attain their meaning content from their particular position vis-à-vis other signifiers. So far, post-structural discourse analysis has not tried to establish any kind of heuristic framework to describe, classify, and categorize different types of signifiers. Post-structural discourse analysis has been focused on the explication of empty signifiers instead of trying to re-construct entire discursive structures (Angermüller 2007). Extending the analytical focus from empty signifiers to an entire discursive system of signifiers makes it meaningful to not only describe the signifiers unified by empty signifiers nominally, but to try and classify and categorize them. Following the suit of governmentality studies (e.g., Dean 1999), it should be possible to establish a heuristic system or taxonomy of signifiers, which makes it possible to describe the function that a signifier has in a particular discourse.

A heuristic system of signifiers would make it possible, in a manner similar to governmentality studies, to not only ask what signifiers act as empty signifiers, but also to inquire what signifiers are attributed uppermost ethical value as objects of collective desire, the function of active social agency or means, technologies and resources of agency, and so on. Even though it is possible now to draw, for instance, on the Foucauldian discourse analysis or the governmentality studies and establish heuristic systems that allow for the classification of signifiers, it remains questionable whether the analyst might really know what meaning a particular signifier has in an articulation. First of all, it should be noticed that even though the meaning content of a signifier depends on its relation to other signifiers, we cannot know exactly what meaning the articulating subject derives from that relation. Even though Howarth (2005: 319) suggests that post-structural discourse analysis is about "second-order interpretations of social actors' own self-understandings," we do not have access to these understandings: we can only describe how the discursive structure of these understandings is organized. In other words, the attempt to classify signifiers contained in articulations appears problematic since we cannot know exactly what these signifiers mean to subjects of articulation.

A strictly relational and functional analysis might provide a means to classify signifiers without really knowing the meanings social subjects attach to them. Even though I am very well aware of the fundamental ontological differences between the post-structural discourse theory and Greimas's (1987, 1990) structural semiotics, Greimas's system of actants provides a means for a non-substantial classification of signifiers. Greimas's universalistic system of *Narrative Grammar* aimed at providing a system of narrative positions (*actants*) that "recur[s] from one text to another" (Greimas 1990: 113). The system of narrative positions would facilitate the "study of the discursive organization of signification" and make it possible to identify the functions and roles that particular signifiers played in a particular text (Greimas 1990: 12). For Greimas, every narrative is structured around a limited number of narrative positions, and these positions can be occupied by different signifiers.

Moreover, similar to the post-structural discourse theory, Greimas also argued that a particular signifier has a specific narrative position only in relation to other positions. In other words, in order to learn what narrative position the entrepreneur has, for instance, we do not have to know what meaning entrepreneur has for the subject of articulation. Instead, we can understand its narrative position from its relation to other narrative positions (Greimas 1971: 171, 175; 1987: 106ff). For instance, a narrative element performs the role of "traitor" when it is set into a negative relation toward "subjects" who want to reach certain "objects of desire." According to Greimas, there are altogether six different narrative positions of *destinator, receiver, subject, adjuvant, traitor,* and *objects*, as well as two isotopes of *space* and *time* that give situational framing for the narrative (Titscher et al. 1998: 164). Instead of applying Greimas's system of narrative positions strictly, the following discussion draws loosely on the six narrative positions and the two isotopes of space and time to four discursive levels of ethics, technologies, subjects, and spatio-temporal framings.

According to Greimas, the ethical level of discourse refers to the objects of desire, which social subjects are keen on achieving and protecting. Illustrative of ethics is Foucault's association of the ethos and the telos of society (Dean 1996: 224). In this regard, the telos—the desired, wanted, and appreciated—is intimately related to the idealized social condition of being. Ethos motivates the coordination of various social conducts, practices, rationalities, programs, and techniques so as to guarantee the achievement and maintenance of the conceived good of the "good, beautiful and honourable" (Foucault 2004: 883). Ethos is, in this regard, a foundation of reflexivity and makes it possible to measure and evaluate possible deviations and discrepancies between the actual state of social being and the idealized state of being. Ethos and telos are intimately interrelated because the ethos provides the coordinates, objectives, "ideals or principles to which government should be directed—freedom, justice, equality, mutual responsibility, citizenship, common sense, economic efficiency, prosperity, growth, fairness, rationality and the like" (Rose and Miller 1992: 179). Whereas ethos defines the socially good and valuable, telos defines the future direction of the social practices, and institutions required to either realize or maintain the ethically valuable. The liberal discourse, for instance, appreciates individual freedom as the highest ethical good of society. Freedom, as the ethical principle, instructed the political government to conduct itself in such a manner that individual subjects were capacitated to exercise their freedom actively (Rose 1993: 291). The collective "national objective of the good citizen will fuse with the personal objective for the good life" (Rose 1993: 291). In contrast to liberalism, a communitarian ethos places considerably more weight on membership and active participation in different kinds of social communities. In place of the liberal ideal of "the individualized and autonomized actor," we now encounter a subject-ideal of actors with their "unique, localized and specific ties to their particular family and to a particular community" (Rose 1996a: 334). As these two examples illustrate, ethos is neither something purely collective nor individual, but instead an ethical interface that coordinates conducts of collective institutions and individual subjects in accordance with their common ethical fundament. However, ethics is not just something that motivates political governments and individual subjects to conduct themselves in a particular manner, but also something that establishes them within a common horizon of coexistence.

In terms of post-structural discourse theory, the ethical level refers to the discursive levels of empty signifiers and nodal points. Empty signifiers and nodal points are not only symbols that represent the systemic identity of the discourse, but they also epitomize unquestionable values and principles associated with the ideal social being. It is therefore reasonable to assume that the ethical level is accessible in articulations in the form of either desired objects or signifiers that unify particular signifiers and motivate and justify their being together. In this regard, we have to know already what the common good of the society might have to be (e.g., freedom, democracy, social welfare) so as to be able to identify the ethical level of discourse. However, not every object of desire functions necessarily as an empty signifier or a nodal point. Greimas (1990: 130) has observed that objects of desire possess desirability due to their conceived objective or subjective value. When objects have an objective value, they are conceived to be valuable and desirable in themselves. On the contrary, the subjective value of objects means that these are perceived as something valuable or desirable because they lend subjects certain capacities. Taking into consideration the earlier discussion of the empty signifiers, it seems likely for empty signifiers to appear in articulations in the form of objects that have objective values. For instance, social welfare would not be a resource to achieve certain desirable social ends: instead, it is the superordinate goal for social practices. Employability would be a possible example of an object conceived to possess a subjective value. Employability is desired and valued because it capacitates subjects to find work and stay in employment. The distinction between objective and subjective values is crucial for empirical discourse analysis because it facilitates the identification of different ethical levels and helps to distinguish between objective values—empty signifiers and nodal points—and other desirable objects that figure either as means, strategies, and devices that subjects may mobilize and make use of in order to attain the desired ethos of society.

The non-subjective and non-agential strategies, institutions, tactics, devices, and so on refer to the discursive level of technologies, which consists of all those resources that are conceived to support the attainment of the uppermost ethical values. The meaningfulness of these technologies originates from their assumed capacity to support the attainment of ethical values. In terms of Rose and Miller (1992: 175), "technologies [are] the complex of mundane programs, calculations, techniques, apparatuses, documents, and procedures through which authorities seek to embody and give effect to governmental ambitions." However, technologies not only capacitate social agency. According to Foucault, social technologies both capacitate and restrict possible social conducts. Technologies allow social subjects to act on their own conducts and those of other subjects "so as to transform in order to attain a certain state of happiness, purity, wisdom, perfection or immortality" (Foucault 1988: 18). In terms of Greimas, technologies appear in narrative structures as the adjuvants enhancing the subjects' capacity to grasp and attain the objects they desire. It is nonetheless useful to distinguish between two different types of technologies: the "technologies of the other" and "technologies of the self." According to Foucault, the technologies of the other embrace the ensemble of means that make it possible to act on the others' conducts of themselves so as to govern them in line with the desired ethical objectives (cf. Dean 1996: 222f; Foucault 2004: 875f). Technologies of the self refer to various ways of how individual subjects arrange their own conducts so as to support and facilitate the attainment of the ethical objectives of government (Foucault 1988: 18).

However, the distinction between the two types of technologies is analytical at most, which Cruikshank's (1996) analysis of the discourse on "self-esteem" also illustrates. Concerns on individual self-esteem proliferating in California in the 1990s were far from being an ethical objective only: The latter also figured as a means of political government to mobilize individual subjects to work on their self-esteem as well as a guideline for individual subjects work on themselves. For Cruikshank (1996: 233), "[s]elf-esteem is a technology in the sense that it is a specialized knowledge of how to esteem our selves, to estimate, calculate, measure, evaluate, discipline, and to judge our selves." However, the "problem" of self-esteem and subsequent collective efforts to increase the general level of self-esteem appeared within a collective discourse that observed an insufficient level of liberation, self-responsibility, and personal self-fulfillment. In this regard, the self of the "self-esteem" discourse is far from being a private self, a personal subject, but far more symbolizes "the product of power relations, the outcome of strategies and technologies developed to create everything from autonomy to participatory democratic citizenship" (Cruikshank 1996: 248).

The discourse on self-esteem indicates that technologies are not necessarily governmental programs, policies, regulations, or the like, but also include definitions about the being of social subjects. In other words, identity policies and various forms of subjectivation and subject-constructs are essential types of technologies of the other, which political government makes use of in order to govern society toward the idealized ethical objectives. As Rose (1990: 213) argues, the "complex and heterogeneous assemblage of technologies" functions as a relay that brings "the varied ambitions of political, scientific, philanthropic, and professional authorities into alignment with the ideals and aspirations of individuals."

Taking into consideration the earlier described antagonistic and dichotomic organization of discourse, it is reasonable to suggest that the technological level of discourse not only embraces the complex of beneficial and productive technologies, but also technologies that are conceived to impede the attainment of ethical objectives. In other words, just like the ethical level is divided between ethical principles charged with positive and negative meanings, so are the technologies. It is therefore reasonable to assume that articulations not only describe functioning and beneficial technologies, which appear *admissible* with regard to the ethical objectives, but also define *non-admissible* technologies hindering the attainment of ethical objectives or even making it completely impossible. The admissible and non-admissible technologies are singled out by their respective positive and negative association with the ethical objectives of discourse. This argument should be plausible against the backdrop of the earlier discussion about how empty signifiers assign particular signifiers their respective position within the discursive edifice. Whether a technology is conceived of as functional or dysfunctional, productive and non-productive, rational or irrational depends on its articulated relation to the empty signifiers.

The same kind of antagonistic and dichotomic organization of discourse applies to the discursive level of subjectivity. The power of discourse determining social reality depends essentially on its capacity to subjectivate individual subjects into subject positions within the discourse and to make them accept the discursive perspective of reality as their subjective point of view (cf. Foucault 2004: 888). Regarded in this way, the political power of government depends on the extent to "which individuals are willing to exist as subjects" of the discourse represented by the government (Gordon 1991: 48). An essential element of the subjective level of discourse concerns the construction of the "allegiance between individuals and communities in the service of the [political] projects, regulation, reform or mobilization" (Rose 1996: 334). However, the establishment of allegiance between political government and the individual subjects is but one type of subjectivation. If we follow Greimas, every discourse arranges at least five different subject positions of destinator, receiver, subject, traitor, and adjuvant. Destinator refers to the world view or the principles in whose name articulations are made (Titscher et al. 1998: 164). Destinator can be an abstract ideal or ethical principle, as well as a group of subjects, in whose name articulations are made. Receiver, in contrast, symbolizes the consignee and pre-supposed owner of the world view represented by the destinator. In general terms, destinator denotes the sender of the articulation, whereas receiver refers to the addressee (Greimas 1971: 118, 163).

Greimas (1971) explains the distinction between the destinator and the receiver by drawing on the Marxist theory, in which receiver is the entire "humanity" (*Menschheit*), on whose behalf the subject (*man*) is assumed to act. A characteristic feature of the discursive construction of the receiver is the pre-supposed shared identity between the subject of articulation and the receiver of the articulation. In Marxist theory, the subject of articulations speaks on behalf of a community (*nation, workers, humanity*), whose identity defines the articulation at the same time. Whereas the receiver is the passive addressee of the articulation, Greimas describes the subjects as the group of social agents to whom the articulation attributes the responsibility and the duty to act in order to attain or reproduce the social order idealized by the articulation (cf. Greimas 1971: 161; 1990: 121). Subjects possess, according to Stichweh (2005), the "role of performance" so as to secure the attainment or retention of the idealized social state of being. Greimas divides the agential subjects into two primary types of agency: the instituting and the controlling subject. An instituting subject is assigned the capacity or potential to bring society in tune with the idealized state of social being. The controlling subject, on the other side, figures as the maintainer of the already achieved social order (Greimas 1990: 126f). In legal discourse, the legislator appears as an instituting subject when it is assigned the task to provide better legal codes. On the other side, the same subject becomes a controlling subject when it is assigned the role to maintain the existing legal order. Both types of subjects are essential for achieving ethical objectives. However, they have rather different kinds of responsibilities and functions.

The subject roles of destinator (the subject of articulation), receiver (subject addressed by the articulation), and subjects (agents assigned by the articulation) constitute the coalition of social subjects assigned the objective to achieve and maintain the discursive representation of the social order. Against the backdrop of the earlier described antagonistic structure of discourse, the discursive level of subjectivity is also divided between subjects conceived to either support or impede the implementation and maintenance of a discursive order. The major relation of antagonism is located between the above described discursive coalition of destinator, receiver, subjects, and adjuvants and the conceived traitors of this coalition. In terms of Greimas (1971: 164), traitor refers to social subjects who, in some way, impede the realization of the idealized discourse. The traitor is defined in relational terms as the antagonistic other of the discourse coalition. Moreover, the traitor is always identified within the perspective of the idealized discourse. A traitor is observed from a position within a discourse as the potential or real force that may hinder society from attaining its discourse-specific conception of the ideal state of being. As a consequence, the conceived traitor becomes such through its conceived negativity and radical otherness to the discourse, whose realization it impedes.

It is useful to distinguish further between two levels of primary and secondary traitors. In accordance with Greimas, both subjects and traitors are supported by adjuvants that either support subjects to fulfill their assigned discursive role or assist traitors to play their harmful roles. In this regard, both the traitor and adjuvants of the traitor figure as two different types of anti-subjects who restrain subjects from attaining the idealized social condition of being. However, anti-subjects are not necessarily individual subjects, social roles, or the like, but can equally well relate to abstract conditions (e.g., unemployment), social institutions (e.g., finance market regulation), or social practices (e.g., taxation). A common feature of all types of anti-subjects is their association with aggravating conditions, hindrances, and obstacles that render the attainment of ethical principles difficult, if not even impossible. Another crucial aspect in the discursive denomination of anti-subjects regards their temporal embeddedness. Anti-subjects can refer to existing, already encountered, or potential and expected future grievances. In other words, the anti-subjects can be articulated as either a real or a potential threat to the discourse coalition. A common aspect of all types of anti-subjects is their association with conceivably inadmissible consequences for society.

The fourth and concluding discursive level consists of the spatio-temporal framings that define the spatial and temporal setting of the discourse. The temporal dimension defines the historical and chronological context of the discourse and makes it possible to distinguish other historical events, processes, and entire historical epochs. Moreover, the temporal setting also provides a connection between past, present, and future and, therewith, defines the temporal similarities, differences, and changes. Furthermore, different narrative approaches to discourse have emphasized the dynamic and processual dimension of time and argued that temporal framing goes beyond the temporal location of the discourse, static comparisons, and even embraces conceptions of diachronical changes (cf. Viehöver 2001, 2003). Temporal setting also denotes attitudes, judgments, and expectations associated with temporal changes. The spatial framing, on the other side, sets up the coordinates of the social place, in which social practices, institutions, and processes take place (cf. Titscher et al. 1998: 164). According to Greimas (1971: 196f), the spatial framing is not just one among many other narrative structures, but actually the most central means to provide narrative coherence. According to Ricoeur (1991) and Link (1984), among others, social myths play a central role in the construction of spatial framings. It is typical of myths to establish how they depict imaginaries of primordial collective coexistence by elevating symbols into the status of collective symbols that incorporate and represent the pre-supposed endemic essence of the social community. As Ricoeur (1991: 483) claims, myths function as a social cement that conceived naturalness of the given social organization. The nation, for instance, is but one historically contingent political myth that provides an imaginary of the people as the inheritors of a historically determined social space. Foucault's (2007: 11) analysis of the logics of political power has observed further how spatial framings and the "problematics of space" legitimize and rationalize particular governmental technologies and institutions by associating them as reflections of an underlying objective social order (Rose 1996: 329). Consider, for example, how the spatial conception of the community legitimized the respective political strategies of the Thatcherite and Blairite governments. In the Thatcherite discourse, society could not figure as the explanation for individual mishaps and problems for the sheer reason that society did not exist at all as a meaningful spatial setting of individual subjects. As Thatcher argued:

> Too many people . . . are casting their problems on society. And you know, there is *no such thing as society*. There are individual men and women, and there are families. And no government can do anything except through people, and people must look to themselves first. (in Shore and Wright 1997: 24; italics added)

As this citation manifests, spatial framing is not a discursive ornament but much a point of reference that articulations apply to manifest the rationality or irrationality of certain political practices. Indeed, one essential point of difference between the Thatcherite and Blairite discourses referred to their way of conceiving of the social bonds between individual subjects. One reason for the possibility of the Blairite discourse to appeal to the social solidarity between individual subjects derived from the pre-supposed natural embeddedness within particular communities. I do not argue that such communities do not exist, but rather that the knowledge about the presence of communities, which the Thatcherite discourse lacked, was an essential premise for the rights and duties that individual subjects had toward their respective communities in the New Labour discourse (cf. Reyes 2005: 235). There is an additional reason for the uppermost discursive importance of spatial framings. This is that articulations on behalf of a particular order, such as the community, "abolish[es] the difference between sender and receiver" and therewith induce a sense of commonality between the subjects of articulations and the receivers (Greimas 1990: 33).

The above outlined four levels of discourse and their respective sub-dimensions make it possible to not only describe the signifiers contained in articulations nominally, but also to classify and categorize these signifiers and therewith detect discursive changes on different levels of the discourse. This chapter's concluding discussion provides an overview of different types and extents of discursive change.

DIACHRONIC CHANGES OF DISCOURSE

If we are to observe changes in the discursive construction of the entrepreneur, it appears inevitable to set up a heuristic framework that allows for the identification and classification of different kinds of discursive change. The genealogical analysis of the origin of discursive changes is exacerbated by the fact that discursive changes become tangible only against the backdrop of the previous discursive structures. In other words, we not only have to describe the change that took place, but also in what sense the new discursive structure was installed as the result of "substitutions, displacements, disguised contests and systematic reversals" (Foucault 1977: 151). Åkerstrøm Andersen (2003) has pointed out that genealogical analysis of discourse cannot be restrained to an analysis of change only. It must also "distinguish discontinuity in that which presents itself as continuity and examine possible continuities in that which presents itself as new, different or unique" (Åkerstrøm Andersen 2003: 20). However, against the backdrop of the earlier described indeterminate and undecidable nature of discourse, variegation must be considered the normal condition of being of discourse. Regarded in this way, the analyst has to define the base line for the analysis of discursive change and define what kinds of changes are extensive enough to attach any analytical interest. Following the discussion about the different kinds of discursive undecidability, as carried out in the initial part of this chapter, it is possible to distinguish two kinds of discursive changes that subvert the existing systematicity of discourse. It is meaningful to start speaking of the systematicity of discourse undermining change when articulations begin to dissolve existing discursive limits and subvert the discourse/environment distinctions, alter the predominant relations between signifiers, or either question the meaningfulness of empty signifiers and nodal points or require their radical re-interpretation and re-substantiation.

Following the earlier discussion regarding decisions about and within the discursive structure, we can distinguish between two moments of discursive change: first, moments in which the social order representing empty signifiers and nodal points are subjugated to critique and become replaced by new ones; and second, moments in which the system of signifiers represented, unified, and organized by empty signifiers and nodal points becomes radically revised and re-interpreted. The first type refers to *offensive* articulations, which subvert the entire discursive system and aim at replacing it by another one. The second type denotes *defensive* articulations that aim at re-arranging and supplementing the existing discursive order. While the offensive articulations are enabled by the empty place of the social, the defensive articulations reflect the essential undecidability, openness, and indeterminacy of empty signifiers and nodal points. Offensive articulations are engaged in constituting the imaginaries of the ontologically "absent fullness of the community" (Laclau 1996b: 42; cf. 2000a:

58). Social subjects of offensive articulation claim the access to "privileged access to knowledge" about the essential and ideal organization of society (Laclau 1990b: 77). On the other side, defensive articulations aim at sustaining social organization represented by the empty signifiers and nodal points by re-arranging the system of signifiers associated with them.

The incessant need and possibility of defensive articulations derives from the substantial openness and contestability of empty signifiers and nodal points. In other words, both offensive and defensive articulations reflect an underlying ontological undecidability, which generates the necessity of discursive determinations of the social. Whereas offensive articulations are involved in establishing imaginaries of the social, which cover the radical absence of the social determining principles at least partially and temporally, the defensive articulations are involved in continuous substantial determination of these "constitutively inadequate" discursive representations of society (Laclau 1996a: 56; cf. 1996b: 39; Žižek 1989: 99). Whereas the offensive articulations are tangible in the denomination of the principles on which the collectively shared "common sense" or "general will" can be founded, defensive articulations try to figure out those social institutions, practices, and identities that most adequately allow the substantiation of these principles (cf. Gramsci 1971: 181f; Mouffe 1993: 53).

According to Dyrberg (1998: 31), the need for offensive and defensive articulations is reproduced by the impossible substantiation of the empty place of the social and its representation by means of empty signifiers and nodal points (cf. Laclau 2005b: 85). A common feature of all offensive articulations is the subjects' discontent with the prevailing social order and their intention to identify and introduce another, in some sense better, order. Offensive articulations are therefore both destructive, as they contest and aim at replacing the existing discursive representation of the social, and also productive, since they introduce another discursive system of representation that re-substitutes the empty place of the social. In contrast to offensive articulations, defensive articulations are involved in stabilizing the existing discursive representation of the social. There at three primary functions to defensive articulations. First, defensive articulations continuously defend the set of empty signifiers and nodal points to provide the most appropriate symbolization of the social. Second, defensive articulations consistently replenish and re-substantiate, and therewith continuously re-actualize, the meaning of empty signifiers and nodal points. Thirdly Nonhoff (2007) argues that defensive articulations not only try to re-actualize the discursive structure, but also determine the social subjects and groups that most authentically represent the actual substance of empty signifiers symbolizing the social.

The analysis of the offensive and defensive articulations is complicated considerably by the fact that discourses are predominated "by the principles of equivalence and difference" (Stavrakakis 1999: 76). Following the terminology of the post-structural discourse theory, discourse organized by the relations of equivalence can be described in terms of a *popular* discourse, whereas a discourse predominantly structured by the relations of difference refers to an *institutional* discourse. Depending on whether the prevailing discourse is a predominantly popular or institutional one; whether the discursive change-inducing articulations are offensive or defensive; and whether they reproduce or change the previous popular or institutional structure of discourse, we encounter quite a range of different types of discursive change. To begin with, we can single out two nominal kinds of popular and institutional articulations. Whether these are to be characterized as offensive or defensive articulations depends on their respective impact on the prevailing discourse. The earlier argument that a discourse is either dominated by relations of difference or equivalence means that the discursive representation of the social is predominated by either a popular or an institutional kind of discourse. The Thatcherite discourse of the 1980s is one of the most characteristic cases of popular discursive construction of the social. On the other side, the subsequent Blairite New Labour discourse was a typical example of an institutional discourse. Marquand (1998: 19 in Stavrakakis 1999: 78) describes the logic of the respective discourse rather well when arguing that "Thatcherism was exclusionary; New Labour is inclusionary. Margaret Thatcher was a warrior; Tony Blair is a healer. Where she divided he unites, where she spoke of 'enemies within', he speaks of the 'people.' "

A popular discourse is characterized by its binary division of the discursive space of representation between an "us" and an antagonized "them." As Laclau (2005b: 74) argues, the popular structure of discourse is the result of the "formation of an internal antagonistic frontier." The characteristic aspect of *every* popular type of discourse is the presence of antagonistic limits of discourse, the organization of signifiers into two mutually opposing chains of equivalences, and the denomination of the antagonistic other as the origin for the "absent fullness" of society (Laclau 1996b: 42, 57). As we learned in Chapter 3, antagonistic limit overdetermines/overrules relations of difference by relations of equivalence. A binary division of the social along the opposition between we/them, good/bad, and just/unjust radically simplifies the discursive structure into two mutually contrary chains of equivalences. In popular discourse, every signifier belongs to either of these chains (Laclau 2000b: 250; Torfing 1999a: 97). The more signifiers are articulated as constituents of the mutually antagonistic chains of equivalences, the more extensive does the popular construction of the social become (Laclau 2005b: 74).

Whereas popular discourse is characterized by a binary division of the social space between two mutually antagonistic chains of equivalences, the institutional discourse is characterized by the absence of the relations of contrariety. In terms of the post-structural discourse theory, popular discourse is structured around metaphorical condensation of particular signifiers to either substantiate the valued ethical principles of the social or the depreciated principles of the antagonistic other. In contrast, the institutional discourse "multiplies the differential-syntagmatic positions and, as a result, reduces the equivalential movements that are possible within a certain social formation" (Laclau 2000c: 194). In other words, particular signifiers are not reduced to constituents of either side of the antagonistic divide, but may instead take up a number of different relations with other signifiers. When the discursive representation of the social centers on the antagonistic division, singular signifiers are reduced to symbols of either side of the divide between us and them. As Laclau (1980: 91) argues, "the more the determinations of the antagonistic force are incorporated into the chain of equivalence, the more the discourse will be a pure discourse of antagonism" (cf. Laclau 2000b: 239; 2005b: 89).

The situation in the institutional discourse, like the Blairite New Labour discourse, is rather different than that of popular discourse. In accordance with Marquand, an institutional discourse is characterized by its attempt to establish a symbolization of society that represents all social institutions, identities, and practices in overtly positive and inclusive terms. It should be kept in mind that each and every discourse consists of relations of difference and equivalence. What characterizes the institutional discourse is that the mutual substitutability (i.e., equivalence) of particular signifiers either comes without a reference to an antagonistic other, or, what appears more realistic, the antagonistic other remains without any clear substantiation. This implicates that, contrary to popular discourse, particular signifiers are not subjugated to a positively charged us or a negatively charged them. Instead, an institutional discourse aims at coinciding with the community and therefore the principle of difference covers the entire socio-political landscape (Laclau 2005b: 81). The discursive representation of a "nation" or a "people" are two rather typical ways that the institutional discourse tries to represent all social subjects and identities without exception and without an utterly represented antagonized and excluded other. Žižek (1989) notices how the political mobilization of protests was facilitated in the former GDR by the all-inclusive representation of the individual subjects as a "people." In other words, in institutional discourse the boundaries of discourse tend to coincide with the boundaries of the community. In the Great Britain of the late 19th century, Prime Minister Disraeli's vision of the "one nation" free of social conflicts is characteristic of an institutional discourse that aims at the "absorption of all social divisions into an ever-expanding system supported by the illusion of a society encompassing all differences and demands" (Stavrakakis 1999: 77). The social democratic political discourse presented later in this book (Chapters 7 and 8) is another characteristic example of an institutional discourse. The social democratic discourse replaced the previous popular construction of the social represented by the liberal-conservative government by an all-inclusive representation of the active society, in which all social subjects were invited to participate in productive work on behalf of the sustained social welfare.

The distinction between popular and institutional discourse is not only a matter of the nominal definition of the characteristics of the prevailing discursive construction of the social. Far more, the comparison of popular and institutional discourses makes it possible to describe whether the discursive change reproduces either type of the discourse, or replaces the popular discourse by an institutional one, or the institutional discourse by a popular one. In the first case, the discursive change can be related to an "institutionalization," whereas the second case refers to a process of "popularization." We encounter the process of popularization when articulations introduce unprecedented representations of an antagonistic other. On the other side, articulations lead to discursive change qua institutionalization when they erase the prevailing representations of the antagonistic other by an all-inclusive discourse representing the entire social space positively. Of course, processes of popularization and institutionalization can consist of either offensive or defensive articulations, depending on the extent to which they contest and replace the existing discursive edifice. The Keynesian political regime based on corporative cooperation and coordination of employer and employee interests can be used as a historical case of replacement of earlier antagonistic conflict between capital and labor within the political vision representing and embracing both sides positively. For example, in the Swedish welfare state discourse, the economic interests of the employers and the social interests of the employees were recognized as two distinctive yet equally respected social positions. They were not set into mutually antagonistic relations with regard to the realization of the primary ethical principle of the welfare state. Instead, their cooperation and coordination was considered essential for the attainment of the welfare society. In contrast, a new articulation of the incommensurability and mutual contrariety of the interests of employers and employees would re-establish an antagonistic division between these two social camps and replace the prevailing institutional discourse by a popular one.

SUMMARY: THE ORDER OF POLITICAL DISCOURSE

The concept of political discourse elaborated in this chapter refers to three characteristics of articulation. First, articulations are involved in representation of the social representing empty signifiers and the subsets of nodal points they represent. Whereas defensive articulations reproduce and support prevailing empty signifiers, offensive articulations contest and aim at replacing these. Second, articulations are involved in continuous re-arrangement and re-structuration of discursive systems of signifiers represented by empty signifiers and nodal points. Re-arrangement of signifiers involves re-actualization of the discursive relations that either unify (representation, difference, equivalence) or separate (contrariety, hyper-difference) signifiers. Depending on the relative dominance of the relations of difference and equivalence, respectively, and on the presence of the antagonistic construction of the other, articulations produce either popular or institutional types of discourse and result in a popularization or institutionalization of the discursive representation of the social. Third, articulations not only rearrange discursive relations, they also denominate and arrange signifiers on different levels of discourse.

Whenever the combination of discursive relations and discursive levels makes it possible to reconstruct a discursive order produced in a number of articulations, the distinction between offensive and defensive articulations and the comparison between popular and institutional discourses allows for identifying various general types of discursive change. Altogether, the heuristic framework presented in this chapter provides a heuristic network of coordinates that allows us not only to describe the discursive structures involved in the social construction of the entrepreneur, but also to identify, describe, and compare diachronic changes in the discourse of the entrepreneur. This chapter has supplied an overview of the discursive structures in which the social function of the entrepreneur is articulated. The elucidated discursive relations (*representation, difference, equivalence, contrariety, hyper-difference*), discursive levels (*ethical substance, technologies, subjects, spatiotemporal framings*), general types of discourse (*popular and institutional*), different extents (*offensive and defensive*), and types of discursive change (*popularization and institutionalization*) allow for the heuristic analytical model embedded in the post-structural discourse theory to analyze the discursive construction of the entrepreneur empirically. The multi-dimensional and multi-level conception of discourse, together with the observed undecidability and openness of discourse to change, means that the presented overview of discourse provides only a number of a priori ideas about how the discursive construction of the entrepreneur might be structured.

However, even though the objective has been to translate the highly abstract model of discourse, as presented in Chapter 3, into a number of empirically observable properties and characteristics, we are but left the option to conduct minutely detailed and empirically arduous elaborations of the discursive structures reproduced in the articulations about the social function of the entrepreneur. Moreover, against the backdrop of the considerable undecidability and the resulting contestability and changeability of discursive structures, we have to move beyond the mere nominal descriptions of discourse and also point out the moments of discursive change and the impact that these have on the prevailing conceptions of the entrepreneur. According to the presented quadrinomial scheme of discourse, the articulated signifiers belong to either the level of ethics, technologies, subjectivity, or spatiotemporal framing. It is noticeable that the ethical level containing of empty signifiers and nodal points justifies, motivates, and legitimizes the structural order of signifiers. Moreover, the ethical level also provides the reasons for the antagonistic relations of contrariety. This means that in the popular discourse the binary division of society arranges the signifiers into two mutually opposed chains of signifiers on each of the discursive levels. On the other side, these relations of contrariety are either absent or at least less predominant in the institutional discourse. The objective of Chapter 5 is to operationalize the represented heuristic model of discourse into a system of semantic codes, and thus allow for the translation of the semantic structure of articulations into the structural properties of discourse described in this chapter.

5 Discourse Analysis

Post-structural discourse theory has so far been strongly associated with the methodology of deconstruction. Laclau (1996a: 90) observes, for instance, that while the post-structural discourse theory provides an epistemic perspective that emphasizes the historically "contingent character" of discourse and "the role of the decision [caused by] . . . the undecidability of the structure," deconstruction aims at manifesting "the moment of decision that underlies any sedimented set of social relations" (Laclau 1996a: 78; cf. Åkerstrøm Andersen 2003: 58). Without intending to delve too far into the differences between Foucault's genealogical analysis and Derrida's deconstruction, they can be claimed to have in common the analytical interest to manifest the historical origins and conditions of possibility of later social formations. However, where Foucault's analytical interest seems to have been focussed on the interplay of historical discursive continuities and discontinuities (Foucault 1977), deconstruction is obviously keener on achieving persistent reversal and problematization of any social objectivity.

As Åkerstrøm Andersen (2003: 20) argues, Foucault's genealogical analysis could be neither reduced to an analysis of discontinuity nor to that of continuity. Instead, its focus was on the observation of "discontinuity in that which presents itself as continuity and to examine possible continuities in that which presents itself as new, different or unique" (Åkerstrøm Andersen 2003: 20). In other words, genealogical analysis tries to observe historical events by identifying how social practices transgress, contest, and reverse prevailing social objectivities. From the deconstructivist perspective, the analysis of the interplay between structure and event appears considerably more difficult because the history of the present now consists of nothing but consistent supplements and representation that associates "repetition to alterity" (Derrida 1977: 7). In other words, discourses are repeated and retained in a manner of temporal differences. However, Laclau and Mouffe (2001: 112) reject that new social practices of articulation would completely replace and subjugate existing significations. In other words, even though we cannot expect the existence of relatively stable discourses, as Foucault does, neither is there complete absence of any discursive structures. As a consequence, the post-structural discourse analysis can be neither reduced to a deconstructive analysis of the trace of historical differences nor to a reconstruction of spatiotemporally stable discourses. In this regard, it seems necessary to question the division of empirical discourse analysis into either a "deconstructive" or "reconstructive" type of inquiry and instead search for a common ground that allows for the observation of the discontinuity against the backdrop of the previous discursive continuity (cf. Angermüller 2005: 23f.).

However, even though the following analysis of the discursive construction of the entrepreneur aims at reconstructing relatively stable and diachronically continuous discourses of the entrepreneur as well as the moments of their replacement and reversal, the analytical logics and methods of reconstruction should be motivated by the epistemological possibilities and limitations of the post-structural discourse theory. First of all, a reconstructive discourse analysis can be carried out in the form of a hermeneutic analysis, which aims at reconstructing the knowledge contents and meanings (i.e., the social sense, which social subjects associate with objects of knowledge, such as that of the entrepreneur). On the other side, a deconstructivist analysis aims at analyzing the forms, distinctions, and organizations of meanings without yet claiming access to the produced meanings themselves (cf. Angermüller 2005: 39). Focus on the formal structure of meaning-generating articulations does not mean that the analyst abandons any interest in the meanings produced. Instead, the post-foundational ontology of meaning and signification (cf. Chapter 3) postulates that the meaning content of a signifier is the outcome of the formal organization of signifiers. The epistemological priority attached to the formal structure rather than the meaning content of articulations reflects the underlying assumption that the formal organization of signifiers is responsible for their respective meaning contents (Angermüller 2005: 41). However, there is also another and possibly even more pressing reason as to why post-structural discourse analysis should be carried out in the manner of a formal-structural analysis of articulations. Even though Howarth (2005: 319) has argued that reconstructive post-structural discourse analysis is about "second-order interpretations of social actors' own self-understandings and interpretations of their situations and practices," there are a number of reasons that the analyst cannot access social subjects' "self-understandings and interpretations" and, furthermore, as to why the formal structure of articulations must be prioritized to that of meanings produced in articulations.

First, cognitions including those of the analyst are made within particular epistemic limitations (cf. Marttila 2010). This means that the analytical reconstructions of social meanings and social subjects' own understandings coincide only when they are located within the same epistemic structures. In this situation, obviously, there is no need of interpretation: we are perfectly capable of accessing social subjects' understandings without any need of a theoretical framework that bridges the gap between the observer and the object of observation. Second, post-structural discourse theory distinguishes among the locutionary, illocutionary, and perlocutionary levels of articulation (Angermüller 2007; Hetzel 2001: 240; Ricoeur 1979: 72). Analysis of the locutionary level interprets articulation as a practice of signification and understands the meaning content. On the other side, an analysis of the illocutionary level penetrates the immediate visibility of the articulation and analyzes it as an expression of an underlying social convention, social norm, or, in our case, a discourse. The third level of articulation, the perlocutionary level, refers to the individual and social consequences of articulation (Hetzel 2001: 240). If our theoretical point of departure is located in the assumption that articulations are not voluntary and individual social practices, but rather acts both regulated and facilitated by underlying discursive conditions of possibility, there is hardly any reason to try and understand the meaning content of articulations. Against the backdrop of the post-foundational ontology of the social, discourse must be considered the general social logic and form, which any singular articulation-persisting signification has to take (cf. Chapter 3; Marttila forthcoming). This means that every subjective self-understanding is already the outcome of that subject-constituting discursive structure. In this light, post-structural discourse analysis is not interested in articulations for the sake of their meaning contents, but instead because they provide analytical access to these articulations in the first place, allowing discursive structures. The general methodological aspiration to not describe meanings produced in articulations or their immediately accessible and cognizable characteristics also means that post-structural discourse analysis edges its way to the level of illocution and, against the backdrop of the post-structural discourse theory, observes discursive structures expressed and reproduced in articulations.

The earlier (Chapter 3) described transitive character of knowledge implicates that the discursive structures described in the preceding chapter are not immediately observable by the analyst. Although it might seem counterintuitive, the discursive logic of knowledge also counts for the post-structural discourse analysis. In other words, we are capable of observing in articulations contained illocutionary level of discourse only against the backdrop of a priori knowledge about discourse, as provided by the post-structural discourse theory. As Marttila (2010: 91) argues,

post-structural discourse analysis is itself a social practice that, at the same time, departs from certain (theoretical) preconditions preceding practice, applies these internal possibilities and constraints to observing reality in order to make new propositions about the constitution of the (discursive) being of objects observed.

The epistemological possibility of discourse analysis is accordingly located in the a priori assumption "about the different *kinds* of things in the world and the *being* of these things" (Glynos and Howarth 2008: 10). This means that post-structural discourse analysis departs from a number of theoretically based assumptions, and this theoretical knowledge makes it possible to transgress the social objectivities, conventions, and everyday knowledge and observe a more fundamental level of discourse beyond the visible surface of articulations. In the place of post-modern epistemological relativism and pragmatism (cf. Lyotard 1986; Rorty 1980), which restrains from representations of social subjects' own representations and interpretations of their reality, post-structural discourse analysis has to interpret, represent, and reconstruct the empirically analysed social reality in accordance with the theoretical pre-suppositions of the post-structural discourse theory. Marttila (2010) compares post-structural discourse analysis to "constrained constructivism" (cf. Hayles 1995) that translates the theoretical model of the discourse into an analytical and heuristic framework that allows for the observation of contextually particular discursive structures. In other words, the contact between the analyst and the analyzed reality is intermediated by the epistemological possibilities of discourse theory. Considering the fundamental analytical importance of theoretical knowledge, the first stage in the operationalization of post-structural discourse theory into post-structural discourse analysis of the discursive construction of the entrepreneur consists of the elucidation of theoretical propositions and assumptions for the empirical analysis of discourse.

INTERPRETATIVE ANALYTICS

As Marttila (2010) argues in "Constrained Constructivism in Post-Structural Discourse Analysis," empirical post-structural discourse analysis must be operationalized in a manner that allows for the empirical observation of the theoretically proposed and described discursive structures. Since all cognitions are, at the same time, facilitated and constrained by epistemological limitations, post-structural discourse analysis is confronted with the question as to how the empirical analysis can visualize and manifest the assumed discursive construction of reality. There is not only one epistemological limit, but rather a plurality of limitations. After all, discourse theory assumes that all social subjects are embedded and informed by supra-individual social norms and objectivities. However, from the point of view of post-structural discourse theory, social embeddedness is not any kind of embeddedness whatsoever, but rather a distinctive kind of discursive embeddedness. In other words, even though the post-foundational ontology of the social, as described in Chapter 3, postulates the relative nature of all cognitions and understandings of reality, our knowledge is not only biased: it is biased in accordance with our particular cognitive resources. Even though we cannot avoid the perspectival limitations of our cognitions, our perceptions can still more or less well reflect the consciously accepted theoretical representations of reality. For the empirical post-structural discourse, this means that, instead of an "anything goes" kind of methodological pragmatism, methods, gathering of material, empirical interpretations, and decisions about the research strategy must be motivated and justified by their assumed contribution to the analytical visibilization of the discursive structures.

Even though Laclau was never really interested in making a contribution to the operationalization of the post-structural discourse theory (cf. Laclau 2004: 231), he still claimed that empirical discourse analysis is essentially about analyzing "the ontical level in terms of the distinctions brought about by [our discourse theoretical] ontology" (Laclau 2004: 323). Instead of departing from the hermeneutical ideal of an undistorted glance at social processes, institutions, and practices that, in accordance with Rorty (1980), withdraws from scientific representation of social subjects' own representations of their reality, post-structural discourse analysis needs to generate representations that represent the observed social reality in accordance with the representative possibilities provided by post-structural discourse theory (cf. Alvesson and Sköldberg 2000: 61). In contrast to Fuchs's (2001: 24) idea of critical cultural analysis as a second-order "observation of an observer's observation of the world," post-structural discourse analysis must become a third-order observation that not only observes how social subjects observe their own world, but actually observes these observations in accordance with the observational possibilities provided by its own theoretical fundament (cf. Åkerstrøm Andersen 2005: 141; Luhmann 1993).

Even though the methodological position of "interpretative analytics"[1] has been closely associated with the works of Foucault, and although a number of differences exist between the post-structural discourse theory and Foucault's theory of discourse, Diaz-Bone's (2005, 2007) as detailed as instructive conceptualization of the reflexive methodology of the interpretative analytics provides a number of ideas about how the a priori discourse theoretical knowledge should be operationalized in order to enable theoretically consistent and coherent interpretations of the discourse object. First of all, interpretative analytics departs from the assumption of the ever-present discursive construction of reality. Operationalization of the model of discourse does not aim at any kind of testing (falsification or verification) of the a priori theoretical propositions about empty signifiers, nodal points, or the general form of organization of discourse. Instead, theoretical knowledge is a device to understand and interpret empirical reality in accordance with our theoretical model of reality. According to Diaz-Bone

(2006a), theoretical knowledge is a means of achieving an "epistemologi-cal break" from social conventions, tacit pre-suppositions, and conceptions of reality guided by common sense. In terms of Bourdieu and Wacquant (2006: 100), an epistemological break makes it possible for the analyst to "regress from the world" and replace the uncontrolled and non-reflected relationship between the analyst and the object of analysis by a controlled and theoretically guided and determined bias (Diaz-Bone 2006a, 2007: Marttila 2010). Theoretical knowledge points out the set of meaningful themes, relations, and objects, toward which the empirical analysis can be geared (Diaz-Bone 2006b: 246).

Theoretical knowledge capacitates the analyst to avoid nominal re-description and reproduction of the characteristics of articulations that are immediately accessible even for the untrained eye and instead reconstruct only those discursive structures contained in articulations supplied by the post-structural discourse theory (Diaz-Bone 2002: 190ff). Discourse analy-sis differs from other nominal analyses of texts in the sense that texts are analytically interesting only as containers of discursive structures.[2] In other words, an analysis of texts becomes a discourse analysis only when it suc-ceeds in penetrating and transgressing characteristics of the text available for immediate cognitions and in observing and visualizing the phenom-enological structure of discourse described by discourse theory (Diaz-Bone 2006b: 257). In other words, before we are capable of analyzing any dis-course, we must begin with the definition of not only the phenomenologi-cal structure of discourse and how it becomes empirically accessible. Even though Foucault has been accused of general disinterest in methodological questions, he had a clear conception of the phenomenological structure and organization of discourse, and this a priori knowledge about discourse was the precondition for Foucault's empirical analysis of discourse (cf. Foucault 1981: 68; 2002a: 28, 41). For Foucault, the analysis of the his-torical discourse of sexuality could not be reduced to observations of how sexuality was performed or understood in different times and contexts. Instead, discourse analysis of sex required that the analyst observed "the way[s] in which sex is 'put into discourse' " (Foucault 1998: 11). However, before Foucault could say anything about the discursive construction of sex, there had to be a priori conceptions about the organization, structure, and practices of reproduction of discourse (cf. Diaz-Bone 2006a: 77). In other words, Foucault's (2002a: 41) definition of the discourse as a "reg-ularity of dispersion" "between objects, types of statement, concepts or thematic choice" was a fundamental a priori definition that made the dis-course analysis possible in the first place. Foucault's notion of the discourse and the assumed discursive construction of knowledge made it possible to achieve an epistemological break from social subjects' own observations of reality and instead retrace discursive structures located, actualized, and reproduced in these observations.

Any discourse analysis that aims at transgressing characteristics of articulation available and accessible immediately for cognitions needs an analytical penetration of the textual surface facilitated by discourse theory and an observation of the discourse object created by discourse theory only (Diaz-Bone 2006a: 76). In contrast to the hermeneutic kind of interpretation of texts, discourse analysis cannot refrain from an initial, theoretically based representation of social subjects' own representations of their reality. On the other side, however, the described necessity of commensurability between the theoretically defined discourse object and the analytically observed discourse engenders the need of two types of analytical *askesis*. First, the analyst has to abandon his own familiarity with the analyzed themes and problematize the socially accepted self-evidentiality, necessity, or normality of certain knowledge, institutions, practices, and so on. This previously described epistemological break is an inevitable pre-condition for the possibility of cognitions that break with socially conventional and objective ways to understand and interpret the world (Burchell 1993: 277). Second, and perhaps even more important, the analyst has to avoid any kind of interpretations, understandings, and explanations that go beyond the epistemological possibilities of the chosen theoretical framework. For Diaz-Bone (2006b: 179), this second type of askesis is achieved by means of a holistic methodology, which basically means that the analytically available and meaningful phenomena and their structural properties are derived from the consciously and transparently applied theoretical framework only. Departing from these two methodological premises of post-structural discourse analysis, the subsequent step is to elucidate how the multi-relational and multi-level structure of discourse described in Chapter 4 can be made accessible to empirical analysis.

SEMANTIC STRUCTURE ANALYSIS

The previous section located the most pressing methodological problem of post-structural discourse theory in the translation of the earlier (Chapter 4) described and elucidated model of discourse into empirically observable properties of articulations. The question as to how discourses become tangible in articulation does not only concern this research account. It also points out a general and so far unsolved problem in post-structural discourse analysis (Marttila forthcoming). The general aim of this section is to elaborate how discursive structures become observable textual structures produced in articulations. If, following the argument, obvious and immediate properties of text are not properties of discourse, the level of discourse must be different to the salient characteristics of text. In order to search for the discursive level of texts, it seems useful to distinguish different levels of texts. The most salient—and for every observer tangible—level consists of the textual surface of lexical elements.

The phenomenological level located beyond the textual surface combines lexical elements with qualitative relations that determine the connections between elements as well as their respective characteristics. The phenomenological level of texts becomes manifest and tangible in the narrative structures. For example, Prince (1999: 46) argues that phenomenological structures of the world originate from narrations that "make that world coherent and intelligible by evoking a network of relations—causal links, psychological motivations, goals, plans—among the entities and events." Narrations create images and knowledges of the world through a combination of lexical elements with qualitative relations that connect these with each other. For Somers (1994: 616), narrative "emplotment" is by no means a neutral and objective activity that neutrally and objectively represents the essential being of reality. Narrations not only engender knowledges of the world: they actually also determine the order of the world. Emplotment determines, for instance, the mutual commonality of disparate social events and therewith subjugates these under "chronological order[s]" (Somers 1994: 616). Hajer (2003: 104) observed later that, similar to narrations and narrative emplotment, also so-called "story lines" go beyond the neutral representation of reality and instead strongly "channel political thought and action in certain directions."

While the phenomenological (or narrative) structure of texts provides an epistemological access to the discursive structure, these two levels are by no means identical. On the other side, discourse is located neither beyond nor underneath the phenomenological structure of text, which, for instance, the Foucauldian concept of discourse suggests. Following the French structuralist writings of Roland Barthès, Claude Levi-Strauss, and Georges Dumezil (cf. Dosse 1999), Foucault (2002a) assumed that statements were regulated by discursive rules that remain beyond the knowledge of social subjects and without representation in statement. The existence of such discursive rules is manifested by the shared homology of a set of statements. In the Foucauldian discourse analysis, discourse is something that goes beyond the phenomenological structure. In a way, Foucauldian discourse analysis reconstructs the discursive level in statements by describing rather hypothetically the kinds of unspoken und unconsciously reproduced rules that must exist if we are to explain the regularity and homogeneity of statements. In contrast to the Foucauldian discourse analysis, post-structural discourse theory gives no reason for an analysis of discursive rules or the deep structures located beyond and underneath statements. However, post-structural discourse analysis is not constrained to reconstructing the phenomenological structure of texts either, like the narrative analysis does. The level of discourse is manifested in the homology of statements made to certain social themes, objects, and problems, and this homology, again, is a combined structural effect of the empty signifiers, nodal points, and discursive limits (cf. Chapter 3). In other words, general regularity and mutual commonality of articulations is a means of identifying the shared discursive identity of these articulates. The following step is to manifest how this shared regularity is enabled by re-activation and re-actualization of the same empty signifiers, nodal points, and discursive limits. An urgent analytical question is, of course, how the shared discursive identity of articulations becomes manifest.

First, the indeterminate character of discourse described in the previous chapter indicated that if a set of articulations about the entrepreneur belong to the same discourse, it is unlikely that these are identical. Second, it must be expected that articulations belong to the same discourse only insofar as they are organized and structured by the same empty signifiers, nodal points, and conceptions of discursive limits. Third, Angermüller (2007: 163) has rightly criticized the objectivist aspirations of earlier post-structural discourse analysis to identify empty signifiers and nodal points immediately without first analyzing what textual elements actually provide the coherence between singular signifiers. In other words, empty signifiers, nodal points, and discursive limits cannot be analyzed without starting from the reconstruction of the structural homology of articulations. Thereafter, the analysis can move to identifying the textual elements, which seem to function in a number of mutually homological articulations as empty signifiers and nodal points, respectively. Regarded in this way, post-structural discourse analysis cannot refrain from reconstructing the points of shared commonality between articulations. An urgent analytical question is how this shared structural homology of articulations becomes manifest in texts. Taking into consideration that the general focus of post-structural discourse analysis is geared to the formal-structural organization of articulations, the range of applicable methods of analysis is limited considerably. Nonhoff (2006: 242ff) has argued that, considering the formal-structural focus of post-structural discourse analysis, the semantic structure analysis conducted by Van Dijk (1985) could well be one possible way of elucidating discursive structures. Similar to post-structural discourse analysis, the semantic structure analysis also emphasizes the formal organization of texts to their contentual level (Van Dijk 1985: 105).

However, the semantic structure is analytically interesting only as some material in which the discursive structures become tangible and manifestable. In this regard, the interest in the semantic structure is rather similar to Stäheli's (1997, 1998) and Åkerstrøm Andersen's (2005) efforts to visualize functionally differentiated social systems by means of textual communications reproducing and retaining these systems.[3] Semantic structures are of interest for an analysis of social systems due to the assumption that "semantic development always follows the differentiation form of society, that is that compression of meaning into concepts in individual social systems follow each other in parallel movements" (Åkerstrøm Andersen 2005: 145). In systems theory, semantic structure is not only a textual expression of the systemic organization, but far more, it also provides a systemic memory in the sense that semantic structure makes it possible to re-copy and retain systemic organization from one act of communication to another (cf. Stäheli 1997: 131). Semantic representation of the systemic structure is therefore essential for the diachronic "procession of the procession of meaning" (Luhmann 1980 in Stäheli 1997: 134). However, an analysis of the semantic structure is meaningful for systems theoreticians only if they can translate the non-textual systemic organization into analogical semantic expressions (cf. Åkerstrøm Andersen 2005; Stäheli 1998: 326). Consider, for example, the earlier discussion about the differences between the system and the environment constituting functionally differentiated social systems (see Chapter 3).

An analysis of semantic structure becomes a meaningful way of analyzing the retention of the system/environment distinctions only insofar as these have semantic expressions (cf. Åkerstrøm Andersen 2003: 87). In a similar manner, the semantic structure of articulations is a meaningful object of analysis for the post-structural discourse analysis only if we can unmistakably observe analogies between the theoretically elucidated form of discourse and the empirically observable semantic structure of texts. Even though semiotics and in particular the analysis of the use of tropes (e.g., metaphor, metonomy, synecdoche, etc.) offers a method to identify and describe the different functions of lexical elements (cf. Glynos 2001; Hetzel 2001), a particular semantic function or trope is by no means immediately translatable to, for instance, the discursive concept of the empty signifier. In this regard, it seems of limited usefulness to try to establish an a priori system of correspondences between, for instance, rhetorical figures and discursive roles of lexical elements.[4] After all, whether, for example, a signifier plays the role of an empty signifier cannot be derived from its metaphorical or synecdochic function only. I prefer a more pragmatic approach that applies discursive relations, levels of discourse, and different types of diachronic change as a system of heuristic codes for which the empirical analysis tries to locate corresponding semantic expressions. In Chapter 4, the multi-dimensional model of discourse is broken down into a system of theoretically derived analytical codes, which again the empirical analysis tries to re-locate and identify in the semantic structure of the articulations about the entrepreneur (Strauss 1994: 63ff).

Earlier defined discursive relations and discursive levels of articulations provide an analytical and heuristic framework to detect an order of discourse contained in articulations. For instance, on the semantic level, empty signifiers and nodal points correspond to semantic elements that motivate the substitutability of particular elements and give reason for their mutual commonality or separation, respectively. In contrast to inductive abstraction and reduction of textual elements into "codes," a methodology preferred by grounded theory, the applied analytical procedure organizes semantic configurations of elements contained in texts into discourse-theoretically defined structures. However, the earlier described inter-relational and inter-dependent character of the different discursive constituents implicates that heuristic codes cannot be analyzed in isolation. For example, when we try to identify the signifiers that play the role of empty signifiers and nodal points, respectively, we must try to observe how antagonistic relations are justified, what explains the relation of contrariety between subjects and traitors, and why something appears as a desired object while something else is regarded as an inadmissible consequence of social practice. Similarly, also the conceived rationality and irrationality of sets of technologies depend on their respective connection with the ethical level of discourse.

Therefore, it should be rather clear that in place of a unilinear process of interpretation, which starts from the denomination of theoretical codes, operationalizes these into empirically observable characteristics and thereafter identifies empirical correspondences with theoretical codes, we are dealing with a non-linear, messy interpretation (cf. Law 2004). However, even though interpretation remains messy in the sense that we cannot choose a definite method to empirically reconstruct the discursive structures, the object of analysis—*the discourse*—remains anything but unclear. However, in contrast to Law's (2004: 2f) argument that science is messy due to the indeterminate, heterogeneous, and diffuse nature of the things analyzed, post-structural discourse analysis has quite a fair idea about what it analyzes. In other words, we cannot content ourselves with an "anything goes" kind of analytical pragmatism (Marttila 2010). On the other side, the analytical object of discourse is indefinite enough to allow a number of different ways of using different empirical approaches. In other words, the quality of the post-structural discourse analysis is not determined by the usage of a particular method, but by the appropriateness of the method in the empirical manifestation of the discourse object. Taking the discourse analytical co-construction of reality into consideration, Marttila (2010) has argued that not only should discourse analysis analytically reconstruct the discourse object, but it should also be carried out in a transparent manner that makes it possible to understand, contest, and question the results of discourse analysis. As Glynos and Howarth (2008: 15) argue, the incessantly contingent nature of all cognitions, including those of scientific inquiries, requires us "to develop a style of research that builds contingency into its very modus operandi." The objective of analytical transparency in the use of the described heuristic codes is facilitated by the explicit manifestation of the usage of heuristic codes and indication of the semantic structures that were associated with the respective code (see Table 5.1).

Table 5.1   Categories of Discursive Codes

Categories of Codes	Codes
Discursive Relations	• Difference • Equivalence • Contrariety • Hyper-difference • Empty Signifiers • Nodal Points
Levels of Discourse	
Ethics	• Empty Signifier • Nodal Points • Objects of Desire • Non-admissible Consequences
Technologies	• Technologies of the Other • Technologies of the Self • Non-admissible Technologies of the Other • Non-admissible Technologies of the Self
Subjects	• Destinator • Receiver • Subject • Adjuvant • Traitor • Adjuvants of the Traitor
Spatiotemporal Framing	• Spatial Setting • Temporal Setting

ANALYTICAL STRATEGY

This research project has both a diachronic and synchronic focus since it aims at distinguishing diachronic changes into the discursive construction of the entrepreneur as well as reconstructing relatively stable sequences in the conceived social functions, roles, and utilities of the entrepreneur. The concept of discursive "event" constitutes the point of intersection between discursive change and stability. An event is the point of distinction between two discursive continuities: the first being the one that it brings to an end and the second being the continuity that it initiates. If we consider discourse to be a relatively stable and invariable system or organization of signifiers, the event refers to an articulation that institutes a discontinuity in the prevailing continuity (cf. Diaz-Bone 2005: 186). However, a change is only a change within an existing discursive structure, and as a consequence, such changes are possible to observe only in retrospect to what has already prevailed. Even though Foucault (1977: 151) has argued that human history is nothing but a succession of events—of "substitutions, displacements, disguised contests and systematic reversals"—not every event is equally important for the course of history. Discursive events are not there just to be located and observed: they have to be constructed by means of clarifying their disruptive and constructive discursive impact. Moreover, events are analytically interesting only against the backdrop of the research interest.

The following analysis of the discursive construction of the entrepreneur aims at observing both the historical origins (i.e., events) that resulted in a conception of the entrepreneur lasting for a limited period of time as well as the discursive organization of these mutually different and distinguishable conceptions. When taking into consideration that these different conceptions of the entrepreneur are not mutually exclusive, but instead, in different regards draw on each other, I find it more accurate to speak of different discursive sequences rather than of different discourses of the entrepreneur. Currie's (1998) work on narrative sequences is highly indicative of the identification of discursive sequences. As Currie (1998: 82) suggests, analysis of historical (narrative) sequences is a process of unravelling of narrations in the search for "the first moment in a historical sequence . . . [that] at the time it occurs . . . has not yet been marked by subsequent moments." Currie argues that the "first moment" of a historical sequence can be observed only in relation to the subsequent "moments," in which the formative impact of the inaugural moment was confirmed and reproduced. Accordingly, then, origins of discursive sequences are possible to identify only through the reconstruction of the sequence. However, if we take into consideration that there are no absolute origins, but only discontinuities in the historical continuity (cf. Åkerstrøm Andersen 2003: 20; Derrida 1979: 146), we are left with the pragmatic decision to determine where a sequence begins and when it ends. In terms of post-structural discourse theory, the original moment of a discursive sequence consists of the contestation and re-activation of the political logic of the existing discursive representation of the social (Glynos and Howarth 2007: 141).

A new sequence sets on from the displacement of the existing discursive structure (Laclau 1990b: 33f). Whereas the stabilization and reproduction of discourse originates from the process of sedimentation, which Laclau (1990b: 34) describes as "forgetting the contingent origins," reactivation makes the absent objective necessity of a particular discursive representation tangible. The durability of a discursive sequence is delimited by the original moment that, at the same time, contests and questions the appropriateness of the prevailing discourse and provides a discursive representation that is, in some sense, better or more adequate and that, again, in the case of its sedimentation, leads to a new, relatively stable discursive sequence. The aim of the following analysis of the discursive construction of the entrepreneur aims at locating, reconstructing, and comparing mutually different and distinguishable discursive sequences. Every sequence contains its particular discursive system that determines the utilities, functions, identities, and expected social consequences of the entrepreneur. Moreover, different sequences are mutually distinguishable and differentiable due to their systemic differences. Of course, different discursive sequences of the entrepreneur are not there just waiting for their discovery: they must be actively constructed, compared, and justified with regard to their systemic differences. Against the backdrop of the heuristic model of discourse, different diachronic sequences in the discursive construction of the entrepreneur are manifestable by means of their mutual variations with regard to discursive relations, signifiers located on the different discursive levels, and their predominant institutional or popular logic (see Chapter 4). In terms of the initial discussion, each of these sequences contains a particular "subject fiction" of the entrepreneur, and every fiction is organized in accordance in the form of a discursive system.

A diachronic analysis of the historical sequences requires a priori limitation of the analysis to a delimited spatial context, in which the diachronic interplay of continuity and discontinuity becomes possible to manifest. Following Diaz-Bone (2006, 2007), discourse analysis must start from a delimitation of the analyzed set of articulations. However, taking into consideration that the discursive structure is the endpoint of the empirical study, discourse analysis must begin with some kind of a priori knowledge about the social contexts and social subjects responsible for and essentially involved in the establishment of the analyzed discourse. In other words, discourse analysis cannot be carried out without initial limitations of the meaningful social context of analysis. Of course, initial research questions, problems, and general analytical interests are essential resources for defining the kind of discourse that we intend to analyze. I argue in line with Diaz-Bone (2005, 2007) that we cannot determine the spatial limitations of the analyzed discourse without first having clear ideas about the contextual coordinates of the discourse analyzed. In contrast to any objectivist idea that a discourse analysis could more or less adequately inquire the discursive order, or even that the selected material of analysis could more or less well represent the whole amount of articulations that reproduce the analyzed discourse, we still need to justify and explain the material we decide to analyze. The following three sections justify the decision to analyze the governmental discourse, motivate the compilation of the text corpus analysed, and indicate how the empirical findings are presented so as to guarantee maximum transparency.

Discourse Genre

A first and obviously most fundamental analytical decision is to determine the spatial and temporal limits of the following study. The spatial delimitation is based on decisions about the social subjects, whose articulations about the entrepreneur deserve foremost interest. However, even though the initial decision to analyze the discursive construction of the entrepreneur in governmental discourse considerably constrains the number of social subjects analyzed, we still need to see what kinds of articulations should be analyzed: books, letters, leaflets, debates in newspapers, policy papers, and so on. Schneider and Hirseland (2005) argue that the material of discourse analysis may include either written or spoken texts, symbols, signs, and visual material, such as film and pictures, architecture, and so on. The argument of Laclau and Mouffe (1990: 103) claiming that all social objects, whether textual, material, or abstract ones, "are never given to us as mere existential entities; they are always given to us within discursive articulations," indicates that all social practices function as articulations and can be analyzed as such. The decision about the analyzed "genre" of discourse is a means to reduce the extent of analysis to a particular type or kind of articulation (Keller 2001: 136).

Foucault observed that the discursive construction of meaning proceeds within different, mutually more or less exclusive, social contexts such as different scientific disciplines. The totality of knowledge, accessible at a given point of time, is the result of several parallelly prevailing discursive formations (cf. Foucault 1981, 2002a; Keller 2008: 239). In this manner, discursive production of meaning is regulated by historical differentiation of discourses (Link 1988: 288). Foucault assumed that each and every discourse contained its particular order of knowledge, modalities of production, and control of knowledge and a set of rules that regulated the access of social subjects to subject positions authorizing them to speak on behalf of the discourse. The differentiation or—in terms of Foucault—the "individuation" of discourse resulted from their capacity to control their particular production of meaning. This relative autonomy of a discourse generated over time sustained a differentiation of various discourses (cf. Link 2005: 80). While Foucault emphasized the spatial (i.e., contextual) differentiation of discourse, Link (1988, 2005) has argued that besides the horizontal differentiation of discourses, we must also take into account a vertical dimension that embraces the relative societal extents of different discourses. It should be obvious that while scientific discourses, such as biology, have a rather restricted social relevance beyond the community of the biologists, there are, on the other side, more popular and extensive discourses that draw, for instance, on the knowledge produced by different scientific discourses. Link (1988: 288) mobilizes the concept of "inter-discourse" to describe discursive configurations embracing themes, objects, ideas, and theories from a number of different contextually limited discourses.

Inter-discourse has, in two regards, a more public and open character than a special discourse. First, there are less formal requirements to participate in public discourse, which increases the general accessibility to participation (Keller 2008: 229). Participation in popular science, popular literature, and popular music requires lower formal qualifications than publishing in distinguished academic journals. Second, inter-discursive articulations are accessible and receptible among a wider audience. However, due to the appropriation and selection of material from different special discourses, special discourses are popularized in inter-discourse. It has been argued that Foucault's assumption of differentiation of different discourse formations and institutional fields of social practice was accompanied by disinterest in the analysis of inter-discursive interchanges of meaning and the observation of inter-discursive conflicts as instances for constructing a general order of the society (cf. Keller 2008: 229; Link 2005; Schwab-Trapp 2001). Recent post-Foucauldian studies have shifted the focus of interest from socio-historic regularities of special discourses to an investigation of (inter-)discourse coalitions (e.g., Griggs and Howarth 2002; Hajer 1995), struggles between different problem narratives within particular thematic fields (e.g., Viehöver 2001, 2003), and the emergence of new socio-political problematizations supported by the scientific community.

Research accounts focusing on socio-political contestations between different problem narratives or analyzing the hegemonization of different subject cultures benefit from the focus on inter-textual origins of the hybrid and inter-discursive system of knowledge (e.g., Reckwitz 2006: 19f). Also, this particular research project, which focuses on the establishment of the entrepreneur and the diachronic variation of its meaning in the discourse on rational political government, should detect the inter-textual and inter-discursive construction of the entrepreneur. According to Link, inter-discourse fulfills a particular social function in the sense that it integrates knowledge produced in different social contexts and fields of practice into a profane and popular system of meaning. The discursive production of meaning is located between two mutually opposing tendencies of differentiation into special discourses and de-differentiation of special discourses into inter-discourse. De-differentiation and generalization of knowledge facilitate the access of a general public to knowledge generated by groups of scientific experts (Link 2005: 90). In our case, the culture of enterprise and its leading figure, which is the entrepreneur, draw on the scientific insights of economic science (cf. Foucault 2006). However, the present-day dissemination of the culture of enterprise into contexts beyond economic system and private business bears witness to a considerable process of generalization of the initially theoretical economic ideas of concepts of organizational rationalities, individual happiness, organization of private lives, and so on.

The culture of enterprise functions as an inter-discourse in the sense that, even though it derives from the neoliberal economic theory, it has become mixed and enriched with elements from other scientific disciplines (psychology, organization and management studies, human engineering, etc.), social and political problems (unemployment, structural change, demographic change, globalization, etc.), and so forth (cf. Bröckling 2003, 2007a; Reckwitz 2006). The inter-discursive logic of the culture of enterprise points out that each and every particular configuration of the culture of enterprise consists of a temporary and precarious arrangement of meanings that were initially articulated within different social contexts. Regarded in this way, the culture of enterprise must be understood as the outcome of a continuous process of re-articulation of its limits. For Link (cf. 2005), the indeterminate and open character of inter-discourse implicates that inter-discourses can to a greater or less extent reflect a special discourse. Depending on the context, the culture of enterprise can reflect the orthodox ideas of the neoliberal economic theory more or less clearly. Both Reckwitz (2006) and Williams (1977) have pointed out that initially a relatively marginal cultural system becomes a socially dominant and hegemonic one only insofar as it is capable of asserting itself beyond its original social location.

Following Link (2005: 92) and Reckwitz (2006: 67), increasingly dominant and socially extensive discourses have to establish themselves either in the place of or in connection with existing discourses. However, it is reasonable to assume that some social institutions and groups of social subjects are better placed to determine and evaluate the respective social value of different discourses and to play a decisive role in the constitution of cultural systems embracing more or less the entire society. A limitation of the analytical focus on governmental discourse departs from the assumption that governmental institutions and subjects play an essential role as an instance of consecration that weights the general social relevance of different discourses and amalgamates them asymmetrically into a society-wide discourse of the social articulated in governmental policies and documents. Accordingly, the configuration of governmental discourse is not just a reflection of the relative social validity of different discursive meanings, but far more, it actively arranges inter-discourses that are authoritative and valid for the entire society. It is therefore reasonable to assume that governmental discourse plays a prominent role in the identification and determination of social values, utilities, and functions of entrepreneurs. It is crucial to notice that governmental discourse does not coincide with politics, which Keller (2008: 22) refers to any "political-argumentative contestation" carried out in and through the mass media. Even though inter-discourse is a typical feature of political discourse, it is considerably more difficult to delimit. Political discourse is diffused over time and space, and it is distributed over different media (TV, newspapers, radio, internet, books). Governmental discourse, on the other side, is institutionally limited to a set of governmental practices (e.g., policy-making), a relatively clear set of articulations (white papers, green papers, consultations, etc.), and standardized processes of interactions and practices that generate articulations (debates, interpellations, committee meetings). And yet, despite its seemingly exclusive, routinized, and institutionalized logic of articulation, governmental discourse contains also traces of different special discourses (economic theories) and asymmetrical influence of social subjects, institutions, and organizations. In this regard, we can analyze governmental discourse as an inter-discourse and try to locate indications of the social, institutional, and discursive origins of different governmental conceptions of the entrepreneur.

Text Corpus

Definition of the discourse genre is a first means to limit the analyzed textual material. However, even though it is relatively uncomplicated to denominate the criteria for the selection of texts, the preceding discussion of the absence of transparent diachronic limits of discourse constitutes a considerable problem for the compilation of the text corpus. Indeed, the text corpus can be expanded *ad infinitum* in both diachronic (*temporal*) and synchronic (*spatial*) dimensions. Following suit of Keller (2001: 136) and Diaz-Bone (2007), discourse analysts are left with the option of a contingent and by the research interest motivated starting point of analysis. The diachronic starting point of the following analysis derives from an initial exploration of recent developments in Swedish governmental discourse. Research accounts of Johannisson (2003), Rothstein and Westerhäll (2005), Garsten and Jacobsson (2004), Mahieu (2006), Benner (1997), and Lindvall (2006) provided an overview into the meta-narratives of Swedish governmental discourse since the early 1980s. It turned out soon that first problematizations of the lacking socio-political support of entrepreneurs occurred at the beginning of the 1990s only. Above all, Benner's (1997) analysis of the transformation of the regime of growth and Mahieu's (2006) study of the introduction of "entrepreneurship education" at schools gave reason to assume that entrepreneurs had received limited interest in the post-war governmental discourse. Indeed, it was only the liberal-conservative government elected in autumn 1991, and headed by Premier Carl Bildt, that, in a fashion not unlike the Thatcherite government in the England of the 1980s, proclaimed the arrival of an *entrepreneurial era*. More precisely, it was the political program of the Liberal party (Folkpartiet) and the Conservative party (Moderaterna)—*New Beginning for Sweden* (En ny start för Sverige)—as well as the government declaration of Carl Bildt in October 1991 that planted concerns entrepreneurship at the core of the governmental discourse.

Starting with the liberal-conservative government installed in 1991, the following study analyzes governmental discourse in order to identify different stages in the discursive construction of the entrepreneur, reconstructs the discursive structure of each of these discourses, and points out the moments of change (i.e., discursive events), which initiated the transition into the subsequent discursive sequence. Even though the decisions about the diachronic (from 1991 on) and synchronic limits of the analysis (governmental discourse) provide criteria for the limitation of the material analyzed, it was still necessary to reduce the text corpus further. One possibility of weighting the relative discursive significance of texts is to judge whether they can be considered to constitute "key texts" reproducing the systematicity of the analyzed discourse. According to Åkerstrøm Andersen (2005: 146), key texts stand out from the totality of articulations in the sense that they deal with the systematicity of the functionally differentiated social systems. Following Stäheli (1997), key texts can be understood as referring to texts that contain so-called "serious semantics," which, in contrast to "popular semantics," "tries to represent the functional identity of the system" (Stäheli 1997: 140). Translated into the terminology of post-structural discourse theory, key texts can be understood to deal with the systematicity of the discourse constituting empty signifiers, nodal points, and discursive boundaries.

According to Laclau's (2005: 117) distinction between "social logics" referring to rule-following and "political logics" that denote principles of "the institution of the social," key texts not only elucidate the institutional forms, means, and instruments of government, but also the more general political logic of the inevitability associated with a particular conduct of government. Even though key texts are not immediately observable with regard to their senders or receivers, or the themes, general aims, and so on contained therein, it is still possible to identify types of articulations whose role it is to re-actualize and reproduce the constitutive principles of governmental discourse. It is a fair assumption that white and green papers, documents explaining the general political agenda, texts authored and directly authorized by key personnel of the government such as speeches of the Premier, as well as comprehensive position papers, are more likely to reflect the constitutive structures of governmental discourse than, for example, notes from committee meetings and short press briefings. However, the relative weight of different types of articulations must be judged for each and every context and must be motivated by the research interest. Useful indications of the key texts are comments in research literature as well as cross-references between primary texts, which both point out the focal texts of the governmental discourse. Key texts include, for instance, policy papers and documents that describe long-term governmental strategies and reflect on the historical status of present policies. A characteristic feature of Swedish policy process is its rigidly standardized procedure of consecutive steps, which enables the analyst to retrospectively locate preceding texts and stages of articulations as well as the participation of different social actors in political discussion. Having reduced the totality of the texts by means of key texts, the remaining text corpus can be delimited further by means of browsing them for the relative centrality of themes related to entrepreneurs and entrepreneurship.

Presentation of Empirical Findings

The contingency of all social cognitions described initially in Chapter 3 also applies to post-structural discourse analysis. The incessant contingency of discourse analysis does not implicate that empirical results could be presented in any form whatsoever. Instead, in order to avoid that the knowledge generated by discourse analysis is observed as non-contestable and objective knowledge, which it can never become due to its own epistemological limits, it is necessary to provide the reader with insights into the process of analytical interpretation. The following three empirical chapters observe three discursive sequences in the discursive construction of the entrepreneur in Swedish governmental discourse and reconstruct the discursive organization of each of these sequences. Even though the process of interpretation cannot be presented entirely due to its complexity, these chapters will try to go beyond the description of the discursive structure and indicate how the semantic structures of articulations were translated into the terminology of post-structural discourse theory. To make the congruence between discourse theory and empirical analysis more graspable and to make the attainment of the research results more comprehensible, direct citations are added to underline interpretations. Moreover, direct citations are also contained in the observed discursive structures such as relations and empty signifiers. These notifications indicate the observed correspondences between the semantic structure of texts and the theoretically derived properties of discourse.

The observed correspondences between the semantic structure and the properties of discourse are shown in squared brackets. A further means to increase the transparency of interpretations was to underpin empirical findings with passages of texts that support the respective interpretation. Moreover, instead of merely providing "texts over texts," which discourse analysis ultimately does, the following chapters will be accompanied with graphical displays of the observed discursive structures. These graphical presentations combine discursive relations and different discursive levels described earlier in Chapter 4. The general aim of the aspired transparent and inter-subjectively comprehensible presentation of empirical results is to allow the reader to comprehend the results of the analysis against the backdrop of the adopted epistemological lens of post-structural discourse theory. In order to further increase the respective structure of the observed discursive sequences, the findings of every empirical chapter are summarized in a table that provides an overview of the observed discursive structure.

6 Liberal-Conservative Politics for Functioning Market Economy 1991–1994

During the post-war years, Sweden developed into one of the most progressive, but also one of the most thoroughly politically planned, bureaucratically organized, and corporatively controlled societies (Johansson and Magnusson 1998; Lindvall 2006; Rothstein and Vahlne-Westerhäll 2005). Institutionalized political reason displayed rather well the governmentality form of sovereignty, as characterized by the sovereign government of territory, economy, and population (Dean 1999). Johansson and Magnusson (1998) have illustratively defined the Swedish post-war economic model to have been based on "a vision of 'capitalism without capitalists' " in which private entrepreneurship and private economic initiatives were subordinated to the intention to unify collectivism and market dynamics (Henrekson and Roine 2007: 70).

Yet, on the eve of the 1990s, the Swedish welfare state was criticized by several social groups. One such source was the group of economists affiliated with the SNS state model, and the post-war mode of political government became increasingly criticized, the policy think-tank closely affiliated with the Swedish industry (Blyth 2001; Lindvall 2005, 2006). Other sources were parliamentary committees and, above all, the "Productivity Delegation" (SOU 1991: 82) and the "Competition Commission" (SOU 1991: 59 and SOU 1991: 104), which were both inspired by new conceptions of free competition and economic dynamics of unbound private economic initiatives (cf. Lundquist 2005). In February 1989, the social-democratic government assigned the Civic Department the task to build a committee to make suggestions on how the competition policy could be improved to achieve designated political objectives (cf. SOU 1991: 104, *Foreword*). Concentration of capital, lack of competition, a relatively great share of state-owned enterprises, the ineffective use of resources, lacking structural modification toward a new economy, and the absence of entrepreneurship were only some of the problem descriptions unveiled (cf. Lundquist 2005; Steinmo 2005).

Problems observed with the political reason of sovereign government were responded to in numerous public committees proposing more "market-oriented solutions." This general shift in political mentality, as Svensson (2001; cf. Elander 1999) defines it, can be described in terms of "marketization." Illustrative of marketization are, among other things, the introduction of a free choice of services, the introduction of private service providers in public sector, and public sector implementation of management strategies aligned to private business (Elander 1999; Rövik 2000: 241f). Competition policy is the sector, where the new governmentality reason of "advanced liberalism" reached recognizable institutional impact most tangibly (e.g., Blomqvist and Rothstein 2000; Lundquist 2005). In a path-breaking parliamentary inquiry into conditions of competition (SOU 1991: 59), an intensification of competition was considered crucial for the future possibility to maintain the thus far reached levels of social welfare (Steinmo 2005: 163). The institutional break-through of marketization occurred during the early 1990s, and especially during the period of liberal-conservative government (1991–1994). Beliefs in the progressive potential of the sovereign state were partially replaced by liberal reasoning emphasizing the progressive and thus far untapped potential of unbounded competition (cf. Blomqvist and Rothstein 2000: 9; Rothstein 1992).

Criticism of the Swedish political model was not confined to the structure of the public sector and forms of political regulation and steering of market, but also considered the sharing of responsibilities, personal autonomy, and forms of democratic participation (cf. Blomqvist and Rothstein 2000). Since the 1970s, different parliamentary committees and civic society associations had criticized how the Swedish political model had restricted democratic participation, and how the distance between the civil society and the state had resulted in a corresponding discrepancy between citizens' needs and services and assistance provided by the state (cf. Jacobsson 1999). According to Jacobsson (1999) and Boréus (1994), the political debate of the 1980s was in general more critically reflecting on bureaucratic organization and more positively minded toward citizens' direct participation in public administration and alternative forms of market-oriented and cooperative organization of the public sector services. Jacobsson (1999: 189) observed an ideational change of the conception of democracy during the 1980s, which was more positive about direct participation, freedom of choice, and extension of the space of civil society activities. As Lundquist (2001) describes, at the end of the 1980s, the traditional Swedish social and political organization did not appear as self-evident as before.

Both "marketization" and emphasis on extended citizen participation in political government symbolizes the constituents of a general epistemological transformation of political reason toward an "advanced liberal" form of governmentality, which, in contrast to a "sovereign" form of government, recognizes the economic sphere as a quasi-natural and autonomous realm beyond the capacity of political government (cf. Foucault 2006; Du Gay 1991, 1996). The extent of possible objects and areas of society that are controllable by the political government is curtailed by the epistemology. Aligned to the neoliberal theory of social life, the latter assigns the collective government the role to engender virtuous spontaneous social and economic processes emerging from below, through rational conduct. One of the most tangible manifestations of the transition toward the advanced liberal conception of government is the implementation of external, impartial, and objective norms of government (Blyth 2001; Lindvall 2005; Lundquist 2005l). The centrality of corporatist negotiations, interest presentation, and pragmatism in decision making were to some extent replaced by the self-restraint of politics, now "acting at a distance" after having installed rules of *coherence, impartiality,* and *legality* (Blyth 2001; Lindvall 2005; Lundquist 2005). The opening for more competition, the abolition of interest representation in market regulating bodies, and the appreciation of the rule of law all manifest the political reason of advanced liberalism (Dean 1999: 169ff). The turn to advanced liberalism in Sweden epitomizes how the political reason in advanced liberal governments demands the state to confess to the inherent nature of things and to govern in accordance with the organic processes in economy and society (Dean 1999: 113f; Foucault 2006; Gordon 1991: 48).

RESURGENCE OF THE ENTREPRENEUR

Following suit of Hall (1993), political government is located within epistemological paradigms that consist of overarching policy objectives, such as societal norms, techniques and policy instruments, and precise settings of the instruments. In Sweden, the transition toward the advanced liberal forms of political reason has been observed to take place on the level of instruments and organizations as early as the 1980s (cf. Blomqvist and Rothstein 2000). A full-scale dislocation on the level of "objectives" and relative prioritization between different objectives occurred during the first years of the 1990s. Traditionally, the primary objective of the Swedish political government had been the maintenance of full employment. Full employment was superordinate to any other singular objective since it was trusted to facilitate the achievement of further objectives of efficient production, efficient resource allocation, and efficient utilization of human capital (Blyth 2001). Employment was to be achieved through state-led and initiated macro-economic measures aligned to the Keynesian model of government, which counteracted business cycle downturns and acts as a broker between business and labor interests. A central element is the "solidaristic wage policy" invented by two labor union economists, Gösta Rehn and Rudolph Meidner, having been labeled thereafter as the "Rehn-Meidner-Model," which set enterprises under the pressure to realize a consistent productivity increase through technological change (cf. Blyth 2001; Stephens 1996: 39). Economic growth and competitiveness was supported by occasional currency depreciations (Stephens 1996: 40). Depreciation was a constituent element of the third-way model of government practiced by the social-democratic governments in the 1980s (Stephens 1996). The traditional macro-economic model also assigned large companies a crucial role in the achievement of economic growth (Blyth 2001: 6; Steinmo 2005).

The most significant change in Swedish political reason occurred at the turn of the 1990s. Svensson (2001) describes this discursive change in terms of transition from Keynesian macro-economic political management to "norm politics" (see also Lindvall 2006). Some authors relate the abandoning of the Swedish model to materialist-structural changes. For instance, Timonen (2001) argues that it was the fiscal and economic crises that constituted the context in which earlier welfare state aspirations were partly abandoned. Similarly, Bergmark and Palme (2003) argue that economic crises at the beginning of the 1990s and a rapidly deteriorating budget deficit triggered institutional changes. What a structural explanation overlooks is the subtle epistemological change of political reason that occurred in the Swedish political field after the late 1970s. Especially worth emphasizing is Lindvall's (2005, 2006) content analysis of the ideas held by central political and economic decision makers, and how epistemological changes became persistent already during the 1980s, only to unfold into tangible institutional changes during the 1990s. Similarly, Blyth (2001) and Boréus (1994) observe the 1980s to have been a decade of ideational and ideological changes, especially among the economists, who successively adopted a public-choice model for understanding the welfare state (Blyth 2001: 17). In the 1970s, Keynesianism provided the epistemological frame for conceiving the functioning of the economy and corresponding ideas on efficient political government of economy and market (Lindvall 2005: 120). At the beginning of the 1980s, the chief economist of SNS, Assar Lindbeck, adopted a "norm-based, non-discretionary [conception of] macroeconomics that would bypass and indeed render obsolete traditional social-democratic institutions" (Blyth 2001: 18).

The then social-democratic government took a conclusive step from the prioritization of the full employment to the combat of inflation around 1990. Transition was preceded by proliferating reports from economists affiliated to SNS, the organization, and the policy think-tank of the Swedish industry. In this context, Svensson (2001) stresses especially the importance of a report of SNS economist in 1986—"New Rules of Game for Growth." In light of the experiences of rising inflation and instability of prices, this report accentuated the introduction of objective, permanent, and transparent political norms to lower the expectations of inflation. Criticism uttered by SNS economists was based on neoclassical and public choice arguments that observed the aspiration of the objective of full employment as subjugation of the state to partial interests, which led to a stabilization of employment above the normal and natural rate for a market economy (Blyth 2001: 18). The problem of full employment was caused by its price distortion, inflation tendencies, and irrational allocation of economic resources (Blyth 2001: 18). Norm politics, on the other side, intended to establish objective and rigid economic circumscriptions for economic government, which would decrease rent seeking behavior and facilitate the state to follow long-term economic rationality. Inflation rate, not employment, was elevated to an objective point of measure of conduct of government.

The ideas of SNS economists were adopted by the liberal and right wing parties that constituted the government from September 1991 on. Yet, as Svensson (2001) and Lindvall (2005, 2006) point out, social democrats were far from repulsive, especially the former finance minister, Kjell Olof Feldt, but also representatives from labor unions, recognized and advocated norm politics before 1991. For instance, "supply side" economic ideas promoted by Feldt were introduced into the program of the then social-democratic government in 1989. Yet, the final stage toward the implementation of "norm politics" was reached in the spring of 1991 in the financial plan of the social-democratic government (Government Bill 1990/91: 100, see sections 1–5). In the Government Bill 1990/91: 100 (chapter 1), inflation and expectations of future inflation based on past inflation are observed as the most severe economic problem and source of decreasing economic growth, investments, and development of productivity. Therefore, "politics aimed at securing justice and full employment must prioritize the combat of inflation to any other aspirations and demands" (Government Bill 1990/91: 100). From this moment on, a low rate of inflation took the role of the decisive objective of economic policy and held a superordinate position to that of full employment. In the 1991 report by the Department of Industry [Industridepartement], a low level of inflation was articulated as being essential for the competitiveness of Swedish enterprises. Competitiveness was considered crucial for economic growth, welfare, and employment (Department of Industry 1991: 6). Norm politics was also resonant to new conceptions of social subjects as contributors to societal well-being and welfare.

At the turn of the 1990s, policy documents of the social-democratic government expressed concerns about the Swedish third-way economic policy model, which had been applied after the takeover of government from the liberal-conservative coalition in 1982. In the Government Bill 1989/90: 88 on a new industrial policy, the social-democratic government problematized the functionality of the third-way policy model as it was assumed to endanger the socio-economic balance and overheat the economy. These negative outcomes were supposed to have led to the deteriorated budget balance and the rapid rise of inflation. In the Government Bills 1990/91: 100 and 150 on the economic budget, the social-democratic government defined inflation as the most severe economic problem. Government Bill 1990/91: 87 further argued that:

> The central short-term economic and political problem is inflation that causes increased insecurity, a less functioning economy, the arbitrary redistribution of propriety and decreased competitiveness. (chapter 1.2)

The problem with the earlier third way mode of government was two-fold. First, in the opened international financial market, the trustworthiness of the Swedish economy depended on its capacity to control inflation and maintain the balance of trade (cf. Department of Industry 1991). Second, due to restricted expenditure and the possibility of attaining the objectives of the balance of trade, and of developing and maintaining welfare, the level of economic growth must necessarily be increased. As Government Bill 1989/90: 88 argued, the freedom of action depends on the resources and economic free-zone provided by economic growth. Inflation distorts rational economic conduct by disturbing economic incentives, interests, and activities, which again lower the level of investment and sever improvement of productivity. In contrast to the later liberal-conservative government, the social-democratic government did not establish competition and inflation in a relation of antagonism set against a "functioning market economy" (cf. Government Bills 1989/90: 88 and 1990/91: 87). Inflation was established in antagonistic relation to welfare:

> The price and wage-cost development of the Swedish economy must be disrupted if welfare and employment are to be maintained. Combating inflation must be superordinate to any other aspirations and demands. (Government Communication 1990/91: 50)

The problematization of inflation accentuated the corresponding rationality of stabilization policies, whose foremost objective is to limit inflation expectations by establishing rigid rules and norms that help economic actors to make long-term risk and cost calculations and to anticipate the future prices and costs. Receivers of the norm politics were, above all enterprises, especially smaller enterprises, which the Department of Industry (1991: 4) report observed as the source for general dynamics and, more specifically, for occupations. Maintenance of social welfare was subsequently made dependent on complex economic processes residing beyond direct political control, which under beneficial macro-economic contexts would lead to more efficient resource allocation, improvement of productivity, international competitiveness, and, hence, new occupations (cf. Government Bill 1989/90: 88; Department of Industry 1991).

Macro-economic government through stable price levels and restricted wage increases corresponded to an industrial policy with an unprecedented focus on the situation of smaller enterprises. The objective of the government's industrial policy was to provide a macro-economic context in which private businesses would be able to realize the political objective of economic renewal, higher level of productivity, and efficient allocation of resources conducted autonomously by market actors (Government Bill 1989/90: 88). An unprecedented focus was now attached to smaller enterprises as the forerunners of economic renewal. Government Bill 1989/90: 88 suggests that the focus should rest on the smaller enterprises, and this intention was to be realized by "offensive industrial policy," which observed above all the general socio-economic and political context of enterprises. In the Government Bill 1990/91: 87, this strategy was further specified as one endeavoring to develop Swedish enterprises by supporting their consistent adaptation to changing market requirements considering demands, technological development, and the development of markets. In the Government Bill 1990/91: 87, industrial policy was denoted as concerning such factors as access to a well-educated labor force, a beneficial environment of research and development, functional infrastructure, and well-functioning markets.

Another context of supporting smaller enterprises was the labor market and employment policy. The earlier conception of the sources of employment was characterized largely by industry-scale thinking and the dominance of beliefs in larger companies' capacity to generate economic growth and employment (Johannisson and Lindmark 1996: 11). The dislocation of the epistemology on economic growth appears as one of the reasons for the political resurrection of small enterprises. The traditional support along with industrial policies oriented toward large companies is argued to hinder the expansion possibilities of smaller enterprises (cf. Lundell 1998). The traditional welfare state, and especially the traditional privileging of the interests of larger companies, was now problematized to hinder the development and realization of entrepreneurial mindsets and cognitive capacities in the population (cf. Henrekson 1999).

Lately, new attempts and efforts have appeared to sponsor and facilitate the situation of small enterprises and new business start-ups (see Table 6.1). The background for this is the massive number of unemployed in Sweden (Johannisson and Lindmark 1996). In the mid-1990s, economic and political debates were dominated by beliefs in the capacity of small enterprises to renew the economy and provide new occupations. Policy areas involved in both enterprise support and the general industrial policy are, above all, business development, regional policies, and labor market policies. One of the areas with the most evident focus on entrepreneurship is labor market policy, and especially active labor market policy. In the report originating from the group of economists on public and social economy (Department Report 1995: 14), different forms of labor market policies that simultaneously count as measures for enterprise support embrace *recruitment support, enterprise education*, *Vocational training* and *Educational internships, Youth internships, Labor market fund*, and *Working life environment fund*. Still, all policy areas included, the most tangible manifestation of the unprecedented importance of the entrepreneur in Swedish political discourse is illustrated by the expansion of the labor market policy "Start your own," which stands for the major part of the financial costs for the support of entrepreneurship in Sweden (Johannisson and Lindmark 1996: 204). According to the parliamentary report SOU 1996: 34, the most important function of labor market politics as concerns its relation to the objectives of the support of new entrepreneurship and small enterprises is to provide enterprises effectively with appropriate employees. However, both the direct financial support and the number recipients of entitled to "start your own" have expanded vastly over time (Government Bill 1990/91: 100; SOU 1993:70).[1]

Table 6.1   Funding of the Enterprise Allowance Scheme

Year	Funding in Mn. SEK	Government
1985–1989	430	Social-democratic
1990/91	101	Social-democratic
1991/92	272	Liberal-conservative
1992/93	400	Liberal-conservative
1993/94	450	Liberal-conservative
1995/96	1,300	Social-democratic

In 1984, Public Employment Services (PESs) implemented measures to create new potential entrepreneurs among those who had become unemployed. Unemployment grants entitled the unemployed to obtain a self-employment grant[2] to start their own company or to work as self-employed. According to Thedvall (2004), this represents a shift in traditional Swedish labor market policy in several ways. Traditionally, the salaried employee with a full-time position constituted the Swedish employment norm. The introduction of self-employment represents, among other things, untypical forms of occupations, such as part-time and temporary work, another form of the flexibilization of work. More interestingly, the introduction of new measures to raise the number of self-employed and business-starters symbolizes a novel type of use of PESs in cultural engineering and construction of citizens. Individuals are increasingly conceived of as subjects whose potentials can be mobilized by public institutions and small enterprises, which—though earlier judged as inefficient—became evaluated to possess great economic potentials (Thedvall 2004: 136). Thedvall (2004; cf. Garsten and Jacobsson 2004) interpreted the introduction of the self-employment grant in 1984 as the beginning of the individualization of employment governance. A fundamental imaginary that fostered the implementation of new forms of employment measures was, according to Thedvall (2004: 137), "that individuals are, at the core, entrepreneurial."

POLITICS OF A FUNCTIONING MARKET ECONOMY

In autumn 1991, a liberal-conservative coalition under the auspices of the Conservative Party leader Carl Bildt replaced the social-democratic government, which had constituted the government after 1982. In contrast to suggestions regarding a dislocation of the conception of a rational form of governing, Blyth (2001; cf. Lundquist 2005; Svensson 2001), among others, regards the policies of the liberal-conservative government as an institutionalization of ideas that have been assumed by the social-democratic government. For instance, the liberal-conservative government adopted the tax reform of 1990, which the social-democratic government has implemented, and continued the norm politics, whose primary objective was the "permanent reduction in inflation" (Blyth 2001: 20). Yet, the liberal-conservative government problematized both the tax reform and the thus far initiated norm politics as being insufficient in stimulating economic growth and entrepreneurship (Government Bill 1991/92: 60). According to Benner (1997: 165), the essential point of this criticism was the intention "to stimulate the group of entrepreneurs to enhance and sustain economic growth." Norm politics already adopted by the social-democratic government was then combined with an unprecedented emphasis on small enterprises as the "spearheads" of future economic development (Benner 1997: 165). In the declaration of the new liberal-conservative government, the new Premier Carl Bildt claimed that "entrepreneurship must become the spearhead of economy towards the future" (Parliamentary Minutes 1991/92: 6). A characteristic feature of the new government was the assumption that the future economic development would depend to an unprecedented extent on their capacity to stimulate and extend entrepreneurship as expressed in Government Bill 1991/92: 51:

> Of most crucial importance for Sweden's economic development in the 1990s [*object; Time*—future] is the renaissance of small enterprises and new entrepreneurship [*subject; object; adjuvant*]. It is in these enterprises [*subject*] that new occupations [*object*] are located. New entrepreneurship [*adjuvant*] must become the spearhead of economy towards the future.

The growth strategy promoted by the liberal-conservative government was in several respects inspired by the entrepreneurial culture of the Thatcherite government in Great Britain. Emphasis was not merely placed on private initiatives, incentives, and entrepreneurship as sources of economic development, but future welfare was observed to depend on a new culture of entrepreneurship. This, again, required a new social contract between private actors and the political government (cf. Benner 1997: 212).

The socio-political discourse of the liberal-conservative government operates through a primary relation of antagonism between "economic growth" and "economic stagnation." In its first Government Bills in autumn 1991, the government explained its two most prioritized objectives to be bringing Sweden into a European cooperation through membership in the European Union (EU) and "disrupting the economic stagnation and preparing the ground for a new period of growth, entrepreneurship and development" (Government Bill 1991/92: 38). Already, entrepreneurship appears as a central tenet of the economic policy (e.g., Parliamentary Minutes 1991/92: 6). The antagonistic other of the liberal-conservative discourse is symbolized by social-democratic economic policy, which caused stagnation of the economy. The opposition between growth and stagnation symbolizes the substantiation of a more general opposition between a "functioning" and a "dysfunctioning" market economy. The assumption can be made that a "functioning market economy" constitutes the imaginary of the fullness of society, which would be realized through future growth and endangered by future economic stagnation. Among the documents analyzed, the inaugural speech of the new Premier Carl Bildt on October 6 most clearly supports this suggestion:

> At the beginning of the 1990s our economy was characterized [*time*; past] by a rapid loss of employment [*inadmissible consequence*] and enterprises [*inadmissible consequence*], a decrease of investments in the private sector [*inadmissible consequence*], a diminishing production of goods and services [*inadmissible consequence*] and deteriorating public finances [*inadmissible consequence*]. It is crucial for Sweden's future [*empty signifier*; growth] to disrupt this development [*strategy*]. If the crises of economic growth [*empty signifier*] cannot be stopped [*strategy*], the 1990s will be characterized by even increasing unemployment [*inadmissible consequence; Time*—future] combined with increasing difficulties to fund public objectives [*inadmissible consequence*; welfare]. The central objective of government's economic policy [*adjuvant*] is to regain the vigor of development [*empty signifier*] and growth [*empty signifier*] in the Swedish economy [*receiver*]. (Parliamentary Minutes 1991/92: 6)

In the previous text, the empty signifier is not expressed through a singular word and semantic symbol. It is located in notions like "vigor" and "growth" that symbolize the natural outcomes of a functioning economy. In contrast, the decrease of "employment" and "investments" and the "deteriorating public finances" symbolize the outcomes of a dysfunctional market economy. A central dimension of a "functioning economy" is constituted by the temporal becoming, such as development, renewal, and change. Becoming and change is attained through the utilization of potential chances and resources by economic actors, such as new entrepreneurs and small and medium-sized enterprises (SMEs).[3] As Table 6.3 illustrates, the function of a "functioning economy" as an empty signifier of the liberal-conservative discourse organizes an antagonistic relation between two opposed chains of signifiers (A≠B).

The antagonistic relation between the two opposed imaginaries of functioning and dysfunctioning economy are based on a conception of movement and progress. What characterizes a functioning economy in analyzed texts is its movement and process, expressed through repeatedly applied semantic signs of "developing," "growing," "efficient," and "free." This initial opposition between "functional" and "dysfunctional" as constitutive antagonistic relation generates further particular relations of equivalence between singular signifiers. The semantic elements used to describe the functional economy

Table 6.2 Functioning Market Economy

Discourse Formation A: Liberal-Conservative Discourse 1991–1994

Functioning Market Economy (Es)

A (eth.) (—)	Developing Economy *(object)*	/=	Growing Economy *(object)*	/=	Efficient Economy *(object)*	/=	Free Economy *(object)*	(—)
			/=		/=			
B (eth.) (—)	Stagnating Economy *(inadmissible consequence)*	/=	Distorted Economy *(inadmissible consequence)*	/=	Restricted Economy *(inadmissible consequence)*	/=	Inefficient Economy *(inadmissible consequence)*	(—)

Dysfunctional Market Economy (Es)

Discourse Formation B: The Antagonistic Other

Abbreviations/
Symbols

Difference	|
Equivalence	=
Antagonism	.....
Empty Signifier	(Es)
Nodal Point	(Np)

A (px.): Level of Practices in Discourse Formation A (techniques; subjectivities; adjuvants; receivers)
A (eth.): Ethical substance of Objects of Desires in Discourse Formation A
B (px.): Level of Practices in Discourse Formation B (Traitor)
B (eth.): Ethical substance of inadmissible Consequences Caused by the Discourse Formation B
(. . .): Continued Relations of Difference/Equivalence

(developing, growing, efficient, free) are connected to signifiers that define the range of determination of each semantic entity. "Developing Economy" as an equivalent of "Functioning Economy" is defined in terms of "renewal," "dynamics," and "innovativeness" (see Table 6.3).

This, in liberal-conservative discourse, frequently repeated configuration of mutually equivalent descriptions of "Functioning Economy" is opposed to the imaginary of a stagnating economy—one that has lost the normal and possible pace of progress. A slackening pace of growth is repeatedly described by the metaphor of "slipping-off," which symbolizes that the Swedish economy loses not its capacity for growth, but its capacity to partly live up to the endemic dynamics of a functioning economy,[4] and partly to meet the demands to development set by the ever fiercer international competition (Government Communication 1994/95: 22).[5] Measurement of the actual economic pace of development and the slipping-off is conducted nominally through statistical numbers. However, the internationalization of the economy, international economic development, increasing international competition, and expectation of an accentuation of internationalization provide possibilities to problematize the slackening development (e.g., Department of Industry 1991; Government Bill 1991/92: 51; NUTEK 1991). International levels of wages and taxation, for instance, are observed as benchmarks for a rational conduct of government (Government Bill 1991/92: 38). In this respect, Government Bill 1991/92: 60 on the taxation reform discusses the need for internationally competitive regulation. The domestic capacity to sustain welfare is connected to the capacity to keep pace with the development abroad. It is observed that "our capacity to realize our aspirations does not suffice" (Department Report 1994: 35).

The conception of the functioning market economy as a system of constant change and progress also elucidates why the primary objective of government is to "provide the foundation for revival in economy and future stable growth" (Government Bill 1991/92: 38, p. 5). Such a political strategy must be "cohesive," "long-term" (e.g., Government Bill 1991/92; 60, p. 80), "pervasive" (Government Bill 1991/92: 60; Conservative Party and Liberal Party 1991), and "rigid and permanent" (Government Bill 1991/92: 51; Conservative Party and Liberal Party 1991). Actual politico-economic strategies for the realization of the functioning market economy act as a structural support to economic activities. The political program of the

Table 6.3 Semantics of a Functioning Market Economy

Developing	Growing	Efficient	Free
Renewal	Future growth	Resource allocation	Freedom of activity
Dynamics	Growth potential	Resource use	Freedom of choice
Innovative	Sustainable growth	Functioning market	Free entre-preneurship

liberal-conservative government is constructed around the nodal point of "beneficial economic climate of business" (e.g., Government Bill 1991/92: 38). The government intends to enhance the growth potential of the economy and to mobilize all the potential resources to increased future growth through a new "industrial policy," whose primary objective is to improve the climate of enterprises and entrepreneurs. In Government Bill 1993/94: 40, this objective is defined in the following manner:

> Through a climate [*Nodal point; space*] benefiting entrepreneurs [*subject*] with a functioning structure [*adjuvant*] and rules [*adjuvant*] for the small and medium size enterprises [*receiver; subject*] may the renewal [*empty signifier*] be attained, new occupations [*consequence*] created and markets vitalized [*strategy*= "vitalization"].

Moreover, in Government Bill 1993/94: 140, the aspect of indirect mobilization through an increase of incentives and contextual improvement of likelihood of interests is defined even more precisely. Here, the liberal-conservative government argues, "the necessity that the government's sectorial policies [i.e. regional policy] are designed in a way that leads distribution of resource in such a way that the growth potential in all parts of the country is mobilized" (chapter 7.1). The dual function of enterprises is observable as these play the role of "receivers" of government policy, but they are also assigned the responsibility to realize the objective of renewal and growth of economy. Enterprises and entrepreneurs are incentives attributed to "innovations," "renewal," and "growth." In Government Bill 1993/94: 40, this "sublimation" of entrepreneur is expressed in the following terms:

> It is only the individual entrepreneur [*subject*] and his employees [*adjuvant*] that through their efforts [*technique of the self*] may realize a growing Sweden [*time*; future][*object; empty signifier; space*].

Similarly, in Government Bill 1991/92: 60, p. 60), SMEs are sublimated as the subjects that will, and are even obliged to, realize the collective want of growth: "The small and medium-sized enterprises [*subject*] must largely take responsibility [*adjuvant; technique of the self*] for future [*time*; future] growth [*empty signifier*]."

The socio-economic climate that the government observes to benefit the attainment of functioning market economy is characterized by its capacity to facilitate renewal and growth in enterprises. This climate is characterized by a further relation of antagonism between "'beneficial'" and "disadvantaging" climate. A beneficial climate improves the total situation of existence and activity of business actors, such as enterprises or entrepreneurs. In NUTEK's (1991) report, such a climate is "benign" for enterprises; in Government Bill 1992/93: 51, it is defined as "more benign" than earlier situations, and in the report of the Department of Industry (1991), the degree of benignity is determinable through the actually realized frequency of new start-ups of enterprises. In Government Bill 1991/92: 60, a beneficial climate is similarly defined as socio-economic and political structures, which are beneficial for economic activities, such as investment, innovation, and growth. On the contrary, a "disadvantaging" climate distorts conditions, "has harming consequences," and constitutes a "burden for entrepreneurship and new entrepreneurship" (Government Bill 1991/92: 60, p. 61). As a consequence, such a disadvantaging climate was expected to "deter many growing enterprises from entering the share market" (Government Bill 1991/92: 60, p. 62).

In a way, characteristic of a hegemonic strategy, the liberal-conservative government posits the pre-suppositions for the need of a "new industrial policy" by defining, partly, the need of the beneficial climate in general, and partly, by defining what such a climate must necessarily consist of. New industrial policy symbolizes (Government Bill 1991/92: 38) the hegemonic strategy for the realization of the "functioning market economy" as its objective is to "foster economic growth." The general imaginary of the "functioning market economy" (empty signifier) is constructed through a relation of equivalence between "enterprise" and "entrepreneurship." A "positive climate of entrepreneurship" is assumed to generate business start-ups and small enterprises, which, again, figure as the pre-condition for a general "vitalization" of the economy (NUTEK 1991). A benign climate for SMEs benefits competition, which for its part is the prerequisite of "economic growth," "force of development," "functioning economy," and "market economy" (Government Bill 1991/92: 51). The actual quality of the present climate is also articulated to determine the conditions for "employment," "welfare," and "growth" (Government Bill 1993/94: 40). In this regard, the social imaginary of "functioning market economy" is defined as superordinate to the further social objectives of "welfare," "growth," and "justice." In this regard, the articulation of the primacy of the "functional economy" is posited to realize other general objectives, which would remain beyond realization without a functioning economy (Table 6.4).

The distinction between a beneficial and a non-beneficial climate is defined through definitions of the origins, forces, and adjuvants of economic growth, which further defines and restricts the susceptible, functional, and rational objectives, forms, and modes of political government. In this regard, "climate of entrepreneurship" functions as a nodal point (Np) as, on a lower level of abstraction, it provides distinctions between possible/impossible, rational/irrational, and functional/dysfunctional forms, strategies, and institutions of political government. A good climate of entrepreneurship functions as a nodal point in the political discourse of the liberal-conservative government by organizing and distinguishing sets of adjuvants, subjects, consequences, techniques, and strategies supporting liberal-conservative governmental rationality from a corresponding set of

Table 6.4 Contrariety Functioning/Dysfunctioning Market Economy

Discourse Formation A: Liberal-Conservative Discourse 1991–1994

Functioning Market Economy (Es)

l/=

(—) Sufficient Competition (Np) l/= Climate of Entrepreneurship (Np) (—)

l/=

(—) Insufficient Competition (Np) l/= Poor Climate of Entrepreneurship (Np) (—)

l/=

Dysfunctional Market Economy (Es)

Discourse Formation B: The Antagonistic Other

Abbreviations/ Symbols:

Difference	|	A (px.): Level of Practices in Discourse Formation A (techniques; subjectivities; adjuvants; receivers)
Equivalence	=	A (eth.): Ethical substance of Objects of Desires in Discourse Formation A
Antagonism	....	B (px.): Level of Practices in Discourse Formation B (inadmissible techniques; traitors)
Empty Signifier	(Es)	B (eth.): Ethical substance: Inadmissible Consequences of the Discourse Formation B
Nodal Point	(Np)	(. . . .): Continued Relations of Difference/Equivalence

elements, which hinder the realization of the liberal-conservative imaginary of fullness of society.

"Climate of entrepreneurship" stands in a relation of equivalence to a further "nodal point" of "competition" (Np). As Government Bill 1991/92: 51 (cf. Government Bill 1993/94: 40) illustrates, a good climate is inseparably linked with competition. Indeed, it appears as if there were a mutual resonance between the two, since entrepreneurship is enabled through competition, and competition, for its part, functions as the pre-condition of entrepreneurship. Illustrative of this is the antagonistic relationship between competition and monopoly/limitation of competition with regard to the "free market economy," which functions as a limitation of the expression of the signification of the empty signifier of "functioning market economy" (e.g., Government Bill 1991/92: 51, 1991/92: 38). The objective of "new industrial policy" is to improve the climate of entrepreneurship, enterprises, and business in general by facilitating competition and abolishing restrictions and hindrances to competition (e.g., Government Bill 1991/92: 38). In the following two chapters, I will explicate the discursive construction of the two nodal points of "climate of entrepreneurship" and "competition" by looking at them separately.

Climate of Enterprises and Entrepreneurship

Assuming that the "climate of enterprises and entrepreneurship" functions as a nodal point in the political discourse of the liberal-conservative government indicates that it acts as a condensed point of reference, that is to say as a signifier that sustains the signification of the social imaginary articulated in governmental discourse. Indeed, two antagonistic chains of signifiers appear to be organized through their reference to a "beneficial" and a "disadvantaging" climate of economic activities. These two mutually opposed chains are further specified in the table below. The function of the "climate of enterprises and entrepreneurship" as a condensed point of reference for the liberal-conservative discourse is, among others, illustrated in Government Bill 1993/94: 40:

> Through *a climate* [*Nodal point*] *benefiting enterprises* with well-functioning frames and rules [*adjuvant*] for the small and medium-sized enterprises [*subject; receiver*], may the renewal [*empty signifier*] be attained, new occupations developed [*consequence*] and markets vitalized [*consequence*]. (italics added)

One of the previously indicated oppositions organized around the "climate of enterprises and entrepreneurship" consists of antagonism between "freedom" of market and "restrictions"/"regulation" through politics. In Government Bill 1991/92: 51, the SME-friendly climate is defined through an analogy to "free competition" and "free trade" as contrasted to "distorting regulations" and "market distortion." Especially, market distortion plays a central role by setting the limits for admissible (no distortion) and inadmissible political strategies (distortion). It is not the political regulation of the market that is prohibited, but rather such regulations, which are expected to have harmful consequences on the functioning of the market. Distortion means that the natural or normal balance of the market as regards competitiveness, production, but also the assumed endemic dynamic market processes of renewal, become dislocated (see Government Bill 1992/93: 82, 1993/94: 40; Government Communication 1994/95: 22). For this reason, currency devaluation is considered an inefficient political strategy, as it distorts the calculability of risks and profits (SOU 1993: 16; Government Bill 1991/92: 38).

The phenomenological construction of "distortion" is most clearly expressed in Government Bill 1991/92: 60, where "market balance" and "market distortion" are established as being in binary opposition with regard to the imaginary of the natural and normal course of the economy. Opposition does not follow an either/or logic, but instead it expresses inclining stages as "the less distorting" political activities, and institutions are defined better than the "more distorting" ones (see Government Bill 1991/92: 60, p. 84). What cause the distortion are activities that restrict the interplay of market price mechanisms. Such distorting elements, which can be classified as "traitors," as they hinder the realization of the imaginary of fullness of society, include above all "taxation pressure," "selective and partial interests supporting economic policy," "business and branch support," and "direct state involvement in economy." Taxation pressure embraces the taxation of capital—property, savings, and shares, all of which are problematized through the constructed analogy and relation of equivalence between "restriction of market" and "taxation pressure" (Parliamentary Minutes 1991/92: 6; SOU 1993: 16). Traditionally, the expansive public sector and the width of the Swedish welfare state as concerns its share of the economy are problematized due to their demand to high rates of taxation, which in turn leads to the distortion of markets (e.g., SOU 1993: 16). The welfare state's sole focus on distributional aspects is argued to be one of the major reasons for the actual economic and employment crises that the Swedish state experienced in the early 1990s:

> Moreover, labor market legislation [*traitor*] prioritized short-term security aspects [*inadmissible technique + object*] regarding the cost of the flexibility and dynamics [*inadmissible consequence*], that is decisive for the enterprises' [*subject*] capacity to adjustment and renewal [*technique of the self*] and hence, also for the living standard [*object*] in the longer term [*Time—future*]. (SOU 1993: 16, p. 15)

The most severe consequence of the distorted market is the distortion of prices, which would implicate that the general potential of economy, economic resources, as well as cognitive capacities of creativity and innovativeness of enterprises and entrepreneurs cannot be mobilized to attain maximum productivity and growth. As the prior quotation illustrates, long-term market freedom is assumed to provide more distributed resources than short-term external political regulation. What all the harmful political activities, regulations, and institutions have in common is their "disturbance" of the functioning of market in a natural and normal way.[6] The governmental strategy for a free market consists of, above all, the new competition law, which was implemented in Government Bill 1992/93: 56 (see chapter 6).

Another opposition covers the antagonism between beneficial and the development potential of the market supporting "market plurality" and "diffusion of economic power" as contrasted to "concentration of power" (e.g. Government Bill 1991/92: 38). Plurality of market actors, that is, enterprises, producers, and entrepreneurial subjects, constitutes itself a beneficial climate for innovation and, as such, appears as a pre-condition for economic dynamics. As the next section on the nodal point of "competition" illustrates, this assumption is based on a specific epistemological point of view on the origins of economic growth. Contrariwise, a market climate that supports innovation also induces innovative activities among the market participants and supports the start-up of new enterprises and the commercialization of new ideas (see NUTEK 1991). Market plurality is closely linked to the extent and functioning of competition as the regulation of competition per se also withholds possible actors from market entrance through business start-ups (NUTEK 1991). In this regard, market plurality is linked to subjective incentives to creativity and innovativeness, which are hindered by a concentration of power on the market, lower investments due to high costs, and lack of capital and inflation, as all these aspects cause insecurity about the future. As Government Bill 1992/93: 56 articulates, political regulations of the market and monopolies induced by regulations constitute entrepreneurship, which again is the prerequisite of economic dynamics, renewal, and growth (Government Bill 1992/93: 56). The plurality of market actors appears as an "adjuvant" of economic incentives and activities that lead to productivity increase and general renewal of the economy. One of the roles played by an entrepreneur is to induce competition, invigorate markets, animate competition, and increase the number of market participants through further business start-ups and thus to involve animation and vitalization of the market in general (see Government Bill 1991/92: 38).[7] Therefore, it is appropriate to argue that an entrepreneur and subjects possessing entrepreneurial capacities play the role of "subjects" who enable the liberal-conservative government to realize the imaginary of the "functioning market economy" and with it the subordinated collective objectives of growth, employment, and welfare.

A further opposition organized by the nodal point of "climate of enterprises and entrepreneurship" prevails in the form of the antagonistic relation between "transparent" and "intransparent"/"complex" rules (e.g.,

Department of Industry 1991; Government Bills 1991/92: 38 and 51; NUTEK 1991). Transparency of rules relates to the general efficient institutional framework that supports the most rational and efficient allocation of resources, and in this way also contributes to the general extent of economic production, efficient use of resources, and increase in the extent of competition. On the opposite side, complexity of rules, often defined as "trouble" or "multitude" of rules, is generalized as a hindrance to development, which prevents enterprises from realization of their endemic potential of development (e.g., Department of Industry 1991; Government Communication 1994/95: 22). In the Department of Industry (1991: 12) report, the complexity of rules is defined in the following manner:

all too complicated system of rules [*traitor*] causes unnecessary costs [*inadmissible consequence*] for enterprises [*receiver; subject*], impedes new establishment [*inadmissible consequence*] and impairs the functioning of the market.

Transparency of rules describes the inherent quality of rules and legislation, whereas the "rigid" and "objective" rules accentuate the temporal aspect: that rules must remain possible to anticipate and calculate by economic actors (Government Bill 1991/92: 51; Parliamentary Minutes 1991/92: 6). A functioning market economy (empty signifier) depends on the presence of effective rules, which are defined as rules inducing cost reduction, effective and productive resource allocation enabling information, and stable economic expectations enabling institutional contexts (e.g., Government Bill 1991/92: 51). On the opposite side, complex and opaque rules cause high economic costs and inefficient investment and allocation of economic resources (e.g., Government Bill 1991/92: 51). The stability of rules appears especially important, as this facilitates the calculation of the long-term consequences, costs, and profitability of economic investments for market actors (e.g., Government Bill 1991/92: 38). Another problematization of the complexity of rules concerns the unjust distribution of administrative burdens they may cause for small and larger enterprises. The complexity of rules exerts a more severe impact on small enterprises than on large companies (e.g., Government Bill 1991/92: 51, 1993/94: 40). Equal conditions of competition, which accentuates the quality, productivity, and prices as a means of competition, induce activities of renewal, development, and innovations, which, when accumulated, count for the economic growth (Government Communication 1994/95: 22). In this manner, the need for more transparent rules is motivated not only by the increased effectiveness of the use of resources, but also by its positive contribution to the small enterprises' capacity to compete. The pre-supposition of the value of small enterprises and the corresponding support of entrepreneurial activities, and even more so the start-up of new enterprises, was supported by the conceived relation of inter-dependence between the intensity and scope of competition and the endeavored renewal of the economy (e.g., Department of Industry 1991; Government Bill 1993/94: 40; SOU 1993: 16). Therefore, SOU 1993: 16 (p. 81) articulates that "it is of the utmost significance for new enterprises [*receiver; subject*] to be provided with stable and transparent conditions [*adjuvant*]."

A further antagonistic relation constituted in context with the "climate of enterprises and entrepreneurship" consists of the opposition between "risk-capital supply" and "shortage on risk-capital" (e.g., Government Bill 1993/94: 140). Government Bill 1993/94: 140 motivated not only the implemented reforms of capital taxation, but also the institution of state-owned venture capital companies (ATLE and BURE and six regional companies) as a means to support new business start-ups and smaller enterprises, whose risk capital supply by the market was observed to be insufficient. What deteriorates the supply of risk-capital are principally taxation on savings, capital, and social costs, which all lower the level of investment and cause capital flows abroad (Parliamentary Minutes 1991/92: 6; Government Bill 1991/92: 60). These problems symbolize traitors in the political discourse that are considered "burdens" for enterprises, which under more "beneficial circumstances" would provide higher economic growth and guarantee future welfare (Government Bill 1991/92: 60). In Government Bill 1991/92: 60, burdens are defined in terms of "hindrances of possibilities," "causes harming effects," and "obstacles to new entrepreneurship and enterprises." Improvement of risk-capital supply defined as "working" and "active capital," through a reduction of capital taxation, improved matching of capital supply and demand are emphasized as "adjuvants" in the achievement of higher economic growth through SMEs (Department of Industry 1991). Table 6.5 summarizes the primary connections made around the nodal point of "climate of enterprises and entrepreneurship" and shows how these are linked to the empty signifier of "functioning market economy."

Competition

As Table 6.5 illustrates, "competition" is another nodal point in the political discourse of the liberal-conservative government. As with the nodal point of "climate of enterprises and entrepreneurship," competition also functions in accordance with an either/or logic between two opposed chains of signifiers, which is typical of popular types of discursive formations (see Chapter 4). The primary opposition to "competition" is that among "plurality of market actors," "economic concentration," and "monopoly" (e.g., Department of Industry 1991; Government Bill 1991/92: 51; Parliamentary Minutes 1991/92: 6). "Competition" is defined in an equivalent relation to both "free market economy" (empty signifier) and private entrepreneurship. Private entrepreneurship is observed as the guarantee and stabilizer of the free market economy, whereas "competition" is the necessary condition for the presence of private entrepreneurship (e.g., Government Bill 1991/92: 38).

Table 6.5 Discursive Structure of the Functioning Market Economy

Discourse Formation A: Liberal-Conservative Discourse 1991–1994
Functioning Market Economy (Es)

(—) Sufficient Competition (Np) /= Climate of Entrepreneurship (Np) (—)

/= /=

A (px.) (—) New Competition Law/ /= Information/Knowledge on /= Undistorted Competition /= Entrepreneurship (*subject*)/Political (—)
Swedish Competition markets (*adjuvant*)/Calcu- (*adjuvant*)/Transparent and Government (*adjuvant*)/Competi-
Authority (*adjuvants*) lable Yields of Risks (*object*) Stable Rules (*adjuvant*) tion (*technique*)

/= /= /= /=

A (eth.) (—) Competition Supporting /= Rational and Efficient /= Vigorous Enterprises (*object*) /= Competitiveness (*object*) (—)
Political regulation (*object*) Resource Allocation (*object*)

....

B (eth.) (—) Competition Distorting /= Irrational and Inefficient /= Feeble Enterprises /= Incompetitiveness (—)
Political Regulation (*inad-* Resource Allocation (*inad-* (*inadmissible consequence*) (*inadmissible consequence*)
missible consequence) *missible consequence*)

/= /= /= /=

B (px.) (—) Restricted Freedom of Con- /= Waste of Resources and /= Intransparent Rules, Social /= Hindrances to Realization of (—)
sumption and Production Inefficient Utilization of Costs/Taxation Pressure Entrepreneurship and Economic
(*traitor*) Resources (*traitor*) (*traitor*) Incentives (*traitor*)

(—) Insufficient Competition (Np) (—)

/= /=

Dysfunctioning Market Economy (Es)
Discourse Formation B: The Antagonistic Other

Abbreviations/ Symbols:
Difference |
Equivalence   =
Antagonism   .....
Empty Signifier   (Es)
Nodal Point   (Np)

A (px.): Level of Practices in Discourse Formation A (techniques; subjectivities; adjuvants; receivers)
A (eth.): Ethical substance of Objects of Desires in Discourse Formation A
B (px.): Level of Practices in Discourse Formation B (inadmissible techniques; traitors)
B (eth.): Ethical substance: Inadmissible Consequences of the Discourse Formation B
(. . .): Continued Relations of Difference/Equivalence

The appreciation of private entrepreneurship derives from the imaginary that the growth potential and the economy's endemic capacity for development depend on the presence of a plurality of market actors and the economic activities of investment, production, and innovations conducted by these (e.g., Government Bill 1991/92: 51). The relationship between "competition" and the scope of private entrepreneurship appears as a tautology, since effective competition requires a multitude of market actors, but is itself the pre-condition for the establishment of business start-ups, and the presence of a multitude of competing economic actors achieved in this way. In other words, the establishment of new enterprises through entrepreneurial subjects is a prerequisite for effective competition (Government Bill 1991/92: 51). This tautological relation can be summarized as follows:

plurality of market actors > competition < > competition > plurality of market actors

Similar to the definition of the "climate of enterprises and entrepreneurship," the value of "competition" and its facilitating or preventing conditions is also effectuated through relations of antagonism and equivalence. The signifier of competition that functions as a nodal point is located between valorized "free competition" and opposed "distorted competition." What is accentuated in competition is not primarily the nominal activity and interaction of competition, but the economic pressure enacted by competition that emanates into innovations, productivity increase, and general economic renewal. Government Bill 1992/93: 56 on new competition law (cf. Lundquist 2005) contains several references to other documents in which competition in the Swedish economy was problematized. Above all, in its report SOU 1991: 82, the parliamentary committee labeled as "Productivity Delegation" identified competition as being the driving force in economic growth and productivity increase. In its report SOU 1991: 82, the "Competition Committee," just like several reports from the OECD and the European Commission, observed an insufficient extent of competition in the Swedish economy in general (see Government Bill 1992/93: 56). In congruence to these reports, the government observes various competition-preventing regulations along with welfare state institutions limiting the extent of the competitive sector, restrictions on foreign direct investment, and market concentrations as conditions restricting the actual competitive pressure in the Swedish economy (e.g., Government Bill 1992/93: 56). As Government Bill 1992/93: 56 on the new competition law argues, the earlier competition law is insufficient since it exerts sanctions and prosecutes reactively. A functioning competition law must be able to proactively prevent the economic activities that harm competition (Government Bill 1992/93: 56).

The absence of sufficient competition is problematized due to the corresponding absence of economic growth, which, under higher competitive pressure and a resulting induced productivity increase, would have been significantly higher. A discourse-specific observation of competition and the emphasis of its inter-dependence with growth and productivity provide possibilities to problematize existing political regulation of the economy. The epistemology of competition in the liberal-conservative discourse is characterized by two mutually antagonistic chains of signifiers around competition. The general antagonistic relation is installed between mutually opposed ethical poles of "sufficient competition" and "insufficient competition." The first opposition embraces political regulation that either facilitates or distorts competition. On the positive side, competition-supporting political measures provide beneficial structural and judicial frames for the market. Public risk-capital supply, rigid and transparent rules, public sector privatization, and the introduction of mechanisms for competition between private service providers as well as public investments in infrastructure and communications provide objective and equal conditions for all market actors. On the opposite side, political price regulations, direct economic subventions and protections, prioritization of large companies, inflexible and partial interests following institutions, public sector monopoly, and taxation pressure ("skattetryck") symbolize conditions that distort competition. The general rationale of this complex configuration of elements is well expressed in the report of a parliamentary committee (SOU 1993: 16):

> Our opinion [*destinator*] is that the role of the state [*adjuvant*] is to set up frames [*strategy*] for the civil society [*receiver; subject*] and to create generally good conditions [*adjuvant; strategy*] for the activities of households [*receiver; subject*] and enterprises [*subject*].

Subjects of "household" and "enterprise" are not just any subjects, but subjects who make economic decisions on consumption and investment that maintain the extent and intensity competition. SOU 1993: 16 observes the need to redefine the sharing of responsibilities and roles between the state and the private sector. The actual employment crisis was observed to symbolize the state's neglect of its natural role as provider of objective and an egalitarian institutional and judicial set-up to facilitate the realization of individual incentives (e.g., SOU 1993: 16, p. 15). In this context, the new competition law implemented in Government Bill 1992/93: 56 was motivated by the assumption that freedom of entrepreneurship and consumption would enhance the rationality and efficiency in allocating resources (see Government Bill 1994/95: 16). Allocation of resources is not only a matter of production, and of producers' decisions on investments, but also embraces considerations on the capacity of consumers to realize their personal incentives. One of the principles of the government's consumer policy is therefore to:

> support households' [*strategy; receiver*] capacity to utilize their resources [*object; strategy*] in accordance with their future interests [*object; time:* future], including the possibility to make contemplated

decisions [*strategy; consequence*] enabled by the transparency of the market [*adjuvant*]. (Government Bill 1994/95: 16)

Both producers and consumers are emphasized subjects who effectuate an efficient allocation of resources. In the prescription for the Swedish Competition Authority installed on July 1, 1992, the latter was assigned the objective to evaluate potential distortions of competition as caused by legislation and public sector regulation, and to suggest measures that would increase competition (Government Bill 1994/95: 16). What is conceived to hinder the rational allocation of resources is, besides insufficient information, the insufficient freedom of producers and consumers. Competition is accentuated as a mechanism that guarantees rational resource allocation and thereby sustains the effective use of accessible economic resources, with optimal economic growth being the outcome (cf. Lundquist 2005; Svensson 2001). Efficient resource allocation indicates free allocation of resources in activities observed to provide the highest expected returns on invested capital (e.g., Government Bill 1992/93: 56; SOU 1993: 16). Efficient allocation of resources is contrasted with a "waste of resources" (e.g., SOU 1993: 16). This implicates that the total potential of the Swedish economy will not be completely utilized until efficiency in resource allocation has been attained. Rational resource allocation also means that resources and responsibilities are dislocated from the public sector to the private sector (Government Bill 1991/92: 38). This is chiefly attained through an accentuation of consumers' freedom of choice of service, privatization, and deregulation of public services.

A further relation of opposition articulated in the framework of the nodal point of "competition" is that between "vigorous" and "feeble" enterprises. Competitive pressure functions as an "adjuvant" for the natural evolutionary course of market economy, in which competition provides the source of verification of the economic potential of enterprises. This is most clearly expressed in Government Bill 1991/92: 38 (p. 8), which argued that "Government [*subject*] will not carry out any attempts to resuscitate enterprises [*receiver; inadmissible strategy*], which do not fulfill the demands set by the market [*destinator*]." The discourse of the liberal-conservative government expresses an imaginary of competition as a validation of the rationality in actualized resource allocation. "Vigorous" enterprises succeed in normal economic competition, whereas "feeble" enterprises survive only in economic anomalies (Government Bill 1991/92: 51, p. 10; 1993/94: 40). Political regulations and policies that secure the existence of enterprises through subventions and market protection were rejected because they were conceived to contradict the principle of economic renewal based on free competition.

The liberal-conservative government argued therefore that it is "crucial to note that loans et cetera, are not given to rescue employment feeble enterprises" (Government Bill 1993/94: 40). Industrial policies are therefore restricted to support enterprises and to embrace forms of support that do not distort competition and neither strengthen nor weaken the endemic potential of economic profitability: "An essential aspect in each singular case is that an enterprise [*receiver*] is expected to be or become economically profitable" (Government Bill 1992/93: 82, p. 10). In other words, the market itself validates the factual rationality in resource allocation, and, as such, undistorted competition also figures as the guarantee of the highest possible levels of economic growth and productivity attained. New enterprises and entrepreneurial subjects perform the role of social agents who maintain, vitalize, and stabilize competitive pressure; and in this role, they guarantee the optimal level of economic renewal. In Government Communication 1994/95: 22, the competitive pressure is analogous to the "pressure on transformation" that guarantees that the Swedish economy does not slip-off the economic pace endemic to a functioning market economy.

A last relation of opposition established around the nodal point of "competition" is that between "competitiveness" and "incompetitiveness" (cf. Conservative Party and Liberal Party 1991; Department of Industry 1991; Government Bill 1991/92: 51 and 38). Competitiveness is the objective of the political strategy, whereas noncompetitiveness figures as the inadmissible consequence of the political government (cf. Conservative Party and Liberal Party 1991). Like the earlier described logics of signification of a "functioning market economy," competitiveness also functions in accordance with an either/or logic ensuring that pre-conditions of competitiveness are determined through a distinction between factors that generate and hinder competitiveness, respectively. The objective of the liberal-conservative government is to achieve the resurgence of Sweden as an industrial nation (cf. Parliamentary Minutes 1991: 6; Government Bill 1991/92: 38).

Resurgence refers to the resurgence of international competitiveness of the Swedish economy (e.g., Government Bill 1991/92: 38). Competitiveness of the national economy is the contingent outcome of economic actors who realize the chances offered by the liberal-conservative government (Government Bill 1992/93: 82). As such, competitiveness is achieved as a reciprocal outcome of economic "subjects" who possess the capacity for "entrepreneurship," referring to economic decisions on production investment and functioning competition as established by political institutions that act as an "adjuvant" of entrepreneurs (Government Bill 1991/92: 38). The government of economy is consequently considered most effective when it pursues "stimulation" and "vitalization" of the business life and provides it with incentives and a beneficial climate to stimulate renewal and economic development (Government Bill 1993/94: 40). "Subjects," who realize the beneficial climate for realizing chances of competitiveness, are "entrepreneurs," defined here as either subjects who initiate new businesses or make entrepreneurial decisions in the form of decisions on renewal, development, and innovations (Government Bill 1993/94: 40). Entrepreneurs are those agents who are imagined to utilize the full potential of the economy (SOU 1993: 70).

Table 6.6   Nodal Point of Competition

Discourse Formation A: Liberal-Conservative Discourse 1991–1994

Functioning Market Economy (Es)

|/=

(—) Sufficient Competition (Np) |/= Climate of Entrepreneurship (Np) (—)

|/=

A (px.) (—) Lowering of Taxation Pressure *(technique)*/ Government *(subject)*	|/= International Inst. Adjustment *(technique)*	|/= Transparency of Rules & Calculable Rules *(technique)*/Government *(subject)*/Enterprises *(receiver)*	|/= Taxation Reform/De-regulation of Finance Market *(technique)*/ Entrepreneurs, SEs, & SMEs *(receiver)* (—)
|/=		|/=	|/=
A (eth.) (—) Free Competition/Free Trade/Free Price Setting *(object)*	|/= Diffusion of Economic Power *(object)*	|/= Efficiency & Productivity of Resource Use *(object)*	|/= Access to Risk-Capital *(object)*
|/=	|/=		|/=
B (eth.) (—) Distorting Market Regulations/ Market Distortion *(inadmissible consequence)*	|/= Concentration of Power & Market Domination *(inadmissible consequence)*	|/= Inefficient Resource Use & Allocation *(inadmissible consequence)*	|/= Insufficient Risk Capital Supply/Insufficient New Entrepreneurship *(inadmissible consequence)*
|/=		|/=	|/=
B (px.) (—) Taxation/Political Wage Bargaining/Public Budget Deficit/Inflation *(traitor)*	|/= Market Regulations/Selective Econ. Support/Subventions *(traitor)*	|/= Complexity of Rules/Intransparent Rules *(traitor)*	|/= Taxation of Capital and Savings *(traitor)*

|/=

(—) Insufficient Competition (Np) (—)

|/=

Dysfunctioning Market Economy (Es)

Discourse Formation B: The Antagonistic Other

Abbreviations/ Symbols:

Difference	|	A (px.): Level of Practices in Discourse Formation A (techniques; subjectivities; adjuvants; receivers)
Equivalence	=	A (eth.): Ethical substance of Objects of Desires in Discourse Formation A
Antagonism	....	B (px.): Level of Practices in Discourse Formation B (inadmissible techniques; traitors)
Empty Signifier	(Es)	B (eth.): Ethical substance: Inadmissible Consequences of the Discourse Formation B

A number of previously described institutions, socio-economic factors, and political strategies figure as the pre-conditions for competitiveness. Among these are "simplification of rules," "de-regulation of markets," "stimulation of enterprises," "international contacts," and "efficient risk capital supply" (e.g., Department of Industry 1991). As traitors (i.e., as hindrances to the achievement of competitiveness), figure social factors that hinder the burgeoning of economic incentives, which under more beneficial conditions would lead to decisions of product and service development, innovations, and realization of new ideas (Government Bill 1991/92: 38). Competitiveness is related to political regulations and institutions that are observed as either internationally "competitive" or uncompetitive (Government Bill 1991/92: 60; 1992/93: 56 and 82). At this point, it is worth emphasizing that competitiveness in general refers to competitiveness in an increasingly internationalized economy. Table 6.6 summarizes the field of differences around the nodal point of competition and how the mutually antagonistic poles of "sufficient" and "insufficient" competition are used to define competition and the sufficient conditions of competition that support the attainment of the "functioning market economy." The two antagonistic chains of signifiers symbolize "competition supporting" *and* "competition distorting and restricting" types of political regulation.

THE GOVERNMENTAL FUNCTION OF ENTREPRENEUR

Liberal-conservative discourse departed from an observed ineluctable necessity of more and more profitable and competitive enterprises. To realize the ethical substance of government (i.e., the functioning market economy), entrepreneurs were observed to be economy's "spearheads towards the future" (Government Bill 1991/92: 38, p. 41). Rationality in political strategies supporting entrepreneurs resides in the assumption of economic renewal and progress achieved through entrepreneurs. The Department of Industry report (1991, p. 5; cf. Government Bill 1991/92: 38) observed "new entrepreneurship," defined as activities leading to business start-ups, as a pre-condition for dynamics in the Swedish economy. Similarly, the NUTEK (1991) report observed that economic vitality depended on "strong entrepreneurship." In 1990, a program [insatsområde för nyföretagande] was installed at the Department of Industry to increase the growth in SMEs (NUTEK 1991). The assumed advantages in entrepreneurship and SMEs resided in the assumption that these are geared toward innovation, product, and service development, which further promotes the intensity of competition, involves a decrease in price level, and leads to economic modernization of the production apparatus, which is accompanied by growth and international competitiveness. What facilitates entrepreneurial activity is above all the beneficial economic climate, but additionally also positive societal attitudes toward entrepreneurship and enterprises (Government

Bill 1991/92: 51). As early as the early 1990s, the liberal-conservative discourse emphasized the need of a "culture of enterprise" that was described in terms of positive attitudes to entrepreneurs and enterprises, established through school education and disseminated by campaigns and associations, such as "Youth Entrepreneurship."

Industrial, competition, and economic policies depend on conditions for new entrepreneurship and entrepreneurship in SEs (Government Bill 1991/92: 38, p. 6).[8] Moreover, reductions in taxation, intensification of competition, improvement of risk-capital supply to SEs, and introduction of the Enterprise Allowance Scheme in 1991 as an alternative to unemployment benefit all intend to support entrepreneurs as "subjects" to realize their assigned roles. Above all, entrepreneur as subject is anticipated to utilize potential resources and contextual conditions most efficiently so as to optimize the national capacity to economic growth. The political government plays a supportive role and performs as an "adjuvant" vis-à-vis entrepreneurs, most of all, through stimulation and vitalization of entrepreneurship. Chances of entrepreneurs and entrepreneurship are enhanced through policies that "vitalize" and "stimulate" the business life by improving its institutional, material, and cooperative context (e.g., Government Bill 1993/94: 40 and 140; SOU 1993: 16 and 70). SOU 1993: 70 (p. 13) explains this role of the state: "governmental measures can never replace the competent entrepreneur but facilitate his activities." The new competition legislation was explicitly structured to facilitate activities and the market entrance of SEs:

> The objective of the new competition law [*adjuvant*; *technique*] is by and large to keep the market open [*object*] for small enterprises [*receiver*] and new entrepreneurship [*receiver*; *subject*]. Prohibitions [*technique*] focus therefore on conditions that have negative consequences [*traitor*] for small enterprises [*receiver*] and new entrepreneurship [*receiver*]. (Government Bill 1992/93: 82; p. 16)

The Department Report 1994: 35 criticizes the earlier systems of taxation and redistribution as they are considered to affect the individuals' willingness to "make extra efforts." This is problematic in as far as "every person's will to grow constitutes the capacity of the entire nation" (Department Report 1994: 35). Moreover, the individual endemic spirit and will to learn and create is the most important driving force behind the willingness to achieve personal initiatives. Vitalization and stimulation of entrepreneurship as two rational strategies of government depart from the pre-supposition that entrepreneurs are driven by the aspiration to develop, innovate, and improve themselves. This elucidates the government's aspiration to provide a beneficial climate in which individuals can try their wings and take risks to realize their personal objectives (Government Bill 1991/92: 38, p. 41). The quality of the climate is measured in the absolute number of enterprises started in Sweden and in comparison with the number of enterprises started abroad (e.g., Department of Industry 1991). Entrepreneur is the subject who—through activities, incentives, and willingness to creativity and innovations—utilizes the potential located in the economy (e.g., Parliamentary Minutes 1991/92: 6). Endemic personal creativity and incentives are realized under the social climate of "free entrepreneurship." This conception of analogy between general economic prosperity and renewal and individual incentives is well defined in the following observation:

> It must be worthwhile for the individual [*subject*] to do what benefits the entire society [*receiver*: society; *object*]. This requires both general lowering of taxes [*technique*] and above all, a conscious combat of inflation [*technique; object*] [*destinator*: economic theory]. (Government Bill 1991/92: 38, p. 40)

Individual activities emanate from personal material and economic interests, which also elucidates the emphasis placed on the material dimension of the "climate of entrepreneurship." The liberal-conservative government defines the climate of enterprises and entrepreneurship in terms of *institutions* (rules, information, functioning markets, property rights, taxation), *material factors* (infrastructure, transportation, risk-capital supply, costs on employment and production), and *forms of cooperation* between societal actors (networks with R&D, information on funding opportunities) (e.g., Department Report 1994: 35; Government Bill 1991/92: 38; 1992/93: 56). Similarly, culture, soft non-material factors such as human capital, and cognitive mindsets are reflected, but they seem to be subordinated to institutional and material factors.

Considering the observed inter-dependence among entrepreneurial activities, the general societal climate, and the extent of economic growth, the government argues the necessity of a coherent, cohesive, and mobilizing political strategy (e.g., Government Bill 1991/92: 38 and 51; 1993/94: 40;; Government Communication 1994/95: 22; NUTEK 1991). Summarizing its competition policy, the liberal-conservative government is claimed to have had a "comprehensive" focus on economy as its primary objective (Government Communication 1994/95: 22). A central aspect is the political objective of "efficient resource use" (Parliamentary Minutes 1991/92: 6). Efficiency neither expresses that all resources are used nor that the management of resources is efficient. Rather, two other aspects appear more central. First, efficient resource use implicates that economic actors make the most of a given politically supported socio-economic situation. Second, efficiency refers to the optimization of potential, capacity, and applicability of resources in the sense that the same amount of resources leads to either a higher valued added or quantitatively higher number of products. In this regard, efficiency is intimately connected to productivity. Entrepreneur is the subject who realizes the given context-specific chances (e.g., Government

Table 6.7 Discursive Construction of the Entrepreneur 1991–1994

	Discourse Formation A: Liberal-Conservative Discourse 1991–1994							
				Functioning Market Economy (Es)				
	(—) Sufficient Competition (Np)			/=	Beneficial Climate of Enterprises and Entrepreneurship (Np) (—)			
				/=				
A (px.) (—)	Lowering of Taxation Pressure (*technique*)/ Government (*subject*)	/= International Inst. Adjustment (*technique*)	/= Transparency of Rules/ Calculable Rules (*technique*)/ Government (*subject*)/Enterprises (*receiver*)	/= Taxation Reform/ De-regulation of Rinance Market (*technique*)/ Entrepreneurs, SEs, & SMEs (*receiver*)	/= New Competition Law (*technique*)/ Swedish Competition Authority (*subject*)/ Entrepreneur (*receiver*)	/= Calculable Yields on Risks (*adjuvant*)/ Enterprise (*receiver*)	/= Undistorted Competition (*adjuvant*)/ Transparent and Stable rules (*adjuvant*)	/= Competition (*technique*)/ Political Government (*adjuvant*)/ Entrepreneurship (*subject*) = (—)
	/=	/=	/=	/=	/=	/=	/=	/=
A (eth.) (—)	Free Competition/ Free Trade/ Free Price Setting (*object*)	/= Diffusion of Economic Power (*object*)	/= Efficiency & Productivity of Resource Use (*object*)	/= Access to Risk-Capital (*object*)	/= Competition Supporting Politics (*object*)	/= Rational and Efficient Resource Allocation (*object*)	/= Vigorous Enterprises (*object*)	/= Competitiveness (*object*) (—)
	/=	/=	/=	/=	/=	/=	/=	/=
B (eth.) (—)	Distorting Market Regulations/ Market Distortion (*inadmissible consequence*)	/= Concentration of Power/ Market Domination (*inadmissible consequence*)	/= Inefficient Resource Use & Allocation (*inadmissible consequence*)	/= Insufficient Risk Capital Supply/ Insufficient New Entrepreneurship (*inadmissible consequence*)	/= Competition Distorting Political Regulation (*inadmissible consequence*)	/= Irrational and Inefficient Resource Allocation (*inadmissible consequence*)	/= Feeble Enterprises (*inadmissible consequence*)	/= Internat. Incompetitiveness (*inadmissible consequence*) (—)
	/=	/=	/=	/=	/=	/=	/=	/=
B (px.) (—)	Taxation/Political Wage Bargaining/ Public Budget Deficit (*traitor*)	/= Market Regulations/ Selective Subventions (*traitor*)	/= Complicated and Intransparent Rules (*traitor*)	/= Taxation of Capital and savings (*traitor*)	/= Restricted Freedom of Consumption and Production (*traitor*)	/= Waste of Resources/ Inefficient Resource Utilization (*traitor*)	/= Intransparent Rules/ Social Costs/ Taxation Pressure (*traitor*)	/= Hindrances to Realisation of Entrepreneurship (*traitor*) (—)
				/=				
	(—) Insufficient Competition (Np)			/=	Poor Climate of Entrepreneurs and Entrepreneurship (Np) (—)			
				Dysfunctional Market Economy (Es)				
				Discourse Formation B: The Antagonistic Other				

Abbreviations/ Symbols:

Difference	|	A (px.):	Level of Practices in Discourse Formation A (techniques; subjectivities; adjuvants; receivers)
Equivalence	=	A (eth.):	Ethical substance of Objects of Desires in Discourse Formation A
Antagonism	.....	B (px.):	Level of Practices in Discourse Formation B (inadmissible techniques; traitors)
Empty Signifier	(Es)	B (eth.):	Ethical substance: Inadmissible Consequences of the Discourse Formation B

Bill 1993/94: 40). Rational conduct of political government intending to achieve economic growth therefore exerts politics that provides chances for entrepreneurs. The more beneficial the climate, the more entrepreneurs may achieve in a given context. For instance, Government Bill 1992/93: 56 (cf. Government Bill 1993/94: 40) argues that the actual extent of entrepreneurship depends on individual incentives to entrepreneurial activities such as the start-up of new enterprises, which again is the result of the "climate of enterprises and entrepreneurship." A beneficial climate enables economic actors to calculate, envisage, and base present economic decisions, such as investment and production, on the expectations of future conditions. "Stability" and "permanence" of the economic structure provide business starters and entrepreneurs with "clear" conditions (Government Communication 1994/95: 22; Parliamentary Minutes 1991: 6; SOU 1993: 16).

In liberal-conservative discourse, the function of entrepreneur is comparable to functionally differentiated business starters and subjects located within the economic sector, who either build up enterprises or make path-breaking decisions on investment and innovations in existing enterprises, who realize and commercialize new ideas and utilize structural chances optimally. It is the entrepreneur who maintains the intensity and societal extent of competition and in this way exercises pressure on costs and price levels and increases productivity in resource allocation. The entrepreneur also provides alternatives to public sector services and realizes the customers' "freedom of choice" and, as such, capacitates the government to fulfill the intended "freedom of choice revolution" and the improvement of the quality of public services (e.g., Conservative Party and Liberal Party 1991; Government Bills 1991/92: 38; 1992/93: 82; Parliamentary Minutes 1991/92: 6) and thus enables the state to withdraw from activities that distort the market. These different discursive interfaces between entrepreneurs and political government are presented in Table 6.7.

TOWARD AN EXTENDED CULTURE OF ENTERPRISE

The liberal-conservative government was not involved in the "making up" of entrepreneurs. Individuals are observed to either have or not have the natural capacity to act as entrepreneurs, and therefore "A failing entrepreneurial capacity cannot be replaced through external measures" (SOU 1993: 70, p. 23). Equally so, the qualification to the Enterprise Allowance Scheme was linked with a presence of "genuine" interests for business start-ups (SOU 1993: 70, p. 79f). However, toward the end of the liberal-conservative discourse, there appeared an unprecedented problematization of the number of subjects who were actively supported in their aspirations to become entrepreneurs. The preceding demands for a more positive climate of entrepreneurship had focused on collective attitudes toward private enterprises, business managers, and entrepreneurs. Lacking entrepreneurial culture was not considered the reason for the lack of entrepreneurs as compared with other European countries. After all, incentives and interests to the pursuit of entrepreneurial activities were presumed to depend on material and institutional circumstances: entrepreneurial aspirations were regarded as either naturally present or absent and beyond the scope of external control. The government was not involved in the "making up" of entrepreneurs but provided support for existent interests to start-ups.

This narrow view on the "natural" origins of entrepreneurs was partially changed and revised in Department Report 1994: 35 and Government Bills 1993/94: 40 and 1993/94: 140. Government Bill 1993/94: 140 observed existing strategies for regional development as insufficient, as they did not recognize the dissimilar economic and entrepreneurial needs and interests of men and women. A problematization of the underrepresentation of women among entrepreneurs also considers women as a social group possible to mobilize:

> Women [*receiver*] make an unutilized resource [*inadmissible consequence*] concerning entrepreneurship [*adjuvant*], and increased entrepreneurship [*adjuvant*] among women can be expected to contribute to creativity [*object*] within entrepreneurial activities [*subject*]. (Government Bill 1993/94: 140, chapter 8)

The underrepresentation of women among entrepreneurs was problematized by the report *The Other Side of the Coin* from the Swedish National Rural Development Agency in 1993. This report observed that only 17% of total business start-ups in 1992 were initiated by women. Primarily the Center Party (see Motion 1990/91: N355; 1991/92: A805; see also motion of Social Democrats 1991/92: A435) thematized women's absence in entrepreneurship. In December 1991, the liberal-conservative government mandated NUTEK to elaborate measures of how women's entrepreneurship could be supported in regions with structural problems. Yet, it was only in Government Bill 1993/94: 140 that entrepreneurship was discussed as a form of activity and subjectivity that could be expanded to further groups and through which the potential of individuals could be utilized to achieve political objectives. Also, earlier texts observed the relative underrepresentation of women among business starters (e.g., Government Bill 1991/92: 51, p. 10; NUTEK 1991).

The new aspect on the nature entrepreneurs as introduced in Government Bill 1993/94: 140 concerns the "origin" of entrepreneurial incentives. Incentives were now differentiated and regarded as independent of the material and institutional context since men and women were supposed to have different interests despite their location within the same social context. Therefore, it was argued that, "Such efforts [of regional development] must especially notice that women and men have partly different needs, and in the following work special measures for women must be continuously taken into consideration" (Government Bill 1993/94: 140). This suggests that during the later period of the liberal-conservative government, entrepreneurial subjects were not taken for granted, but there appeared assumptions of a further potential for entrepreneurship beyond the statistically measurable number of individuals who start businesses. The focus on utilization of subjective resources and cognitive skills is more central for the subsequent discourse of the social-democratic government.

Department Report 1994: 35 elucidates some reasons for an accentuated focus on the mobilization of subjective resources. The individual "capacity to act" is an essential constituent of the collective capacity to realize the national goals of "welfare," international economic competitiveness, and economic renewal. Defining individual "learning" as the constituent of the general competence level, the driving forces in economic growth are "joy" or "inspiration" experienced in personal development. Efforts to competence development made in education systems are in vain insofar as "the incentives and driving forces for human growth and development are insufficient" (Department Report 1994: 35, p. 52). Incentives for personal development are not given by the institutional and material contextual factors; mobilization of the assumed individual interests and incentives to personal development is necessary. As Department Report 1994: 35 argues, entrepreneurs are those individuals who utilize and transform their possessed and acquired competences and knowledge into practical and economic activities, such as product and service development and innovations.

Entrepreneurship is now conceived of as one of the possibilities in which the individual's will to develop could be realized. Correspondingly, the capacity to economic competitiveness and growth, which Sweden was argued to have lost in comparison with other countries, could be utilized and mobilized by improving conditions for business start-ups and business life in general. Incentives to do more have been affected by combination of taxes and equalization of wages (Department Report 1994: 35, p. 24). Government Bills 1993/94:40 and 1993/94:140 as well as Department Report 1994: 35 accentuate the individual mindset beneath incentives and interests. An assumed analogy between the extent of individual commitment and the general level of welfare generating economic growth requires correspondingly individuality, recognizing and promoting institutions and forms of government. A government benefiting such individual development is opposed to a way of governing that "commands life." Among other things, such institutions aid the development of individual competence and "learning" supporting education system, more flexible forms of working organization. Also, a culture of "learning" and "knowledge development" is defined as a contextual factor that would enable the mobilization of individuals on behalf of collective objectives. This once more opposes forms of collectivizing to forms of political government restricting individual incentives.

The liberal-conservative government aspired toward an extension of the group of individuals active as entrepreneurs, and above all women

were observed as a thus far unrecognized group of potential future entrepreneurs. For this reason, the government assigned NUTEK to organize
and carry out a three-year program to support female entrepreneurship
in areas of particular importance of regional policy (NUTEK 1995; see
also Government Bill 1993/94: 140). Worth mentioning is also the program "Consultants for Female Entrepreneurs" implemented in a total of
sixty-two municipalities in 1992, whose objective was to increase the number of women as entrepreneurs by improving consultancy and information (Memorandum 1992/93: BoU17; cf. Government Bill 2001/02: 4, p.
161). The absence of women as entrepreneurs was also problematized by
the Social-Democratic Party during the liberal-conservative government
(Motion 1993/94: A56), and there was cross-party consensus on the need
to increase the number of female entrepreneurs. In this regard, the later
position of the social-democratic government was a continuation of its earlier position, which observed that "International statistics [*destinator*] displays that it is the number of female entrepreneurs [*subject*] that increases
most among the new small and medium-sized enterprises [*subject*]. For this
reason, industrial policy [*adjuvant; strategy*] must prioritize efforts that
increase women's entrepreneurship [*object*]" (Motion 1993/94: A56). All in
all, there was a line of continuity between the later culturalist conception
of entrepreneurship as adopted by the liberal-conservative government and
the explicit efforts of the later social-democratic government to actively
make subjects into entrepreneurs.

7 Social-Democratic Politics for Full-Employment 1994–1997

After the elections to Swedish parliament in September 1994, the parliamentary majority of liberal and conservative parties ended with a victory of the Social-Democratic Party, the Socialist Party (*Vänsterpartiet*), and the Green Party (*Miljöpartiet*). In October 1994, Ingvar Carlsson, the leader of the Social-Democratic Party, was elected prime minister of a social-democratic minority government. Contrasts between the social-democratic government and the liberal-conservative government became obvious already in the Motion 1993/94: Fi208, in which the Social-Democratic Party attacked the then liberal-conservative government for its insufficient management of the economic and unemployment crises. The Social-Democratic Party positioned itself as the contender of a new politics for Sweden's re-unification. The liberal-conservative government was observed as the cause of a general societal crisis symbolized by Sweden's emerging binary division between the unemployed and socially disadvantaged groups, on the one hand, and growing export enterprises and the group of the employed, on the other hand.

At first sight, social-democratic political discourse appears to distance itself from the discourse of the liberal-conservative government. The "resurrection of Sweden as nation of growth and entrepreneurship with a strong and growing economy" intended by the liberal-conservative government (Parliamentary Minutes 1991/92: 6) is observed by social democrats to have resulted in a negative development of growth, a non-optimal realization of the economic potential,[1] a high budget deficit, an unprecedented extent of public expenditure, a high extent of unutilized labor force, and mass unemployment (Motion 1993/94: Fi208). Yet, the social-democratic government does not criticize the liberal-conservative discourse in what concerns the logics of functioning of the economy, the interdependence between welfare and economic growth, and economic growth as the pre-condition for realizing all other political objectives. Sustainable and persistent growth also figures in social-democratic discourse as a pre-condition for the capacity to meet political objectives of employment and welfare (e.g., Government

Bill 1995/96: 25; 2001/02: 4; Government Communication 1996/97: 41; Social Democratic Party 1994). What the Social-Democratic Party criticized instead was the free market dogmatism, political passivity, and exaggerated beliefs in the inherent and independent capacity of the market to achieve economic growth (Motion 1993/94: Fi208; Social Democratic Party 1994). The social-democratic government makes the state an "adjuvant" of economy. Figuring as the destinator of these convictions is the Clinton administration in the United States and its "offensive" and "coordinating" industrial policy in contrast to political passivity as it is demanded in the liberal-conservative discourse. Furthermore, the active role of the state in the governance of markets assigned by the U.S. economist Paul Krugman and the "new growth theory" referred to epistemologies that supported the social-democratic imaginary of an active government of the economy (Government Bill 2001/02: 4; Motion 1993/94: Fi208; Social Democratic Party 1994; SOU 1996: 34).

In contrast to the liberal-conservative discourse, which operated similar to a popular hegemonic strategy by instituting various antagonistic relations, the subsequent social-democratic discourse has the character of an institutional discourse.[2] A characteristic feature of the institutional discourse is the pre-dominance of syntagmatic relations over metaphoric ones manifested by weak antagonistic relations. It also implicates that empty signifiers have the status of "floating signifiers." As with Disraeli's conception of the fullness of society in terms of "one nation," so too the discourse of the social-democratic government operates through the production of imaginaries of the society without an antagonistic other that would obstruct the realization of the imagined fullness of social order. By contrast, like an institutional articulatory strategy, social-democratic discourse appeals to the entire population; it emphasizes the necessity of a national mobilization of all accessible human resources for the sake of optimal level of employment and economic progress. Illustrative of this strategy is the intention to realize a new "active" social contract among government, economy, and society.[3]

The spatial imaginary is set by the expected paradigmatic transition from the industrial society to the knowledge society and the knowledge-based economy (KBE).[4] Two of the central policy programs—the program for "Development of Small Enterprises, Renewal and Growth"[5] announced in Government Bill 1995/96: 207 and the national program for Knowledge Boost launched in 1997 as an implementation of the "Education Revolution" announced in Government Bill 1995/96: 207—endeavored to adapt the Swedish society as a whole to the era of KBE. Similarly, the repetitive emphasis on a mobilization of all resources for employment and growth also symbolizes the "absorption of all social divisions into an ever expanding system supported by the illusion of a society encompassing all differences and demands," which is typical of institutional articulatory strategies (Stavrakakis 1999: 77). As Government Bill 1994/95: 161 argues, "A small country like Sweden cannot afford to omit the growth potential in any part of the country." Equal and pervasive mobilization stands in a relation of equivalence to equal standards of welfare (e.g., Government Bill 1994/95: 100 and 150).

In contrast to the liberal-conservative popular discourse, social-democratic institutional discourse does not clearly articulate a singular empty signifier. Rather, during the first few years after 1994, social-democratic discourse is centered around two overarching symbols of "employment" and "growth" that constitute the axiomatic axis of social-democratic discourse (e.g., Government Bill 1995/96: 222, chapter 5). The primary objective of the government was to halve unemployment by the year 2000, which was also the title of Government Bills 1995/96: 207 and 1995/96: 222 on general policy measures (e.g., Government Communication 1996/97: 41; Parliamentary Minutes 1995/96: 74). The intention to cut unemployment in half is an expression of a wider intention to unify and consolidate Sweden (e.g., Government Bill 1995/96: 222; 1996/97: 150D2).[6] In a speech before the parliament, Premier Göran Persson argued that the combating of unemployment was the government's primary objective:

> Present unemployment [*Time:* present; *inadmissible consequence*] undermines the foundation of a good society [empty signifier; object]. Social economy [*adjuvant*], the moral [*adjuvant*] and the will [*adjuvant*] are weakened [*inadmissible consequence*]. First and foremost, the campaign for employment is a matter of *keeping Sweden unified* [*empty signifier; Time:* future]. (italics added)

As the quotation illustrates, empty signifier is ambiguous as symbolized by both "good society" and "unified society." Yet, unification consists of an axiological and a praxeological side. In axiological regard, unification is a general imaginary of fullness of social integration consisting of equally shared standards of living and regional and spatial unification as concerns the pace of development; local standards of living; and, above all, social inclusion of individuals through their labor market participation. In praxeological terms, the norm of unification sets the objectives for a range of social agents and spheres of activities. The rationality concerning the unification of all forces on behalf of employment and growth is located in an imaginary of economic growth to be beyond the reach of direct political government and to result from the totality of social activities, investments, aspirations, and incentives. The "maximal mobilization of resources" appears as the only way of attaining the desired set of objectives. Whereas the liberal-conservative government prioritized low inflation to all other objectives, at the initial stage of the social-democratic government, fighting unemployment is declared the primary objective:

> The combat of inflation [*object*= stable prices; *traitor*= inflation] shall no longer be superordinate to other ambitions and aspirations. Instead, there is a new norm for economic policy [*strategy*]: that unemployment

[*traitor; inadmissible consequence*] will at least be halved [*object; consequence*] before the end of the 1990s [*time:* future]. (Social Democratic Party 1994)

The government's program for halving unemployment (see Government Bill 1995/96: 25, 207, and 222; 1996/97: 150D6; Parliamentary Minutes 1995/96: 74) contains four precepts in all. Firstl stabilization of public finances with balanced public finances by 1998 is the goal. Second, good and beneficial conditions for enterprises and entrepreneurship are desired (cf. Government Bill 1995/96: 207 and 222). Similar to the liberal-conservative discourse, the social-democratic government also stressed the intention to make Sweden a "good country for entrepreneurship":

Sweden is a good country for entrepreneurship [*object; adjuvant* = climate of entrepreneurship; *subject* = entrepreneur]. We have a flexible economy [*adjuvant*], a constructive climate of cooperation [*adjuvant*] and competent and well-educated labor force [*adjuvant*]. The government [*subject*] will further improve the conditions of entrepreneurship [*object*]. (. . .) The number of small and medium-sized enterprises has increased substantially [*consequence; object* = increase of number of enterprises]. It is a healthy development [*time:* consistent] that will be strengthened further through competence development [*technique*], support of innovations [*technique*], provision of capital [*technique*] and enterprise support [*technique*]. The government's [*subject*] cohesive policy [*strategy*] will improve the conditions [*technique*] for business starts [*receiver; consequence*], development [*object; consequence*] and expansion [*object; consequence*].

Third, similar to the liberal-conservative discourse, and despite its institutional strategy of articulation, the social-democratic discourse posits its own pre-suppositions by defining the limits for possible political conduct through a relation of antagonism. The only possibility to achieve competitiveness is located in competence development effectuated through a culture of "life-long learning" and expansion of the education system. There are two possible methods of achieving economic growth: the low wage strategy and cost competitiveness, and the competence and productivity-based strategy (Government Bill 1994/95: 100 and 150; Parliamentary Minutes 1995/96: 74; Social Democratic Party 1994). Only the second strategy is observed as compatible with the objective of welfare. Fourth, there is a new social contract on "collaboration" aimed at the attainment of full employment (cf. Department Report 1999: 32; Government Bill 1995/96: 207; 2001/02: 04).

Social consensus [*adjuvant*] has been on the foundation for the stability [*object*] and the faith [*object; adjuvant:* of people] in the future that so long characterized the Swedish society [*space:* society]. Collaboration [*strategy; adjuvant*] is the key in the struggle for full employment [*object; consequence*]. (Parliamentary Minutes 1995/96: 74)

Collaboration is connected to a particular imaginary of conditions of economic growth. Above all, the central role is played by human capital aligned initially to the "new growth theory," which is supplemented later by the theory of regional economic clusters. Again, like the liberal-conservative government, the social-democratic government also connects the rational mode of government with the implementation of institutional, cultural, and legal frameworks that sustain activities emerging from below through individual and entrepreneurial incentives, which, when aggregated, lead to processes benefiting employment and economic growth. In a similar manner, the rational mode of government is observed as being aligned to the "increasing demands on 'comprehensive solutions' " (Government Bill 1995/96: 222, chapter 5). This initial description of the social-democratic discourse of government provides an inaugurating network of semantic codes that are further elaborated on in the subsequent sections. It is obvious that the social-democratic government accentuates far more than the preceding liberal-conservative government the willingness and preparedness of individual subjects to participate in, engage in, and make their contribution to general societal development. As Department Report 1999: 32 argues, everybody "must take his or her responsibility for development." The focal point of the subsequent analysis is to identify how the subject position of entrepreneur is constructed in relation to the general political objective of national mobilization.

SOUND PUBLIC FINANCES

Objective and external limits for the capacity and extent of political government are set by the norm of "sound public finances." This norm was effectuated in 1997 through an absolute and inevitable limit to public expenditure that was externalized as if located beyond the possibility of political negotiation. The decision on the norm of an absolute limit to public expenditure was made with the support of the Green Party and the Center Party (Government Bill 1995/96: 25). The norm of expenditure set absolute external limits to the imagined possible conduct of government (e.g., Department Report 1999: 32; Government Bills 1995/96: 25 and 207, 1996/97: 150D2; 1997/98: 62). One crucial aspect is the international norm of budget balance as comparisons are consistently made with the level of budget deficit in other countries. The solid budget process is seen as a comparative and systemic economic advantage over other countries (Government Bill 1995/96: 207). Sound public finance is regarded as a constituent of the international "systemic competitiveness" of the Swedish economy (cf. Messner 1996, 1997).

Budget norm is definable in absolute terms as the maximum level of allowable budget deficit and as the share of public sector expenditure of the Gross National Product (GNP) (e.g., Government Bill 1996/97: 150D2). Yet, the symbolic construction proceeds though a set of antagonistic relations. Sound public finances is contrasted to the "budget mire" of the liberal-conservative government symbolized by a historically unprecedented budget deficit (Government Bill 1995/96: 207), which took Sweden to the brink of economic bankruptcy (Government Bill 1996/97: 150D2). Yet, the actual imagined value of the norm of expenditure develops through a set of further antagonistic relations defined in Table 7.1.

The overarching antagonistic relation appears between the international "economic trustworthiness" of the Swedish economy, high interest rates, and inflation (Government Bill 1995/96: 25). The foremost objective to be reached by restricting public expenditure is "transparency," that is, the capacity to anticipate the price and cost development (Memorandum 1994/95: FiU20). In the parliamentary debate on the regulative norms for public expenditure, the social-democratic government accentuated that the implementation of the norm of long-term budget regulations increases the faith in economic policy and facilitates growth, which again is crucial for improving public finances (Parliamentary Minutes 1994/95: 106). Whereas the Socialist Party claims the budget norm to induce tolerance toward a high level of unemployment and to limit the regulatory capacity of the government, the social-democratic government praised the budget as the precondition for active employment politics (Parliamentary Minutes 1994/95: 106, remarks 72–77). The introduction of the nominal budget limit is also an expression of the prioritized objective of stable price development and low inflation, as already introduced under the liberal-conservative government (cf. Lindvall 2005). Faith in economic policy is construed as an essential constituent of economic growth, and, as such, politics for low inflation is presented as being essential for politics for economic growth (Parliamentary Minutes 1994/95: 120, remark 62).

Sound public finances are in three important and inter-related ways connected to the capacity to achieve the objectives of employment and growth. First, political discourse of the social-democratic government expresses the uncertainty concerning the future economic development due to the entanglement of the international economy. Sound public finances provide the capacity to face and overcome future economic down-turns (cf. Government Bill 1995/96: 25 and 207). Second, like liberal-conservative discourse, the social-democratic discourse observed that enterprises and subjects pursuing enterprising activities demand stable and assessable institutional and fiscal conditions. Third, commitment of financial policy to a norm on expenditure lowers interest rates "which is the perfect way of stimulating investments" (Social Democratic Party 1994). The faith of enterprises in economic policy is observed as a prerequisite for the realization of economic growth (Government Bill 1995/96: 207). In this assumption, the

Table 7.1 Antagonism Sound Public Finances/Budget Deficit

Discourse Formation A: Social Democratic Government 1994–1998

Sound Public Finances (Np) /= Utgiftstak /= Budget Discipline

/=

A (eth.) (——) Economic Trustworthiness/low interest rates *(object)* /= Stabilization of Debt *(object)* /= Economic Recovery *(object)* /= Price Stability*(object)*/Low Inflation *(object)* (——)

B (eth.) (——) High Interest Rates *(inadmissible consequence)* /= Lost Economic Competitiveness *(inadmissible consequence)* /= Unemployment *(inadmissible consequence)* /= Inflation *(inadmissible consequence)* (——)

/=

Budget Deficit (Np) /= Budget Mire

Discourse Formation B: The Antagonistic Other

Abbreviations/ Symbols:

Difference	|	A (px.): Level of Practices in Discourse Formation A (techniques; subjectivities; adjuvants; receivers)
Equivalence	=	A (eth.): Ethical substance of Objects of Desires in Discourse Formation A
Antagonism	.....	B (px.): Level of Practices in Discourse Formation B (inadmissible techniques; traitors)
Empty Signifier	(Es)	B (eth.): Ethical substance: Inadmissible Consequences of the Discourse Formation B
Nodal Point	(Np)	(. . .): Continued Relations of Difference/Equivalence

social-democratic government was supported by the Conservative Party, which equally observed remedying the budget deficit as the most important condition for a good climate of enterprises and entrepreneurship and which further generates a positive accumulative process of economic growth and employment (cf. Conservative Party 1994). In all three regards, sound public finances is conceivable as a constituent of an internationally competitive economic system and supports economic processes emanating to general economic development.

CLIMATE OF ENTREPRENEURSHIP

Similar to the liberal-conservative discourse, the social-democratic government declared the "climate of enterprises" as an inevitable objective of the rational conduct of government. Aligned to this objective and with the Clinton administration as a role-model, the "active industrial policy"— as opposed to the "passive industrial policy" of the liberal-conservative government—was designed to improve the situation of, above all, smaller enterprises offensively. Akin to liberal-conservative discourse, the quality of the climate is defined in institutional and material terms of level of taxation, social costs, and costs of production. Moreover, low inflation, sustained among other things by the norm of budget regulation, institutional context assessable by economic actors as concerns the development of public expenditure, but also the institutional and legal "rules of the game" and "transparency" of rules are observed as indispensable for the quality of the climate of entrepreneurship (e.g., Government Bill 1996/97: 150D). Particular importance is attached to re-designing a taxation system better aligned to needs of the SMEs (Government Bills 1995/96: 222, chapter 4; 1996/97: 45).[7] The costs on labor and rigid labor law were also observed as potential hindrances for furthering occupations and growth in SMEs (Government Bill 1995/96: 207 and 222).

The imaginary attached to such a climate is the imaginary of an accumulative process in which the establishment of new enterprises and growth of existing enterprises result in general economic growth and employment. The opposition between a good/sufficient and an inappropriate/insufficient climate is constructed in accordance with an institutional articulatory pattern emphasizing the heterogeneity of mutually interdependent and reciprocal factors, outcomes, strategies, and activities. One of the few clearly articulated antagonistic limitations of the definition of a "sufficient climate" for enterprises is constructed through an opposition to "inflexible and outmoded structures" (Government Bill 1995/96: 207 and 222). Outmoded can be related, partly, to the expected transformation of the economy toward the KBE and, partly, to the unprecedented role of SEs as engines of the economy. The KBE figures as a general imaginary on the future in which, considering the attainment of economic growth, the external limits of government capacity (e.g., sound public finance and low inflation), is equal to the capacity to achieve welfare and employment. On the way toward a KBE, we meet ever increasing demands for "knowledge," "competence," and "life-long learning" (cf. Government Bill 1996/97: 150D2).

Within this imaginary of the economy and society, SEs and newly established enterprises figure as "subjects" who realize the shift to a knowledge- and competence-intensive production system by demanding a well-educated, competent, and skilled labor force. As such, entrepreneurs are the "subjects" who realize the "adaption" and realization of the knowledge society by demanding and employing a qualified labor force (Government Bill 1995/96: 207). The observed necessity in transition to a more knowledge-intensive production was articulated as the "only way" to combine international competitiveness and welfare. In an international context, there are two strategies to achieving growth: a low-wage strategy and a strategy based on productivity and KBE[8] (Government Bill 1994/95: 100 and 150; Parliamentary Minutes 1995/96: 74; Social Democratic Party 1994). Economic growth through knowledge-intensive production is observed as the "means in our endeavor to develop welfare" (Social Democratic Party 1994: 10). The imaginary of the welfare society and the conceptual limits of welfare set the restrictions for the rational mode of government.

Illustrative of the construction of SEs as "receivers" of the assignment to realize KBE is the program for "Development of Small Enterprises, Renewal and Growth" (Government Bill 1995/96: 207) launched in 1996 and the Campaign "Ljusåret" ("light Year") in 1997. Both public initiatives observed SEs, entrepreneurial culture, and attitudes as vanguards of economic growth. The destinator of both initiatives is the "new growth theory" that attaches attention to knowledge and innovation as being essential yet immaterial factors of production and facilitators of growth (see Government Bill 1995/96: 222, chapter 5). Besides the new epistemological conception of economy in the KBE, another reason for the valuation of SEs appears in reflections of decreasing a future expansion of employment in larger industries, which traditionally dominated the Swedish economy (e.g., Government Bill 1996/97: 45). In light of the new growth theory and decreasing trust in larger industries as sources of future employment, the government emphasized the necessity of an economic and a social climate that induces better chances for expected future "knowledge and innovation oriented" enterprises (Government Bill 1996/97: 45). Economic growth emerges from new enterprises and SEs supported by individual initiatives and creativity. For instance, Ljusåret—a public campaign to stimulate long-term economic and societal renewal—emphasized the role of societal attitudes:

> The objective is to stimulate and support processes [*object*] that are of importance for the economy's [*receiver*] long-term capacity of renewal [*object*] and pace of development [*object*] by means of influence on attitudes [*technique; receiver* = population] and clarification [*technique*] of

the connection between innovations, growth and welfare [*destinator*]. Also, to activate [*technique*] individuals [*receiver*], enterprises [*receiver*] and organizations [*receiver*] to take initiatives to improvement [*adjuvant*: of economic renewal; object]. (Memorandum 1996/97: NU1)

This quotation illustrates how the social-democratic government, in contrast to the earlier liberal-conservative discourse, interprets the culture and general societal attitudes as crucial economic factors. Attitudes have a formative impact on the renewal of business-life and general "conditions of entrepreneurship and innovations" (Government Bill 1996/97: 45). Entrepreneur is located within the business life and entrepreneurship is enacted in and by enterprises. Yet, in contrast to the liberal-conservative discourse, a culture supporting entrepreneurship is defined as a society-wide attitudinal structure. Government Bill 1995/96: 25 on politics for "Work, Security and Development" observed economic progress as efforts made across the society and—"that people actively and permanently commit themselves to work and society; that employees as well as the individuals invest in education and—through competition on domestic and international markets—create and sustain a pressure of transformation in the economy" (Government Bill 1995/96: 25). In other words, the climate of entrepreneurship is conceived of in wider and more cultural terms than before: very social subjects' attitudes, mentality, and initiatives constitute the aggregate national capacity to realize the imagined fullness of society. Even though SEs are observed to perform pivotal roles in channeling material, institutional, and cultural resources to concrete economic production and occupations (e.g., Government Bill 1994/95: 218), the realization of entrepreneurship facilitating personal growth, commitment, initiatives, and attitudes must be utilized across the entire society (Government Bill 1995/96: 25, chapter 5).

CULTURE OF COMPETENCE AND LEARNING

The first policy papers of the social-democratic government expressed the expectation of an imminent transition to a knowledge society and a corresponding KBE (e.g., Government Bill 1995/96: 25, 207, and 222; cf. Social Democratic Party 1994). The imaginary of the knowledge society is constructed in the manner of a self-fulfilling prophecy through which the knowledge society is presented as pre-supposed and external, and from above direction of transformation determined by the "rapid technological development" (Government Bill 1994/95: 100 and 150). First, the expectation of the transformation toward the knowledge society imposes demands to adapt economic system, work, education, and socio-political institutions to demands set by the knowledge society. Second, the initiated adjustment to the knowledge society fulfills the prophecy of its becoming and motivates the already enacted measures of adjustment (e.g., Government

Bill 1995/96: 207). It was noted previously that enterprises, through their increasing demands for qualified labor force, were to realize the upgrading of the economy from industrial production to a service- and communication-based economy. The Social-Democratic Party adopted relatively early the conviction that "It is knowledge and ideas that provide growth" (Social Democratic Party 1994: 20). Yet, the long-term economic competitiveness is not located in the actual and measurable knowledge and competence, but in its consistent upgrading (Government Bill 1997/98: 62, chapter 4). The unprecedented imaginary of the knowledge society also opened new demands to adapt the political government of employment and growth to new pre-conditions of growth rooted in knowledge and competences. The liberal-conservative government relied on material and institutional conditions of market and endemic incentives and cognitive constitution of individuals to lead to a fulfillment of entrepreneurial intentions and an increase of the general societal level of entrepreneurship. In contrast, the social-democratic government's attention to growth through knowledge and competence could not focus on single institutions (e.g., taxation system) or discernible hindrances to investment (e.g., production costs, interest rates, inflation) and measurable conditions.

The imaginary of the knowledge society is not an open and a variable conception but departs in several documents from the perspective of the "cluster theory," which functions beside the "new growth theory" (e.g., Government Bill 1995/96: 222) as the economic epistemology and "destinator" in social-democratic discourse (e.g., Department Report 1999: 32; Government Bill 2001/02: 4 and 100). Government Bill 1997/98: 62 (chapter 4) defines the central assumption of the "cluster theory": "enterprises [sustain] their competitiveness by being innovative and consistently upgrading their knowledge base." Akin to the "cluster theory," the "new growth theory" emphasizes soft and cultural factors and conditions and, above all, innovations and knowledge as essential constituents of the economic growth facilitating social contexts (e.g., Government Bill 1995/96: 222). In documents from 1994 to 1998 already, knowledge and competence do not appear recognizable as nominal and clearly determinable factors or resources. Rather, knowledge and competence function as nodal points as they constitute a layer of knowledge that is imposed on and recognized within several existing institutions. In this regard, the imaginary of the knowledge society caused an overdetermination of a range of prevailing social practices and institutions. Illustrative of this is Government Bill 1995/96: 207: "Educational revolution for Sweden towards the 21st century" [Utbildningsrevolution för Sverige inför 2000-talet] (Government Bill 1995/96: 207), which was to be realized, among other things, through a nationwide program for "Knowledge Boost" [Kunskapslyft] that would enable all adults to achieve the secondary-school competence level. A typical feature of the pervasiveness of the imaginary of the knowledge society was also the re-naming of the "work-principle" dominating the labor market policy with "work and competence orientation" (Government Bill 1995/96: 207). Also in 1997, implemented individual action plans to activate the unemployed were motivated due to their assumed capacity to improve the competence development of the unemployed (cf. Government Bill 1994/95: 218, p. A2).

The primary limit to the social-democratic discourse on government appears through the antagonistic relation between the two opposed strategies for economic growth combined with increasing employment: the "low-wage strategy" and "productivity and knowledge-based strategy of which only the latter was conceived as being consistent with the endeavored "welfare society." Another source of restriction was set by the above described externalized limit to public expenditure, which rejected the possibility to increase employment through public sector expansion (e.g., Government Bill 1994/95: 218). A further destinator for limits to the rational conduct of government was the parliamentary committee called "Edin-group," composed of economists from both labor unions and employer organizations. In its report *Out of Time with Employment* [I otakt med Sysselsättning] (1997), economists observed that international economic competitiveness could be maintained only through the adjustment of a domestic wage increase to comparable levels in other OECD countries (cf. Government Bill 1996/97: 150D6). In Government Bill 1995/96: 25, the social-democratic government expressed its sincere intention to support the wage norm. Wage development was connected to concerns on domestic price development in accordance with the European level.

In contrast to material resources and physical factors of production, the new growth theory attached to the imaginary of the future KBE accentuated the role of cognitive subjective competencies as factors increasing economic performance. Yet, competencies are complex and difficult to transform, allocate, and canalize to economic activities. Illustrative of the pervasiveness of the new growth theory and the imaginary of the KBE are recurrent concerns of the social-democratic government on "hidden" and "potential" resources, which have not yet been utilized (e.g., Government Bill 1994/95: 100 and 150). Another characteristic feature is the conception that individuals possess inherent qualities that, when aggregated, constitute the society-wide force of growth as well as the recognition of competence as a subjective and an individual resource (e.g., Government Bill 1997/98: 62, p. 161). Such a conception of competence similarly constructs the rational political government in terms of "stimulation," "mobilization," and "vitalization." It is noteworthy to look at the discussion led in Government Bill 1997/98: 62 on rational political organization for regional development. Rational organization is defined as "recognizing different competences and perspectives," and "[i]t is important that the local development groups experiences and competencies are utilized" (Government Bill 1997/98: 62, p. 161). In Department Report 1999: 32, economic growth is defined as the outcome of the totality of efforts and attempts made, which is why every person's capacity and competence must be mobilized. Knowledge and competence are not static and measurable resources and factors of production but procedural and emerging properties that develop and expand parallel to personal development. Personal learning and initiatives to creativity appear as resources within the imaginary of the knowledge society. The relationship between "welfare" and "growth" now becomes more complex, as economic growth neither stands in opposition to welfare nor is just a means to realize welfare. Rather, social security appears as an adjuvant of the economic system since it constitutes the general cultural breeding ground that generates individual incentives, which again constitute essential resources for economic growth (cf. Government Bill 1995/96: 25; Social Democratic Party 1994, p. 10; SOU 2000: 87).

ACTIVE SOCIAL CONTRACT

Akin to an institutional hegemonic strategy, the social-democratic discourse promotes an all-inclusive form of societalization. Yet, this mode of inclusion is not determined and justified by a singular and monolithic conception of society, nor by a certain norm on social inclusion. Rather, it configures several mutually inter-linked sets of ideals, strategies, techniques, and objectives of government. Social-democratic government aspires toward the realization of a new and active social contract between the state and society, not least because the government's capacity to achieve economic growth is increasingly conceived as depending on individual incentives, investment, mobilization, and activation (e.g., Social Democratic Party 1992: 61f; 2002: 27).[9] Cultural, cognitive, and epistemological coherence is recognized as a pre-condition for the realization of the ideal of "A Nation at Work," which is positioned in a relation of contrariety to the massive unemployment of the early 1990s (e.g., Government Bill 1994/95: 100 and 218). A characteristic feature of the new social contract are articulations that "we all must cooperate and join forces" (Department Report 1999: 32) and collaborate in the combat of unemployment (Parliamentary Minutes 1995/96: 74). According to Prime Minister Persson:

> Consensus [*adjuvant:* of government] has been the foundation for the stability [*consequence*] and faith in the future [*consequence*] that for such a long time have characterized the Swedish society [*space*]. Cooperation [*adjuvant:* of government] is the key [*technique*] in the struggle for full employment [*object; empty signifier*]. (Parliamentary Minutes 1995/96: 74)

The government's strategy to attain a "national gathering" is linked to the capacity of governing work and economy (cf. Government Bill 1995/96: 207). The mobilization of social actors strives toward an encouragement of social subjects' self-responsibility and duties toward society. It would be too hasty an assumption to interpret this as merely an expression of a new active solidarity consisting of a mix of rights and duties. It also mirrors a new epistemology on the government of economy. The capacity of the government was regarded as limited by several contextual factors, which appeared as external and given objective facts. Traditional policy instruments of exchange rate depreciation, economic subventions, and temporal government debts were considered dysfunctional within the internationalized economy. When analyzing their political defeat in the parliamentary elections of 1991, the Social-Democratic Party observed that achieving full employment would, due to the government's limited capacity, have to be compensated for by increased individual commitment (Social Democratic Party 1992: 59ff; cf. Green Party 2000: 11; 2002: 10 and 43).

The realization of limited political sovereignty was within the limits of the imaginary consisting of the knowledge society and new growth theory, producing a new epistemology of economic growth based on the general mobilization of subjects. Both the Social-Democratic Party and the Green Party emphasize the creativity of the subject. Accordingly, the role of the state will be to generate socio-cultural conditions in which subjects may realize their innovativeness. An interesting comment can be found in the report of the Social-Democratic Party from 1992, which even argues that it was the misconception of the subjects' need of freedom that made voters elect liberal and conservative parties (Social Democratic Party 1992: 91). The conception of the subject as being intrinsically creative was most obviously expressed in the Department Report 1999: 32:[10]

Growth policy [*technique*] must be based on every person's participation [*destinator; adjuvant*] in the production system [*adjuvant*] and in the distribution of the results of production [*adjuvant*]. Growth [*Object*] is attained, not just through the competence of experts [*adjuvant; inadmissible technique*] and the highly educated [*adjuvant; inadmissible technique*]; sustainable growth [*object*] is achieved when everybody's [*subject:* all] capacity [*adjuvant:* subjectivity] and competence [*adjuvant*] is utilized [*strategy:* "tas tillvara"; *consequence*]. If we [*destinator*] are to realize these competent and committed efforts [*object*] throughout the working life [*space*], then the working life [*space*] must provide secure and developing conditions [*technique:* welfare; *adjuvant*], and hindrances [*traitor*] such as prejudices [*traitor*] and discrimination [*traitor*], must be abolished [*technique*]. (Department Report 1999: 32, p. 5)

As the previous quotation shows, the political government must be exercised in a way that activates subjects, which also supports the argument that "we all must cooperate and head into the same direction" (Department Report 1999: 32, p. 15). In the report of the parliamentary committee that investigated the sharing of responsibilities among central, regional, and local levels, a few years later it was observed that: "It is difficult to realize the public sector objectives, if the citizens are not participating in collective life in other ways than before, and in some cases even accept more responsibilities" (SOU 2003: 123). In other words, it is essential that the state is capable of utilizing and mobilizing the full potential of social subjects (Government Bill 1994/95: 100 and 150). The focus on the regional level as an arena for the implementation and realization of the politics for employment and growth appears, within the imaginary of economic growth, as an outcome of a virtuous and an accumulative process emerging from below through individual initiatives and local cooperation. In this light, every region is observed to "possess its own growth potential and this must be utilized in order to make the general development as positive as possible" (Government Bill 1995/96: 207). For this reason, the objective of the government is to "mobilize a great number of actors in the country o attain a regional and local mobilization for image building and growth" (Government Bill 1995/96: 207). The government's strategy for "Halving Unemployment" as presented in Government Bill 1995/96: 222 also shows that the virtuous process of growth originates from inter-subjective dynamic synergies emerging in networks and cooperation: "There are many examples of the dynamic forces that can be freed in cooperation between the different local actors" (Government Bill 1995/96: 222, chapter 5). In this context, local "individuals," "enterprises," "organizations," and "institutions" figure as "adjuvants" of the social-democratic government, which observed local solutions and forms of cooperation as the possibility to "create new employment through growth in enterprises" (Government Bill 1995/96: 222, chapter 5; cf. Government Bill 1997/98: 62).

Whereas the institution of regional cooperation can be understood to install an active social contract between the central government and local and regional actors, the government also intends to realize a social contract directly with social subjects. Women are especially recognized as a social group, whose commitment and participation could be extended. A functioning welfare society requires the dedication of both men and women (Government Bill 1995/96: 25). The level of economic growth is seen in a relation of analogy to the extent to which resources and experiences of both men and women are utilized (Government Bill 1995/96: 207). Government Bill 1995/96: 25 presents the reason for the abolition of possible hindrances to a mobilization of women's unutilized resources in a straightforward way:

> By breaking up the gender-related labor markets [*traitor*] the unutilized resources [*inadmissible consequence*] of women [*subject; receiver*] may better contribute to the increase of productivity [*object*]. (Government Bill 1995/96: 25)

In a similar fashion, the later *Program of the Social-Democratic Party* (Social Democratic Party 2002: 28) problematizes socio-cultural discrimination as a "traitor," which "implicates that competencies and willingness to work of different individuals are either underestimated or will not be utilized at all, which again is an irresponsible waste of human resources." The problem of unutilized resources is a specter that seems to haunt the social-democratic government. The problem as such is not the lacking utilization, but what the parliamentary report (SOU 1996: 4) observed as a gap between potential and actual levels of economic growth. The role of the entrepreneur is to close this gap by guaranteeing that all socio-economic opportunities and available resources are utilized in the most efficient way.

ENTREPRENEUR: THE ACTIVE SUBJECT

The performative role of the entrepreneur is connected in two inter-linked respects to the government's capacity to achieve the aspired societal mobilization. First, mobilization can be conceived of in terms of a quantitative increase of resources, potentials, commitment, and competencies available, which particular social actors then canalize into economic activities that generate employment. Entrepreneur is the social agent who utilizes the chances and resources created by the general societal mobilization (cf. NUTEK 1995a). Second, mobilization also has a more qualitative dimension concerning the method in which mobilization materializes through maximal and optimized utilization of available resources. The quantitative dimension is expressed in straightforward terms by the Department Report 1999: 32 (p. 36), which argued that "[g]rowth results from human efforts and all growth policy must intend to engage as many people as possible in productive work." In other words, the growth potential of the economy could be exhausted by means of a maximal mobilization of people, and in this regard, "[t]he more social commitment the working life succeeds in mobilizing and utilizing, the more growth will there be in the economy" (Department Report 1999: 32, p. 92).

The social-democratic discourse sets the number of new enterprises and entrepreneurs into a positive causal relation to the number of occupations (e.g., Government Bill 1994/95: 100 and 150). SMEs are observed to offer the largest potential for future occupations, and, consequently, the number of new SMEs is related to the number of new occupations (Government Bill 1994/95: 218). The quantitative increase of enterprises is also set into positive reciprocity to the level and intensity of economic competition. Similar to the liberal-conservative government, the social-democratic government also observes entrepreneurial activities, new entrepreneurship, and new enterprises as guarantees of maintained competition, which again counteracts the "inherent tendency of the economy to monopolization" (Government Bill 1999/00: 140, p. 67). An interesting reference is made in Government Bill 1995/96: 222 to McKinsey's (1995) report *Sweden's Economic Performance*, which observed vast differences in productivity between sectors operating under intense competition and protected sectors. Entrepreneurs who realize innovations and introduce new techniques are seen as *adjuvants*, who break up existing low-productive production systems by increased value added in production and efficiency of resources (e.g., Government Bill 1995/96: 222). Like the liberal-conservative government, the social-democratic government discourse maintains that the functioning of competition, as opposed to a distortion of competition, is an inevitable demand and defines efficient competition as the prerequisite of optimal allocation of resources (Government Bill 1995/96: 222).

In social-democratic discourse, entrepreneurs are projected as possessing the capacity to both surmount and sooth the economic crises. The generic capacity of entrepreneur is defined in terms of its capacity to initiate the virtuous process of "dynamics," which appears intelligible in light of the observation that economic growth emanates from, and is maintained through, a consistent "productivity increase," which again requires the presence of a consistent "pressure of transformation" (e.g., Government Bill 1995/96: 25; Motion 1993/94: Fi208; Social Democratic Party 1994).[11] Moreover, entrepreneurs are attributed the capacity to realize necessary technological investment and to demand a competent labor force, which together facilitate the realization of the *knowledge society* considered necessary for maintaining the welfare society in the future (Government Bill 1995/96: 207). Like the observation of the new enterprises as "spearheads to the future" in liberal-conservative discourse, so social-democratic discourse posited entrepreneurs as adjuvants of the government, as subjects who conduct innovations and invest in economically sustainable and increasing employment generating knowledge-intensive production (e.g., Government Bill 1995/96: 222). Yet, it must be noticed that the social-democratic sublimation of the entrepreneur was starkly criticized in a report from NUTEK (1995a). First, NUTEK questioned whether current political support would generate a suitable subset of entrepreneurs and business plans that, as a consequence, could survive competition and even generate economic growth (NUTEK 1995a). Second, NUTEK also divided new enterprises into "subsistence enterprises," which were intended to merely provide subsistence for a singular person, and growth-oriented and capital intensive enterprises that generated employment for third parties. The NUTEK report questions the government's intention to stimulate economic growth by supporting SEs. This criticism is indicative of the sublime emphasis the entrepreneur placed on the general expectation of the socio-economic change that "all" new enterprises and the sheer quantity of new enterprises would generate. Yet, Government Bill 1995/96: 25 had already problematized the absent growth in the number of SEs and observes that only 10–15% of SEs actually registered any growth at all. Moreover, more than 60% of all enterprises had no employees other than the business starter. Still, subsequent

Government Bills from the same year (e.g., Government Bill 1995/96: 207 and 222) sustained the sublime projections of the smaller enterprises:

> In order to guide the country out of the employment crisis [*empty signifier*: employment; inadmissible *consequence*] a comprehensive renewal of business life [*technique; object*] is required. Renewal [*object*] must be based on investments in new knowledge [*adjuvant; technique*], a better utilization of competence [*technique*: utilization], new technology and innovation [*technique*: innovation]. The government [*subject*] therefore assigns 1 bn. SEK to the program on 'Development of Small Enterprises, Renewal and Growth' [*technique*]. This program, which has a clear focus on small enterprises [receiver: SEs], intends to facilitate the development of Sweden into a knowledge society [object; time:future; space: knowledge society], make it easier to be an entrepreneur [receiver and subject: entrepreneur] and initiate an adaption [strategy] towards sustainable development [object]. The program embraces, amongst other things, the assignment of a delegation for simplifying the establishment of small enterprises [*adjuvant*; *technique*: simplification; *receiver*: SEs], whose objective is to present suggestions of how to stimulate business start-ups [*object; technique*: stimulate] and show possibilities of how to simplify rules [*technique; object*] for small enterprises [*receiver*: SEs]. Beside the program for small enterprises [*receiver*: SEs; *technique*], the government [*subject*] also intends to initiate comprehensive cooperation in regions [*space*: region; *technique*: mobilization] to setup an effective industrial and regional policy [*technique*] directed towards the smaller enterprises [*receiver*: SEs]. (Government Bill 1995/96: 20, italics added)

Whereas the liberal-conservative government relied on the natural presence of entrepreneurs, the social-democratic government is far more concerned with the "making up" of entrepreneurial subjects. The strategy of the social-democratic government to support entrepreneurship can be divided into strategies, techniques, instruments, and programs that improve the general socio-economic climate for business start-ups and smaller enterprises; and instruments that involve either the general social construction of an entrepreneurial climate consisting of "positive attitudes to growth, entrepreneurship, entrepreneurialism and innovations" or the support of individuals who are or may become entrepreneurs (Government Bill 1995/96: 222, chapter 5). The subject of entrepreneur is situated within the political discourse both in existing enterprises and beyond enterprises as subjects who are either planning or potentially initiating their own enterprises. The general political strategy of national mobilization toward employment and growth is also intended to evoke activities, incentives, and creativity. Entrepreneur is the subject who makes use of, allocates, directs, invests, channels, and materializes resources assembled through national mobilization by transferring both hard (*capital, technology, labor*) and soft (*human capital, competence, initiatives, ideas, creativity*) capital to employment and growth. The foremost measure of the social-democratic government, which was intended to improve the general climate of growth and entrepreneurship, was the three-year program for the "Development of Small Enterprises, Renewal and Growth" assigned a budget of 1 bn. SEK. Furthermore, the government also assigned an expert committee (Committee on Small Enterprises) to investigate how to improve the contextual conditions for SMEs to support their endemic growth processes (Government Bill 1995/96: 222; SOU 1997: 186). Also worth mentioning is the institution of SIMPLEX, a group of experts on business life and the impact of legislation in terms of the administrative burdens of enterprises, which in analogy to a previous audit organization on competition—the Swedish Competition Authority—has as its objective to "evaluate all draft law with regard to their effects on small enterprises" (Department Report 1999: 32, p. 69). The social-democratic government's aspiration to establish an entrepreneurial culture is a logical consequence of the imagined inter-dependence between the capacity of the political government and the extent of societal mobilization of initiatives and participation. A characteristic feature of the social-democratic conception of reciprocity between rational political conduct of government and the entrepreneurial subject is that the quantity of entrepreneurs was proportional to the corresponding increase in the capacity of the political government. As Government Bill 1994/95: 100 and 150 pointed out, having more women as entrepreneurs is a condition necessary for attaining more enterprises, increased growth, and more employment (SOU 1996: 34, p. 278).

In the social-democratic discourse, entrepreneur is not merely an actor who starts a new enterprises but, far more, an agent who initiates a virtuous accumulative process that can be summarized in the form of a linear causal relation: *entrepreneur → enterprise → number of enterprises → growth → employment*. The expansion of the group of entrepreneurs was motivated since it was expected to lead to a corresponding increase in national economic growth (cf. NUTEK 2001b: 10). Under-representation of various social groups among those who had already started their own businesses was interpreted as a result of hindrances, which obstructed the "natural," as generic stance of subjects represent the entrepreneurial mindset (cf. NUTEK 2001b: 10f). Not only women but also cultural minorities[12] and youth were observed as groups possessing "vast and inner entrepreneurial reserves" (Government Bill 1996/97: 150D2; NUTEK 2001b: 10f). The liberal-conservative government had already problematized the under-representation of women, youth, and cultural minorities as a possible source of future extension of entrepreneurs. However, in contrast to the social-democratic government, it did not define this under-representation as an obstacle to the conduct of government. In this regard, the social-democratic government problematized in an unprecedented way the actual composition of the group of entrepreneurs. Reflecting the increasing concerns about the number of entrepreneurs, and whether the potential of different social groups (*women, immigrants, youth*) was fully utilized, the social-democratic government focused on instruments that would enable the realization of the maximum intensity and quantitative scope of entrepreneurship. It would be impossible to summarize all the instruments applied, not least because the policy measures and instruments serve multiple objectives.

However, we should emphasize some novel techniques that the social-democratic government applied to increase the number of entrepreneurs. Similar to the epistemology of the politics for full employment, the economic growth theory also constitutes the imaginary within which the extension of entrepreneurship to new groups was estimated. As the Government Bill 2001/02: 4 argued, "It is one of the core factors of economic growth [*object*] that more enterprises [*object*; *subject*: entrepreneur] are started [*object*], not just by persons who already regard it as a possibility [*subject*: all], but that entrepreneurship [*subject*] also reaches new groups [*adjuvant*]" (p. 160). Increased concerns about the expansion of the group of entrepreneurs are reflected on the level of designed institutional strategies, techniques, and programs. During its first years, the social-democratic government raised the funding for the Enterprise Allowance Scheme substantially, which covered 1.3 bn. SEK in 1995/96 as compared with 450 m in 1993/94, the last year of the liberal-conservative government. In August 1994, the then liberal-conservative government introduced a 50 m. "loan scheme" for female entrepreneurs that reflected the problematizations of earlier programs for funding business start-ups, which had discriminated women who in general needed less start-up capital than men and therefore remained beyond the scope of the loan schemes (Government Bill 1994/95: 100 and 150; 1995/96: 25; Government Communication 1996/97: 41). The subsequent social-democratic government extended the existing funding to 149 m. SEK in 1995/96.

Special attention has also been devoted to the support of women's entrepreneurship in rural areas, which was stimulated through programs and policy measures that provided training in information technology. One such measure was the establishment of specific "resource centers" in 23 out of 24 geographical administrative units. In 1998, the number of local resource centers increased from 59 to 120 (Government Bill 1998/99: 1D18). The establishment of resource centers for women was demanded by the Social-Democratic Party in 1994 (Motion 1993/94: A254). The initial motivation for creating resource centers was to guarantee a more equal distribution of state support to men and women. The objective of the resource centers was to provide platforms for the exchange of experiences and building of networks, evaluation, competence development, coordination, and initiation of local development programs (Government Bill 1994/95: 161; 1997/98: 62). Resource centers, it was argued, would release "women's vigor" (Government Bill 1994/95: 161; 1997/98: 62) and mobilize women as a "resource for regions" (Government Bill 1997/98: 1D19). Moreover, in 1992, programs of consultants for female entrepreneurs were assigned in 62 municipalities, which were adapted and continued by the social-democratic government during 1994–1996 and 1997–2000 (cf. Government Communication 1996/97: 41; SOU 2001: 44, p. 161). The "Enterprise Allowance Scheme" launched in the framework of the labor market policy was the foremost measure to subjectivate the unemployed to entrepreneurs. Besides the quantitative increase in funding, an interesting change occurred considering qualification to this policy measure. In 1996, the earlier criterion of a preceding 24-month period of unemployment as an entitlement was lowered to 6 months to avoid the concern that women most qualified as entrepreneurs might be excluded from the program.

It is also most interesting to see how the previous liberal-conservative government and the social-democratic government connected entrepreneurship to the norm of equality. The liberal-conservative government mentioned equal rights to entrepreneurship as being one of the main objectives of its politics for gender equality (e.g., Government Bill 1993/94: 147). However, under-representation of women among business starters was not problematized as an expression of inequality. Indeed, women's entrepreneurship was observed as a resource within the regional development programs, but the absence of women as entrepreneurs was not problematized as lacking mobilization of socio-economic potential, as the social-democratic government argued (e.g., Government Bill 2001/02: 4). In this regard, political concerns on women's entrepreneurship intensified within the social-democratic discourse. In its criticism of the liberal-conservative government's failure to re-install full employment, the Social-Democratic Party observed the expansion of the number of women as entrepreneurs both as a measure to increase equality and as a source of employment (Motion 1993/94: A254).

Women's entrepreneurship was regarded as a possibility to re-introduce employees released in the wake of public sector cut-downs to economic and labor market participation (Government Communication 1996/97: 41). The norm of gender equality is the pre-supposition of women's entrepreneurship, but equality is also defined as equal opportunity to participate in the economy. This relation of equivalence between entrepreneurship and gender equality has been a constituent element of the social-democratic government. Already Government Bill 1994/95: 100 had articulated that:

> In order to promote gender equality [*object*; *adjuvant*] in working life [*space:* work] there are measures suggested on women's entrepreneurship [*object*]. Having more women as entrepreneurs [*object*] is crucial for achieving the objective of more enterprises [*object*], growth [*object*] and employment [*empty signifier:* employment].

Even the Parliamentary Committee SOU 1998: 6, which criticized the publicly dominating patriarchal gender culture harshly, problematized women's exclusion in terms of the lost and non-utilized potential and "reserve of talent that is not used" claiming that "a great deal of competence is lost since women and men are not mobilized to their full potential" (SOU 1998: 6, p. 3; cf. Government Bill 1995/96: 25).

Whereas women's entrepreneurship was recognized relatively early in the 1990s, the value of entrepreneurship among cultural minorities was recognized only during the social-democratic government. In a manner similar to the socio-political value of entrepreneurs in general, the value of entrepreneurship among cultural minorities also consists of a configuration of mutually supportive meanings. First, as SOU 1996: 55 announces straightforwardly, "There is also a societal interest in utilizing the resources and competencies of those who migrated to Sweden" (SOU 1996: 55, p. 11; cf. Government Bill 1997/98: 1 and 16). Second, regarding the externally imposed restrictions of the possibility to raise the number of occupations within the public sector, expansion of the private sector, and especially new SEs were observed as the source of a considerable number of future occupations. Both objectives of increased growth and lowered unemployment were considered possible to achieve through increased entrepreneurship among immigrants:

> Immigrants [*receiver*] as entrepreneurs [*adjuvant*] are now very much desired and they have received a lot of public attention from politicians [*destinator*] and other decision-makers [*destinator*]. This can be explained, amongst other things, with a higher level of entrepreneurship among immigrants [*adjuvant; receiver* = immigrant] being increasingly regarded, partly as an important way of decreasing unemployment [*object; empty signifier:* employment] among immigrants, and partly, as a source of renewal [*object*] and growth [*object*] in the economy. (SOU 1996: 55, p. 15)

The imaginary, within which the construction of "immigrant entrepreneur" is located, is the limitation of the capacity of the political government. This is supported by the suspicion of an inherent potential of expansion of resources and competencies utilized thus far that "may be lost forever" if they are not mobilized in a more efficient manner (SOU 1996: 55, p. 84). As a consequence, increasing attention has been paid to information campaigns, information distribution, and the institution of networks and supporting institutions, all of which create general positive attitudes toward immigrants as entrepreneurs. Similar to the articulation of the social necessity to recognize women's entrepreneurship, the social-democratic government has also aspired to the change of attitudes that facilitates the recognition of socio-cultural plurality as a strength and an engine of development (cf. Social Democratic Party 2002: 28). As SOU 1996: 55 and Government Bill 1997/98: 16 observed, "cultural plurality" must be recognized as a social and economic resource:

In a society of ethnic and cultural plurality [*space:* plural society] people [*subject:* all] should complement each other and mutually contribute their competences [*adjuvant*] and experiences [*adjuvant*] so that the potential of cultural plurality [*adjuvant*] can be released and appropriated [*technique:* utilize potential]. (Government Bill 1997/98: 16, p. 20)

It appears to have been international competition and globalization that posited external and inescapable demands requiring "that all resources in the country must be utilized" (Government Bill 1997/98: 16, p. 46; cf. Department Report 2000: 69; Government Bill 1997/98: 16). In this socio-economic context, "unutilized human capital and other capital must begin to work for the growth of the country" (Government Bill 1997/98: 16, p. 46). Demands to the entrepreneur-friendly political government support-ing entrepreneurship, which are based on external and inescapable global conditions and the inherent logic of economy and economic growth, are supported by the cultural projection and "sublimation" of both women and the immigrants as natural entrepreneurial subjects. First, immigrants are recognized as having come from cultures more aligned to "entrepre-neurship" (SOU 1999: 49). Second, due to the more precarious labor mar-ket situation of immigrants, they are assumed to be more ready to start their own enterprises. These two assumptions are supported by statistical data that observe an ever increasing share of immigrants starting their own businesses (Government Bill 1997/98: 1; NUTEK 2001; SOU 1996: 55; 1999: 49). Third, the increase in the number of immigrant-owned enter-prises is associated with the increasing number of women as entrepreneurs (see NUTEK 1995) and is expected to invigorate Swedish business life (cf. NUTEK 2001). Considering women, the abolition of the gender-segre-gated labor market and male-dominated cognitive patterns in economy, for instance, in regard to the conception of the entrepreneur (e.g., SOU 1997: 87) are expected to increase the share of enterprises started by women (e.g., Government Bill 1996/97: 150D2).

NUTEK's (2001) report put the finger on the illusionary construction of women and immigrants as entrepreneurs.[13] As the report argues, recent pub-lic debates have produced undifferentiated and exaggerated assumptions of the roles played by both women and immigrants as entrepreneurs, which have overdone their vitalizing influence on the economy. Government Bill 2001/02: 4 expresses that the social-democratic government's conception of the entrepreneur has emphasized the quantitative side of entrepreneur-ship measured by the number of entrepreneurs, which also explicates the motivation to extend entrepreneurship to new social groups. The destinator supporting this aspiration is, above all, the theory on economic growth, which pre-supposes as

one of the constituting factors of growth [*object*] that enterprises are started [*adjuvant*] not only by persons who already regard it as an option [*subject:* all] but that entrepreneurship is extended to new groups [*technique:* extension of entrepreneurship; *adjuvant:* all. (SOU 2001: 44, p. 160)

Expansion of the activity of entrepreneurship to new socio-cultural groups becomes intelligible once it has been located within the configuration of the elements that suggestively constitute the hegemonic imaginary of the social-democratic government. The government's intention to "act from a distance" by mobilizing and coordinating social activities and actors is supported by an epistemology of economic growth largely congruent with the "new growth theory" that defines economic growth as the result of individual and local incentives, activities, and creativity resulting from innovative economic processes.[14] A newly activated contract of citizenship unifies this governmental and economic epistemology with full employment as the primary political objective.

Meaningfulness in the quantitative extension of the group of entrepreneurs derives from the connection to the equal quantity of personal "growth" and mobilization of personal potential.[15] The central constituents of the social-democratic government's politics for full employment are summarized in Table 7.2. Due to the complexity of discourse formations and the multiplicity of connections between discursive elements, it is only possible to illustrate what appears to be the central constituent relations of social-democratic discourse. In the manner of an institutional pattern of articulation, as contrasted to the popular strategy of the preceding liberal-conservative government, social-democratic discourse exerts an all-inclusion of social interests and issues on behalf of the welfare society. The main relation of antagonism observed is located between the two poles of *activity* and *passivity*. For instance, the active government is contrasted to the passive political government, which is argued to rely to an inadmissible extent on the rationality of the market, and on its generic capacity to generate growth. Another aspect of the opposition between active and passive relates to the participation and commitment of social subjects.

The main form of dislocation in the construction of the entrepreneur in political discourses of the liberal-conservative and social-democratic governments regards the problematization of the scope of societal participation. Whereas the liberal-conservative government took the presence of subjects intending to act as entrepreneurs for granted, the social-democratic government has been far more concerned with the actual extent of social subjects who are capable of and willing to mobilize themselves as active citizens and entrepreneurs. In social-democratic discourse, entrepreneur appears both as the mode of subjectivity, which mobilizes both hard and soft capital of economic activities, and also as the subject, who makes use of and channels capacities and competencies of other active citizens in a way that initiates a virtuous process of economic renewal. The origin of this problematization is primarily located in the novel epistemology on economic growth,

Discourse Formation A: Social-Democratic Discourse 1994–1998

Nodal points / empty signifiers (connected by l/= = Difference/Equivalence):

(—) Optimal Resource Use/Mobilization (Np) · Welfare Society (Es) l/= Full-Employment (Es) l/= A Nation in Work (Es) · Persistent Growth (Np) l/= Economic Renewal (Np) (—)

Level	(connected by l/=)							
A (px.) (—)	Active Industrial Policy/Canalisation of Ideas/Creativity to New Enterprises (*technique*)	,Utgiftstak'/ Budget Discipline/ Disciplin-ation of Public Sector Funding (*technique*)	Disciplination of the State Expenditure (*technique*)	,Programme for Development of Small Enterprises, Renewal and Growth' (*technique*)	Education Revolution/ Know-ledge Boost/ Life-Long Learning (*technique*)	Acceptance of Personal Responsibilities/ Local & Regional initiatives (*technique*)	Rapid Technological Change/ Technological Innovations (*technique*)	Societal Mobilization of Entrepreneurial Reserves/ ,Starta-Eget Bidrag' (*technique*) (—)
A (eth.) (—)	Expansion of the Scope of Economy (Object)/ Increased Number of Enterprises & Econ. Actors (*object*)	Sound Public Finances/ Stable Price & Cost Development (*object*)	Stable Price Development/ Low Rate of Inflation/ Competitive Wage Development (*object*)	Optimal Utilization and Allocation of Resources to Growth and Employment (*object*)	Knowledge Society/ Qualified Labor Force (*object*)	Absorption of Socio-Cultural Divisions/ Equal National Standards (*object*)	Up-Grading of Economy to Knowledge Intensive Production (*object*)	Active Social Contract (Object)/ Social Consensus on Socio-Econ. Participation (*object*) (—)
B (eth.) (—)	Negative Growth Development & Lost Chances of Growth (*inadmissable consequence*)	Lost International Trust in Swedish Economy & Government (*inadmissable consequence*)	Unutilized Economic Potential (*inadmissable consequence*)	Unutilized Potential of Entrepreneurs (*inadmissable consequence*)	Under-Representation of Social Groups as Entrepreneurs (*inadmissable consequence*)	,Tudelning' of Sweden (*inadmissable consequence*)	Out-moded Economic Structures (*inadmissable consequence*)	Lacking Pressure for Transformation/ Lacking Renewal (*inadmissable consequence*) (—)
B (px.) (—)	Exaggerated & Unrealistic Trust in the Rationality of the Market (*traitor*)	High Budget Deficit & ,Budget mire' (*traitor*)	Insufficient Socio-Political Mobilization (*traitor*)	Hindrances to realisation of entrepreneur-ship (*traitor*)	Cultural Prejudices & Discrimination/ Neglect of Entrepreneurial Capacities (*traitor*)	Lost Faith in Justice, Security & Welfare (*traitor*)	Political Focus on Material and Institutional Conditions of Econ. (*traitor*)	Exaggerated Faith in the Market Forces/ Monopolisation of Economy (*traitor*)

(—) Free-Market Dogma (Np) · Passive Political Government (Np) (—)

Mass-Unemployment (Es)

Discourse Formation B: The Antagonistic Other

Abbreviations/ Symbols:

Difference	|
Equivalence	=
Antagonism	.....
Empty Signifier	(Es)
Nodal Point	(Np)

A (px.): Level of Practices in Discourse Formation A (techniques; subjectivities; adjuvants; receivers)
A (eth.): Ethical substance of Objects of Desires in Discourse Formation A
B (px.): Level of Practices in Discourse Formation B (inadmissible techniques; traitors)
B (eth.): Ethical substance: Inadmissible Consequences of the Discourse Formation B
(. . .): Continued Relations of Difference/Equivalence

which has broadened the conception of "resources"; "capital" composition and utilization would generate the aspired economic growth and full employment. The liberal-conservative government observed, above all, the material and institutional conditions as constituting the socio-structural context decisive for individual decisions on conduct of the self. In contrast to this, the social-democratic discourse has emphasized individual cognitive and attitudinal resources, which can, and indeed should, be mobilized politically. Similar to an institutional form of discourse (see Chapter 4), the social-democratic government has intended to mobilize all subjects under the auspices of "national mobilization." An extension of the group of entrepreneurs to embrace a greater number of women, young people, and immigrants is positioned within the more general discourse on activating government. The antagonistic relation that divided susceptible and rejected modes of political government originates from the opposition between high productivity and high-wage economic growth, in contrast to low productivity and low-wage economic growth. The opposition between these two roads to prosperity in an internationalized economy is constructed with a reference to "welfare,", which as such appears as the empty signifier of the governmental discourse of the social-democratic government.

The intention to achieve increased societal mobilization, as symbolized by the "active social contract," also reflects the realization of new restrictions set on the political government. Besides the realization of cognitive resources and human capital as the constituents of economic growth, government through activation reflects the government's limited capacity to realize the endeavored universal imaginary of a "nation at work" through traditional policy measures. The introduction of "budget discipline," but also the rejection of the possibility to raise employment within the public sector, symbolizes limits set to the government that are considered external. Entrepreneur is a central, yet not the superordinate subject of governmental rationality required by the social-democratic program. Entrepreneur is one of the roles, yet not the only performative role, in which individuals may cooperate with the political government. However, the social-democratic government problematizes the absence of entrepreneurship in society to an unprecedented extent and has become concerned about the "making up" of entrepreneurial subjects, which is also manifested by the previously described implementation of numerous techniques of subjectivation.

8   Securing the Welfare in the KBE
1997–2004

The third discursive sequence in the construction of entrepreneur that will be described now is an endemic development within the social-democratic discourse between 1997/98 and 2004. There are clear parallels to the second discursive sequence, and indeed, the connection between the "knowledge society" and sustained "welfare" as it is illustrated in Table 8.1 attains an even more central position during the post-1998 period. A typical aspect of the social-democratic discourse between 1997/98 and 2004 is the universalization of the entrepreneur to become a role model of an active subject in the "knowledge-based economy" (KBE). The earlier presented second discursive sequence manifested the attention paid by the social-democratic government to the mobilization of all material, cultural, and subjective resources in order to realize the objective of a high-wage and high-productivity society, defined as a pre-condition for the welfare society.

This general mobilization was realized chiefly through the "active social contract." Even in more recent policy documents such as, for example, the report from the parliamentary committee on the sharing of societal responsibilities [*Ansvarskommittén*][1] (SOU 2003: 123), the transfer of more responsibilities to individual subjects has remained a central principle. In line with the second discourse, there is also the intention to extend the group of active entrepreneurs to include more women, immigrants, and young people. In 2002, the "National Program for Entrepreneurship" was implemented for the first time and was carried out between 2002 and 2004, From 2005 to 2007, the focus was again explicitly on young people as a social group whose positive attitudes toward entrepreneurship were considered decisive for the realization of the objective of more new enterprises and more subjects being active as entrepreneurs (cf. Memorandum 2001/2: NU4; 2002/3: NU7).

However, what changes in this third discursive sequence is the emergence of a socio-spatial imaginary on the advent of the KBE along with the emergence of analogous demand to provide an adequate form of societalization in the form of the "knowledge society." The presence of the knowledge society also changes the governmental reason, as the society becomes more and more knowledge-intensive [*space*: knowledge society; *time*: transformation; *destinator*], and an important task for the state [*receiver*] is to provide conditions of life-long learning [*technique*: learning]. Investments in education on all levels [*technique*] are carried out in order to create better chances for people [*receiver*] to acquire competences [*object*: knowledge] and skills [*object*: skills] demanded by working life [*destinator*: KBE]. (Government Communication 2003/04: 129, p. 98)

In the previous quotation, knowledge society and KBE are externalized as "destinators," as supposedly natural and inevitable developments that impose on the government the demand to "adjust" the national economic system to knowledge and innovation intensive production. Moreover, the new economic imaginary also imposes new demands on individuals to adjust their personal development to macro-level development in order to live up to the knowledge and competence demands set by working life in the KBE. As Government Communication 2003/04: 129 (p. 86) argues, "the knowledge society must be open for all." In the context of the knowledge society, an unprecedented synergy appears between individual learning and societal well-being since "[i]n the knowledge society the demands on education increase, and the individual and individual knowledge become the ever increasing driving forces for sustainable growth" (Government Bill 2003/04: 1, p. 33).

There is general consensus between political parties that Sweden must become a leading nation within the KBE. For instance, the opposition parties agreed with the social-democratic government on the fact that Sweden must become a "world-class knowledge nation" (cf. Motion 2000/1: Ub260; cf. Government Communication 2003/04: 129, p. 86).[2] The objective for the education policy as defined in Government Bill 2000/01: 1 was that "Sweden shall be a leading knowledge nation characterized by high quality of education and life-long learning for growth and justice" (Government Bill 2003/04: 1D19, p. 33). The ambition of the EU, as expressed in the Lisbon strategy in 2000, to become the world's leading KBE appears as an imperative in Swedish discourse, which confirms the rationality of national aspirations to proceed towards knowledge-intensive production. In 2004, the social-democratic government launched the innovation strategy "Innovative Sweden." Its objective was to make Sweden the most "competitive and dynamic KBE of Europe and thus one of the world's most attractive countries for investments" (Department Report 2004: 36, p. 1; cf. Government Bill 2004/5: 1D).

The supporting pillars of this strategy were, among other things, "stronger basis of knowledge," "innovative business life," "knowledge-intensive entrepreneurship," "innovative public sector," "stimulation of subjects' initiatives," and "utilization of personal competences" (Government Bill 2004/5: 1D1). As, for instance, Government Bill 2004/5: 1D18 notices, the global knowledge society, and economic competitiveness determined by the levels of competence and innovativeness, induce an ineluctable demand to mobilize subjects as innovators, as learning subjects, who pursue personal competence development and have faith in their own capacity, creativity, and potential to improve and renew (Government Bill 2004/5: 1D18, chapter 6). It was the synergy among the general spatial imaginary of the KBE, the central role of innovation and knowledge for internationally competitive economic production, and the conception of subjects as primary agents of the realization of competence and knowledge upgrading that installed the entrepreneur as the subject that sustains the transition of society to a knowledge society. It is above all this universalization of the entrepreneur as a general "Role Model of the Creative Subject" (see Chapter 9), alongside the paralleling universalization of the culture of enterprise, which symbolizes the most central changes in political reason after 1997/1998. In order to conceive this transformation of the conception of the entrepreneur, it is worthwhile making a further analysis of two particular discursive formations: regional and education policy appear as contexts in which the new conceptions of entrepreneur and entrepreneurship were initially developed and which also serve as sources for the dissemination of the culture of enterprise. The following two sections describe the evolution of these two logics within the contexts of the social-democratic discourses on regional development and education policy, respectively.

ECONOMIC GROWTH IN THE KBE

In line with the partnership model assigned to the national administration of the structural fund programs by the EU, the social-democratic government initiated in Government Bill 1997/98: 62—*Regional Growth for Employment and Welfare*—a novel model of governance for regional development policies. In this new model of the government, regional growth agreements implemented first for the period, 2000–2002, turned to a primary modus of regional governance and entailed an increasingly decentralized mode of government (cf. Government Bill 2001/02: 7).[3] These new regional strategies consisted of a heterogeneous ensemble of strategies, techniques of government, and organization models connected to a new economic epistemology connected with the general epistemology of the "endogenous growth theory." Rationality assigned to regional growth agreements was supported by expectations of intensification of international competition, globalization of the economy, and technological development. In the Swedish context, earlier concerns about the beneficial climate of enterprises in terms of national institutional configuration were supplemented with new concerns about local socio-cultural conditions of enterprises. Especially the activation of local initiatives, civic society commitment, the strength of the community level, and the functionality of local partnership models of public-private and local-national cooperation were all conceived of as being constituents of local environments beneficial for the economic development (cf. Department Report 1999: 32; Government Bill 1997/98: 62, p. 154). This epistemology on "regionalized" economic growth was supported by both the European Spatial Development Perspective (ESDP) and the endogenous growth theory, both of which emphasized the role of locally specific soft factors of production, such as competence, knowledge, social capital, networks, and partnership.[4]

Regionally based growth policies as the overarching technique to sustain the welfare society should be located within the observation of the necessary "period of transition" to the KBE (cf. Government Bill 1997/98: 62, p. 164; 2001/02: 4, p. 7; SOU 2000: 87, p. 302ff). The transition to the KBE was expected to increase the importance of extensive knowledge-based production (Government Bill 1997/98: 62, p. 150; Parliamentary Committee SOU 1996: 4). The Government Communication 1996/97: 112 argued that only technology and knowledge-intensive production could be considered compatible with the realization of the desired welfare society. Changes implemented in the economic role played by regions, set-up of regional level "growth plans" [*tillväxtavtal*], accentuation of social networks and partnerships as factors of good economic climate, as well as the intention to mobilize individuals to invest in their creativity, innovativeness, and competence all draw their rationality from the meta-narrative of the KBE. It is reasonable to define both the "knowledge society" and the "KBE" as nodal points within the third discursive sequence.

While the knowledge society appears as a necessary societal adjustment to expected economic and technological changes, the KBE assumes the role of a "destinator" since it provides an unprecedented form of an epistemology about economy, subjectivity, and political government. Above all, theories on economic "clusters," which define systems of production in terms of spatially limited and complex networks and "innovation systems," appear as a theoretical source that motivates the regionalization of growth policies (cf. Department Report 1999: 32; 2001: 15). For example, Government Bill 2001/02: 2 (chapter 4)—*R&D and Cooperation in Innovation Systems*—confirms that regional growth agreements are based on the conception of the economic system as a polyvalent and poly-nodal system of production clusters. The functionality and relative competitiveness of such clusters as a "home-base" of enterprises depends on a complex configuration of institutional, legal-judicial, material, and cultural factors. Economic results of clusters achieved in terms of products, services, processes of renewal, productivity increase, and general international competitiveness all emanate from the quality of interfaces and interchanges between the nodes of a network. In contrast to the classical theory on growth that accentuates exogenous factors of production, such as savings, risk capital, but also institutional contexts of rules as determining the competitiveness of firms, implemented regional growth agreements and efforts to develop economic clusters symbolize the epistemological impact of the new endogenous growth theory that emphasizes the role of soft, invisible, and cognitive factors of production, such as attitudes, cultural values, competence, and knowledge (Government Bill 2001/02: 4, p. 67ff). Indeed, Department Report 2001: 15 articulates that the central motivation for growth agreements was their assumed support in establishing new clusters from "below," through regional initiatives based on region-specific development potentials. In this regard, every enterprise is located within "a system consisting of all those enterprises, organizations and other actors with which these enterprises interact" (Government Bill 2001/02: 4, p. 163). Consistently, every political measure to support the competitiveness of enterprises must "see enterprises as parts of a system—innovation system and cluster" (Government Bill 2001/02: 4, p. 163). Moreover, regarded from the perspective of the adapted "cluster theory," every successful cluster is characterized by the "[s]ocial capital, which encourages a spirit of entrepreneurship" (Government Bill 2001/02: 4, p. 68).

The "spirit of entrepreneurship" is regarded as a generic resource that induces synergies, innovations, and complementary activities, but it also destroys existing networks in order to install new and more competitive ones (Government Bill 2001/02: 4, p. 61ff). Adaption of the cluster theory as an epistemology to understanding the economy extends the subset of factors decisive for the competitiveness of enterprises. Both the cluster theory and the endogenous growth theory accentuate the role of invisible, cognitive, soft, and context-specific factors of production (Government Bill 2001/2: 4, p. 67). This plurality of largely invisible factors of production emerging from inter-subjective communications impose on the government the task to generate, sustain, support, and coordinate local social networks. Emerging economic activities can, accordingly, not be reduced to outcomes of static and durable subsets of available material or institutional resources. Far more important is the social and cultural capital, which emerges from spatially specific dynamics in local interactions and networks. Moreover, the local "entrepreneurial culture" is increasingly important that is related to "creative, dynamic and chaotic environments" (Government Bill 2001/02: 4, p. 67). Hence, Government Bill 2001/02: 2 (p. 6, italics added) argues that "[a]n increasing *entrepreneurship* and *creative environments*, where possibilities for growth and cooperation are especially explicit, ensure that *good ideas* may grow and create new occupations and new enterprises."

The conception of initiatives, creativity, and mobilization of knowledge as processes emerging from below, and which must be provided a free space to proliferate, also ascribes to the political government the objective to "create good conditions for an innovative climate in which enterprises are established and grow" (Government Bill 2001/02: 2, p. 30). Such a climate is defined as quasi-institutional networks and clusters of mutually supporting activities, also in terms of innovations and growth fostering social culture that motivates social actors to mobilize their "endemic" capacities of

innovativeness (cf. Government Bill 2001/02: 2, p. 6). Local culture, values, attitudes, a propensity to path-breaking visions, and new ideas are the
engine of economic growth, and this entrepreneurial social capital is what
emanates the innovative, productivity, and competitiveness enhancing utilization and creation of resources, such as capital, technology, and raw material (cf. NUTEK 2002). The social-democratic government's suggestion
that regional business life must be allowed to develop in accordance with
specific regional circumstances does not mean that such circumstances are
fixed once and for all (cf. Government Bill 2001/02: 4, p. 179). As a matter
of fact, cluster theory points out how shared visions, consensual points of
view, and common identities emerge through synergies within local and
regional networks. Therefore, the regional actors must be presented with a
possibility of social entrepreneurship so that individual creative and innovative visions can be collectively and consensually materialized in the form
of local and regional projects.[5]

This emphasis on the cultural and inter-subjective nature of economic
growth induces two particular logics of rational government. First, intentions appear to decentralize the national growth policy and replace the
cohesive national growth strategy with regionally embedded growth agreements. Decentralization symbolizes the overarching intention to adjust the
government to local circumstances and chances (e.g., Government Bills
1997/98: 62, p. 148; 2001/2: 4, p. 70; SOU 2000: 87, pp. 266f and 293).
This intention is again interlinked with the belief that the economy's capacity for development and most productive utilization of available resources
requires the release of entrepreneurial spirits. Therefore,

> competitiveness of enterprises [*object; subject*] is determined to an
> increasing extent by the capacity to rapidly adjust products and ser-
> vices to customers' demands [*destinator*: KBE]. This requires innova-
> tion [*adjuvant*], flexibility [*adjuvant*] and constant learning [*adjuvant*],
> which are competencies [*adjuvant*] that largely develop in an interplay
> between actors [*destinator*: intersubjective capital]. (Government Bill
> 2001/02: 4, p. 61)

Second, local mobilization is an emergent factor of production that originates from individuals' willingness to engage and participate.[6] Local
mobilization is, in this regard, a prerequisite for the previously described
local capacity to generate competitiveness, "innovation," "flexibility," and
"learning." An example of this argument is NUTEK's (2002: 5) report on
cluster development that defines clusters in wider terms than mere physical
networks and emphasizes the constitutive role of shared ideas and visions
about the cluster (NUTEK 2002: 15). The conception of cluster as a configuration or network of actors, institutions, activities, and processes based
on shared visions accentuates the role played by creative and innovative
subjects in general (cf. Government Bill 2001/02: 2). As Government Bill

2001/02: 4 (p. 119) argues, "All efforts to development must set out from people's creativity and will to change. For the regional development policy it is crucial that this force can be utilized." The earlier described "active social contract" aspired to the general nationwide mobilization of citizens on behalf of the ethical substance defined in terms of the "welfare society" and "a nation at work." Now, this mobilization is maintained yet at the same time re-located into regional and local spaces (Department Report 2000: 7, p. 2).[7] Regionalization is not equal to individualization because the inter-subjective and cultural nature of clusters requires subjects who participate as members of a network. In this regard, networks are the means to observe both regional strategies and arenas for their implementation (e.g., Government Bill 2001/2: 4 and 7).

However, it is also recognized that the central responsibility for the establishment and maintenance of regional networks is carried by so-called "Grassroot Leaders"[8] and "Social Entrepreneurs," who exercise societal leadership by inducing new forms of connections between enterprises and public bodies and contribute to a "dynamic socio-economic development" in general (NUTEK 2002: 19). These subjects perform the role of network entrepreneurs who create and disseminate visions of the direction of a cluster, have skills to co-ordinate cluster activities, and possess an entrepreneurial spirit in general (NUTEK 2002: 7). The cluster perspective on regional economies adopted by the political government identifies network entrepreneurs as engines of clusters and innovation systems. Network entrepreneurs evoke collective visions that enable "consensual" visions about regional resources, potentials, and "knowledge and experience with regard to means that generate the best effects" (Government Bill 2001/02: 7, chapter 6). The centrality of network entrepreneurs reflects an observed need of regional learning, which, in the context of regional growth policies, appears to mean a general readiness to evaluate present social organization and receptiveness toward improvement (Government Bill 2001/02: 7, chapter 4). The attractiveness of particular contexts of production is related to their unique configuration of "networks, patterns of cooperation, attitudes and capacity of individuals to gather around visions and solve problems" (Department Report 2004: 36, p. 22). In the context of regional growth policies, entrepreneur becomes equivalent to the general capacity to "make things happen."

The "Innovation Strategy for Sweden" elucidated in Department Report 2004: 36 describes an antagonistic relationship between economic growth achieved through societal innovativeness and renewal, on the one side, and imitation and copying of other enterprises and nations, on the other (Department Report 2004: 36, p. 13). Permanent economic growth is considered possible only when one succeeds in "staying at the very front" and "leading the development" (Department Report 2004: 36, p. 13). Imitation of and satisfaction with the economic success achieved are defined as a position contrary to constant renewal. The push forward toward constant economic renewal through innovations and creativity is defined as the only possibility to achieve growth and maintain "welfare" and "employment" (e.g., Department Report 1999: 32; Government Bill 2001/2: 4; NUTEK 2003a). Activities performed by entrepreneurial subjects are conceived as constituents of the macro-level process of socio-economic renewal (Department Report 2004: 36, p. 24; NUTEK 2003a: 12). The reciprocity between entrepreneurial activities as the ethical substance of welfare imposes an imperative on general entrepreneurial culture since

> society [*space*] must to a higher extent than today [*time:* future] be characterized by positive attitudes to entrepreneurship [*adjuvant; subject:* entrepreneur] in all its different forms. More entrepreneurial individuals [*subject; object*], who see the possibility to contribute to societal development [*object; empty signifier*], are needed to create regional development [*space*: region; *object*]. It includes to an increasing extent, amongst other things, the mobilization [*technique*] of those possibilities that are created for innovation [*adjuvant; object*], development [*adjuvant*] and marketization [*adjuvant*] of new products, services, processes and cooperative solutions [*objects*]. (Government Bill 2001/02: 4, p. 187)

Developing an entrepreneurial culture symbolizes a means of global economic competition (cf. Department Report 2004: 36, p. 1). First, the observed transition toward the KBE requires flexible and innovative products and services. The innovative climate is interchangeable with an "entrepreneurial climate" that facilitates the attainment of innovative and flexible production (Department Report 1999: 32, p. 12; 2004: 36, pp. 1 and13). Second, an internationalized economy and intensification of competition make the consistent renewal of the national productions system an inevitable prerequisite of international competitiveness. The capacity to upgrade skills and sustain learning and innovativeness depends on the general socio-cultural attitudes toward development and renewal. Third, the capacity of the political government to achieve employment depends on the presence of adequate mentalities of societal actors and individuals, and, as such, adjustment to the KBE is also dependent on the "subjects' willingness and capacity to try something new" (Department Report 2004: 36, p. 13; cf. NUTEK 2003a: 10). Fourth, Sweden's transition to the KBE and to global competition is observed as potentially endangered by a too much restricted SME sector and entrepreneurship, a situation that could be improved by more business start-ups (NUTEK 2003a: 13).

These four points describe complex inter-dependencies and synergies observed to exist between the entrepreneur and the now increasingly decentralized political government of the economy. Entrepreneurial capacities and mindsets are not regarded as endemic to individuals but are observed to emerge from inter-subjective networks and cultural contexts embedding individuals (NUTEK 2003a: 12). The role of the political government is consequently to foster the emergence of entrepreneurship because while "[s]ome regions in Sweden have an environment characterized by the spirit of entrepreneurship others are weaker. A local culture characterized by the spirit of entrepreneurship emerges through synergies between different competencies and through mobility of the labor force between both regions and enterprises, and new entrepreneurship" (Government Bill 2001/02: 4, p. 68). In other words, the entrepreneur is no natural and biologically determined being of the self but the contingent result of certain beneficial socio-cultural contexts. In other words, entrepreneur denotes a generally accessible and possible individual character, and, as such, entrepreneurial conduct can be assumed to become a general "driving force in every citizen's work, in society and leisure time" (Department Report 2004: 36, p. 13; Government Bill 2004/5: 2, chapter 12; e.g. NUTEK 2003a: 10, 12).

If the competitiveness of enterprises depends on their endemic capacities for innovation and learning, and if such capacities emerge from below through the development of individual subjects, the political government is correspondingly required to provide spatial conditions in which entrepreneurs may evolve (cf. NUTEK 2003a: 11; SOU 2000: 87, pp. 294, 302). Such conditions cannot be any circumstances whatsoever but must be consistent with the epistemology on socio-economic and cultural circumstances that constitute the positive "climate of entrepreneurship." The political government is involved in supporting entrepreneurship through the institution of a good "climate of entrepreneurship," which is observed as necessary resources in the general political aspiration to "create good conditions of growth in society" (Government Bill 2001/02: 100, chapter 31). Two of the most important factors supporting entrepreneurship are the attractiveness of local environments for the subjects' willingness to live and engage in their immediate environment, and the presence of local cultures that foster innovativeness and creativity (NUTEK 2003a). The social-democratic government defines the positive entrepreneurial climate in terms of attractiveness of localities, intensity of societal participation, cooperation and commitment, and identification with local projects and initiatives (cf. Government Bill 2001/02: 4; NUTEK 2003a: 27).[9] However, there is no general model of how to create a flourishing local and regional entrepreneurial climate because the economic

[a]ttractiveness [of location] is based upon unique conditions [*adjuvant*] that are difficult to copy. Important features are established networks [*adjuvant*], patterns of cooperation [*adjuvant*], attitudes [*adjuvant*] and the capacity of the people to gather round visions and solve problems [*adjuvant; subject:* all]. (Department Report 2004: 36, p. 22)

The quality of the social climate can be either evaluated a posteriori with regard to the number of new enterprises started or, also, with regard to the attitudes of social subjects—for instance, whether they see entrepreneurship "as an equally interesting and possible alternative to that of regular employment" (NUTEK 2003a: 11). An example of the aspiration to measure the entrepreneurial culture is the "Entrepreneurship Barometer," which, for the first time in 2000, measured the extent to which social subjects considered self-employment and business start-up as possible individual projects (NUTEK 2003b). Government Bill 2004/5: 2, as well as policy papers on entrepreneurial school education, emphasize the dual function of school education to both impinge and realize entrepreneurial attitudes and values. In the evaluation of attitudes to entrepreneurship, a survey among the group of 18- to 30-year-olds discovered that more than 71% of those interviewed considered an own enterprise or self-employment as a possible future alternative. Yet, only 11% were actually active as entrepreneurs (cf. Department Report 2004: 36, p. 40; Government Bill 2004/5: 2, chapter 13; NUTEK 2003a). The discrepancy between the extent of entrepreneurial attitudes and activities was problematized as a result of a non-optimal entrepreneurial climate (NUTEK 2005: 11ff).

Another instrument applied to measure and evaluate the "entrepreneurial" quality of local and regional spaces was a SIMPLEX measure initiated by the social-democratic government, which evaluated the impact of new government bills and regulations on smaller enterprises (Department Report 1999: 32, p. 6; Government Bill 2001/02: 100, chapter 31). Also, various information campaigns and public services, such as the "Enterprise Guide," an internet platform that provided actual and potential entrepreneurs with information about legislation, rules, services, actors, and sources of capital, served the purpose of improving the entrepreneurial climate (Government Bill 2001/02: 100, chapter 31). Likewise, measures to adjust the practices of public administration to processes of innovation and growth drew their rationality from the conception of the qualities demanded by the "entrepreneurial free space" (Department Report 2004: 36, p. 32; NUTEK 2003a: 11). Moreover, the social-democratic government also found it necessary to facilitate the access to entrepreneurship by improving, for instance, cultural minorities' information about the possibilities of business start-ups (Government Bill 1999/2000: 1). It must become possible for new social groups to see themselves as initiators of new enterprises (Government Bill 2001/2: 4, p. 160). Also, information campaigns such as "Cooperative Entrepreneurship"[10] bear witness to the general aspiration to realize a society of entrepreneurs, in which the societal participation in the role of the entrepreneur is open to all individuals.

The diversity of measures, strategies, and instruments installed to generate local and regional "entrepreneurial climates" bears witness to the increasingly generalized meanings and functions of entrepreneurs. Individual capacity to entrepreneurship became a generally appreciated social capital because, and as the NUTEK report (2003a: 6) argues,

[e]ntrepreneurial activities [*adjuvant*] and entrepreneurship [*adjuvant*] are not only important from the economic perspective. They are equally important in terms of innovativeness [*objects*] in other parts of the society [*receiver*: society], for example in the public sector [*object*], social activities [*object*], the social economy [*object*] and the school sector [*object*].

In other words, entrepreneurial individuals are now needed in all social sectors, not least because entrepreneurial subjects are expected to induce innovations in the contexts of their interaction (NUTEK 2005: 10). The entrepreneur's generic cognitive mindset,, creativity, capacity to solve problems, preparedness to take responsibilities, and his or her capacity to take initiatives are observed as necessary for individuals who start enterprises, but these qualities are also required for realizing the general political objective to "renew society" (NUTEK 2005: 11). The general impetus that appears to have generated the demand for more entrepreneurship within an increasing number of social contexts was the observed inter-dependence between "welfare" and "renewal" (e.g., Government Bill 2004/5: 2). This hegemonization of entrepreneurs to a dominant social subjectivity was supported by the imagined future transition to a knowledge-intensive mode of production. The KBE was associated with demands for a "stronger basis of knowledge," "innovative business life," "knowledge-intensive entrepreneurship," an "innovative public sector," "stimulation of subjects," "initiatives," and the "economic utilization of personal competence" (Department Report 2004: 36; Government Bills 1997/98: 16, p. 46; 2001/02: 2 and 4; 2004/05: 1D1; NUTEK 2003a;). Moreover, the expected intensification of international economic competition was understood to require an ever better capacity to "utilize the chances of globalization" (Department Report 2004: 36, p. 23; cf. Government Bill 2004/05: 2, chapter 12). Entrepreneur was observed to be the subjectivity that, due to its inner drive to creativity and innovativeness, would generate new enterprises, new products, and new ways of organizing economic and social activities (NUTEK 2003, pp. 6, 10, 13f; Government Bill 2004/05: 2).

An essential discursive change in the social-democratic discourse between 1998 and 2004 concerns the composure of the entrepreneur. The largely economic connotation of entrepreneurship has begun to dissolve steadily and to denote the general innovative, societally committed, and renewal-inducing social subjects (e.g., NUTEK 2005: 11). Entrepreneur is "an individual who utilizes, identifies and develops ideas and innovations within all parts of society in a way that makes enterprises emerge and develop" (NUTEK 2003a: 12). This dissolution of the specificity of the entrepreneur indicates that earlier entrepreneurial activity coinciding usually with the business start-up becomes de-differentiated, since there is no clear location, functional differentiation, or limits of activity for the entrepreneur. In the

Table 8.1 Social-Democratic Growth Policy for the KBE

Discourse Formation A: Social Democratic Discourse 1998–2004
Full-Employment/Welfare Society (Es)

l/=

(---) Economic Renewal (Np)	l/=	Knowledge Nation (Np)	l/=	Entrepreneurial Climate (Np)	l/=	KBE (Np) (---)
					l/=	
A (px.) (---) Construction of Economic Clusters/Innovative Business Sector/ Consensual Economic Visions (technique)/Social Entrepreneurs (subject)	l/=	Regional Growth Agreements (technique)/Local Partnerships & Networks (adjuvant)/ Entrepreneurial Individuals (subject)	l/=	Knowledge-Intensive Enterprises (subject)/ Innovative Economic Climate/ Capacity to Learning (adjuvant)/ SIMPLEX (technique)	l/=	Mobilization of individual (---) and Organizational Competences/ Development of Competencies (technique)/ Innovative Individuals (subjects)
l/=		l/=		l/=		l/=
A (eth.) (---) Knowledge-Based Economy (object)	l/=	Efficient Utilization of Societal Entrepreneurship (object)	l/=	International Economic Competitiveness/Local & Regional Attractiveness for Investments (object)	l/=	Extension of Knowledge- (---) Based Production/Knowledge Society (object)

(---) Low-Wage Mass-Production (Np) l/= Stagnation (Np) (---)

l/=

Unemployment (Es)

Discourse Formation B: The Antagonistic Other

Abbreviations/ Symbols:

Difference	l	A (px.):	Level of Practices in Discourse Formation A (techniques; subjectivities; adjuvants; receivers)
Equivalence	=	A (eth.):	Ethical substance of Objects of Desires in Discourse Formation A
Antagonism	.....	B (px.):	Level of Practices in Discourse Formation B (inadmissible techniques; traitors)
Empty Signifier	(Es)	B (eth.):	Ethical substance: Inadmissible Consequences of the Discourse Formation B
Nodal Point	(Np)	(. . .):	Continued Relations of Difference/Equivalence

framework of the regional growth plans and local initiatives to improve the "entrepreneurial climate," entrepreneur transcended from business starters to denote network entrepreneurs, participants of local and regional growth plans, and subjects who pursue problem solutions and induce renewal. The equal importance, and—expressed in discourse-theoretical terms—their mutual "equivalence" originated from the conception that all these types of entrepreneurship supported the social renewal, optimal utilization of resources, and economic competitiveness related with it and, in the end, sustained social welfare (cf. NUTEK 2007: 3, 12).

Table 8.1 summarizes the system of discourse elucidated in this section. A characteristic feature of the social-democratic discourse on economic growth after 1998 appears to be the absence of a differentiated antagonistic other. The relation of negativity is based on the relation of contrariety between "welfare society" and "unemployment" in the KBE, whereas lacking adjustment of the economy to knowledge-intensive production and the lacking knowledge society are defined as potential origins of the deteriorating welfare and employment. Entrepreneur appears as a general mode of subjectivity, which in its multiple roles as "social entrepreneur," "entrepreneurial individual," and "innovative subject" realizes the ethical substance of the "welfare society."

EDUCATION IN THE KNOWLEDGE SOCIETY

Alongside the regional growth policies, discursive changes within the educational system constitute another source of the de-differentiation of entrepreneur from a business starter to a general role model of the creative subject. In close similarity to the regional industrial and economic policy, the KBE appears as the "destinator" that induces unprecedented demands for development of the knowledge society in which the mobilization of people's initiatives and incentives toward learning becomes increasingly important for attaining national objectives of employment, growth, and welfare (Government Bill 2004/05: 1D18). There is an obvious similarity between the two lines of argumentation of "active social contract" (see Chapter 7) and the demand to conduct oneself as a participant of the knowledge society. In the imagined KBE, knowledge and creative social capital are observed to become necessary conditions for participation in working life. Therefore, the possession of appropriate knowledge appears essential for achieving the national objectives of growth and employment (cf. Government Communication 2001/02: 188, p. 5). Government Communication 2001/02: 188 (p. 55) points out the relationship of inter-dependence between the successful transition into the KBE and the knowledge society, arguing that "[i]n order to continuously develop as a knowledge nation, more individuals must be stimulated to participate in different forms of learning" in Sweden.

The imperative of the transition to a knowledge society is observed to be ineluctable in the context of "globalization" and global competition, which exert constant pressure to increasing international economic competitiveness (cf. Department Report 2002: 47, p. 49). Even though the general intention of the social-democratic government has remained connected to the "utilization of the development potential in entire country." the expected turn to knowledge-intensive production induces new forms of demands for the subjects if the social-democratic government is to realize the ethical substance of a "nation of growth and welfare" (Department Report 2003: 43). While the earlier "active social contract" emphasized the necessity of general consent to the political government within the imagined interdependence of "welfare," "growth," and "knowledge-intensive production"; the general consent is now replaced by an "active" consensual participation as subjects who actively improve their own human capital and as a result on the aggregate level improve the general national "competitiveness":

People's knowledge and competence [*adjuvant; subject:* all], the human capital [*adjuvant*], is the most important factor of production [*object:* production] and therefore decisive for economic growth [*object*]. Technological change [*object*], with increasing complexity and specialization [*space:* differentiated economy; *time:* change; *destinator:* econ. epistemology], in combination with the expansion of service sector production [*space:* service economy; *time:* change] has increased the demands to *knowledge* [*technique*], *competence* [*technique*], and *flexibility* [*technique*]. For a country's competitiveness [*object; ethical substance*] it is therefore crucial to ensure that the population has a high level of education [*adjuvant:* of competitiveness] and a *well developed spirit of entrepreneurship* [*adjuvant:* of competitiveness]. (Government Bill 2001/02: 2, chapter 5, italics added)

As the previous quotation illustrates, the conduct of the self as a subject of reproduction and improvement of individual social capital is connected with the capacity to achieve national political goals of economic growth and competitiveness (Government Communication 2001/02: 188). Therefore, the conduct of government requires the presence of individual aspirations to develop oneself and conduct individual learning (Department Report 2002: 47, p. 7). The social-democratic government expected the inclusion in the future working life to require quite different competences than had been the case before. Therefore, rational conduct of government interested in the sustainment of a high level of employment involved the utilization, mobilization, and improvement of the competences of the entire population (Government Bill 2003/04: 1). In light of the unprecedented focus on the development of competence, it is hardly surprising that the education system attains a central role in accommodating the individual and collective ethical objectives. One example of this is that school education is not only a provider of formal skills but is also an institution that is trusted to generate appropriate attitudes toward personal learning:

> Education [*adjuvant:* of subjects] shall promote thirst for knowledge [*object; receiver:* people], creativity [*object; receiver:* people] and critical thinking [*object; receiver:* people], give pupils [*receiver; subject*] the possibility to personal development [*object*] and provide good basic knowledge [*adjuvant*] required in further studies, work and participation in society [*object:* processual competence; inclusion]. (Government Bill 2003/04: 1, p. 33)

The observed demand for consistent personal learning is above all related to the observation of future occupations being to an ever increasing extent located within "learning organizations" (Government Communication 1996/97: 112, p. 12). Preparedness to learn and willingness to develop oneself become generic skills and competencies (Government Communication 1996/97: 112, p. 8). General positive attitudes toward personal "learning" become the criteria of inclusion into the KBE (Government Communication 1996/97: 112, p. 8). It is also observed that, due to the individual nature of learning and because of the rapidly changing working life, school education cannot provide qualifications that will outlast the entire course of one's working life (Department Report 1997: 78, p. 16f; Government Communication 1996/97: 112). Therefore, the reproduction of sufficient skills and competencies becomes increasingly the responsibility of individual subjects (Department Report 1997: 78; Government Communication 1996/97: 112, p. 15). Moreover, the expected transition to the KBE is associated with "increasing competence requirements on each employee" (Government Communication 1996/97: 112, p. 12). New demands imposed by the KBE consist, above all, of intensification and expansion of the knowledge content in production, shorter, more flexible, and customized production series, expansion of the service sector, increasing demands to communicative skills, and social competence of the labor force (Department Report 2000: 62; Government Communication 1996/97: 112, p. 12; SOU 1997: 121, p. 250).

The introduction of ideas about "entrepreneurial education" and education in entrepreneurship is located in this general context of unprecedented and largely individually harnessed demands imposed by the KBE. "Entrepreneurship" is, in this context, associated with a generic skill and a processual competence required if subjects are to deal with unprecedented demands of the knowledge-intensive economy.[11] An education system adapted to the demands of the KBE must generate entrepreneurial competencies since entrepreneurship is observed as a generic competence required in competitive enterprises (Department Report 2000: 62, p.76; SOU 2000: 28, p. 150; cf. Government Communication 1996/97: 112, p. 15).

Working life changes ever faster [*destinator*]. The OECD [*destinator*] has presented a study on employment that shows that every year, 10% new occupations evolve with demands to higher qualifications, at the same time as unqualified tasks, above all in industrial production, disappear [*destinator*: work; *Time*: consistent change; *consequence*: working life change]. The development points towards the need of interdisciplinary competences [*adjuvant*: of people]. In this perspective, there is a need for a flexible secondary school education [*adjuvant*: of people] that changes concurrently with the development [*object*: adjust to change]. (Government Bill 1995/96: 206, chapter 8)

As the prior quotation illustrates, school education must adapt to general societal change and provide all citizens with competencies that adjust personal qualifications to the technological and organizational changes in the economy (Government Communication 1996/97: 112). The "destinator" appears to be the observed and pre-supposedly inevitable changes in the economy and the parallel transformation of the working life, which impose "increasing demands on the employees' disposition to change, to quality consciousness and the capacity to adopt comprehensive points of view and observation of processes" (Government Bill 1995/96: 145, chapter 4).

The primary logic behind the inevitably of the adjustment is the rejection of the political alternative to sustain international economic competitiveness through low-cost mass production due to its incompatibility with the imagined welfare society (Government Communication 1996/97: 112). Only knowledge and innovation-intensive production is observed to sustain an appropriate level of welfare. In other words, in order to support the attainment and maintenance of the welfare society, the educational system must "create possibilities for a personal development of skills" that increase the personal competitiveness of individuals (cf. Government Communication 1996/97: 112, p. 15). The personal competitiveness depends, among other things, on capacities to "problem solution, critical and creative thinking, adjustment to new situations and problems, the competence to negotiate and competence to team-work" (Government Bill 1995/96: 206, chapter 4). These capacities are observed to characterize entrepreneurs, and, moreover, it is expected that an increasing number of persons will be active in future in entrepreneurship-like activities:

As a preparation for such a development [*technique*: adaption to future], for example in order to be able to start and manage an enterprise [*object; subject*: entrepreneur], a specific subset of competences and skills [*adjuvant*: entrepreneurial skills] are required. Therefore, there is a need to direct the education programs of the secondary school towards entrepreneurship [*technique*: education; *object*: entrepreneurial competences; *adjuvant*: schools]. (Government Communication 1996/97: 112, p. 70)

The definition of entrepreneurship as a generic competence is supported by the observation of two changes in working life. First, there is an observation of the increasing dedifferentiation of work, employment, and forms of labor market participation (Department Report 1997: 78; SOU 1997: 121). This differentiation can be described appropriately in terms of "dissolution" of work. Government Communication 1996/97: 112 notices a consistent development toward more people working as entrepreneurs or participants of project and team work. Entrepreneurial competence is regarded as a key asset in the differentiated future working life in which regular employment is but one possible form of work (Department Report 1997: 78, p. 90). Second, and aligned to the first change, an entrepreneurial subject is not restricted to a differential-functional position since capacities, skills, cognitive mindsets, and attitudes characteristic of entrepreneurs are appreciated as new socio-economic roles and functions. The entrepreneurial subject becomes dislocated, de-differentiated, and consequently universalized through the inclusion of "entrepreneurial characteristics" into a set of characteristics necessary for all citizens in the KBE. In other words, within the general imaginary of the KBE, entrepreneur turns into a role model of the creative subject. In the manner of a nodal point, entrepreneur now appears to function as a condensing point of reference that unifies and, at the same time, over-determines different competencies and individual skills, such as "creativity," "sense of responsibility," and "capacity to co-operate" (SOU 1997: 121, p. 250; cf. SOU 2000: 28, p. 45). The notion of the entrepreneur as a nodal point in the late social-democratic discourse is manifested in relations of equivalence that appear between skills such as the "capacity to obtain a comprehensive view," "capacity to take responsibility for planning and exercise in various tasks," "leadership of the self," "development-mindedness," "disposition to learning," "creativity," and "capacity to problem solving" (SOU 2000: 28, p. 45).

Entrepreneurship is also seen as a definite way of conduct of the self that becomes manifested well with regard to the concept of learning. The capacity to learn is a central competence demanded from the subjects of the knowledge society, and, interestingly enough, learning is understood as an *intra-individual* capacity based on a certain emotional and cognitive composition of the self (Department Report 2000: 62, p. 240; SOU 1999: 141). The idea of learning as "knowledge creation"—"kunskapande"—defines knowledge as an emergent property that "is regarded as something that 'resides in-between' the individual and the environment" (SOU 2000: 19, p. 139; cf. SOU 1999: 93, p. 100). This notion of learning as the "creation" of something new pre-supposes the presence of attitudes and kinds of preparedness and motivations necessary for creativity. Learning becomes largely individualized and supported by the education system, which yet cannot replace the individual's responsibility for learning (SOU 1999: 141, p. 70). For instance, the Conservative Party argues that the "individual subject must be put in the focus of a completely different way than is the case today" in the education system (Motion 2000/01: UB260). Schools are therefore not only asked to provide standardized skills but also to generate individual creativity supporting mindsets (cf. Government Bill 2000/01: 72). What must be supported is the subjects' "faith in their own capacity and will to develop" (Government Bill 2000/01: 72, chapter 6). Interestingly enough, a parallel is drawn between being a creative subject and being an entrepreneur, which is well described in the following quotation from SOU 1997: 40 (p. 90):

> Schools [*adjuvant*] must to a greater extent than today [*time*: future] prepare pupils [*subject; receiver*] for their own entrepreneurship [*object; subject*: entrepreneur]. All programs in the secondary school [*adjuvant*] shall develop the creative capacity [*object; subject*: entrepreneur] and spirit of entrepreneurship [*object; subject*: entrepreneur]. School education [*adjuvant*] must encourage pupils' [*subject; receiver*] commitment to school enterprises [*consequence*], school cooperatives and similar activities [*object*: entrepreneurs] by integrating these activities as natural constituents of their work [*adjuvant*: conceived normality of entrepreneurship].

The previous quotation illustrates how the normalization of "entrepreneurial education" at school is supported by the observation of the general socio-cultural benefits of knowledge on how to start-up and manage an enterprise. As Department Report 1997: 78 (p. 16, cf. NUTEK 2003b: 35) argues, entrepreneurial competences

> are not only qualities needed by an individual [*subject*] who starts an enterprise [*object; subject*: entrepreneur]. They are also competencies [*adjuvant; receiver*: people] that are required for the development of an activity within an enterprise or organization [*object*], for example, competence to '*get something done*' [*object*] and *take self-initiative to solve problems* [*object*]. (Department Report 1997: 78, p. 16, italics added)

The meta-narrative that constitutes the imperative to learning is located in the conception of the knowledge society as the socio-cultural equivalent of the KBE. It is imagined that social capital demanded in working life in the future KBE bears remarkable resemblance with entrepreneurial skills such as readiness to take initiatives, creativity, bravery, and personal preparedness to continuous learning (NUTEK 2003b: 51ff). When these competencies are defined as the outcomes of "intra-subjective" cognitive and attitudinal stance, the education system should teach individuals the general social value of being creative. The imperative to be a creative, learning, and entrepreneurial subject is supported by the general hegemonic project of the social-democratic government to maintain the future competitiveness of the Swedish economy, and hence also the level of employment, by mobilizing the innovative and creative social capital. As NUTEK (2003b: 51) argues, the capacity of the political government to attain competitiveness is contingent on individual subjects' investments in their own capacity to entrepreneurship. Therefore, it is

> important that in a *knowledge society* [*space*; *object*] all [*receiver*: all; *subject*: people] are educated [*technique*: education] to have the possibility to train, experience and be confronted with the distinctive character of entrepreneurship [*adjuvant*: entrepreneurial skills]. However, this is not in the first instance for individuals to become entrepreneurs. In contrast, everybody should be given the sense and understanding of what entrepreneurship may be [*adjuvant*: entrepreneurial competence] in order to experience the driving force of entrepreneurship in a *knowledge society* [*object*: knowledge society]. (NUTEK 2003b: 51, italics added)

As the prior quotation illustrates, entrepreneurship is both the "engine" in the development of the society toward a knowledge society and the general competence and capacity of individual subjects within the knowledge society. This discursive system includes ethical principles (*competitiveness, welfare, work*), knowledge of the ontological foundations of learning (*individual, cognition, attitudes*), assumption of the knowledge society to constitute the socio-cultural foundation of the KBE, and knowledge that the entrepreneurial spirit of subjects is possible to mobilize by means of right institutions, which together ascribe the entrepreneurial educational a remarkable and unprecedented social importance. After all, entrepreneurial education is trusted to facilitate the establishment of the highly idealized knowledge society by means of teaching subjects the "joy to do," "fantasy," "motivations," and "knowledge theoretical curiosity" (NUTEK 2003b: 55).

The so far described social-democratic idea of the micro-macro link between learning to be creative and the competitiveness promoting knowledge society can be further illustrated with regard to the "Municipal Entrepreneur and Technique School" [*Kommunala Entreprenör—och Teknikskolan*] (KomTek) initiated in 2003 (NUTEK 2003b, 2009). KomTek complements the institutions of formal education, and, similar to the school education in entrepreneurship, it is also expected to inspire the creativity among children and youth, something that is believed to increase the future level of economic growth further (SOU 2001: 44, p. 29). The key idea behind KomTek was to enable interaction between social subjects in general and the societal actors engaged in technique and entrepreneurship, such as teachers, parents, innovators, entrepreneurs, and municipal officials. This network would make "a complement for learning at schools and in working life [and] . . . provide comprehensive technical knowledge and lust and capacity to entrepreneurship" (NUTEK 2009). In general, the "profanation" and universalization of the culture of enterprise supported by KomTek was expected to result in more innovations, improved commercialization of ideas, new enterprises, increased employment, and growth (cf. Answer on a Written Question 2001/02: 1259; 2003/04: 1037; NUTEK 2003a).

This chapter has so far described the intersections among the imaginary of the KBE, the knowledge society as its socio-cultural foundation, the changing role of school education as the adjuvant of the culture of enterprise, and the observed inter-dependence between the sustained welfare and the individual subjects' entrepreneurial conduct of themselves. The observation of the reciprocal connection between the KBE and the knowledge society seems to have supported the recognition of the further relation of inter-dependence between the entrepreneurial conduct of the self and the collective capacity to sustain the pace of development in the global economy (Government Bill 2000/01: 72; NUTEK 2003b: 37). In other words, the importance of entrepreneurial subjects in general, and hence also of the universalization of the culture of enterprise, derives from the observed reciprocity between the social aggregation of entrepreneurial competences and the extent of economic competitiveness within the KBE. In the social-democratic discourse entrepreneur developed to a hegemonic mode of subjectivity, which is also shown by the previously described function of the entrepreneur as a "nodal point." After all, being entrepreneurial became a synonym for "capacity to take initiatives," "faith in personal capacity," "creativity," "competence to problem solution," and "preparedness to take responsibility" (Government Bill 2004/05: 1D18, chapter 6; cf. NUTEK 2005: 11). At a closer look, there appear altogether three different "entrepreneurial functions" within the social-democratic discourse as described earlier. First, one function of the entrepreneur subject is to conduct him or herself as a learning subject who habitually adjusts his or her personal human capital to sustain its demand within working life. Second, the entrepreneur also symbolizes a creative and innovative subject whose cognitive and attitudinal assets make it flexibly adjustable to the demands imposed by working life within the KBE. Governmental documents observe the youth to possess creative, initiative-driven, and culturally open mindsets. Younger people are considered to have attitudes that contradict the traditional societal norms of regular employment. This has motivated the design of socio-political measures that fostered subjective creativity and will to personal self-fulfillment (e.g., Government Bill 1998/99: 115, p. 8ff; NUTEK 2003b: 9). Third, the entrepreneur is also the subject who observes self-employment and business start-up as chances to evolve his or her individual interests of self-fulfillment.

Table 8.2 summarizes the empirical findings presented earlier. A noteworthy feature is the maintained ethical substance of "full employment" and "welfare society," in the name of which entrepreneurial education was implemented. There is also a maintained antagonistic relation between the desired "welfare society," which appears to have the function as an empty signifier, and "low-wage economic competitiveness" and "mass production," which symbolize the insufficient techniques to sustain the welfare society in the context of the KBE.

Table 8.2 Social-Democratic Discourse on Education in the KBE

Discourse Formation B: Social Democratic Discourse 1998–2004

Full-Employment/Welfare Society (Es)

(---) Economic Renewal (Np) l/= Knowledge Nation (Np) l/= Entrepreneurial Climate (Np) l/= KBE (Np) (---)

|= |= |= |=

A (px.) (---)   Mobilization of Personal Learning/Individualization of Education/Entrepreneurial Education (technique)   l/=   Transition from 'Formal' to 'Informal Learning'/New Secondary School/KomTek (technique)   l/=   Dissemination of Entrepreneurial Skills/New Secondary School (technique)/The Learning Subject (subject)   l/=   Adaption of Education System to KBE/School-Business Partnerships (technique)   (---)

|= |= |= |=

A (eth.) (---)   Life-Long Learning/Personal Working-Life Competitiveness (object)   l/=   Culture of Learning/'Kunskapande'/Spirit of Entrepreneurship (object)   l/=   International Economic Competitiveness (object)   l/=   Accumulation of Social Capital for the KBE/Knowledge based Production (object)   (---)

|=

(---) Low-Wage Mass-Production (NP) l/= Relative Economic Stagnation (Np) (---)

Unemployment (Es)

Discourse Formation B: The Antagonistic Other

Abbreviations/ Symbols:

Difference	l	A (px.): Level of Practices in Discourse Formation A (techniques; subjectivities; adjuvants; receivers)
Equivalence	=	A (eth.): Ethical substance of Objects of Desires in Discourse Formation A
Antagonism	.....	B (px.): Level of Practices in Discourse Formation B (inadmissible techniques; traitors)
Empty Signifier	(Es)	B (eth.): Ethical substance: Inadmissible Consequences of the Discourse Formation B
Nodal Point	(Np)	(. . .): Continued Relations of Difference/Equivalence

POLITICAL HEGEMONY OF THE CULTURE OF ENTERPRISE

This concluding section relates the hegemonization of the culture of enterprise advanced by the social-democratic government so far to the general tendencies within Swedish politics after 1998. The various objectives to achieve "an innovative Sweden," to establish a "wider knowledge base," to increase the number of "innovative businesses," to install an "innovative public sector," and to improve the "innovativeness of people" stand in a relation of analogy as particular steps of development toward a knowledge-intensive economy (cf. Department Report 2004: 36, p. 13; Government Bill 2004/05: 1D1 and 175). Within this hegemonic imaginary, entrepreneur became the *popular* mode of subjectivity—that is, the role mode of subjectivity as such (see Chapters 2 and 9; cf. Parliamentary Minutes 2003/04: 96, remark 1; 2004/05: 79). The popular construction of the entrepreneur is reflected, among other things, in the general socio-cultural imperative of more creative and innovative individuals (Parliamentary Minutes 2003/04: 2 and 5, remarks 2, 6, 7). The following statement by Prime Minister Persson is illustrative of the society-wide imperative of creativity defined in analogy to entrepreneurship:

> Ultimately, growth [*object*] is the result of people's faith in the future [*subject*; *adjuvant*], the innovative entrepreneurs [*subject*] in socially coherent contexts [*space*: community],[12] the willingness of the majority of people to work [*adjuvant*] and the aspiration to develop and trespass boundaries [*adjuvant*]. (Parliamentary Minutes 2003/04: 2)

When economic growth is defined as an outcome of complex cultural, economic, social, and cognitive factors, the role of a *rational* political government is correspondingly curtailed to the systemic governance of the maintenance of a beneficial socio-cultural context for innovations and creativity. The following statement by the Minister of Finance is indicative of the new "systemic" nature of government (cf. Government Bill 2001/02: 100, p. 31).

> Growth [*object*] results from a complex and successful interaction between different factors [*destinator*: econ. epistemology; *adjuvant*], such as education [*adjuvant*], well-functioning social welfare [*adjuvant*] and public sector services [*adjuvant*], system of taxation and benefits [*adjuvant*], which encourage education [*adjuvant*] and work [*adjuvant*], good conditions of entrepreneurship [*object*; *adjuvant*], a good climate of social cooperation [*adjuvant*], and much more. (Parliamentary Minutes 2003/04: 96, remark 1)[13]

Within the systemic approach to political government, entrepreneur appears to have become both the *adjuvant*—which can be trusted to support the political government—as well as the *subject* who carries the responsibility for attaining the collective objectives of growth and welfare.

The central performative function of entrepreneur as an "adjuvant" of political government means that:[14]

> Sweden [*destinator*] needs more enterprises and more entrepreneurs [*object:*]. It is the entrepreneur [*subject*] that is the hope of us all [*receiver*] that require development [*object*] and change [*object*] in different areas. It is the entrepreneur [*subject*] who shall create the new [*consequence:* of entrepreneur] and solve problems [*consequence:* of entrepreneur] . . . It is the entrepreneur [*subject*] who makes the world a better place to live. (Parliamentary Minutes 2003/04: 121, remark 59)

This binary function of entrepreneur is present in the "National Program for Entrepreneurship" that was implemented for the first time in 2002–2004 and whose primary objective was to "create a better entrepreneurial climate, contribute to positive attitudes towards entrepreneurship and entrepreneurialism and increase the extent of entrepreneurship" (Government Bill 2001/02: 100, p. 31; cf. Department Report 2004: 36; Government Bills 2001/02: 4; 2004/05: 2, chapter 12, 1D1, and 1D18; ; NUTEK 2003a).

The prerequisite of the systemic governance by means of the entrepreneurial conduct of individual subjects, enterprises, and private as well as public organizations is that social actors are first observed to possess the required "will and capacity to try something new" (Department Report 2004: 36, pp. 13, 19). In other words, the popular construction of the entrepreneur as the role model of the (creative) subject was preceded by an epistemological change, which observed subjects to be essentially entrepreneurial, which as such made it possible to "utilize the individual's competence and capacity to take initiatives" (Department Report 2004: 36, p. 13; cf. Parliamentary Minutes 2003/04: 2; 2004/05: 79). This epistemological change has become more and more dominant in Swedish political discourse. Already around the mid-1990s, one of the first documents that expected the paradigmatic transition toward the KBE noticed that the "Capacity of innovation in the widest sense is a matter of singular individuals' or groups' ideas, initiative and creativity in all parts of the society" (Motion 1996/97: N242). The positive relation between the number of "entrepreneurial individuals" and from their entrepreneurship, emanating economic growth, and new occupations has been acknowledged by all political parties (cf. Parliamentary Minutes 2001/02: 103, remarks 25, 27, 28, 29, 30; 2003/04: 2; 2004/05: 79, remark 3). A representative of the Social-Democratic Party argued that, "I think *we all* agree that a good climate of enterprises is important for the preservation of the Swedish welfare society" (Parliamentary Minutes 2001/02: 103, remark 31, italics added).

There is also general political consensus that the imperative of more, more extended, and more differentiated forms of entrepreneurship is supported by the necessary future transition to an internationally competitive KBE. There is, for instance, wide political agreement that Sweden must become a "world-class knowledge nation" (Motion 2000/01: Ub260; cf. Parliamentary Minutes 2000/01: 45, remarks 132, 136, 175). The observed urgency to adapt to the KBE is, above all, motivated by the possible increase of employment. The ethical substance of employment as a constituent of the fullness of the social was acknowledged by the social-democratic government, which declared that fighting unemployment was the overarching objective. A few years later, the same priority was confirmed in Government Bill 2001/02: 1 (p. 28), which acclaimed that "[t]he best politics for increasing welfare is through increased employment. The economic policy is constantly aimed at full employment." The leading two ethical principles of employment and welfare have been acknowledged by other parties. The Conservative Party argues in this regard that "*Entrepreneurship is the engine of growth.* Politics that facilitates entrepreneurship increases the demand to the labor force and increases welfare" (Motion 1999/2000: N340; cf. Motion 2000/01: N385, italics added).[15] Moreover, different political parties also define the economic social-economic climate that generates growth as a context to facilitate and inspire mobilization, utilization of individual incentives, ideas, and creativity. Such a climate results in new enterprises and provides new occupations and increased welfare.[16] Political parties also agree on the observation of the reciprocal relation among individual learning, personal competence development, an aggregated level of creativity, and the level of economic competitiveness in the global economy (see Parliamentary Minutes 1999/00: 92, remarks 1, 182, 183, 185; Motion 1999/2000: N340; 2000/01: N385).[17]

Even though all political parties emphasize the importance of an optimal climate of entrepreneurship that "fosters new entrepreneurship and growth in existing enterprises," there are still different definitions about the constituents of the good climate of entrepreneurship (Department Report 2003: 62, p. 35). Differences between various political positions consist of conflicting standards, measures, and factors of the context supporting entrepreneurship.[18] As the following ensconce of the Conservative Party illustrates, the differences between the political positions concern the ensemble of techniques assumed to engender a beneficial "climate of entrepreneurship":

> Rigid rules [*traitor*] make entrepreneurship [*subject; receiver*] less profitable [*inadmissible consequence*]. We get less enterprises [*inadmissible consequence*], less growth [*inadmissible consequence*], less employment [*inadmissible consequence*] and less welfare [*inadmissible consequence; empty signifier:* welfare]; that will say everything that characterizes today's Sweden [*space; empty signifier:* welfare]. More generous rules generate [*adjuvant*] an opposite situation [*object:* growth; employment; welfare]. More individuals decide to become entrepreneurs [*object*]. We get more enterprises [*object*], enterprises that grow faster [*object*], increased employment [*object*] and, in the long run, faster growth [*object*]. (Parliamentary Minutes 2003/04: 51, remark 43)

Political dissonances do not question the performative role of the entrepreneur as such, but they disagree with the socio-economic context in which the endemic creativity and innovativeness of entrepreneurial subjects is best released (cf. Motion 1999/00: N340; Parliamentary Minutes 2003/04: 51, remarks 9 and 25; 121, remarks 19, 30, 50, 58, 59).[19] Instead, the political struggle is localized on the level of definitions of the appropriate definition of the beneficial "climate of entrepreneurship." On the ethical level of empty signifiers, it is agreed that only a good climate of entrepreneurship can generate social welfare (Parliamentary Minutes 2001/02: 103, remarks 28–31; 2004/05: 79, remark 9). On the level of techniques, strategies, programs, and maneuvers, political parties associate the "climate of entrepreneurship" with a heterogeneous configuration of factors, standards, qualities, and conditions that together constitute the socio-economic context facilitating growth and supporting welfare. Among these elements figure conditions of competition and consumption, level of competence, education of the labor force, level of research and innovations, taxation, quality of rules, legislation, and administrative structures (Government Communication 2004/05: 48; Memorandum 2002/03: Fi20, pp. 60–65; cf. Memorandum 2002/03: NU7).

An interesting feature of the debates about the optimal constitution of the climate of entrepreneurship is how different political parties position themselves as "true" contenders of the entrepreneurs and, as such, claim to represent the "true" needs and interests of entrepreneurs. A typical example in this regard is the remark of the Liberal Party that the social-democratic government has misconceived the sincere needs of the entrepreneur (cf. Parliamentary Minutes 1999/00: 92, remarks 182, 185).

> Entrepreneurship [*subject*] and SMEs [*subject*] play a crucial role in the offensive for sustainable growth [*strategy; object*] and increased employment [*object*] that the government [*destinator*] presented for the first time in Government Bill in 1998, and which has been followed up consistently [*time*: no change] in budget bills ever since. (Memorandum 2002/03: FiU20)

The Conservative Party claims that the "climate" is not a conceptual or definitional matter but a matter of the sincere needs and demands of entrepreneurs (Parliamentary Minutes 2001/02: 103, remark 44; 2004/05: 79, remark 18). The social-democratic representatives in the committee of finance respond to the liberal-conservative critique of the social-democratic government to reject the needs of the entrepreneurs, arguing now that

> Decisive for Sweden, for the growth [*object*] and employment [*object*], are high competitiveness [*adjuvant:* of growth] and a good climate of enterprises [*adjuvant:* of entrepreneur]. In contrast to what is argued in motions Fi14(m), Fi15(fp), Fi16(kd) and Fi17(c)[20] the committee regards

> [*destinator*] the general *climate for entrepreneurship* [*adjuvant*] expansion and higher employment as relatively good. (Memorandum 2002/03: Fi20, p. 60, italics added)

Whereas the social-democratic government focuses on taxation, rules, regulations, administrative costs, and risk-capital supply as the constituents of the good climate of entrepreneurship, the liberal and conservative parties set greater store by a decrease of administrative work-load, administrative burdens, general conditions of individual and economic freedom, and the general socio-cultural standing of entrepreneurs (Parliamentary Minutes 2001/02: 103; remarks 25, 27, 30, 31; 2003/04: 2; 14, remark 1).

An interesting aspect, which must as yet remain beyond further discussion, concerns the role of international institutions and benchmarking in measuring the entrepreneur-friendly political government. In Swedish political discourse, international standards and criteria of a beneficial climate of entrepreneurship appear as objective facts that enable a depoliticized determination of the necessary political measures to improve domestic economic competitiveness (e.g., Department Report 2003: 62). As a consequence, the political government's evaluations were based on objective measurements provided by international institutions on the rate of entrepreneurship, measuring the "growth potential" of the domestic economic system and international comparisons of the administrative costs of SMEs (cf. Parliamentary Minutes 2001/02: 103, remarks 44 and 45; 2004/05: 79, remark 11). For instance, national efforts to simplify rules through the SIMPLEX function have the Simpler Legislation on the International Market (SLIM) as their role model, which was implemented by the European Commission in 1996 (cf. NUTEK 2003a).[21] Moreover, OECD surveys, evaluations, and country studies are accepted as objective benchmarks for the national political government in its efforts to reduce administrative costs of SMEs and expand the sector of SEs and SMEs (cf. Government Bill 1999/00: 140, p. 65; Government Communication 2002/03: 8, p. 3ff; NUTEK 2003a; SOU 1997: 186). International surveys and ratings foster the domestic debate by providing different indications of the "climate of entrepreneurship," and as such, international standards and objective indicators are imposed from outside, which sustain different political positions. An example of the politicized function of standards is the argument posited by the Center Party:

> In its budget bill, the government [*traitor*] wrote that we have had increasing entrepreneurship [*object*] during a number of consequent years. I argue that this is not true, and it depends on the statistic measures upon which the facts presented by the bill were based. . . . We have a poor climate of entrepreneurship [*traitor; inadmissible consequence*] in Sweden. (Parliamentary Minutes 2003/04: 14, remark 1)

Table 8.3   Discursive Construction of the Entrepreneur 1998–2004

Discourse Formation A: Social-Democratic Discourse 1998–2004

Full-Employment l/= Welfare Society (Es)

(---) Economic Renewal (Np) l/= Entrepreneurial Climate (Np)   l/=   l/=   Knowledge Nation (NP) l/= KBE (Np) (---)

A (px.) (---)	Construction of Economic Clusters/Innovative Business Sector/ Consensual Economic Visions (technique)/Social Entrepreneurial Individuals (subject)	l/= Regional Growth Agreements (technique)/ Local Partnerships & Networks (adjuvant)/ Entrepreneurial Individuals (subject)	l/= Knowledge Intensive Enter-prises (subject)/ Innovative Economic Climate (adjuvant)/ Capacity to Learning (adjuvant)/ SIMPLEX (technique)	l/= Mobilisation of individ-ual and Organisational Competences/ Develop-ment of Competencies (technique)/ Innovative Individuals (subject)	l/= Mobilization of Personal Learning/ Individualisation of Education/ Entrepreneurial Education (tech-nique)	l/= Transition from 'Formal' to 'Informal' Learning'/ New Secondary School/KomTek (technique)	l/= Dissemination of Entrepreneurial Skills/New Sec-ondary School (technique)	l/= Up-Dating of the Education System to the KBE/ School-Economy Partnerships (technique) (---)
	l/=	l/=	l/=	l/=	l/=	l/=	l/=	l/=
A (eth.) (---)	Knowledge-Based Economy (object)	l/= Efficient Utiliza-tion of Societal Entrepreneurship (object)	l/= International Economic Competitiveness/ Local & Regional Attractive-ness for Investments (object)	l/= Extension of Knowledge-Based Production/A Knowl-edge Society (object)	l/= Life-Long Learn-ing/Personal Working-Life Competitiveness (object)	l/= Culture of Learn-ing/'Kunska-pande'/ Spirit of Entrepreneurship (object)	l/= International Economic Competitiveness (object)	l/= Accumulation of Social Capital for the KBE/ Knowledge-Based Production (object) (---)

. . . .

(---) Low-Wage Mass-Production (Np)   Stagnation (Np) (---)

l/=
l/=
l/=

Unemployment (Es)

Discourse Formation B: The Antagonistic Other of the Social-Democratic Discourse

Abbreviations/Symbols:

Difference	l	A (px.): Level of Practices in Discourse Formation A (techniques; subjectivities; adjuvants; receivers)
Equivalence	=	A (eth.): Ethical substance of Objects of Desires in Discourse Formation A
Antagonism	....	B (px.): Level of Practices in Discourse Formation B (inadmissible techniques; traitors)
Empty Signifier	(Es)	B (eth.): Ethical substance: Inadmissible Consequences of the Discourse Formation B
Nodal Point	(Np)	(. . .): Continued Relations of Difference/Equivalence

Despite the seemingly different ideas about the essential socio-cultural, legal, economic, and bureaucratic conditions that best benefit entrepreneurial conduct, Swedish political discourse is still characterized by a remarkable consensus that future welfare depends on the subjects' entrepreneurial conduct of themselves. Moreover, there seem to be no limits to contexts, situations, and social sectors in which entrepreneurship would not be needed. Table 8.3 provides a snap-shot view of the discursive order evolving between 1997 and 2004, which, in terms of Gordon (1991: 42), enabled the hegemonization of the culture of enterprise by diffusing "the enterprise form throughout the social fabric" until society itself became "a range of different enterprises." As indicated in Tables 8.1 and 8.2, the primary antagonistic relation exists between the "welfare" (society) and "unemployment." Moreover, and this is arguably the discursive dislocation of the earlier social-democratic discourse, the maintenance of welfare has now become equivalent to the attainment of the internationally competitive KBE. Social-democratic imaginary articulates the presence of a knowledge society, where entrepreneurship has become a natural role of all social subjects, as a pre-condition of the KBE. At this stage of the entrepreneur's development, the being of the entrepreneur is located within numerous social activities, entrepreneurship now being a societal rather than an economic phenomenon.

9   The Specters of Entrepreneurship

This account has analyzed the genealogy of the discursive construction of the entrepreneur in Swedish political discourse between 1991 and 2004. The point of departure as presented in Chapter 3 suggested that subject forms consist of heterogeneous bundles of social practices, identities, ethos of the self, and so on, and that these, again, must be considered the outcomes of different discursive systems. A particular knowledge about the functions, utilities, and values of entrepreneur is essential for the neoliberal entrepreneurial government because subject forms establish an interface between the government of the conducts of other and subjects' government of themselves. Like Hutter and Teubner (1994; cf. Teubner 2006), Stäheli (2007b) and advocates of the so-called "governmentality studies" initially argued, there is no institution that does not actively and selectively observe, establish, and reproduce positive synergies between their own operations and those of individual subjects. Political government is in this regard no exception. The objective of the preceding empirical discourse analysis was to re-construct discursive systems that made it possible to observe particular relations of inter-dependence between government and entrepreneurs.

The results of the empirical discourse analysis highlight two different dimensions in the spectral being of the entrepreneur (cf. Chapter 1). First, the previous three chapters illustrated that there have been numerous changes in the governmental conception of entrepreneurs. Empirical discourse analysis identified altogether three different and mutually distinguishable *spectral apparitions* of entrepreneurs, each of which was characterized by its particular system of notions about the social functions, practices, potential consequences, and endemic characteristics of the entrepreneur. Second, around the turn of the millennium, entrepreneur transformed into an omnipotent spectre in the sense that governmental subjects were haunted by the possibility that entrepreneurship could be performed in novel contexts (work, school, civic society), carried out by an ever expanding number of subjects, and would, in a more or less conceivable manner, allow the solution to almost any social problem.

FICTIONS OF THE ENTREPRENEUR

The discourse analysis of Swedish governmental discourse covered the period from 1991 to 2004 and observed three discursive sequences, each of which contained a distinctive conception of how the conduct of government had to take into account the particular social practices, utilities, values, and functions of entrepreneurs. As was suggested at the beginning of this book, subject forms should be understood in terms of "actor fictions." First of all, meanings associated with the entrepreneur are not immanent characteristics of the entrepreneur: they are possible to observe only a particular discourse of the entrepreneur. The meaning of the entrepreneur is constructed in accordance with Deleuze and Guattari's (2003: 20f) concept of *chiffré* as a heterogeneous field of associated ideas. Moreover, the historically contingent origin of a particular conception of the entrepreneur means that there is no objective reason that governments should understand and treat entrepreneurs in one manner rather than another. What appears as a rational way to act on the entrepreneur is rational only within a discursive system that rationalizes this behavior. Even the pre-supposedly most rational treatments of entrepreneurs remain fictions, though powerful ones. Furthermore, considering what has been said about the contingent nature of knowledge, necessities conceived by individual subjects to conduct oneself as an entrepreneur fall short of any objective foundation. This means that the adaption of the subject role of the entrepreneur consists of a fiction of oneself.

The discourse theory applied in this study and the methods of discourse analysis made it possible to understand how different actor fictions are constructed and how different conceptions of the entrepreneur are structured as heterogeneous fields of knowledge. However, the analytical-heuristic model of discourse is not only a means of describing the social construction of the entrepreneur; it is also a means of achieving an epistemological break from the social subjects' own conceptions of the entrepreneur, of penetrating them by socially shared ideas about entrepreneurs, and of locating the discursive origins and conditions of possibility of these ideas. The earlier explained transitive nature of knowledge (Chapter 3) and the discussion of discourse analysis as constrained constructivism (Chapter 5) postulated that all social cognitions are facilitated by the perspective that we assume to make sense of the world. This kind of epistemic bias is not something bad or harmful: it is an existential condition that can be dealt with in several different ways. The holistic approach to discourse analysis adopted in this study aimed at making the theoretical bias of the empirical analysis transparent and inter-subjectively conceivable. Against the backdrop of the achieved epistemological break, the re-constructed discursive sequences are necessary and ideally different than the consciously held and reflexively available knowledge of the subjects of Swedish governmental discourse (cf. Diaz-Bone 2007: 16).

However, the analytical-heuristic model of discourse not only facilitates the attainment of the epistemological break, it also provides analytical coordinates for comparing different spatiotemporally particular discourses. The model of discourse provides a framework to identify, re-construct, and compare different discursive structures. The described three discursive sequences could be located and mutually compared with regard to their unique discursive organization. However, the juxtaposition of these three discursive sequences not only facilitates the comparison of their mutual differences and similarities; they also reveal a more general process of universalization (or popularization) of the entrepreneur continuing from one sequence to another. The process of universalization embraces two entangled developments. First, universalization refers to the increasing centrality of the entrepreneurship as a subject form, which more and more social subjects should accept. The belief that entrepreneurship could be performed by so far disregarded social groups paved the way for more or less openly repressive and disciplining "technologies of the other" involved in the active making-up of individual subjects as entrepreneurs.

The social-democratic government was concerned about the lack of entrepreneurs among women, immigrants, and the youth. A problematization of the under-representation of these groups as entrepreneurs was possible within a discourse that understood the lack of entrepreneurship as a potential hindrance to the attainment of the ethical ideals of welfare society and full employment. Second, the comparison of these three sequences also indicates the presence of another type of universalization that allowed entrepreneurship to be performed in unprecedented social practices and within new social contexts, such as in schools and at the workplace. The juxtaposition of the three discursive sequences reveals that entrepreneurs not only had different meanings in the first and third sequence, but also that the domain of meanings, utilities, practices, functions, and social consequences of entrepreneurship became considerably more expanded. With regard to Stäheli's (1997, 2003a: 253; cf. Williams, 1977: 121ff) conceptualization of the popular logic of culture as either transgression from or abandonment of existing distinctions, entrepreneur became an increasingly popular subject form. In the concluding third sequence, a number of previous notions about the distinctive characteristics of entrepreneur were transgressed and supplemented by new ones. However, even though the third sequence described how the entrepreneur became associated with anybody "who just does," the entrepreneur could not be enacted in any manner whatsoever: it remained restricted to social practices that made a positive contribution to the general performance of the economy. The suspicion voiced by Pongratz (2008) that the universalization of the entrepreneur might result in a "society of entrepreneurs" was almost reached in the third sequence.

Post-structural discourse theory cannot offer any general logic that could explain the discursive constructions of the entrepreneur explicated in Swedish governmental discourse. However, this does not make a cross-case analysis of the development of the culture of enterprise obsolete. Even though the heuristic-analytical model of discourse facilitates the re-construction of spatiotemporally limited discourses (cf. Chapter 5), the general validity of the discursive codes makes it possible to compare the empirical results achieved in this study with the discursive constructions of the entrepreneur in other social contexts. There are both similarities and differences in the meanings that entrepreneur had in Swedish governmental discourse in contrast to, for instance, the Thatcherite "culture of enterprise" in the 1980s (e.g., Du Gay 1991; Heelas and Morris 1992; Rose 1996a) and the German labor market reforms after 2001 (e.g., Bröckling 2003; Pühl 2003). A more systematic comparative analysis must remain beyond the scope of this study. However, in order to pave the way for a comparative analysis of different kinds of discursive constructions of the entrepreneur, the following three sections subsume the presented discursive sequences in the form of three ideal-typical conceptions of the entrepreneur as *spearhead of economy*, *active subject of society*, and *creative subject*. The construction of ideal types is, in general, a promising way to prepare the way for cross-case comparisons. For Max Weber (1949: 90), an ideal type was "formed by the one-sided accentuation of one or more points of view" in a manner of which "concrete individual phenomena . . . are arranged into a unified analytical construct." The following types of entrepreneur differ from Weber's concept in the sense that they do not accentuate a particular dimension of empirical reality asymmetrically, as Weber's ideal types did, but a system of mutually enforcing processes and developments characteristic of each of the three sequences.

THE GUARDIAN OF MARKET ECONOMY

The "New Start for Sweden" demanded by the conservative and liberal parties in 1991 reflected the conceived failure of the traditional Swedish third-way model to generate growth, employment, and welfare. The political regulation of the economy was assumed to curtail the autonomy of economic agents and, therefore, to have caused a downturn in economic growth and employment (e.g., Henrekson and Roine 2007; Lindvall 2006; Rothstein and Vahlne-Westerhäll 2005; Steinmo 2005). However, the replacement of the third-way politics did not reflect as much the failure to achieve targeted policy goals as the fundamental disturbance of the functioning market economy. As Lindvall (2005, 2006) and Benner (1997), among others, have observed, the liberal-conservative government did not abandon the ethical values of welfare and full employment. Instead, it was all about getting first things done first and to begin with the fundamental prerequisite of welfare: the performance of the economic system. The liberal-conservative government altered the political priorities and subjugated welfare and full employment to objectives that could be achieved only after the traditionally rigid governmental regulation had been replaced by a widely de-regulated economy. The liberal-conservative discourse was structured around the antagonistic divide between elements that belonged to the functioning or dysfunctioning economy respectively. Entrepreneur was not only conceived to be compatible with the functioning market economy. It was actually ascribed to the most central subject role, the "spearhead of economy," which guaranteed sustained intensity of competition and vitalization of markets (cf. Deutschmann 2008: 98ff). The role of the entrepreneur is that of the *guardian of market economy*, which, in terms of Bröckling (2007: 111–115), "utilizes profit chances" and, in accordance with Casson (2006: 3) and Henrekson and Roine (2007), could be associated with "innovators" and "agents of structural change" that destroy market equilibrium. The discursive interface between the political government and the entrepreneur derived from an epistemic view of the economy that emphasized the interdependence between the individual rational decisions of economic agents and the overall performance of the economy as a whole.

The essential systemic relevance of the entrepreneur has obvious similarities with Schumpeter's (1928, 1961) conception of entrepreneurs as a group of innovators and risk-takers, whose endemic will to prosper generates the evolutionary dynamic of the economy. Following Jessop (2002: 120), the present neo-Schumpeterian conception of entrepreneurship associates entrepreneurial conduct with "the devising and realization of new ways of doing things to generate above average profits." Moreover, the unparalleled and, in the Swedish context, unprecedented importance of entrepreneurs drew on the assumption that the evolutionary dynamics was the result of social practices "within the economic system" instead of being "merely an adaption to exogenous changes" (Elliott 1980: 46). However, the discursive interface between the political government and the entrepreneur not only consisted of a discursive construction of economy as "as a 'natural' . . . unit of analysis, management, regulation" (Jessop 2002: 120), but also the construction of the corresponding entrepreneurial duties, utilities, and characteristics, such as "innovative thinking," which gave reason to concede the entrepreneur its role as a spearhead of economy (cf. Greene et al. 2008: 3; Steyert and Katz 2004: 182). The liberal-conservative discourse was characterized by trust in the ample presence of entrepreneurs.

In contrast to the Thatcherite government of the 1980s, the liberal-conservative government took the presence of the economic vanguard of entrepreneurs for granted (cf. Della-Giusta and King 2006; Jessop 2002: 127). However, a central problem of government concerned the question as to how a sufficient number of individual agents would remain active as entrepreneurs. The line of argumentation about the plurality of entrepreneurs can be described in following manner: levels of welfare and employment depend on the extent of economic dynamics, which again is immediately relatable to the intensity of competition that results from the overall innovative performance of the group of entrepreneurs who set each other under "pressure of change." An essential problem of government concerned the social, structural, and economic conditions most beneficial for the presence of a plurality of entrepreneurs (cf. Elliott 1980: 51; Murphy et al, 1991: 522). The discursive structure of the liberal-conservative government corresponded to the popular logic of discourse (see Chapter 4) characterized by the antagonistic division of the discursive representation of the social along two mutually contrary bundles of signifiers. Typical of a popular discourse, the liberal-conservative government represented and delimited the set of beneficial conditions of entrepreneurship by setting these into an antagonistic relation to conditions that are harmful and distorting for entrepreneurship. The beneficial conditions of entrepreneurship were represented by the nodal point of positive "climate of enterprises and entrepreneurship," which again, was attained by means of four mutually entangled processes of channelling of entrepreneurial talent into the economic system, sustainment of the reward structure of entrepreneurs, utilization of entrepreneurial incentives into profitable economic activities, and maintenance of free competition.

First, the beneficial conditions of entrepreneurship were aimed at guaranteeing the natural selection of entrepreneurially minded subjects to take up the role of the entrepreneur. The liberal-conservative government was therefore concerned about conditions guaranteeing that "high-ability people become entrepreneurs and hire low-ability people in their firms" (Murphy et al. 1991: 507; cf. Bröckling 2007: 111ff; Von Mises 1980a: 30f). Second, beneficial conditions of entrepreneurship were expected to increase the incentives of entrepreneurs to conduct themselves in a truly entrepreneurial, that is, innovative way. It seems that the liberal-conservative government departed from an assumption similar to Baumol's (1990: 894) argument that "[h]ow the entrepreneur acts at a given time and place depends heavily on the rules of the game—the reward structure in the economy." For the liberal-conservative government, the reward structure consisted of a mixture of material and institutional elements, including, among other things, free competition, free allocation of resources, and access to risk capital. On the contrary, the politically regulated and controlled level of prices, costs, capital, and savings, and the political influence of the rate of savings, economic exchanges, and allocation of resources, figured as a bundle of signifiers installed into a relation of antagonism with the positive "climate of enterprises and entrepreneurship." The structural conditions supporting and obstructing the binary division between entrepreneurs induced by means of the relation of antagonism were justified by the conceived and indeed pre-supposed substance of the functioning economy. In other words, it was the reference to the functioning economy that allowed the binary opposition among *growth/stagnation, price stability/inflation, efficiency/inefficiency, access to risk capital/lack of risk capital,* and *objective interests/particular interests.* This binary division made it possible to determine the limitations of the rational conducts of the government depending on whether these made a contribution to the conditions associated with the functioning economy. This either/or logic characteristic of popular discourse implicated that the rationality of governmental actions was possible to deem in accordance with their expected impact on the overall economic dynamics, which again was closely related to the impact they had on the group of entrepreneurs. In a sense, it seems appropriate to argue that the liberal-conservative government treated the entrepreneur as a veto-player, whose needs and interests set the limits for the rational conduct of government.

Third, one obvious reason for the political importance of entrepreneurs can be located in the fact that structural reforms of economic regulation, privatization, and opening of competition could lead to the intended economic dynamics only if there were a number of entrepreneurs available who translated and utilized the beneficial structural conditions into economic growth. As Marttila (2012a: 16) argues, "even though the government could identify the optimal conditions for economic growth, economic chances could be grasped only by the Schumpeterian kind of entrepreneur." Rather paradoxically, if we draw on the earlier described subject positions, which the entrepreneur may possess in the governmental discourse (cf. Chapter 4), entrepreneur appears in the liberal-conservative discourse as both a destinator, whose world view the governmental discourse purports, as well as the receiver or "profiteer" of the improved macro-economic and socio-structural conditions. A similar kind of tautological logic of articulation also applies to the conceived necessity of free competition. There were two justifications for the necessity of largely unbound competition. The first reason was that free competition was considered to be a prerequisite for the presence of a plurality of mutually competing entrepreneurs and enterprises, which again made it possible to attain the desired economic dynamics, productivity increase, and rational allocation of resources conceived to characterize a functioning economy.

The observed relation of inter-dependence between a functioning economy and free competition made it possible to problematize a number of earlier social-democratic policies and the extensive and ever expanding public sector. The overriding antagonistic relation between the functioning and dysfunctioning economy was substantiated by the antagonism between competition supporting and impeding conditions. This overall relation of antagonism arranged, among other things, the relations of contrariety between "competitive private sector" and "non-competitive public sector," competition "supporting" and "distorting" policies, as well as institutional settings that either generated an "efficient allocation of resources" or caused the "waste of resources." The second reason was that entrepreneurs were trusted as a source of *verification* of the rational allocation of capital. Entrepreneurs were trusted to be more capable of making decisions about productive investment of capital and to judge the future potential of business start-ups. In order to fulfill the function as an instance of verification, the political government had to constrain its role of supporting free competition by privatization of the public sector and intensification of competition. In the liberal-conservative discourse, entrepreneurs remained functionally differentiated agents who performed their assigned roles within the framework of the economic system and private business. Moreover, entrepreneur was unmistakably adjacent to the Schumpeterian notion of entrepreneur as a utilizer of the reward structure, risk-taker, and innovator, who guaranteed the overall dynamics of the entire economic system.

Liberal-conservative discourse did not regard the function of the entrepreneur as something that would necessarily have to be open to any social subject, as the subsequent social-democratic government did. The liberal-conservative government appealed for general support of entrepreneurship without yet regarding the dissemination of entrepreneurship to new social groups as a pressing political problem. Even though concerns appeared toward the end of the liberal-conservative period of government that present institutions and policy measures might exclude, for instance, women as entrepreneurs, the liberal-conservative government was not actively making up entrepreneurial subjects. Liberal-conservative and social-democratic discourses departed from two different ontologies of the entrepreneur: the liberal-conservative one was concerned about "the allocation of entrepreneurial talent to the economic system . . . [while] the presence of entrepreneurs was largely taken for granted" (Marttila 2012a: 17). The subsequent social-democratic government was actively involved in making up social subjects as entrepreneurs. This diachronic discursive change reflected the new conception of the ontology of the entrepreneur facilitated by the adaption of the "new growth theory" and knowledge about the reciprocal relation between the level of soft cultural and cognitive resources and the general economic performance.

THE ACTIVE SUBJECT OF SOCIETY

The social-democratic government elected in 1994 attacked the market dogmatism of the preceding liberal-conservative government and replaced its "popular" logic of discourse by an "institutional" one. Moreover, in accordance with the earlier scheme of different types of discursive change, the social-democratic discourse introduced an offensive institutional replacement, which eradicated the popular antagonistic relation between the functioning and dysfunctioning of the economy by an all-inclusive representation of society as expressed by the concept of "a nation at work." However, it would be inappropriate to say that the social-democratic discourse was free from antagonisms. The social-democratic discourse was arranged around the antagonistic relation between realms of *activity* and *passivity*. For example, the political government could be either active (social-democratic government) or passive (liberal-conservative government). The opposition between the active and passive government was substantiated with regard to industrial policies, which could either follow the inspiring example of the Clinton administration in the United States and provide active coordination of the private business sector, or, as in the case of the liberal-conservative government, it could remain inactive and watch passively how the economic agents struggled with structural economic problems. Interestingly enough, the divide between active and passive social conducts also embraced the conducts of individual social subjects, who could either mobilize themselves for the cause of ethical objectives of welfare and employment or disregard any such individual collective responsibility. The active logic of government, whether that of the state or the individual subjects' government of themselves, derived from the conceived antagonistic relation between the idealized ethical principle of the "welfare society" and its antagonistic other: "mass employment." Even though the social-democratic government re-invented the active role of the state in the government of the economy, it did by no means appeal to return to a third-way kind of economic regulations. Moreover, the liberal-conservative government was not criticized for being based on a neoliberal ideology, but rather for having introduced a social division [*tudelning*] that excluded a number of social subjects from "productive work" and "mobilization of energies" [*kräftesammling*] on behalf of the "welfare society" (see Chapter 7).

The apparent aspiration to activate all social subjects bears considerable resemblances with the "project-based" mode of societalization as described by Boltanski and Chiapello (1999: 176; cf. Bröckling 2007: 248). The aspiration of social-democratic discourse to mobilize social subjects to make their contribution to the welfare society reflects the conceived incapacity of the political government to directly act on the economy. Instead, whereas the liberal-conservative government regarded economic output as the immediate result of actions taken by entrepreneurs, the social-democratic government conceived of the economic performance as the aggregated outcome of the totality of interests, practices, and interests in society as a whole. Following Thibaud (1985: 140), the rationale of this governmental strategy required the development of "policies that integrate society into the economy, policies of mobilization, integration, negotiation, which increasingly involve non-management groups in the functioning of the economy." The social-democratic government not only endeavored to establish a "project-based society," but it also defined the rationale of this mode of societalization in accordance with the conceived economic prerequisites of the welfare society. In order to support the ethical ideal of the welfare society, individual subjects had to participate actively in social practices of learning, start-up of businesses, and adapt non-traditional forms of self-employment and innovative conducts of the self-generating, above all, economic innovations (cf. Bröckling 2007: 260ff).

Even though the welfare society appeared as the ethical ideal of the social-democratic discourse, its actual discursive role is much more complicated. The socio-cultural coherence sustained by the welfare society was an essential prerequisite for the willingness of social subjects to activate their slumbering and latent human capital for the sake of full employment. The social-democratic government seemed to have introduced a considerably different conception of social welfare, which no longer focused on the distribution of material social standards, but, in the words of Thibaud (1985: 140), involved instead the "redistribution of the chances for action." The activation policies, one of which was the active making of subjects into entrepreneurs, reflected the assumption that sustained economic dynamics was not the result of an economic elite, but "a matter of single individuals' or groups' ideas, initiative and creativity in all parts of the society" (Motion 1996/97: N242). The conviction that economic dynamics results from below, from the plurality of social actions, explains the rationality behind the "active social contract". While the liberal-conservative government could rely on the almost magical effects that the narrow group of entrepreneurs had on the economy, the social-democratic government had to develop governmental strategies that could mobilize the human capital of all social subjects. A closer look at the conceived prerequisites of the economic growth provides an auspicious starting point to deconstructing the rationality located in the active making of social subjects into entrepreneurs.

The previous liberal-conservative government set economic growth into a relationship of inter-dependency with the quality of the economic, social, and political institutions. For the liberal-conservative government, the external and, above all, political distortion of economic interchanges, decisions on investment, allocation of resources, and so on would inevitably lead to an inefficient use of resources, decrease competition, diminish the general level of economic dynamics, and, in the end, increase the level of unemployment. Active political regulation and control of the economy could only hinder the attainment of maximum economic output, which, ultimately, was the result of the natural endemic capacity of entrepreneurs to make the right choices under the conditions of perfect competition. This neoliberal episteme reduced government to the guarantor of the institutional configuration best compatible with open competition (cf. Casson 1982: 24; Jessop 2002: 96ff). Even the social-democratic activation policies were rationalized by the conceived external and objective fiscal limitations, such as the acceptable levels of "budget deficit" and "inflation" (see Chapter 7). However, these restrictions did not tie the hands of the government. Political government was still trusted to have the capacity to mobilize human capital disregarded by the liberal-conservative government so far. The attention paid to human capital derived from a considerably different understanding of the prerequisites of economic growth.

The new growth theory adopted by the social-democratic government placed an unforeseen emphasis on the cultural and cognitive factors of production, such as innovative ideas, learning, and attitudes. The new growth theory rationalized new forms of activating state intervention in society because it made it possible to cognize the economic relevance of conditions and factors that earlier appeared to be irrelevant for the economy (cf. Boltanski and Chiapello 1999: 208; Jessop 2002: 131). The proliferation of the semantics of "mobilization" and "utilization" observed in Chapter 7 bears witness to the pressing political urgency to release and activate the latent and so far disregarded human capital of individual subjects. It was against the backdrop of the problematization of latent human capital as an economic problem that the social-democratic government "had to figure out strategies to stimulate, mobilize and vitalize the social subjects' utilization of their immanent human capital" (Marttila 2012a: 20). The alternative— the waste of human potential—was conceived of as an inadmissible consequence because it would have implicated abandonment of the ethical ideal of the welfare society based on full employment.

The social-democratic discourse identified two different lines of approach to the welfare society. Both strategies focused on the maintenance of full employment by means of increased economic growth. The *first* alternative was to achieve economic competitiveness through a strategy that combined low wages and international price competition. This strategy was deemed inappropriate because the lowering of wage levels was considered irreconcilable with the welfare society. The *second* alternative combined increasing economic growth, full employment, and an overall high wage level enabled by a general upgrading of the entire economic system toward an increasingly knowledge-intensive production. The endeavored increase of the relative share of knowledge-based production placed an unforeseen emphasis on the general society-wide upgrading of skills, competences, and innovations. Jessop (2002) regards the activation of human capital as constituting the prerequisite of the functioning of late capitalism. In order to make subjects adopt their subject roles in knowledge-intensive production, political governments had to be actively supporting "the individual and collective capacities to engage in permanent innovation" (Jessop 2002: 121). For Jessop (2002), collective cultural characteristics associated with a particular spatial location, such as a region, contribute to the economic attractiveness of that location (cf. Amin and Thrift 1994). Boltanski and Chiapello (1999: 210) go one step further, arguing that being and remaining proactive is not limited to the production system alone, but actually constitutes a general norm with regard to which "undertaking something, taking action, changing oneself . . . are positively estimated as a contrast to inaction and stability." In the social-democratic discourse, the active social contract seems to have been supported by the conceived reciprocity between the individuals' will to develop, learn, and achieve new skills and the level of economic growth. In this light, the rational conduct of government was left no option but try to "stimulate," "vitalize," and "mobilize" the individual accumulation of human capital (see Chapter 7). This kind of disciplining government of the conduct of conducts was supported by the assumption that individual subjects possessed slumbering human capital and, moreover, that they were capable of improving and learning new skills and competences.

Entrepreneur remained a functionally differentiated subject role that was performed in the framework of the economic system and private business. Moreover, similar to the previous liberal-conservative discourse, the social-democratic discourse also regarded the entrepreneur as being the subject indispensable for sustaining the pressure of competition and economic growth achieved with it. As described in Chapter 7, entrepreneurs were trusted to possess the capacities to introduce new ideas, technologies, and innovations and, therewith, initiate the transition toward "knowledge-intensive production." However, the social-democratic discourse differed from the previous liberal-conservative one with regard to its problematization of the insufficient number of individuals being active as entrepreneurs. The most pressing problem of the social-democratic discourse was the question as to how individual subjects could be activated to place their human capital at the disposal of the economic system. The answer was: they should become either entrepreneurs or adopt some kind of self-employment. However, where the liberal-conservative government conceived of the entrepreneur as a spearhead of economy in Schumpeterian terms, social-democratic discourse introduced a number of more differentiated functions to be performed by the entrepreneurs.

First, entrepreneur was a technology of both the other and the self that enabled individual subjects to "conduct themselves in a manner that enabled the political government to realize the ethical objectives of welfare and full employment" (Marttila 2012a: 23). The active making of individual subjects as entrepreneurs was supported by the notion that entrepreneur was the subject form that allowed the government to mobilize the so far passive human capital of women, immigrants, youth, and the unemployed. Political campaigns of the "nation at work" and the "active social contract" along with a number of social institutions, such as the Enterprise Allowance Scheme, loan scheme, and resource centers for female entrepreneurship, are but a few strategies that allowed the government to activate human capital to its full potential (see Chapter 7). In a way, entrepreneurship had a kind of transubstantiating function in the sense that it made something *immaterial*—such as interests, attitudes, incentives—or even *absent*—such as the latent and slumbering potential for individual development—possible to transfer and translate into economic products, decisions on investment, start-up of enterprises, and so on.

Second, entrepreneur also played a "coordinating role" in the very sense of Casson's (1990, 2006) conception of the entrepreneur as coordinator of markets. In this function, entrepreneurs channel social mobilization and development of skills and competencies initiated by the active social contract into occupations and economic products. Entrepreneur was, accordingly, not only a subject form that made it possible to mobilize the human capital of the self, but also that of other social subjects. The start-up of SMEs supported massively by the social-democratic government was a means for entrepreneurs to transfer the human capital of other subjects into internationally competitive employment (cf. Harrison 1994). Third, while the first two functions were aimed at transferring human capital into economic production, the concluding third function of the entrepreneur made the entrepreneur the subject form that counteracted the inherent monopolization tendency of the economy and supported the development toward a knowledge-intensive economy (see Chapter 7). While this third function was rather identical to the function of the entrepreneur as *Guardian of the Market Economy*, the two initially described functions constitute a remarkable difference to the liberal-conservative discourse. All in all, the function that the entrepreneur assumed in social-democratic discourse can be understood in terms of the *Active Subject of Society*.

THE CREATIVE SUBJECT

The second discursive sequence bears witness to a cultural revolution aimed at changing the discursive interface between the political government and the social subjects fundamentally. The third sequence brings this cultural revolution even one step further. The second discursive sequence already expressed the expectation of a future transition into the KBE. Among other things, the two political campaigns of "knowledge boost" and the "Educational revolution for Sweden toward the 21st century" were aimed at upgrading human capital to the level considered necessary in the future KBE. In the third sequence, the aspirations to become a leading KBE were even more intensified. Moreover, even though the political government was still concerned about the possibility of too few social subjects being active as entrepreneurs, there was a considerable change in social practices and social contexts related to entrepreneurship. Furthermore, the attainment of the ethical objectives of welfare and full employment was assumed to require, in part, the transformation of the economy to a worldwide leading KBE and the development of the society into a knowledge society. The sustainment of the welfare society was believed to depend on the establishment of the KBE and the presence of a "world class knowledge nation." While the government argued on the one side that the "knowledge society must be open for all" (Government Communication 2003/04: 129, p. 86), it also requested that entrepreneurship had to become "the driving force . . . in the knowledge society" on the other side (NUTEK 2003b).

Entrepreneurship was no longer an optional and possible way of how individual subjects could conduct themselves. Instead, every subject should ideally assume the "will and capacity to try something new," which is characteristic of the entrepreneur (Department Report 2004: 36, p. 13). In the end, economic growth was seen as the outcome of "the willingness of the people to work and the aspiration to develop and trespass boundaries" (Parliamentary Minutes 2003/04: 2). In the third sequence, entrepreneurship was partly de-coupled from economic practices and now referred to the creative conduct of the self. Characteristically for an institutional discourse, the social-democratic government argued that entrepreneurship had to be available for all subjects. The imperative of society-wide entrepreneurship, whether at schools, in regional partnerships, in economic clusters, or at the workplace, derived from the conceived inter-dependence between the ethical ideal of the welfare state and the assumed prerequisites of the competitive KBE. If subjects were to make a contribution to sustaining the high level of employment, which again was regarded as a pre-condition of the welfare society, they had to be willing to trespass boundaries and conventions and strive toward developing their own skills continuously (see Chapter 8; cf. Department Report 2004: 36, p. 13; NUTEK 2003a: 10; Parliamentary Minutes 2003/04: 2).[1] It was above all the observed relation of inter-dependence between the sustainment of the welfare society and the development toward a competitive KBE that constituted the imperative to upgrade the entire society into a knowledge society characterized by positive attitudes and general preparedness to innovation and creativity.

It was only in this context that entrepreneur should become a subject that consistently improves, develops, and activates itself in order to "experience the driving force of entrepreneurship in a knowledge society" (NUTEK 2003b: 51). It was the assumption that the individual characteristics, capacities, and utilities required in the KBE had to be similar to those of the entrepreneur that generalized entrepreneurship as a universal way for "getting something done" (Department Report 1997: 78, p. 16). In contrast to the earlier two discursive sequences, entrepreneur was neither a functionally differentiated role performed within the economic system (first sequence) nor a way of how individual subjects could put their human capital at the disposal of the economy (second sequence), but a more or less unlimited, universally valid way for all social contexts and practices to conduct themselves. In other words, entrepreneurship not only became an increasingly general way for individual subjects' conducts of themselves, it also became considerably more indeterminate. Now, the indeterminacy of the entrepreneurship also meant that it became considerably more difficult for the political government to make individual subjects entrepreneurs.

In the first and second sequences, particular institutions addressed the conceived needs of the entrepreneur and provided them with capital, knowledge, and information. The general character of entrepreneurship as a way of getting things done required more general cultural and pedagogic measures embracing all subjects. Against the backdrop of the argument that "entrepreneurs can be found everywhere in society" (NUTEK 2003a: 6), and that the sustained welfare society in the KBE indeed required that entrepreneurial subjects be active in all parts of society, the social-democratic government had to develop new governmental technologies of the other that supported the "entrepreneurialization" of the entire society. Association of entrepreneurship with a life-form, or in terms of Boltanski and Chiapello (1999: 209), a general "form" of social capital, required new types of cultural policies that not only addressed business starters or the self-employed, but the entire society without exception. The logic of entrepreneurship as a general form of social capital in the KBE was poignantly expressed by a report from NUTEK (2003a: 6), which argued that, "[e]ntrepreneurial activities and entrepreneurship are not only important from the economic perspective. It is equally important in terms of innovativeness in other parts of the society; for example within the public sector, social activities, the social economy and the school" (cf. Government Bill 2001/02: 2, chapter 5).[2]

Introduction of entrepreneurial education at schools was supported by the idea that participation in the economy, in working life, but also in the civil society would require similar kinds of social skills and competencies to those embodied by entrepreneurs (e.g., Government Communication 1996/97: 112, p. 12; SOU 1997: 121, p. 250). The conception of entrepreneurship as a general life-form considered entrepreneurial education as not being aimed at providing pupils with knowledge about the functioning and organization of private enterprises or how to start-up their own enterprise. In line with the observation of Department Report 1997: 78 (p. 16), claiming that entrepreneurial skills are crucial for "getting something done" and having the capacity to "take initiative to solve problems," entrepreneurial education should be aimed at providing pupils with general entrepreneur-like skills that make them employable in the KBE. In terms of Pongratz (2008), the rationale underlying the introduction of entrepreneurial education seems to reflect the assumption that the society has to become a society of entrepreneurs (*Unternehmergesellschaft*). The concern that the society might not be entrepreneurial enough was reflected by the introduction of the "entrepreneurship barometer" that from 2000 on measured the extent to which pupils had adopted entrepreneurship-friendly attitudes and values.

The third discursive sequence gives reason to assume that the universalization of entrepreneurship to a general type of social capital was supported by a particular discourse on the KBE. Jessop's (2004, 2008) research has manifested that the discourse of the KBE is by no means limited to the conceptions of processes, functions, and practices associated with knowledge-intensive production. Instead, Jessop (2004: 168) refers to the KBE as having "become a master economic narrative" that exerts a considerable impact on the form and logic of societalization. The discourse of the KBE has been effective in "informing and shaping state projects and hegemonic visions on different scales, providing guidance in the face of political and social uncertainty and providing means to integrate private, institutional, and wider public narratives" (Jessop 2004: 168). The discourse on the KBE emphasizes the impact that the entrepreneurial culture—defined in terms of innovativeness and creativity at all social levels—has on the competitiveness of the economic system. In this light, "[a] key element in all areas is the promotion of entrepreneurialism and an entrepreneurial culture" (Jessop 2008: 17). In other words, there is no social location in which the individual subjects would not have to possess "capacities to engage in permanent innovation" (Jessop 2002: 121; cf. Drake 1997).

As the third discursive sequence manifests, human capital is not primarily a measurable qualification or a skill, but a mentality within the KBE. Even though a profound discussion of the conception of human capital in the discourse on the KBE would lead too far away from the actual purposes of this book, the empirical findings in Chapter 8 give reason to suggest that innovativeness and creativity are in at least four different regards linked to the economic logic of the KBE. First, flexible, "just-in-time" production implicates that competitive firms need to have access to creative, innovative intrapreneurs upgrading their skills and competencies continuously. In this regard, entrepreneurship became another "factor input into a production function . . . that improves the allocative efficiency of the economy" (Casson 2006: 9). Second, considering that economic production takes place ideally within local and regional clusters, in each of which competitiveness and relative attractiveness for capital depends on their capacity to identify comparative advantage, clusters need network entrepreneurs who coordinate and re-direct them toward new profit chances. Network entrepreneurs were essential resources because they were conceived as being capable of generating consensual visions *about the cluster* (NUTEK 2002: 15). Moreover, the general level of innovativeness of a cluster requires the presence of "[s]ocial capital, which encourages spirit of entrepreneurship" (Government Bill 2001/02: 4, p. 68). In both regards, the general level of innovativeness and creativity can be understood to be essential for the "systemic competitiveness" of clusters (Messner 1997). For Messner (1997: 23), "[d]ynamic economic locations and zones are marked by general innovation-friendly framework conditions." Third, the differentiation of future working life in the KBE expected by the social-democratic government implicated that an increasing number of subjects would have to be employed in some kind of flexible and project-based employment that required an unprecedented capacity for problem solving, creative thinking, adjustment to new situations, competence to team-work, and so on (Government Bill 1995/96: 206, chapter 4).

Working life was expected to develop in a direction that strengthened the similarities between the entrepreneurs within the economic system and private business and regular employment. In this regard, innovativeness and creativity were means of increasing the general level of employability of the labor force. Fourth, the spirit of entrepreneurship was also regarded as a necessary resource for social subjects' learning and accumulation of their human capital. Rather paradoxically, school education not only taught subjects to increase their human capital, but it also taught them how they could remain actively learning subjects. Social-democratic discourse not only understood learning as an accumulation of skills, but even more as a form of "knowledge creation" that required "the faith in one's own capacity and will to develop" (Government Bill 2000/01: 72, chapter 6). Entrepreneur developed to the role model of the learning subject and indicated how subjects should conduct their process of learning. The common feature of the four spectres of entrepreneurship is the overall idea that entrepreneur is synonymous with the "subjects' willingness and capacity to try something new," whether as employees of private enterprise, in clusters, at work in general, or as learning subjects (Department Report, 2004: 36, p. 13). All in all, in the third sequence, the entrepreneur developed into a general modus or role model of social subjectivity without any spatial, sectorial, or institutional limitations. Entrepreneurship was not only possible to perform in any place whatsoever. The imperative of sustained welfare and employment in the KBE left no other option but to disseminate the subject role of the entrepreneur into unprecedented social contexts. The observed dissemination of the entrepreneur did not take place without reason. The third discursive sequence manifested how the imperative to disseminate entrepreneur-like conducts derived from the imagination that the sustainment of the welfare society in the future KBE requires upgrading of the society into a knowledge society inhabited by entrepreneur-like innovative and creative subjects.[3]

SOME CONCLUDING REFLECTIONS

The dissemination of the culture of enterprise occurring between the first and third sequences resulted from the expansion of the social space within which entrepreneurship became an appropriate and even a necessary way of conducting oneself. However, dissemination of the culture of enterprise also involved increasing conceptual vagueness of the entrepreneur, as the expansion of its characteristics, the social practices it conducted, and the social utilities associated with it and functions illustrate. In this regard, it seems inappropriate to argue that the increasing validity of entrepreneurship as a way of getting things done would have consisted of a cultural transfer of the initial conception of the entrepreneur into novel social contexts and practices. The popularization of the entrepreneur identified in this study consisted of the continuous failure to reproduce existing distinctions between the characteristics, values, utilities, and practices of entrepreneurs and those of other subject forms. In accordance with Stäheli (cf. 2003a, 2003ab, 2007a, 2007b), the failure to draw distinctions is also the origin of the possibility to expand the inner side of the distinction with further meanings. An interesting aspect of cultural change as a popularization is that it indicates how the dissemination of the culture of enterprise actually implicates its own subversion. The dissemination of the entrepreneur observed in the third sequence cannot be restricted to a process of "economization of the social" caused by the subjugation of, for instance, work and learning to the imperative of entrepreneurship. The conceptual excess caused by its dissemination involved a parallel replacement of the initially strictly economic rationale of the entrepreneur. The initially (see Chapter 2) described processes of over-layering and hybridization of cultural codes seem appropriate conceptual frameworks to describe the logics of dissemination of the entrepreneur in Swedish governmental discourse.

This account has been restricted to an empirical analysis of the genealogical process of the construction of the entrepreneur in Swedish governmental discourse. However, the obvious parallels between the process of cultural hybridization and the empirically observed process of dissemination of the entrepreneur into unprecedented social contexts gives reason to start looking for more general cultural patterns and mechanisms that enable a more detailed and sophisticated analysis of cultural hybridization. One possibility would be to elaborate further on the role that nodal points play for the construction of cultural hybrids. Jones and Spicer (2009: 37) argue, the reason that entrepreneur "is essentially indefinable, vacuous and empty" depends on its function as a nodal point in the contemporary culture of enterprise. However, where Jones and Spicer focus on the Lacanian conception of the nodal point as a sublime object of desire, it would be profitable to start discussing the phenomenological structure organized by the nodal point of the entrepreneur. Nodal points play a crucial role in the construction of cultural hybrids because their conceptual openness on the one side and their discursive function to represent the shared commonality of particular discursive elements on the other side make it possible to create inter-cultural (and inter-discursive) configurations among previously incommensurable practices, meanings, codes, and so on (cf. Reckwitz 2006). The notion of the entrepreneur as a nodal point could explain how the entrepreneur became a considerably more indeterminate subject form. In the first and second sequences, entrepreneur remained a subject role that was performed within the economic system.

In the third sequence, entrepreneur became a shared point of reference that symbolized the common point of reference among numerous individual characteristics—such as "will to develop," "creativity," "learning," "innovativeness," "capacity to take initiatives," "faith in personal capacity," and "creativity." Moreover, entrepreneur became related to a number of new subject forms such as pupils, employees, the self-employed, participants of local and regional networks, and grass-root leaders. This extension of the range of subject forms associated with entrepreneurship made it possible to associate them with entrepreneurial characteristics. Jones and Spicer's (2005, 2009) argument that entrepreneur is an indeterminate subject form stands in stark contrast to the rather clear and mutually distinguishable definitions of the entrepreneur observed in this study. Moreover, the argument of the general indeterminate notion of the entrepreneur also disregards the fact that it was only relatively lately that it was possible to associate entrepreneurship with social practices in the context of universities (Grit 1997; Jessop 2008: 19), political government and public sector (Considine 2001), schools (Mahieu 2006), the civic society (Farrell 2001; Henton, Walesh, and Melville 1997), and working life (Boreham 2006; Florida 2002). Obviously, the challenge for the future culturalist and discourse-theoretical analysis will be to further elaborate the mechanisms and processes involved in the diachronic development of the culture of enterprise to an increasingly predominant cultural configuration.

In conclusion, I would like to spend a few words on the empirical validity of the empirical results presented. This study departed from the ontological assumption that all social subjects are positioned within discursive systems that structure their world views. The aim of the analysis was to describe and re-construct discursive structures located in the articulations of governmental subjects. In a frequently overlooked essay titled "Nietzsche, Freud, Marx" (1994b), Foucault observes how modern hermeneutic interpretations involve an infinite process of "interpretation of interpretations." This infinitude of scientific interpretation reflects the disappearance of absolute objective certainties and truths. The absence of objectivity also applies to this study. If the analyst can never fully merge with the object of analysis and discover its immanent properties existing independent of the analytical practice, empirical results remain necessarily confined to a perspectival bias (cf. Foucault 1994a: 678, 732). The insurmountable divide between the analyst and the object of analysis not only allows for different interpretations, it generates the possibility of arriving at an unlimited number of interpretations. As a consequence, "there is nowhere that interpretation stops, where a hard, extra-discursive reality—one which can fix [that interpretation]—takes over" (Szerszynski 1996: 131). However, the incessant relativist logic of interpretation does not mean that discourse analysis comes without any methodological guidelines. If the infinitude of interpretation is the normal condition of science, it becomes—in terms of Glynos and Howarth (2008: 14f)—essential to not only accept that the "ontological framework is itself historical and ultimately contingent and contestable" (cf. Marttila 2010). Discourse analysis must be regarded as a kind of "discourse of a discourse" that produces empirical observations enabled by discourse-theoretical epistemology (cf. Bublitz 2001; Diaz-Bone 2007).

In order to facilitate subsequent re-interpretations, contestation, and critique, the results of discourse analysis should not only refrain from any claims on objective analysis, but also actively instruct the reader about the epistemological bias of the analytical practice. After all, inter-subjective transparency fulfills its purpose only insofar as the reader assumes the role of the critic who questions, supplements, revises, and replaces interpretations by new interpretations. The worst thing that could probably happen to a discourse-analytical study is that it remains uncontested and turns into unquestioned objective knowledge. Obviously, however, the contestation of discourse analysis can be carried out in the framework of discourse-analytical methodology and can, for instance, criticize deviations between discourse-analytical epistemology and methodology, point out inconsistencies in analytical strategies, or address some kind of insufficiency of the achieved empirical results. However, discourse analysis can also be criticized from a scientific point of view that criticizes the discourse-analytical premises as such, postulates the discrepancy between the hermeneutic horizon of the real-life experience and the discourse analytical interpretations, or questions the discursive nature of reality. In this latter case, however, critique does not generate any new interpretations, but it addresses the practice of interpretation itself.

Without any doubt, this study gives reason for both kinds of critical remarks. As concerns the first type of critique of discourse analysis from the community of discourse analysts, the selection of the material is an obvious point of further discussion. One question worth discussing is whether the text corpus challenged by discourse analysis should be compiled in a manner that guarantees some kind of representativity. As regards the second type of critique, post-structural discourse analysis has to achieve an epistemological break from everyday experiences of social subjects and transgress the limits of their own systems of rationality and knowledge (Diaz-Bone 2007; Marttila 2010). In this regard, the presented discourse of the entrepreneur is necessarily different to the self-evident truths and experiences held by the governmental subjects analyzed. In contrast to different types of critical discourse analysis, the post-foundational ontology of the post-structural discourse analysis makes it difficult to conceive how this kind of study could possibly support, evaluate, depreciate, or criticize the empirically observed discourses of the entrepreneur.

Indeed, a general question that remains to be answered concerns the relation between empirical discourse analysis and (ideology) critique (Marttila 2012b). Jones and Spicer (2009: 18) have made use of a post-structural and post-modern theoretical fundament to develop "a critical theory of the entrepreneur" that makes it possible to "question the regimes of domination that are constructed and perpetuated in the name of the entrepreneur." However, even though I do not want to rule out the social importance of critique, I find it difficult to see how post-structural discourse analysis could possibly problematize a particular discourse on entrepreneurship without getting stuck in a contradiction with the discursive nature of critique itself. After all, problematization of, for example, the neoliberal discourse of entrepreneur would have to be carried out on behalf of some equally discursive principles and values. Even the justification of critique as a social practice requires an affirmative discourse on critique (Marttila 2012b).

Considering this general problem of post-structural critique, I lean more toward Ogbor's (2000: 630) deconstructive aspiration that constrains itself to an empirical analysis of "*how* and *why* particular ideational systems, institutions and belief systems produce and shape the pattern of entrepreneurship in contemporary society." I consider this research program challenging and rewarding enough without any clearly expressed intention to criticize the way entrepreneurship is being experienced and performed in contemporary society.

Notes

NOTES TO CHAPTER 1

1. Specter means both "ghost" and "spectrality" of objects. Spectral objects are experienced as disturbing and unclear images.
2. Overdetermination relates to both condensation and transference of meaning.
3. Unless otherwise indicated, all translations from Swedish and German to English have been done by the author.

NOTES TO CHAPTER 2

1. See Mahieu (2006) for a summary of the literature on entrepreneurship.
2. Two of the four pillars of the European Employment Strategy (EES) see enterprises and the spirit of entrepreneurship as the focus of the employment strategy.
3. The debate between Ernesto Laclau and Roy Bhaskar (1998) is most illuminating for the distinction between cultural realism and relativist cultural theory.

NOTES TO CHAPTER 3

1. The discussion in this chapter is carried out more at length in *Political Difference and Social Analysis* (Marttila forthcoming).
2. For summaries of post-structural social theories and their mutual similarities and differences, see Dosse (1999), Phillips and Jörgensen (2002), and Moebius and Reckwitz (2008).
3. Event refers here to repetitive acts of enunciation that construct, sustain, and transform discursive orders of knowledge in the form of singular social practices. In genealogical research, which observes discursive changes, Foucault has also defined "event" in terms interchangeable with discursive change (cf. Foucault 1977: 154). For different types and discursive impacts of events, see Flynn (2004).
4. Foucault's definition of discursive rules beyond discourse has generated general criticism about the "functionalism" and "materialism" on which discursive orders of knowledge are founded (e.g., Derrida 1981; Laclau and Mouffe 2001; Stäheli 2004).
5. Derrida distinguishes the differential ontology of meaning by separating the ontology of *difference* from actualized differences. This distinction is similar to Luhmann's (1997) definition of meaning to have the form of a difference (*Unterschied*) originating from acts of differentiation (*Unterscheidung*).

6. The discussion of the differences between the system-theoretical and the discourse-theoretical conception of discursive limits and different forms and logics of exteriority must be left out here. See Stäheli (2000, 2004) for a comparison between system theory and post-structural discourse theory.
7. The strictly differential logic of meaning means that essence is the contingent outcome of the actualized differences. The potential meaning is the continually lurking possibility of another and different differential relation.

NOTES TO CHAPTER 4

1. In *Hegemony and Socialist Strategy*, Laclau and Mouffe (2001) undertook a deconstruction of the essentialist Marxist proposition that social relations, such as political interest and class consciousness, are ultimately determined by the existing mode of production.
2. For a discussion about the distinction between "discourse" and "ideology," see Purvis and Hunt (1993) and Žižek (1994b).
3. The relationship between misrecognition and identification is discussed more at length in Marttila (forthcoming, chapter 5).
4. Instead of drawing on the Gramscian concept of hegemony as collective will or common sense, a post-ideological and post-political concept of hegemony would instead interpret it in terms of any spatially distinctive and diachronically retained "partial fixing of the relation between signifier and signified" (Laclau 1993: 435).
5. Stavrakakis (1999: 76) argues in a similar tone that political discourse is organized around both "nodal points" (*points de capiton*) and "empty signifiers."
6. This typology of discursive relations is borrowed from Nonhoff (2007).

NOTES TO CHAPTER 5

1. "Interpretative analysis" was coined by Dreyfus and Rabinow (1982) to describe Foucault's methodological position (Diaz-Bone 2005: 181; 2006a: 70).
2. A principle critique of both "content analysis" and analysis of conversation and rhetoric pertains to their nominal analysis of semantic elements (e.g., Diaz-Bone 2006a: 77; Keller 2001). There is also critique that applies to lexicometric and realist analyses of discourse, such as critical discourse analysis.
3. See Stäheli (1998) for a discussion on the interdependence between semantic structure and systemic operations in Luhmann's theory on social systems.
4. This discussion is carried out more at length in Marttila (forthcoming, chapter 7).

NOTES TO CHAPTER 6

1. Information from Government Bill 1990/91: 100 and SOU 1996: 34.
2. The original title was "starta eget bidrag."
3. From now on, the abbreviations SE and SME will be used for small enterprises and small and medium-sized enterprises, respectively.
4. See, for example, Parliamentary Minutes 1991/92: 6; Government Bill 1991/92: 38; Government Communication 1994/95:22.

5. Either the existing international economic competition or expectations of future increases provide a consistently appearing contextual imaginary.
6. The role of imaginaries of the "natural course of market processes in Swedish political discourse" has been discussed in Marttila and Schillinger (2007).
7. It is worth pointing out that an entrepreneur plays the same role as an actor in animating and invigorating competition during all three narratives sequences.
8. The difference between "new entrepreneurship" and "entrepreneurship" refers to "business start-ups" and entrepreneurial activities in existing enterprises, respectively.

NOTES TO CHAPTER 7

1. This is defined as the difference between what could be produced and what has been produced as measured in Gross Domestic Product (GDP).
2. See Chapter 4 for the distinction between popular and institutional discourse.
3. On "active social contract," see Chapter 7.
4. Government Bill 1994/95: 100 and 150; 1995/96: 207 and 222; NUTEK 2003; SOU 1996: 27; 1997: 121; 1998: 51.
5. In Swedish: "Programmet för Småföretagsutveckling, Förnyelse och Tillväxt."
6. On the Swedish government website, it is possible to search the policy documents for different expressions. Illustrative of the argument placed is the fact that the cohesion of Sweden was problematized only in 1994/95, and from then on it appeared at a central place in policy documents that described the general guidelines and orientation of the political government.
7. SMEs were assigned tax reliefs of 3.5 bn. SEK in total from January 1997 on (Government Bills 1995/96: 222, chapter 4; 1996/97: 45).
8. The opposition is defined between the "low-wage model" (*låglönevägen*) and the "high-wage society" (*höglönesamhället*).
9. The Social-Democratic Party distanced itself from the "elitist project" of the liberal-conservative government, which reduced the "activation" of citizens to a small group of the economic "elite." This narrow mobilization of individuals is contrasted to the demand to a society-wide participation of citizens who would advance Sweden and the Swedish economy (e.g., Social Democratic Party 1992: 62).
10. The title of the report was *Development and Participation—Agenda for Growth Policy of the Industrial Department.*
11. Explicit reference is made to U.S. economist Paul Krugman as well as to the "productivity committee" (SOU 1991: 28) that had both argued that stable economic growth was possible only through a corresponding increase of productivity.
12. The term "cultural minority" is used as the Swedish term "invandrare" embraces both persons born abroad and persons with at least one of the parents being of foreign origin.
13. For similar criticism, see Hjelm (2004). For a general criticism of the SME policy, see Stevensson and Lundström (2000).
14. The idea that economic growth is the result emerging from all societal and economic efforts is, for instance, clearly articulated in the analyzed Government Bills, but also in the papers, reports, and programs of the Social-Democratic Party. See, for example, Social Democratic Party 2002 (p. 26) and 1992 (p. 91ff).

15. This is also the title of a NUTEK report on consultancy of female entrepreneurs and the definition of the general objective of these activities to transform "invisible growth" into "visible growth."

NOTES TO CHAPTER 8

1. This would be translated into English as "Responsibility Committee."
2. See, for instance, remarks 132, 136, and 175 in Parliamentary Minutes 2000/1: 45 by the Conservative Party, the Social Democrats, and the Center Party, which all consent on the aspiration to make Sweden a leading knowledge nation.
3. Growth agreements were replaced later in Government Bill 2001/02: 4 by the concept of "Regional Growth Programs."
4. Government Bill 2001/02: 4 describes that work with regionally specified growth agreements and the observation of the importance of networks, clusters, and quality of the home-base emanate from the EU's structural fund programs (Government Bill 2001/02: 4, p. 24).
5. The German word *Unternehmung* would rather well describe the "entrepreneurial" character of such projects since it expresses "risk-taking," "activity," and "mobilization" of actors.
6. Aspirations to constructing regional and local identities could be understood as a means of support for local and regional mobilization and community commitment.
7. Regional concerns about "regional identities," regional capacities to mobilize regional population and expand the total number of social, political, and economic contributions made by the citizens on local and regional levels appearing in the mid-1990s, were very typical of this concern (cf. Government Bill 1996/97: 36, chapter 5; cf. Marttila 2004).
8. NUTEK's report adopted this concept from Henton, Walesh, and Melville (1997).
9. One of the primary objectives for the regional policy designed in the late 1990s was to create new patterns of local and regional identifications, which would facilitate local and regional cooperation (cf. Government Bill 1997/98: 62, p. 97; SOU 1995: 27, p. 325ff).
10. The information campaign *Starta Eget Tillsammans* (English: "Start your own together") was initiated in 1999 to foster employment within the private sector through cooperative enterprises (see Government Bills 1999/2000: 1D15; 2001/02:4, p. 160f).
11. Some inaugurating sources for the discussion of an entrepreneurial education in Sweden were included in the EU's (1995) white paper, "Training and Youth," which evoked debates on the appropriateness of the Swedish education system with regard to the future KBE, as well as Department Report 1997: 3.
12. The original Swedish wording is *sammanhållning*, which refers to social coherence but could also denote societal coherence in terms of solidarity and common patterns of identification. The social-democratic government has repetitively "stressed" the positive relations of reciprocity between social welfare and economic growth: for instance, by elevating the welfare state to a constituent element of the "climate of entrepreneurship" (cf. Parliamentary Minutes 2001/02: 103, remark 31; 2004/05: 79, remark 79).
13. See also Government Communication 2001/02: 172 for a similar description of the role of the political government to "create an improved climate of entrepreneurship by means of information, consultancy, simplification of

rules, capital supply where the private market does not function sufficiently and by means of functioning competition."

14. An example of how the debates are centered around the notion of "climate of entrepreneurship" is how the Conservative Party claims the Social-Democratic Party disregards the sincere needs of the entrepreneur, whereas the Social-Democratic Party accentuates its contribution to increasing the number of entrepreneurs and also emphasizes the direct socialization of individuals to duties characterizing the entrepreneur, such as curiosity, creativity, and inventiveness.

15. See further Government Communication 2001/02: 172, chapter 3; Motion 1999/2000: N340; 2000/01: N385; Parliamentary Minutes 1999/00:92, remarks 1,182, 183, 185.

16. See Parliamentary Minutes 2003/04: 96, remark 3; 12, remarks 19. 28, 226; 13, remarks 99, 100, 102, 207, 208, 236; 14, remarks 1, 47.

17. Compare Parliamentary Minutes 2003/04: 14, remark 27, by the social-democratic Minister for Trade and Industry, Leif Pagrotzky; and Parliamentary Minutes 2003/04: 2, remarks 99, 208 by the Conservative and Centre Party. See also Parliamentary Minutes 2003/04: 13, remark 236; 14, remark 27; 51, remarks 2,6, 7.

18. Debates on what is a beneficial "climate of entrepreneurship" are no novelty as such. The reports of the "SME delegation" especially induced intense debates about the socio-economic climate of SEs. The delegation worked after the EU's role model Business Environment Simplification Task Force (BEST) assigned by the European Commission (cf. Government Communication 1996/97: 83; Parliamentary Minutes 1997/98: 62, remark 25). The delegation made 26 different proposals for a better climate of SMEs, and the acceptance and preparedness to implement these proposals were articulated to symbolize the attitudes toward SMEs in political debates (see Parliamentary Minutes 1997/98:74, remarks 207, 209, 210).

19. This also represents a general shift in the political debate, which in the course of time is more strongly centered around the entrepreneurial subject—the social subject behind the role of the entrepreneur—as contrasted to the previously predominant focus on the situation of enterprises as organizations.

20. M, FP, Kd, and C are abbreviations for the Conservative Party (*Moderata Samlingspartiet*), Liberal Party (*Folkpartiet Liberalerna*), Christian Democratic Party (*Kristdemokratiska Partiet*), and Centre Party (*Centerpartiet*), respectively.

21. SLIM was also part of the Lisbon Strategy of 2001, whose objective was to make the EU the most advanced and competitive KBE.

NOTES TO CHAPTER 9

1. An obvious parallel can be drawn to the predominant management discourse is the 1990s—the strategy of "business process re-engineering"—which according to Boltanski and Chiapello (1999: 114) placed individuals as "creative units" in production processes in order to optimize their productivity and performance.

2. For similar conclusions, see Mahieu (2006), OECD (1989, 2001), and Smyth (2004).

3. Of course, it has to questioned whether a society in which everybody is asked to behave in the manner of an entrepreneur of oneself still deserves the name of welfare society. Nevertheless, an answer to this question—like many others—would go beyond the scope of this book.

Bibliography

Secondary Literature

Agamben, Giorgio, 2007: *Infancy and History: On the Destruction of Experience.* London: Verso.

Åkerstrøm Andersen, Niels, 2005: "Political Administration." In Howarth, David (Ed.), *Discourse Theory in European Politics: Identity, Policy and Governance.* Basingstoke: Macmillan. Pp. 139–169.

Åkerstrøm Andersen, Niels, 2003: *Discursive Analytical Strategies: Understanding Foucault, Kosellack, Laclau, Luhmann.* Bristol: Policy Press.

Althusser, Louis, 1971: *Lenin and Philosophy and Other Essays.* London: NLB.

Alvesson, Mats and Sköldberg, Kaj, 2000: *Reflexive Methodology: New Vistas for Qualitative Research.* London: Sage Publications.

Amin, Ash (Ed.), 1994: *Post-Fordism: A Reader.* Oxford: Blackwell.

Amin, Ash and Malmberg, Anders, 1994: "Competing Structural and Institutional Influences on the Geography of Production in Europe." In Amin, Ash (Ed.), *Post-Fordism: A Reader.* Oxford: Blackwell. Pp. 227–248.

Amin, Ash and Thrift, Nigel, 1994: "Holding Down the Global." In Amin, Ash and Thrift, Nigel (Eds.), *Globalisation, Institutions and Regional Development in Europe.* Oxford: Oxford University Press. Pp. 257–260.

Amiran, Eyal, 2000: "After Dynamic Narratology." In *Style.* Vol. 34, No. 2. Pp. 212–226.

Anderson, Jenny, 2005: "Kritik och Kunskapskamp: Ett Perspektiv på den Starka Statens Fall." In Rothstein, Bo and Vahlne Westerhäll, Lotta (Eds.), *Bortom den Starka Statens Politik?* Stockholm: SNS Förlag. Pp. 24–41.

Andriessen, Daniel and Gubbins, Claire, 2009: "Metaphor Analysis as an Approach for Exploring Theoretical Concepts." In *Organization Studies.* Vol. 30, No. 8. Pp. 845–863.

Angermüller, Johannes, 2007: "Was fordert die Hegemonietheorie? Zu den Möglichkeiten und Grenzen ihrer methodischen Umsetzung." In Nonhoff, Martin (Ed.), *Diskurs, Radikale Demokratie, Hegemonie. Zum Politischen Denken von Ernesto Laclau und Chantal Mouffe.* Bielefeld: Transcript. Pp. 159–172.

Angermüller, Johannes, 2005: "Sozialwissenschaftliche Diskursanalyse in Deutschland. Zwischen Rekonstruktion und Dekonstruktion." In Keller, Rainer—Hirseland, Andreas—Schneider, Werner—Viehöver, Willy (Eds.), *Die Diskursive Konstruktion von Wirklichkeit. Zum Verhältnis von Wissenssoziologie und Diskursforschung.* Konstanz: UVK Verlagsgesellschaft. Pp. 23–47.

Audretsch, David, 2000: "Entrepreneurship in Germany." In Sexton, Donald L. and Landström, Hans (Eds.), *The Blackwell Handbook of Entrepreneurship.* Oxford: Blackwell. Pp. 107–127.

Bachelard, Gaston, 1988: *Der neue wissenschaftliche Geist.* Frankfurt am Main: Suhrkamp.

Bachelard, Gaston, 1978b: *Die Philosophie des Nein: Versuch einer Philosophie des neuen wissenschaftlichen Geistes.* Wiesbaden: Heymann.

Bachelard, Gaston, 1978a: *Die Bildung des wissenschaftlichen Geistes.* Frankfurt am Main: Suhrkamp.

Balibar, Etienne, 1994: *Für Althusser.* Mainz: Decaton.

Bauman, Zygmunt, 1991: *Modernity and Ambivalence.* Cambridge: Polity Press.

Baumol, William J., 1990: "Entrepreneurship: Productive, Unproductive, and Destructive." In *The Journal of Political Economy.* Vol. 98, No. 5. Pp. 893–921.

Baxandall, Phineas, 2004: *Constructing Unemployment: The Politics of Joblessness in East and West.* Ashgate: Aldershot.

Benner, Mats, 1997: *The Politics of Growth- Economic Regulation in Sweden 1930–1994.* Lund: Arkiv.

Berger, Peter and Luckmann, Thomas, 1991: *The Social Construction of Reality: A Treatise in the Sociology of Knowledge.* London: Penguin Books.

Bergmark, Åke and Palme, Joakim, 2003: "Welfare and the Unemployment Crisis: Sweden in the 1990s." In *International Journal of Social Welfare.* Vol. 12. Pp. 108–122.

Bernstein, Richard, J. 1983: *Beyond Objectivism and Relativism: Science, Hermeneutics and Practice.* Philadelphia: University of Pennsylvania Press.

Bertramsen, Rene—Frølund Thomsen, Jens Peter—Torfing, Jacob, 1991: "From the Problems of Marxism to the Primacy of Politics." In Bertramsen, Rene— Frølund Thomsen, Jens Peter—Torfing, Jacob (Eds.), *State, Economy and Society.* London: Unwin Hyman. Pp. 1–34.

Blomqvist, Paula and Rothstein, Bo, 2000: *Välfärdsstatens Nya Ansikte.* Stockholm: Agora.

Blum, Ulrich and Leibbrand, Frank (Eds.), 2001: *Entrepreneurship und Unternehmertum. Denkstrukturen für eine neue Zeit.* Wiesbaden: Dr. Th. Gobler.

Blyth, Mark, 2001: "The Transformation of the Swedish Model. Economic Ideas, Distributional Conflict and Institutional Change." In *World Politics.* Vol. 54. Pp. 1–26.

Bögenhold, Dieter and Schmidt, Dorothea, 1999: "Einleitung: Alte und neue Gründerzeiten." In Bögenhold, Dieter andSchmidt, Dorothea (Eds.), *Eine neue Gründerzeit? Die Wiederentdeckung kleiner Unternehmen in Theorie und Praxis.* Gründungsforschung, Band 1. GtB Verlag Fakultas, Amsterdam. Pp. 1–6.

Boltanski, Luc and Chiapello, Éve, 1999: *Der Neue Geist des Kapitalismus.* Konstanz: UVK.

Boreham, Nick, 2006: "The Knowledge Economy, Work Process: Knowledge and the Learning Citizen—Central but Vulnerable." In Kuhn, Michael—Tomassini Massimo—Simons, Robert -Jan, P. (Eds.), *Towards a Knowledge Based Economy? Knowledge and Learning in European Educational Research.* New York: Peter Lang. Pp. 129–147.

Boréus, Kristina, 1994: *Högervåg: Nyliberalism och Kampen om Språket i Svensk Debatt 1969–1989.* Stockholm: Tidens Förlag.

Bourdieu, Pierre, 2008: *Science of Science and Reflexivity.* Cambridge. Polity Press.

Bourdieu, Pierre andWacquant, Loïc, 2006: „Die Ziele der Reflexiven Sozioanalyse." In Bourdieu, Pierre andWacquant, Loïc (Eds.) (2006): *Reflexive Anthropologie.* Frankfurt am Main. Suhrkamp. Pp. 95–123.

Brenner, Neil, 1994: "Foucault's New Functionalism." In *Theory and Society.* Vol. 23. Pp. 679–709.

Bröckling, Ulrich, 2007a: *Das Unternehmerische Selbst: Soziologie einer Subjektivierungsform.* Frankfurt am Main: Suhrkamp.

Bröckling, Ulrich, 2007b: "Regime der Selbst—Ein Forschungsprogramm." In Bonacker, Thorsten and Reckwitz, Andreas (Eds.), *Kulturen der Moderne: Soziologische Perspektiven der Gegenwart.* Frankfurt: Campus. Pp. 119–139.

Bröckling, Ulrich, 2003: "Jeder könnte, aber nicht alle können." In *Mittelweg 36.* Vol. 11, No. 4. Pp. 6–26.

Brown, Stephen, 2004: "Parasite Logic." In *Journal of Organizational Change Management.* Vol. 17, No. 4. Pp. 383–395.

Bublitz, Hannelore, 2001: "Differenz und Integration. Zur diskursanalytischen Rekonstruktion der Regelstrukturen sozialer Wirklichkeit." In Keller, Rainer—Hirseland, Andreas—Schneider, Werner—Viehöver, Willy (Eds.), *Handbuch Sozialwissenschaftliche Diskursanalyse. Band I: Theorien und Methoden.* Opladen: Leske + Budrich. Pp. 101–118.

Bührmann, Andrea D., 2005: "The Emerging of the Entrepreneurial Self and Its Current Hegemony. Some Basic Reflections on How to Analyze the Formation and Transformation of Modern Forms of Subjectivity." [49 Paragraphs]. In *Forum Qualitative Sozialforschung,* Vol. 6, No. 1. Article 15. http://nbnresolving.de/urn:nbn:de:0114-fqs0501165.

Burchell, Graham, 1993: "Liberal Government and Techniques of the Self." In *Economy and Society,* Vol. 22, No. 3. Pp. 267–282.

Casson, Mark, 2006: "Introduction." In Casson, Mark—Yeung, Bernhard—Basu, Anuradha—Wadeson, Nigel (Eds.), *The Oxford Handbook of Entrepreneurship.* Oxford: Oxford University Press. Pp. 1–30.

Casson, Mark (Ed.), 1990: *Entrepreneurship.* Aldershot: Elgar.

Casson, Mark, 1982: *The Entrepreneur.* Oxford: Martin Robertson.

Clarke, John, 2004: Changing Welfare, Changing States: New Directions in Social Policy. London: Sage.

Considine, Mark, 2001: *Enterprising States: The Public Management of Welfare and Work.* Cambridge: Cambridge University Press.

Cornelissen, Joep P., 2004: "What Are We Playing at? Theatre, Organization, and the Use of Metaphor." In *Organization Studies.* Vol. 25, No. 5. Pp. 705–726.

Coser, Lewis A., 1994: "The Sociology of poverty." In Frisby, David (Ed.), *Georg Simmel: Critical Assessments.* Volume III. London and New York: Routledge. Pp. 140–148.

Cox, Henry Robert, 2001: "The Construction of an Imperative: Why Welfare Reform Happened in Denmark and the Netherlands but Not in Germany." *World Politics.* Vol. 53, No. 3. Pp. 463–498.

Critchley, Simon, 1999: Ethics, Politics, Subjectivity: Essays on Derrida, Levinas and Contemporary French Thought. New York: Verso.

Critchley, Simon and Marchart, Oliver (Eds.), 2004: *Laclau: A Critical Reader.* New York: Routledge. Pp. 241–255.

Cruikshank, Barbara, 1996: "Revolutions Within: Self-Government and Self-Esteem." In Barry, Andrew—Osborne, Thomas—Rose, Nikolas (Eds.), *Foucault and Political Reason: Liberalism, Neo-liberalism and Rationalities of Government.* Chicago: The University of Chicago Press. Pp. 231–251.

Culler, Jonathan, 1986: *Ferdinand de Saussure.* Revised Edition. Ithaca, NY: Cornell University Press.

Currie, Mark, 1998: *Postmodern Narrative Theory.* Basingstoke: Macmillan.

De, Dennis, 2000: "SME Policy in Europe." In Sexton, Donald L. and Landström, Hans (Eds.), *The Blackwell Handbook of Entrepreneurship.* Oxford: Blackwell. Pp. 87–106.

Dean, Mitchell, 1999: *Governmentality. Power and Rule in Modern Society.* London: Sage Publications.

Dean, Mitchell, 1996: "Foucault, Government and the Enfolding of Authority." In Barry, Andrew—Osborne, Thomas—Rose, Nikolas (Eds.), *Foucault and Political Reason: Liberalism, Neo-liberalism and Rationalities of Government*. Chicago: The University of Chicago Press. Pp. 209–229.

Deeks, John, 1993: *Business and the Culture of the Enterprise Culture*. Westport, CT: Quorum Books.

Deleuze, Gilles and Guattari, Félix, 2003: *What Is Philosophy?* London: Verso.

Deleuze, Gilles, 1999: *Foucault*. London: Continuum.

Deleuze, Gilles, 1988: *Spinoza: Praktische Philosophie*. Berlin: Merve-Verlag.

Della-Giusta, Marina and King, Zella, 2006: "Enterprise Culture." In Casson, Mark—Yeung, Bernhard—Basu, Anuradha—Wadeson, Nigel (Eds.), *The Oxford Handbook of Entrepreneurship*. Oxford: Oxford University Press. Pp. 629–647.

Derrida, Jacques, 2004: *Dissemination*. New York and London: Continuum.

Derrida, Jacques, 1999: "Justice, Law and Philosophy—an Interview with Jacques Derrida." In *South African Journal of Philosophy*. Vol. 18, No. 3. Pp. 279–286.

Derrida, Jacques, 1997: *Of Grammatology*. Baltimore and London: John Hopkins University Press.

Derrida, Jacques, 1994: Spectres of Marx: the State of the Debt, the Work of Mourning, and the New International. New York: Routledge.

Derrida, Jacques, 1982: "Différance." In Derrida, Jacques, *Margins of Philosophy*. Brighton: Harvester Press. Pp. 1–29.

Derrida, Jacques, 1981a: *Positions*. Chicago: The University of Chicago Press.

Derrida, Jacques, 1981b: "Semiology and Grammatology: Interview with Julia Kristeva." In Derrida, Jacques, *Positions*. Chicago: University of Chicago Press. Pp. 15–36.

Derrida, Jacques, 1981c: *Writing and Difference*. London: Routledge and Kegan Paul.

Derrida, Jacques, 1979: "Scribble (Writing-Power)." In *Yale French Studies*. No. 58. Pp 117–147.

Derrida, Jacques, 1977: "Signature Event Context." In Derrida, Jacques, *Limited Inc.* Evanston, IL: Northwestern University Press. Pp. 1–23.

Deutschmann, Christoph, 2008: Kapitalistische Dynamik: Eine Gesellschaftstheoretische Perspektive. Wiesbaden: VS-Verlag.

Diaz-Bone, Rainer, 2007: "Die französische Epistemologie und ihre Revisionen. Zur Rekonstruktion des methodologischen Standortes der Foucaultschen Diskursanalyse." [65 Paragraphs]. In *Forum Qualitative Sozialforschung*. Vol. 8, No. 2. Article 6. http://nbnresolving.de/urn:nbn:de:0114-fqs0702241.

Diaz-Bone, Rainer, 2006a: "Die interpretative Analytik als methodologische Position." In Kerchner, Brigitte and Schneider, Silke (Eds.), *Foucault: Diskursanalyse der Politik*. Wiesbaden: VS Verlag für Sozialwissenschaften. Pp. 68–84.

Diaz-Bone, Rainer, 2006b: "Zur Methodologisierung der Foucaultschen Diskursanalyse." In *Historical Social Research*. Vol. 31, No. 2. Pp. 243–274.

Diaz-Bone, Rainer, 2005: "Die 'Interpretative Analytik' als rekonstruktivmethodologische Methodologie. Bemerkungen zur Eigenlogik und strukturalistischen Öffnung der Foucaultschen Diskursanalyse." In Keller, Rainer—Hirseland, Andreas—Schneider, Werner—Viehöver, Willy (Eds.), *Die Diskursive Konstruktion von Wirklichkeit. Zum Verhältnis von Wissenssoziologie und Diskursforschung*. Konstanz: UVK Verlagsgesellschaft. Pp. 179–197.

Diaz-Bone, Rainer, 2002: *Kulturwelt, Diskurs und Lebensstil: Eine Diskurstheoretische Erweiterung der Bourdieuschen Distinktionstheorie*. Opladen: Leske+Budrich.

Dosse, Francois, 1999: *Geschichte des Strukturalismus. Band 1: Das Feld des Zeichens.* Hamburg: Junius.

Drake, Keith, 1997: "Industrial Competitiveness in the Knowledge-Based-Economy: The New Role of Government." In OECD (Ed.), *Industrial Competitiveness in the Knowledge-Based-Economy.* Paris: OECD. Pp. 17–52.

Dreyfus, Hubert, L. and Rabinow, Paul, 1982: *Michel Foucault: Beyond Structuralism and Hermeneutics.* Chicago: University of Chicago Press.

Du Gay, Paul, 1996: *Consumption and Identity at Work.* London: Sage.

Du Gay, Paul, 1991: "Enterprise Culture and the Ideology of Excellence." In *New Formations.* Vol. 13. Pp. 45–61.

Dumézil, Georges, 1989: "Der Götterbote: Interview mit Francois Ewald." In Ewald, Francois (Ed.), *Pariser Gespräche.* Berlin: Merve. Pp. 61–82.

Dyrberg, Torben Bech, 2004: "The Political and Politics in Discourse Analysis." In Critchley, Simon and Marchart, Oliver (Eds.), *Laclau: A Critical Reader.* New York: Routledge. Pp. 241–255.

Dyrberg, Torben Bech, 1998: "Diskursanalyse als postmoderne politische Theorie." In Marchart, Olivier (Ed.), *Das undarstellbare der Politik: Zur Hegemonietheorie Ernesto Laclaus.* Wien: Turia+ Kant. Pp. 23–51.

Dyrberg, Torben Bech, 1997: *The Circular Structure of Power: Politics, Identity, Community.* London: Verso.

Edelman, Murray, 1971: *Politics as Symbolic Action.* Chicago: Markham.

Elander, Ingemar, 1999: "Partnerskap och Demokrati—Omaka par i Nätverkspolitikens Tid?" In *Globalisering. Bidrag till Demokratiutredningens Forskarvolym IX. SOU 1999: 83.* Stockholm: Fritzes. Pp. 327–364.

Elliott, John E., 1980: "Marx and Schumpeter on Capitalism's Creative Destruction: A Comparative Restatement." In *The Quarterly Journal of Economics.* Vol. 95, No. 1. Pp. 45–68.

European Commission, 2003: *Green Paper: Entrepreneurship in Europe.* Brussels: Office for Official Publications of the European Communities.

European Commission, 1995: *Teaching and learning—Towards the Learning Society.* Brussels: White Paper. Office for Official Publications of the European Communities.

Fairclough, Norman, 1992: *Discourse and Social Change.* Cambridge: Polity Press.

Farrell, Larry C., 2001: *The Entrepreneurial Age: Awakening of the Spirit of Enterprise in People, Companies, and Countries.* New York: Allworth Press.

Finlayson, Alan, 2004: "Political Science, Political Ideas and Rhetoric." In *Economy and Society.* Vol. 33, No.4. Pp. 528–549.

Florida, Richard, 2002: *The Rise of the Creative Class.* New York: Basic Books.

Flynn, Thomas R., 2004: "Foucault as Philosopher of the Historical Event." In Rölli, Marc (Ed.), *Ereignis auf Französisch: Von Bergson bis Deleuze.* München: Wilhelm Fink Verlag. Pp. 209–234.

Foucault, Michel, 2007: *Security, Territory, Population.* Lecture at the Collège de France 1978/79. Basingstoke: Palgrave Macmillan.

Foucault, Michel, 2006: *Geburt der Biopolitik: Geschichte der Gouvernementalität II.* Frankfurt am Main: Suhrkamp.

Foucault, Michel, 2005: *Analytik der Macht.* Frankfurt am Main: Suhrkamp.

Foucault, Michel, 2004: "Die Ethik der Sorge um sich als Praxis der Freiheit." In Defert, Daniel (Ed.), *Schriften in vier Bänden.* Vol. 4. Frankfurt am Main: Suhrkamp. Pp. 875–902.

Foucault, Michel, 2002a: *The Archaeology of Knowledge.* London: Routledge.

Foucault, Michel, 2002b: "The Subject of Power." In Faubion, James D. (Ed.), *Power.* London: Penguin Books. Pp. 326–348.

Foucault, Michel, 1998: *The Will to Knowledge. The History of Sexuality,* Vol. 1. London: Penguin Books.

Foucault, Michel, 1994a: "Die Wahrheit und die juristischen Formen." In Defert, Daniel (Ed.), *Schriften in Vier Bänden*. Vol. 4. Frankfurt am Main: Suhrkamp. Pp. 669–792.

Foucault, Michel, 1994b: "Nietzsche, Freud, Marx." In Defert, Daniel (Ed.), *Schriften in vier Bänden*. Vol. 1. Frankfurt am Main: Suhrkamp. Pp. 727–743.

Foucault, Michel, 1994c: *Überwachen und Strafen: Die Geburt des Gefängnisses*. Frankfurt am Main: Suhrkamp.

Foucault, Michel, 1991a: "Governmentality." In Burchell, Graham—Gordon, Colin—Miller, Peter (Eds.), *Foucault Effect: Studies in Governmentality*. Chicago: University of Chicago Press. Pp. 87–118.

Foucault, Michel, 1991b: "Politics and the Study of Discourse." In Burchell, Graham—Gordon, Colin—Miller, Peter (Eds.), *The Foucault Effect*. Chicago: University of Chicago Press. Pp. 53–72.

Foucault, Michel, 1989: *Der Gebrauch der Lüste: Sexualität und Wahrheit*. Frankfurt am Main: Suhrkamp.

Foucault, Michel, 1988: "Technologies of the Self." In Luther, Martin H.—Gutman, Huck—Hutton, Patrick H. (Eds.), *Technologies of the Self: A Seminar with Michel Foucault*. Amherst: University of Massachusetts Press. Pp. 16–49.

Foucault, Michel, 1984a: "Truth and Power." In Rabinow, Paul (Ed.), *The Foucault Reader*. London: Penguin Books. Pp. 51–75.

Foucault, Michel, 1984b: "What Is Enlightenment?." In Rabinow, Paul (Ed.), *The Foucault Reader*. London: Penguin Books. Pp. 32–50.

Foucault, Michel, 1981: "The Order of Discourse." In Young, Robert (Ed.), *Untying the Text: A Post-Structuralist Reader*. London and Boston: Routledge and Kegan. Pp. 48–78.

Foucault, Michel, 1980a: "Language to Infinity." In Bouchard, Donald F. (Ed.), *Language, Counter-Memory, Practice: Selected Essays and Interviews by Michel Foucault*. Ithaca, NY: Cornell University Press. Pp. 53–68.

Foucault, Michel, 1980b: "Preface to Transgression." In Bouchard, Donald F. (Ed.), *Language, Counter-Memory, Practice: Selected Essays and Interviews by Michel Foucault*. Ithaca, NY: Cornell University Press. Pp. 29–52.

Foucault, Michel, 1977: "Nietzsche, Genealogy and History." In Bouchard, Donald F. (Ed.), *Language, Counter-Memory, Practice: Selected Essays and Interviews by Michel Foucault*. Ithaca, NY: Cornell University Press. Pp. 139–164.

Foucault, Michel, 1970: *The Order of Things: Archaeology of the Human Sciences*. New York: Pantheon Books.

Freeden, Michael, 1996: *Ideologies and Political Theory: A Conceptual Approach*. Oxford: Clarendon Press.

Freeden, Michael, 1994: "Political Concepts and Ideological Morphology." In *Journal of Political Philosophy*. Vol. 2, No. 2. Pp. 140–164.

Frick, Siegfried, 1999: "'Kulturen der Selbständigkeit' in Deutschland? Zur theoretischen und empirischen Fundierung eines aktuellen Begriffs der Wirtschaftspolitik." In Bögenhold, Dieter and Schmidt, Dorothea (Eds.), *Eine neue Gründerzeit? Die Wiederentdeckung kleiner Unternehmen in Theorie und Praxis*. Gründungsforschung, Band 1. Amsterdam: GtB Verlag Fakultas. Pp. 7–41.

Fuchs, Stephan, 2001: *Against Essentialism: A Theory of Society and Culture*. Cambridge, MA: Harvard University Press.

Garsten, Christina and Jacobsson, Kerstin (Eds.), 2004: *Learning to be Employable. New Agendas on Work, Responsibility and Learning in a Globalizing World*. Basingstoke: Palgrave Macmillan.

Gehring, Petra, 2004: "Sind Foucaults Widerstandspunkte Ereignisse oder sind sie es nicht?" In Rölli, Marc (Ed.), *Ereignis auf Französisch: Von Bergson bis Deleuze*. München: Wilhelm Fink Verlag. Pp. 275–284.

Gemünden, Hans Georg and Konrad, Elmar D., 2005: "Unternehmerisches Verhalten: Eine kritische Würdigung und Bestandaufnahme verschiedener Erklärungsansätze." In Gemünden, Hans, Georg—Salomo, Sören—Müller, Thilo (Eds.), *Entrepreneurial Excellence: Unternehmertum, unternehmerische Kompetenz und Wachstum junger Unternehmen.* Wiesbaden: Deutscher Universitäts-Verlag. Pp. 1–38.

Gibson, Andrew, 1996: *Towards a Postmodern Theory of Language.* Edinburgh: Edinburgh University Press.

Glasze, Georg, 2007: "Vorschläge zur Operationalisierung der Diskustheorie von Laclau und Mouffe in einer Triangulation von lexikometrischen und interpretativen Methoden." [73 Paragraphs]. In *Forum Qualitative Sozialforschung*, Vol. 8, No. 2, Article 14. http://nbnresolving.de/urn:nbn:de:0114-fqs0702143.

Glynos, Jason and Howarth, David, 2008: "Critical Explanation in Social Science: A Logics Approach." In *Swiss Journal of Sociology*, Vol. 54, No. 1. Pp. 5–35.

Glynos, Jason and Howarth, David, 2007: *Logics of Critical Explanation in Social and Political Theory.* London and New York: Routledge.

Glynos, Jason, 2001: "The Grip of Ideology: a Lacanian Approach to the Theory of Ideology." In *Journal of Political Ideologies.* Vol. 6, No. 2. Pp. 191–214.

Glynos, Jason, 2000: "Sexual Identity, Identification and Difference: A Psychoanalytic Contribution to Discourse Theory." In *Philosophy & Social Criticism.* Vol. 6, No. 6. Pp. 85–108.

Gordon, Colin, 1991: "Governmental Rationality: An Introduction." In Burchell, Graham—Gordon, Colin—Miller, Peter (Eds.), *The Foucault Effect. Studies in Governmentality.* Chicago: University of Chicago Press. Pp. 1–51.

Gramsci, Antonio, 1971: *Selection of Prison Notebooks.* London: Lawrence and Wishart.

Gray, John, 2000: "Inclusion: A Radical Critique." In Askonas, Peter and Stewart, Angis (Eds.), *Social Inclusion: Possibilities and Tensions.* London: Macmillan Press. Pp. 52–80.

Greene, Francis J.—Mole, Kevin F.—Storey, David J., 2008: *Three Decades of Enterprise Culture: Entrepreneurship, Economic Regeneration and Public Policy.* Basingstoke: Palgrave Macmillan.

Greimas, Algirdas Julien, 1990: *The Social Sciences: A Semiotic View.* Minneapolis: University of Minnesota Press.

Greimas, Algirdas Julien, 1987: *On Meaning: Selected Writings in Semiotic Theory.* Minneapolis: University of Minnesota Press.

Greimas, Algirdas Julien, 1971: *Strukturale Semantik. Methodologische Untersuchungen* Braunschweig: Vieweg.

Griggs, Stephen and Howarth, David, 2002: "An Alliance of Interest and Identity: Explaining the Campaign against Manchester Airport's Second Runway." In *Mobilization.* Vol. 7, No. 1. Pp. 43–58.

Grit, Kor, 1997: "The Rise of the Entrepreneurial University: A Heritage of the Enlightenment?" In *Science Studies.* Vol, 10, No. 2. Pp. 3–22.

Grossberg, Lawrence, 2007: "Leben und Zeit der Kultur." In Winter, Rainer (Ed.), *Die Perspektiven der Cultural Studies: Der Lawrence-Grossberg-Reader.* Köln: Herbert von Halem Verlag. Pp. 13–33.

Grossberg, Lawrence, 2006: "Does Cultural Studies Have Futures? Should It? (or What's the Matter with New York?)." In *Cultural Studies.* Vol. 20, No. 1. Pp. 1–32.

Grossberg, Lawrence—Wartella, Ellen—Whitney, Charles D., 1998: *Media Making: Mass Media in a Popular Culture.* London: Sage.

Gülich, Elisabeth and Quasthoff, Uta M., 1985: "Narrative Analysis." In van Dijk, Teun A. (Ed.), *Handbook of Discourse Analysis: Vol II, Dimensions of Discourse.* London: Academic Press. Pp. 169–198.

Hajer, Maarten A., 2003: "A Frame in the Fields: Policymaking and the Reinvention of Politics." In Hajer, Maarten A. and Wegener, Hendrik (Eds.), *Deliberative Policy Analysis: Understanding Governance in the Network Society.* Cambridge: Cambridge University Press. Pp. 88–110.

Hajer, Maarten A., 1995: *The Politics of Environmental Discourse: Ecological Modernization and the Policy Process.* Oxford: Oxford University Press.

Hall, Peter A., 1993: "Policy Paradigms, Social Learning and the State: The Case of Economic Policymaking in Britain." In *Comparative Politics.* Vol. 25, No. 3. Pp. 275–296.

Harrison, Bennett, 1994: "The Myth of Small Firms as the Predominant Job Generators." In *Economic Development Quarterly.* Vol. 8, No. 1. Pp. 3–18.

Harvey, David, 1989: "From Managerialism to Entrepreneurialism: The Transformation in Urban Governance in Late Capitalism." In *Geografiska Annaler; Series B: Human Geography.* Vol. 71, No. 1. Pp. 3–17.

Harvey, David, 1987: "Flexible Accumulation through Urbanization: Reflections on Post-modernism in the American City." In *Antipode.* Vol. 19. Pp. 260–286.

Hay, Colin and Smith, Nicola, 2005: "Horses for Courses? The Political Discourse of Globalisation and European Integration in the UK and Ireland." In *West European Politics.* Vol. 28, No. 1. Pp. 124–158.

Hay, Colin, 2002: *Political Analysis: A Critical Introduction.* Basingstoke: Palgrave Macmillan.

Hayles, Katherine, 1995: "Searching for Common Ground." In Soule, Michael E. and Lease, Gary (Eds.), *Reinventing Nature? Responses to Postmodern Deconstruction.* Washington, DC: Island Press. Pp. 47–64.

Heelas, Paul and Morris, Paul, 1992: "Enterprise Culture: Its Values and Value." In Heelas, Paul and Morris, Paul (Eds.), *The Values of the Enterprise Culture. The Moral Debate.* London: Routledge. Pp. 1–26.

Heidegger, Martin, 2008: *Basic Writings.* London: Routledge and Kegan.

Henrekson, Magnus and Roine, Jesper, 2007: "Promoting Entrepreneurship in the Welfare State." In Audretsch, David—Grilo, Isabel—Thurik, Roy A. (Eds.), *Handbook of Research on Entrepreneurship Policy.* Cheltenham: Edvard Elgar. Pp. 64–93.

Henrekson, Magnus, 2005: "Entrepreneurship: A Weak Link in the Welfare State?" In *Industrial and Corporate Change.* Vol. 14, No. 3. Pp. 437–467.

Henrekson, Magnus, 1999: "Drivkrafter för Entreprenörskap, Nyföretagande och Företagstillväxt." In Calmfors, Lars and Persson, Mats (Eds.), *Tillväxt och Ekonomisk Politik.* Lund: Studentlitteratur. Pp. 373–400.

Henton, Douglas—Walesh, Kim—Melville, John, 1997: *Grassroot Leaders for New Economy: How Civic Entrepreneurs Are Building Prosperous Communities.* San Francisco: Jossey-Bass.

Hetzel, Andreas, 2001: *Zwischen Poiesis und Praxis. Elemente einer kritischen Theorie der Kultur.* Würzburg: Königshausen & Neumann.

Hjelm, Michael, 2004: "Immigrant Entrepreneurship in the Swedish Welfare State." In *Sociology.* Vol. 38, No. 4. Pp. 739–756.

Hjorth, Daniel—Jones, Campbell—Gartner, William B., 2008: "Recreating/ Recontextualising Entrepreneurship." In *Scandinavian Journal of Management.* Vol. 21. Pp. 81–84.

Hodenius, Birgit, 1997: "Neue Leitbilder; alte Tugenden oder: Wie aus dem Unternehmer ein Gründer wurde." In Thomas, Michael (Ed.), *Selbständige- Gründer-Unternehmer.* Berlin: Berliner Debatte Wissenschaftsverlag. Pp. 122–138.

Howarth, David, 2005: "Applying Discourse Theory: The Method of Articulation." In Howarth, David and Torfing, Jacob (Eds.), *Discourse Theory in European Politics: Identity, Policy and Governance.* Basingstoke: MacMillan. Pp. 316–349.

Howarth, David, 2004: "Hegemony, Political Subjectivity, and Radical Democracy." In Critchley, Simon and Marchart, Oliver (Eds.), *Laclau: A Critical Reader.* New York: Routledge. Pp. 256–276.

Howarth, David, 2002: "An Archaeology of Political Discourse? Michel Foucault and the Critique of Ideology." In *Political Studies.* Vol. 50, No. 1. Pp. 117–135.

Howarth, David and Stavrakakis, Yannis, 2000: "Introducing Disocurse Theory and Political Analysis." In Howarth, David—Norval, Aletta—Stavrakakis, Yannis (Eds.), *Discourse Theory and Political Analysis: Identities, Hegemonies and Social Change.* Manchester: Manchester University Press. Pp. 1–23.

Hutter, Michael and Teubner, Günther, 1994: "Der Gesellschaft fette Beute. Homo Juridicus und Homo Oeconomicus als kommunikationserhaltende Fiktionen." In Fuchs, Peter and Göbel, Andreas (Eds.), *Der Mensch—Das Medium der Gesellschaft?* Frankfurt am Main: Suhrkamp. Pp. 110–145.

Jacobsson, Kerstin, 1999: "Den Offentliga Demokratisynen." In *SOU 1999: 77: Demokrati och Medborgarskap.* Stockholm: Fakta Info. Pp. 161–223.

Jäger, Siegfried, 1993: "Text- und Diskursanalyse: Eine Einleitung zur Analyse politischer Texte." In *Diss-Texte.* No. 16. Duisburg: D.I.S.S.

Jakobson, Roman, 1990: *On Language.* Cambridge, MA: Harvard University Press.

Jameson, Fredric, 1990: *Signatures of the Visible.* New York: Routledge.

Jessop, Bob, 2008: "A Cultural Political Economy of Competitiveness and Its Implications for Higher Education." In Jessop, Bob—Fairclough, Norman—Wodak, Ruth (Eds.), *Education and the Knowledge-Based Economy in Europe.* Rotterdam: Sense Publishers. Pp. 13–40.

Jessop, Bob, 2006: "From Micro-Powers to Governmentality: Foucault's Work on Statehood, State Formation, Statecraft and State Power." In *Political Geography.* Vol. 26, No.1. Pp. 34–40.

Jessop, Bob and Sum, Ngai-Ling, 2006: *Beyond the Regulation Approach: Putting Capitalist Economies in their Place.* Cheltenham: Edward Elgar.

Jessop, Bob, 2004: "Critical Semiotic Analysis and Cultural Political Economy." In *Critical Discourse Analysis.* Vol. 1, No. 1. Pp. 1–16.

Jessop, Bob, 2002: *The Future of the Capitalist State.* Cambridge, MA: Polity Press.

Jessop, Bob, 2000: "The Changing Governance of Welfare: Recent Trends in Its Primary Functions, Scale, and Modes of Coordination." In *Social Policy and Administration.* Vol. 33, December. Pp. 348–359.

Jessop, Bob and Peck, Jamie, 1998: "Fast Policy/Local discipline: The Politics of Scale and the Neo-liberal Workfare Offensive." Paper presented at the conference of the association of American geographers. Boston. March 25–29.

Jessop, Bob, 1994: "Post-Fordism and the State." In Amin, Ash (Ed.), *Post-Fordism: A Reader.* Oxford: Blackwell. Pp. 251–279.

Jessop, Bob, 1993: "The Transition to Post-Fordism and the Schumpeterian Workfare State." In Burrows, Roger and Loader, Brian (Eds.), *Towards a Post-Fordist Welfare State.* London: Routledge. Pp. 13–37.

Johannisson, Bengt, 2003: "Entrepreneurship as a Collective Phenomenon." Unpublished Working Paper. *SIRE,* Växjö University.

Johannisson, Bengt and Lindmark, Leif, 1996: "Det Mångfasetterade Småföretagandet." In Johannisson, Bengt and Lindmark, Leif (Eds.), *Företag, Företagare, Företagsamhet.* Stiftelsen för Småföretagsforskning. Lund: Studentlitteratur. Pp. 11–23.

Johansson, Anders L. and Magnusson, Lars, 1998: *LO- Det Andra Halvseklet. Fackföreningsrörelsen och Samhället.* Stockholm: Atlas.

Jones, Campbell and Spicer, André, 2009: *Unmasking the Entrepreneur.* Cheltenham: Edward Elgar.

Jones, Campbell and Spicer, André 2005: "The Sublime Object of Entrepreneurship." In *Organization*. Vol.12, No. 2. Pp. 223–246.

Joseph, Jonathan, 2001: "Derrida's Spectres of Ideology". In *Journal of Political Ideologies*. Vol.6, No. 1. Pp. 95–115.

Keller, Rainer, 2008: *Wissensoziologische Diskursanalyse: Grundlegung eines Forschungsprogramms*. 2ⁿᵈ edition. Wiesbaden: VS Verlag für Sozialwissenschaften.

Keller, Rainer, 2001: "Wissenssoziologische Diskursanalyse." In Keller, Rainer—Hirseland, Andreas—Schneider, Werner—Viehöver, Willy (Eds.), *Handbuch sozialwissenschaftliche Diskursanalyse. Band I: Theorien und Methoden*. Opladen: Leske + Budrich. Pp. 113–143.

Keller, Rainer—Hirseland, Andreas—Schneider, Werner—Viehöver, Willy (Eds.), 2001: *Handbuch sozialwissenschaftliche Diskursanalyse. Band I: Theorien und Methoden*. Opladen: Leske + Budrich.

Kirzner, Israel M., 1973: *Competition and Entrepreneurship*. Chicago: University of Chicago Press.

Knudsen, Sven-Eric, 2006: *Luhmann und Husserl: Systemtheorie im Verhältnis zur Phänomenologie*. Würzburg: Königshausen & Neumann.

Kooiman, Jan, 2003: *Governing as Governance*. London: Sage.

Lacan, Jacques, 1991: *Encore. Das Seminar Buch XX*. Weinheim and Berlin: Quadriga.

Lacan, Jacques, 1977: *Ecrits. A Selection*. London: Tavistock Publications.

Lacan, Jacques, 1976: *The Language of the Self. The Function of Language in Psychoanalysis*. Baltimore: Johns Hopkins University Press.

Laclau, Ernesto, 2006: "Why Constructing of People Is the Main Task of Radical Politics." In *Critical Inquiry*. Summer. Pp. 646–680.

Laclau, Ernesto, 2005a: "Populism: What Is in a Name." In Panizza, Francisco (Ed.), *Populism and the Mirror of Democracy*. London: Verso. Pp. 32–49.

Laclau, Ernesto, 2005b: *On Populist Reason*. London and New York. Verso.

Laclau, Ernesto, 2004: "Glimpsing the Future." In Critchley, Simon and Marchart, Oliver (Eds.), *Laclau: A Critical Reader*. New York: Routledge. Pp. 279–328.

Laclau, Ernesto and Mouffe, Chantal, 2001: *Hegemony and Socialist Strategy*. London: Verso.

Laclau, Ernesto, 2000a: "Identity and Hegemony: The Role of Universality in the Constitution of Political Logics." In Butler, Judith—Laclau, Ernesto—Žižek, Slavoj (Eds.), *Contingency, Hegemony, Universality. Contemporary Dialogues on the Left*. London and New York: Verso. Pp. 44–89.

Laclau, Ernesto, 2000b: "The Politics of Rhetoric." In Cohen, Tom—Cohen, Barbara—Miller, Hillis J.,—Warminski, Andrzej (Eds.), *Material Events*. Minneapolis: University of Minneapolis Press. Pp. 229–263.

Laclau, Ernesto, 2000c: "Structure, History and the Political." In Butler, Judith—Laclau, Ernesto—Žižek, Slavoj (Eds.), *Contingency, Hegemony, Universality. Contemporary Dialogues on the Left*. London and New York: Verso. Pp. 182–212.

Laclau, Ernesto and Bhaskar, Roy, 1998: "Discourse Theory vs. Critical Realism." In *Alethia*. Vol. 1, No. 2. Pp. 9–14.

Laclau, Ernesto, 1996a: "Deconstruction, Pragmatism, Hegemony." In Mouffe, Chantal (Ed.), *Deconstruction and Pragmatism*. Routledge. New York. Pp. 47–67.

Laclau, Ernesto, 1996b: *Emancipation(s)*. London: Verso.

Laclau, Ernesto and Zac, Lilian, 1994: "Minding the Gap: The Subject of Politics." In Laclau, Ernesto (Ed.), *The Making of Political Identities*. London: Verso. Pp. 11–39.

Laclau, Ernesto, 1993: "Discourse." In Goodin, Robert E. and Petit, Philip (Eds.), *Companion to Contemporary Political Philosophy*. Oxford: Basil Blackwell. Pp. 431–438.

Laclau, Ernesto, 1990a: "The Impossibility of the Society." In Laclau, Ernesto (Ed.), *New Reflections of the Revolution of our Time*. London: Verso. Pp. 89–92.

Laclau, Ernesto, 1990b: *New Reflections of the Revolution of our Time*. London: Verso.

Laclau, Ernesto and Mouffe, Chantal, 1990: "Post-Marxism without Apologies." In Laclau, Ernesto (Ed.), *New Reflections of the Revolution of Our Time*. London: Verso. Pp. 97–132.

Laclau, Ernesto, 1980: "Populist Rupture and Discourse." In *Screen Education*. Vol. 34, No. 34. Pp. 87–93.

Latour, Bruno, 1986: "The Powers of Association." In Law, John (Ed.), *Power, Action, and Belief: A New Sociology of Knowledge?* London: Routledge and Paul Kegan. Pp. 264–280.

Lavoie, Dan and Chamlee-Wright, Emily, 2000: *Culture and Enterprise: The Development, Representation and Morality of Business*. London and New York: Routledge.

Law, John, 2004: *After Method: Mess in Social Science Research*. New York: Routledge.

Lawlor, Leonard, 1982: "Temporality and Spatiality: A Note to a Footnote in Jacques Derrida's 'Writing and Difference'." In *Research in Phenomenology*. Vol. XII. Pp. 149–165.

Lee, Jonathan Scott, 1990: *Jacques Lacan*. Boston: Twayne Publishers.

Lefort, Claude and Gauchet, Marcel, 1990: "Über die Demokratie: Das Politische und die Instituierung des Gesellschaftlichen." In Rödel, Ulrich (Ed.), *Autonome Gesellschaft und Libertäre Demokratie*. Frankfurt am Main: Suhrkamp. Pp. 89–122.

Lefort, Claude, 1988: *Democracy and Political Theory*. Minneapolis: University of Minnesota Press.

Lefort, Claude, 1986: *The Political Forms of Modern Society. Bureaucracy, Democracy, Totalitarianism*. Cambridge, MA: Polity Press.

Lemke, Thomas, 2000: "Neoliberalismus, Staat und Selbsttechnologien. Ein kritischer Überblick über die Governmentality Studies." In *Politische Vierteljahresschrift*. Vol. 41, No. 1. Pp. 31–47.

Lessenich, Stephan, 2003a: "Der Arme in Aktivgesellschaft: Zum sozialen Sinn des Förderns und Forderns." In *WSI-Mitteilungen*. Vol. 56, No. 4. Pp. 214–220.

Lessenich, Stephan, 2003b: "Einleitung: Wohlfahrtstaatliche Grundbegriffe— Semantiken des Wohlfahrtsstaates." In Lessenich, Stephan (Ed.), *Wohlfahrtsstaatliche Grundbegriffe—historische und aktuelle Diskurse*. Frankfurt: Campus-Verlag. Pp. 9–22.

Lessenich, Stephan, 2003c: "Soziale Subjektivität: Die Neue Regierung der Gesellschaft." In *Mittelweg*. Vol. 36, No. 4. Pp. 80–93.

Lindvall, Johannes, 2006: "The Politics of Purpose." In *Comparative Politics*. Vol. 38, No. 2. Pp. 253–272.

Lindvall. Johannes, 2005: "Den Starka Statens Ekonomiska Politik." In Rothstein, Bo and Vahlne-Westerhäll, Lena (Eds.), *Bortom Den Starka Statens Politik*. Stockholm: SNS förlag. Pp. 111–133.

Link, Jürgen, 2005: "Warum Diskurse nicht von personalen Subjekten 'ausgehandelt' werden. Von der Diskurs—zur Interdiskurstheorie." In Keller, Rainer— Hirseland, Andreas—Schneider, Werner—Viehöver, Willy (Eds.), *Die diskursive Konstruktion von Wirklichkeit. Zum Verhältnis von Wissenssoziologie und Diskursforschung*. Konstanz: UVK Verlagsgesellschaft. Pp. 77–99.

Link, Jürgen, 1997: *Versuch über den Normalismus*. Opladen: Westdeutscher Verlag.

Link, Jürgen, 1988: "Literaturanalyse als Interdiskursanalyse." In Horhmann, Jürgen and Müller, Harro (Eds.), *Diskurstheorien und Literaturwissenschaft*. Frankfurt am Main: Suhrkamp. Pp. 284–307.

Link, Jürgen, 1984: "Über ein Modell synchroner Systeme von Kollektivsymbolen sowie seine Rolle bei der Diskurskonstitution." In Link, Jürgen and Wülfing, Wulf (Eds.), *Bewegung und Stillstand in Metaphern und Mythen. Fallstudien zum Verhältnis von elementarem Wissen und Literatur im 19. Jahrhundert.* Stuttgart: Klett-Cotta. Pp. 63–91.

Luhmann, Niklas, 1997: *Gesellschaft der Gesellschaft.* Frankfurt am Main: Suhrkamp.

Luhmann, Niklas, 1993: "Deconstruction as Second-Order Observing." In *New Literary History.* Vol. 24, No. 4. Pp. 763–782.

Luhmann, Niklas, 1988: "Wie ist das Bewusstsein an Kommunikation beteiligt?" In Gumbrecht, Hans Ulrich and Pfeiffer, Ludwig K. (Eds.), *Materialität der Kommunikation.* Frankfurt am Main: Suhrkamp. Pp. 884–908.

Luhmann, Niklas, 1984: *Social Systems.* Stanford: Stanford University Press.

Lundell, Elin (Ed.), 1998: *Det Ekonomiska Läget: Näringspolitikens Möjligheter.* Stockholm: Industriförbundet.

Lundquist, Lennart, 2001: *Medborgardemokratin och Eliterna.* Lund: Studentlitteratur.

Lundquist, Torbjörn, 2005: "Konkurrenspolitiken och den Svenska Modellen." In Rothstein, Bo and Vahlne-Westerhäll, Lena (Eds.), *Bortom den Starka Statens Politik.* Stockholm: SNS förlag.

Lyotard, Jean-François, 1986: *Das Postmoderne Wissen.* Vienna: Edition Passagen.

Mahieu, Ron, 2006: *Agents of Change and Policies of Scale. A Policy Study of Entrepreneurship and Enterprise in Education.* Department of Teacher Training in Swedish and Social Sciences, Umeå University.

Majone, Giandomenico, 1989: *Evidence, Argument, and Persuasion in the Policy Process.* New Haven: Yale University Press.

Marchart, Oliver, 2010: *Die Politische Differenz: Zum Denken des Politischen bei Nancy, Lefort, Badiou, Laclau und Agamben.* Frankfurt am Main: Suhrkamp.

Marchart, Oliver, 2007: *Post-Foundational Political Thought.* Edinburgh: Edinburgh University Press.

Marchart, Oliver, 1998: "Einleitung: Undarstellbarkeit und 'ontologische Differenz'." In Marchart, Oliver (Ed.), *Das Undarstellbare der Politik: Zur Hegemonietheorie Ernesto Laclaus.* Wien: Turia + Kant. Pp. 7–20.

Marquand, David, 1992: "The Enterprise Culture: Old Wine in New Bottles?" In Heelas, Paul and Morris, Paul (Eds.), *The Values of the Enterprise Culture. The Moral Debate.* London: Routledge. Pp. 61–72.

Marttila, Tomas, forthcoming: *Political Difference and Social Analysis.* Unpublished book manuscript.

Marttila, Tomas, 2012a: "Governmentalization of the Entrepreneur: A Case Study." Article in Peer Review.

Marttila, Tomas, 2012b: "Kritische Epistemologie der poststrukuralistischen Hegemonietheorie". In Langer, Antje—Nonhoff, Martin—Reisigl, Martin (Eds.), *Diskursanalyse und Kritik.* Forthcoming.

Marttila, Tomas, 2010a: "Constrained Constructivism in Post-Structural Discourse Analysis." In *Sociologia Internationalis.* Vol. 48, No. 1. Pp. 91–112.

Marttila, Tomas, 2010b: "Foucault's Theory of Cultural Transgression." Paper presented at the conference '*Power of Law*,' Helsinki Law School, University of Helsinki. January 28–30.

Marttila, Tomas and Schillinger, Henrik, 2007: "The Governmentalisation of the World Trade Regime: Finding Reason for Institutional Innovation in the Governance of World Trade." Paper presented at Worskshop '*Institutionelle Innovationen*', University of Bamberg. October 20–21.

Marttila, Tomas, 2004: *Refurnishing Regions: Explaining Identity-Policies in Swedish Regionalisation.* Unpublished Master Thesis. Lund University Sweden.

Marx, Karl and Engels, Friedrich, 2003: "The Manifesto of the Communist Party." In Blaisdell, Robert (Ed.), *The Communist Manifesto and Other Revolutionary Writings.* Mineola, NY: Dover. Pp. 123–150.

McKinsey, 1995: *Swedens Economic Performance.* http://www.mckinsey.com/insights/mgi/research/productivity_competitiveness_and_growth/economic_performance_of_sweden. Accessed February 17, 2009.

Messner, Dirk, 1997: *The Network Society: Economic Development and International Competitiveness as Problems of Social Governance.* London and Portland: Frank Cass.

Messner, Dirk, 1996: *Die Bedeutung von Staat, Markt und Netzwerksteuerung für systemische Wettbewerbsfähigkeit.* Duisburg: Gerhard-Mercator-Universität Duisburg.

Miller, Hillis J., 2004: " 'Taking up a Task': Moments of Decision in Ernesto Laclau's Thought." In Critchley, Simon and Marchart, Oliver (Eds.), *Laclau: A Critical Reader.* New York: Routledge. Pp. 217–225.

Miller, Paul Allen, 1999: "Toward a Post-Foucauldian History of Discursive Practices." In *Configurations.* No. 7. Pp. 211–225.

Miller, Peter and Rose, Nikolas, 2008: *Governing the Present.* Cambridge, MA: Polity Press.

Miller, Peter and Rose, Nikolas, 1990: "Governing Economic Life." In *Economy and Society.* Vol. 19, No. 1. Pp. 1–31.

Moebius, Stephan and Reckwitz, Andreas, 2008: "Einleitung: Poststrukturalismus und Sozialwissenschaften: Eine Standortbestimmung." In Moebius, Stephan and Reckwitz, Andreas (Eds.), *Poststrukturalistische Sozialwissenschaften.* Frankfurt am Main: Suhrkamp. Pp. 7–26.

Moebius, Stephan, 2005: "Diskurs—Ereignis—Subjekt. Diskurs—und Handlungstheorie im Ausgang einer poststrukturalistischen Sozialwissenschaft." In Keller, Rainer—Hirseland, Andreas—Schneider, Werner—Viehöver, Willy (Eds.), *Die diskursive Konstruktion von Wirklichkeit. Zum Verhältnis von Wissenssoziologie und Diskursforschung.* Konstanz: UVK Verlagsgesellschaft. Pp. 127–148.

Mouffe, Chantal, 2005: *On the Political.* London: Routledge.

Mouffe, Chantal, 1993: *Return of the Political.* London and New York: Verso.

Murphy, Kevin M.—Shleifer, Andrei—Vishny, Robert W., 1991: "The Allocation of Talent: Implications for Growth." In *The Quarterly Journal of Economics.* Vol. 106, No. 2. Pp. 503–530.

Newman, Janet 2001: *Modernising Governance.* London: Sage.

Nonhoff, Martin, 2007: "Politische Diskursanalyse als Hegemonieanalyse." In Nonhoff, Martin (Ed.), *Diskurs, Radikale Demokratie, Hegemonie: Zum Politischen Denken von Ernesto Laclau und Chantal Mouffe.* Bielefeld: Transcript. Pp. 173–193.

Nonhoff, Martin, 2006: *Politischer Diskurs und Hegemonie. Das Projekt Soziale Marktwirtschaft.* Bielefeld: Transcript.

Norval, Aletta J., 2000: "Review Article: The Things We Do with Words—Contemporary Approaches to the Analysis of Ideology." In *British Journal of Political Science.* Vol. 30. Pp. 313–346.

Nullmeier, Frank and Rüb, Friedbert, 1993: *Die Transformation der Sozialpolitik. Vom Sozialstaat zum Sicherungsstaat.* Frankfurt am Main: Campus Verlag.

OECD, 2001: *Putting the Young in Business: Policy Challenges for Youth Entrepreneurship.* Paris: OECD.

OECD, 1989: *Towards an 'Enterprising' Culture: A Challenge for Education and Training.* Paris: OECD.

Ogbor, John O., 2000: "Mythicizing and Reification in Entrepreneurial Discourse: Ideology-Critique of Entrepreneurial Studies." In *Journal of Management Studies*. Vol. 37, No. 5. Pp. 606–635.

O'Malley, Pat, 2000: "Uncertain Subjects: Risks, Liberalism and Contract." In *Economy and Society*. Vol. 29, No. 4. Pp. 460–484.

O'Malley, Pat—Weir, Lorna—Shearing, Clifford, 1997: "Governmentality, Criticism, Politics." In *Economy and Society*. Vol. 26, No. 4. Pp. 501–517.

Opitz, Sven, 2007: "Gouvernementalität im Postfordismus: Zur Erkundung unternehmerischer Steuerunsgregime der Gegenwart." In Kaindl, Christina (Ed.), *Subjekte im Neoliberalismus—Kritische Wissenschaften 2*. Marburg: BdWi-Verlag. Pp. 93–108.

Osborne, David and Gaebler, Ted, 1993: *Reinventing Government: How the Entrepreneurial Spirit Is Transforming the Public Sector*. Reading, MA: Addison-Wesley.

Pêcheux, Michel, 1982: *Language, Semantics and Ideology: Stating the Obvious*. London and Basingstoke: Macmillan.

Perkin, Harold, 1992: "The Enterprise Culture in Historical Perspective: Birth, Life, Death—and Resurrection?" In Heelas, Paul and Morris, Paul (Eds.), *The Values of the Enterprise Culture. The Moral Debate*. London: Routledge. Pp. 36–60.

Peters, Michael, 1992: "Starship Education: Enterprise Culture in New Zealand." In *Access: Critical Perspectives on Educational Policy*. Vol. 11, No. 1. Pp. 1–12.

Phillips, Louise and Jörgensen, Marianne, 2002: *Discourse Analysis as Theory and Method*. London: Sage.

Pongratz, Hans J., 2008: "Eine Gesellschaft von Unternehmern: Expansion und Profanierung 'Schöpferischer Zerstörung' in kapitalistischen Ökonomie." In *Berliner Journal für Soziologie*. Vol. 18, No. 3. Pp. 457–475.

Pongratz, Hans J. and Voß, Günter G., 2003: *Arbeitskraftunternehmer: Erwerbsorientierung in entgrenzten Arbeitsformen*. Berlin: Edition Sigma.

Pongratz, Hans J. and Voß, Günter G., 2000: "Vom Arbeitsnehmer zum Arbeitskraftunternehmer—Zur Entgrenzung der Ware Arbeitskraft." In Minssen, Heiner (Ed.), *Begrenzte Entgrenzungen: Wandlungen von Organisation und Arbeit*. Berlin: Sigma. Pp. 225–247.

Prince, Gerald, 1999: "Revisiting Narrativity." In Grünzweig, Walter and Solbach, Andreas (Eds.), *Narratologie, Linguistik und Rhetorik*. Tübingen: Gunter Narr. Pp. 43–51.

Pühl, Katharina, 2003: "Der Bericht der Hartz-Kommission und die 'Unternehmerin ihrer selbst': Geschlechterverhältnisse, Gouvernementalität und Neoliberalismus." In Pieper, Marianne and Gutiérrez Rodríguez, Encarnación (Eds.), *Gouvernementalität: ein sozialwissenschaftliches Konzept in Anschluss an Foucault*. Frankfurt am Main: Campus-Verlag. Pp. 111–135.

Purvis, Trevor and Hunt, Alan, 1993: "Discourse, Ideology, Discourse, Ideology . . .". In *British Journal of Sociology*. Vol. 44. Pp. 473–499.

Rabinow, Paul, 1984: "Introduction." In Rabinow, Paul (Ed.), *The Foucault Reader*. London: Penguin Books. Pp. 3–29.

Rasch, William, 1997: "Locating the Political: Schmitt, Mouffe, Luhmann, and the Possibility of Pluralism." In *International Review of Sociology*. Vol. 7, No. 1. Pp. 103–116.

Reckwitz, Andreas, 2007: "Die Moderne und das Spiel der Subjekte: Kulturelle Differenzen und Subjektordnungen in der Kultur der Moderne." In Bonacker, Thorsten and Reckwitz, Andreas (Eds.), *Kulturen der Moderne: Soziologische Perspektiven der Gegenwart*. Frankfurt/New York: Campus Verlag. Pp. 97–118.

Reckwitz, Andreas, 2006: *Das hybride Subjekt: eine Theorie der Subjektkulturen von den bürgerlichen Moderne zur Postmoderne.* Wiesbaden: Velbrück Wissenschaft.

Reckwitz, Andreas, 2002: "Toward a Theory of Social Practices: A Development in Cultural Theorizing." In *European Journal of Social Theory.* Vol. 5, No.2. Pp. 245–265.

Reyes, Oscar, 2005: "New Labour's Politics of the Hard-Working Family." In Howarth, David and Torfing, Jacob (Eds.), *Discourse Theory in European Politics: Identity, Policy and Governance.* Basingstoke: Macmillan. Pp. 233–254.

Ricoeur, Paul, 1991: "Myth as a Bearer of Possible Worlds." In Valdés, Mario, J. (Ed.), *Reflection and Imagination.* New York: Harvester/Wheatsheaf. Pp. 482–490.

Ricoeur, Paul, 1979: *The Rule of Metaphor: Multi-Disciplinary Studies of the Creation of Meaning in Language.* Toronto: University of Toronto Press.

Rorty, Richard. 1980: *Philosophy and the Mirror of Nature.* Princeton, NJ: Princeton University Press.

Rose, Nikolas, 1999: *Powers of Freedom: Reframing Political Thought.* Cambridge: Cambridge University Press.

Rose, Nikolas, 1996a: "The Death of the Social? Re-figuring the Territory of Government." In *Economy and Society.* Vol. 25, No. 3. Pp. 327–356.

Rose, Nikolas, 1996b: *Inventing Ourselves: Psychology, Power, and Personhood.* Cambridge: Cambridge University Press.

Rose, Nikolas, 1993: "Government, Authority and Expertise in Advanced Liberalism." In *Economy and Society.* Vol. 22, No. 3. Pp. 283–299.

Rose, Nikolas and Miller, Peter, 1992: "Political Power Beyond the State: Problematics of Government." In *The British Journal of Sociology.* Vol. 43, No. 2. Pp. 173–205.

Rose, Nikolas, 1990: *Governing the Soul: The Shaping of the Private Self.* London: Routledge.

Rothstein, Bo and Vahlne Westerhäll, Lotta (Eds.), 2005: *Bortom den Starka Statens Politik?* Stockholm: SNS Förlag.

Rothstein, Bo, 1992: *Den Korporativa Staten. Intresseorganisationer och Statsförvaltning i Svensk Politik.* Stockholm: Norstedts juridik.

Rövik, Kjell-Arne, 2000: *Moderna Organisationer.* Malmö: Liber.

Salais, Robert, 2003: "Toward a Capability Approach." In Zeitlin, Jonathan and Trubek, David M. (Eds.), *Governing Work and Welfare in a New Economy.* Oxford: Oxford University Press. Pp. 317–344.

Saussure, Ferdinand, 1966: *Course in General Linguistics.* London: Peter Owen.

Schmid, Günther, 2004: "Gewährleistungsstaat und Arbeitsmarkt: Neue Formen von Governance in der Arbeitsmarktpolitik." *WZB Discussion Paper.* Berlin: WZB.

Schmid, Günther and Kull, Silke, 2004: "Die Europäische Beschäftigungsstrategie. Anmerkungen zur 'Methode der offenen Koordinierung'." *Working Paper.* Berlin: WZB.

Schmidt, Vivien A., 2003: "How Where and When Does Discourse Matter in Small State's Welfare State Adjustment?" In *New Political Economy.* Vol. 8, No. 1. Pp. 127–146.

Schmidt-Wellenburg, Christian, 2009: "Die neoliberale Gouvernementalität des Unternehmens—Management und Managementberatung zu Beginn des 21. Jahrhunderts." In *Zeitschrift für Soziologie.* Vol. 38, No. 4. Pp. 320–341.

Schneider, Werner and Hirseland, Andreas, 2005: "Macht—Wissen—Gesellschaftliche Praxis: Dispositivanalyse und Wissenssoziologie." In Keller, Rainer—Hirseland, Andreas—Schneider, Werner—Viehöver, Willy (Eds.), *Die Diskursive Konstruktion von Wirklichkeit. Zum Verhältnis von Wissensoziologie und Diskursforschung.* Konstanz: UVK Verlagsgesellschaft. Pp. 251–275.

Schumpeter, Joseph A., 1961: *The Theory of Economic Development*. London: Oxford University Press.

Schumpeter, Joseph A., 1928: "Unternehmer." In Elster, Ludwig—Webern, Adolf—Wieser, Friedrich (Eds.), *Handwörterbuch der Staatswissenschaften*. Vol. 4. Jena: G. Fischer. Pp. 476–487.

Schwab-Trapp, Michael, 2001: "Diskurs als soziologisches Konzept. Bausteine für eine soziologisch orientierte Diskursanalyse." In Keller, Rainer—Hirseland, Andreas—Schneider, Werner—Viehöver, Willy (Eds.), *Handbuch Sozialwissenschaftliche Diskursanalyse. Band I: Theorien und Methoden*. Opladen: Leske + Budrich. Pp. 261–283.

Seeleib-Kaiser, Martin, 1999: *Globalisierung und Sozialpolitik: Ein Vergleich der Diskurse und Wohlfahrtssysteme in Deutschland, Japan und USA*. Frankfurt am Main: Campus Verlag.

Serres, Michel, 1982: *The Parasite*. Baltimore: Johns Hopkins University Press.

Shakespeare, William, 2008: *Hamlet: Prince of Denmark*. 8th edition. Edwards, Philip (Ed.), Cambridge: Cambridge University Press.

Shore, Cris and Wright, Susan, 1997: "Policy: A New Field of Anthropology." In Shore, Cris and Wright, Susan (Eds.), *Anthropology of Policy: Critical Perspectives on Governance and Power*. London: Routledge. Pp. 3–40.

Simmel, Georg, 1992: "Der Arme." In Simmel, Georg (Ed.), *Soziologie. Untersuchungen über die Formen der Vergesellschaftung*. Georg-Simmel Gesamtausgabe, Band 8. Frankfurt am Main: Suhrkamp. Pp. 345–374.

Smith, Ann Marie, 1998: *Laclau and Mouffe: The Radical Democratic Imaginary*. London: Routledge.

Smyth, John, 2004: "Schooling and Enterprise Culture: Pause for a Critical Policy Analysis." In *Journal of Education Policy*. Vol. 14, No. 4. Pp. 435–444.

Somers, Margaret S., 1994: "The Narrative Constitution of Identity: A Relational and Network Approach." In *Theory and Society*. Vol. 23. Pp. 605–649.

Stäheli, Urs, 2011: "Decentring the Economy: Governmentality Studies and Beyond?" In Bröckling, Ulrich- Krasmann and Susanne- Lemke, Thomas (Eds.), *Governmentality: Current Issues and Future Challenges*. New York: Routledge. Pp. 269–284.

Stäheli, Urs, 2007a: "Differenzierte Moderne: Zur Heterogenität funktionaler Differenzierung am Beispiel der Finanzökonomie." In Bonacker, Thorsten and Reckwitz, Andreas (Eds.), *Kulturen der Moderne: Soziologische Perspektiven der Gegenwart*. Frankfurt am Main: Campus. Pp. 183–198.

Stäheli, Urs, 2007b: *Spektakuläre Spekulation. Das Populäre der Ökonomie*. Frankfurt am Main: Suhrkamp.

Stäheli, Urs, 2007c: "Von der Herde zur Horde? Zum Verhältnis von Hegemonie—und Affektpolitik." In Nonhoff, Martin (Ed.), *Diskurs, Radikale Demokratie, Hegemonie. Zum politischen Denken von Ernesto Laclau und Chantal Mouffe*. Bielefeld: Transcript. Pp. 123–138.

Stäheli, Urs, 2004: "The Competing Figures of the Limit." In Critchley, Simon and Marchart, Oliver (Eds.), *Laclau: A Critical Reader*. London: Routledge. Pp. 226–240.

Stäheli, Urs, 2003a: "Financial Noises: Inclusion and the Promise of Meaning." In *Soziale Systeme*. Vol. 9, No. 2. Pp. 244–256.

Stäheli, Urs, 2003b: "The Popular in the Political System." In *Cultural Studies*. Vol. 17, Part 2. Pp. 275–299.

Stäheli, Urs, 2001: "Die politische Theorie der Hegemonie: Ernesto Laclau und Chantal Mouffe." In Brodocz, André and Schaal, Gary S. (Eds.), *Politische Theorien der Gegenwart II: Eine Einführung*. Opladen: Leske + Budrich. Pp. 194–223.

Stäheli, Urs, 2000: *Sinnzusammenbrüche. Eine Dekonstruktive Lektüre von Niklas Luhmanns Systemtheorie.* Weilerswist: Velbrück Wissenschaft.

Stäheli, Urs, 1998: "Die Nachträglichkeit der Semantik: Zum Verhältnis von Sozialstruktur und Semantik." In *Soziale Systeme.* No. 4. Pp. 315–339.

Stäheli, Urs, 1997: "Exorcising the 'Popular' Seriously: Luhmann's Concept of Semantics." In *International Review of Sociology.* Vol. 7, No. 1. Pp. 127–145.

Stäheli, Urs, 1995: "Gesellschaftstheorie und die Unmöglichkeit Ihres Gegenstandes: Diskurstheoretische Perspektiven." In *Schweizerische Zeitschrift für Soziologie.* Vol. 21, No. 2. Pp. 361–390.

Stavrakakis, Yannis, 2007: *The Lacanian Left: Psychoanalysis, Theory, Politics.* Edinburgh: Edinburgh University Press.

Stavrakakis, Yannis, 1999: *Lacan and the Political.* London and New York: Routledge.

Stavrakakis, Yannis, 1997: "Green Ideology: A Discursive Reading." In *Journal of Political Ideologies.* Vol. 2, No. 3. Pp. 259–279.

Steinmo, Sven, 2005: "The Evolution of the Swedish Model." In Soederberg, Susanne—Menz, Georg—Cerny, Philip (Eds.), *Internalizing Globalization. The Rise of Neoliberalism and the Decline of National Varieties of Capitalism.* Basingstoke: Palgrave Macmillan. Pp. 56–73.

Stephens, John D., 1996: "The Scandinavian Welfare States: Achievements, Crises and Prospects." In Esping-Andersen, Gøsta (Ed.), *Welfare States in Transition: National Adaptions in Global Economies.* London: Sage. Pp. 32–65.

Stevensson, Lois and Lundström, Anders, 2000: "Dressing the Emperor: The Fabric of Entrepreneurship Policy." In Audretsch, David B.—Grilo, Isabek—Thurik, Roy A. (Eds.), *Handbook of Research on Entrepreneurship Policy.* Cheltenham: Edward Elgar. Pp. 94–129.

Steyert, Chris and Katz, Jerome, 2004: "Reclaiming the Space of Entrepreneurship in Society: Geographical, Discursive and Social Dimensions." In *Entrepreneurship & Regional Development.* Vol. 16, May. Pp. 179–196.

Stichweh, Rudolf, 2005: *Inklusion und Exklusion. Studium zur Gesellschaftstheorie.* Bielefeld: Transcript-Verlag.

Strauss, Anselm L., 1994: *Grundlagen qualitativer Sozialforschung: Datenanalyse und Theoriebildung in der empirischen und soziologischen Forschung.* München: Wilhelm Fink Verlag.

Svensson, Torsten, 2001: *Marknadsanpassningens Politik. Den Svenska Modellens Förändring 1980–2000.* Uppsala: Uppsala Acta Universitatis.

Swedberg, Richard, 2000: "The Social Science View of Entrepreneurship: Introduction and Practical Implications." In Swedberg, Richard (Ed.), *Entrepreneurship: The Social Science View.* Oxford: Oxford University Press. Pp. 7–44.

Szerszynski, Bronislaw, 1996: "On Knowing What to Do: Environmentalism and the Modern Problematic." In Lash, Scott—Szerszynski, Bronislaw—Wynne, Brian (Eds.), *Risk, Environment and Modernity: Towards a New Ecology.* London: Sage. Pp. 104–137.

Teubner, Günther, 2006: "Rights of Non-humans: Electronic Agents and Animals as New Actors in Politics of Law." In *Journal of Law and Society.* Vol. 33, No. 4. Pp. 497–521.

Thedvall, Renita, 2004: "'Do It Yourself': Making Up the Self-Employed Individual at a Swedish Public Employment Office." In Garsten, Christina and Jacobsson, Kerstin (Eds.), *Learning to Be Employable. New Agendas on Work, Responsibility and Learning in a Globalizing World.* Basingstoke: Palgrave Macmillan. Pp. 131–152.

Thibaud, Paul, 1985: "The Triumph of the Entrepreneur." In *Telos.* No. 64. Summer. Pp. 134–140.

Timonen, Virpi, 2001: "Earning welfare Citizenship: Welfare State Reform in Finland and Sweden. In Taylor-Gooby, Peter (Ed.), *Welfare States under Pressure*. London: SAGE. Pp. 29–52.

Titscher, Stefan—Wodak, Ruth—Meyer, Michael—Vetter, Eva, 1998: *Methoden der Textanalyse*. Opladen: Westdeutscher Verlag.

Torfing, Jacob, 2005: "Discourse Theory: Achievements, Arguments and Challenges." In Howarth, David and Torfing, Jacob (Eds.), *Discourse Theory in European Politics: Identity, Policy and Governance*. Basingstoke: Palgrave Macmillan. Pp. 1–32.

Torfing, Jacob, 1999a: *New Theories of Discourse: Laclau, Mouffe and Žižek*. Oxford: Blackwell.

Torfing, Jacob, 1999b: "Towards a Schumpeterian Workfare Postnational Regime: Path-Shaping and Path-Dependency in Danish Welfare State Reform." In *Economy and Society*. Vol. 28, No. 3. Pp. 369–402.

Trubek, David and Mosher, James S., 2003: "New Governance, Employment Policy, and the European Social Model." In Zeitlin, Jonathan and Trubek, David M. (Eds.), *Governing Work and Welfare in a New Economy*. Oxford: Oxford University Press. Pp. 33–58.

Tsoukas, Haridimos, 1993: "Analogical Reasoning and Knowledge Generation in Organization Theory." In *Organization Studies*. Vol. 14, No. 3. Pp. 323–346.

Van Dijk, Teun A., 1985: "Semantic Discourse Analysis." In Van Dijk, Teun, A. (Ed.), *Handbook of Discourse Analysis: Vol II: Dimensions of Discourse*. Academic Press: London. Pp. 103–136.

Viehöver, Willy, 2003: "Die Wissenschaft und die Wiederverzauberung des sublunaren Raumes. Der Klimadiskurs im Licht der narrativen Diskursanalyse." In Keller, Rainer—Hirseland, Andreas—Schneider, Werner—Viehöver, Willy (Eds.), *Handbuch Sozialwissenschaftliche Diskursanalyse. Band II: Forschungspraxis*. Opladen: Leske + Budrich. Pp. 233–267.

Viehöver, Willy, 2001: "Diskurse als Narrationen." In Keller, Rainer—Hirseland, Andreas—Schneider, Werner—Viehöver, Willy (Eds.), *Handbuch Sozialwissenschaftliche Diskursanalyse. Band I: Theorien und Methoden*. Opladen: Leske + Budrich. Pp. 177–206.

Von Mises, Ludwig, 1980b: *Planning for Freedom and Sixteen Other Essays*. South Holland, IL: Libertarian Press.

Von Mises, Ludwig, 1980a: *Nationalökonomie: Theorie des Handelns und Wirtschaftens*. München: Philosophia Verlag.

von Schmidtchen, Dieter, 1995: "Unternehmertum, Wettbewerb und Evolution: Anmerkungen zu Helmut Arndts Theorie der Wirtschaftsentwicklung." In *Jahresbuch für Nationalökonomie und Statistik*. Vol. 214, No. 5. Stuttgart: G. Fischer Verlag.

Weber, Max, 2006: *Die protestantische Ethik und der Geist des Kapitalismus*. München: Beck.

Weber, Max, 1949: "Objectivity in Social Science and Social Policy." In Shils, Edward A. and Finch, Henry A. (Eds.), *The Methodology of the Social Science*. New York: Free Press. Pp. 49–112.

Williams, Raymond, 1977: *Marxism and Literature*. Oxford: Oxford University Press.

Žižek, Slavoj, 1997: *The Plaque of Fantasies*. London: Verso.

Žižek, Slavoj, 1995: *Looking Awry: An Introduction to Jacques Lacan through Popular Culture*. Cambridge, MA: MIT Press.

Žižek, Slavoj, 1994a: *The Metastases of Enjoyment*. London: Verso.

Žižek, Slavoj, 1994b: "The Spectre of Ideology." In Žižek, Slavoj (Ed.), *Mapping Ideology*. London: Verso. Pp. 1–33.

Žižek, Slavoj, 1993: *Tarrying with the Negative. Kant, Hegel, and the Critique of Ideology.* Durham, NC: Duke University Press.
Žižek, Slavoj, 1991a: *For They Do Not Know What They Do. Enjoyment as a Political Factor.* London: Verso.
Žižek, Slavoj, 1991b: "The Truth Arises from Misrecognition." In Ragland-Sullivan, Ellie and Bracher, Mark (Eds.), *Lacan and the Subject of Language.* New York and London: Routledge. Pp. 188–212.
Žižek, Slavoj, 1990: "Beyond Discourse Analysis." In Laclau, Ernesto (Ed.), *New Reflections of the Revolution of our Time.* London: Verso. Pp. 249–260.
Žižek, Slavoj, 1989: *The Sublime Object of Ideology.* London: Verso.

Primary Literature

Reports from Public Agencies

ESO-Report. 2001: "Mycket Väsen för Lite Ull—En ESO-Rapport om Partnerskapen i de Regionala Tillväxtavtalen." Department Report. Finance Department. Accessed March 6, 2009. http://www.regeringen.se/content/1/c6/03/62/89/1b4f50a7.pdf.
NUTEK, 2009: "Kommunal Entreprenörs- och Teknikskola—KomTek." Accessed April 9, 2009. www.nutek.se/sb/d/232.
NUTEK, 2007: "Framtidens Företagande—Om Social Företagande och Utanförskap." Author: Carlberg, Adam. Accessed April 20, 2009. http://publikationer.tillvaxtverket.se.
NUTEK, 2005: "Vem Vill Bli Företagare? Attityder till Företagande i Sverige 2004." R2005: 2. Accessed March 6, 2009. http://publikationer.tillvaxtverket.se.
NUTEK, 2003a: "Ett Starkt Entreprenörskap—Policyskrift om Nya Perspektiv, Ändrade Förutsättningar och Positiva Attityder." Accessed March 5, 2009. http://publikationer.tillvaxtverket.se.
NUTEK, 2003b: "Unga Kvinnor och Män, Morgondagens Företagare? En Skrift om Skolans Roll, Regelverkens Betydelse och Vikten av positiva Attituder." Stockholm: NUTEK.
NUTEK. 2002: "Att Ge Kluster Kraft—En Inspirationsskrift till Klustermotorer." Stockholm: NUTEK.
NUTEK, 2001a: "Invandrarnas Företagande i Sverige: Kartläggning och Analys." Stockholm: NUTEK.
NUTEK, 2001b: "På Tillväxt: Kvinnors Ideer om Innovation." Stockholm: NUTEK.
NUTEK. 2001c: "Marginalisering eller Integration: Invandrares Företagande i Svensk Retorik och Praktik." Stockholm: NUTEK.
NUTEK, 1995a: "Att Stimulera Nyföretagandet. Lägesbeskrivning-Utvecklingsriktningar. En Sammanfattande Analys." Stockholm: NUTEK.
NUTEK, 1995b: "Pengarna och Livet." Stockholm: NUTEK.
NUTEK, 1992: "Att Främja Kvinnors Företagande." Stockholm: NUTEK.
NUTEK, 1991: "Att Skapa Livskraft—Förslag för ett Starkt Nyföretagande." Stockholm: NUTEK.
OECD, 2001: "Businesses' Views on Red Tape. Administrative and Regulatory Burdens on Small and Medium-sized Enterprises." Paris: OECD.
Swedish National Rural Development Agency, 1993: "Den Andra Sidan av Myntet: om Regionalpolitikens Enögdhet. en Idéskrift ur Kvinnligt Perspektiv från Glesbygdsmyndigheten.2." Author: Friberg, Tora. Östersund: Glesbygdsmyndigheten.

Government and Department Documents:

Department Reports (Departementsserie; DS):

Department of Industry, 1991: "Småföretag Ger Tillväxt: en Skrift från Industride-partement om Regeringens Småföretagspolitik." Stockholm: Fritzes.

Department Report, 2004: 36: "Innovativa Sverige: En Strategi för Tillväxt genom Förnyelse." Näringsdepartement. Stockholm: Fritzes.

Department Report, 2003: 62: "Benchmarking av Näringspolitiken 2003—Sverige i ett Internationellt Perspektiv." Näringsdepartement. Stockholm: Fritzes.

Department Report, 2003: 43: "Rapport om Tillväxtavtalen, Tredje Året—Från Tillväxtavtal till Tillväxtprogram." Stockholm: Fritzes.

Department Report, 2002: 47: "Kompetensförsörjning på Arbetsmarknaden—Strategiska Utvecklingstendenser." Stockholm: Fritzes.

Department Report, 2001: 15: "Rapport om Tillväxtavtalen—Första Året." Stock-holm: Näringsdepartement.

Department Report, 2000: 69: "Alla är Lika Olika. Mångfald i Arbetslivet." Stock-holm: Integrations—och Jämställdhetsdepartement.

Department Report, 2000: 62: "Samverkan mellan Skola och Arbetsliv: Om Möjligheterna med Lärande i Arbete." Stockholm: Utbildningsdepartement.

Department Report, 2000: 7: "Rapport om Tillväxtavtalen: Tillväxt i Hela Sver-ige." Stockholm: Näringsdepartement.

Department Report, 1999: 32: "Utveckling och Delaktighet—Agenda för Närings-departementets Tillväxtpolitik." Stockholm: Näringsdepartement.

Department Report, 1997: 78: "Gymnasieskola i Ständig Utveckling." Stockholm: Utbildningsdepartement.

Department Report, 1997: 3: "I Entreprenörskapets Tecken—En Studie av Skoln-ing i Förnyelse." Johannison, Bengt and Madsén, Torsten (Eds.). Stockholm: Närings—och Handelsdepartementet.

Department Report, 1995: 14: "Företagsstödet. Vad Kostar der Egentligen?" A Report from ESO: Expertgruppen för Studier i Offentlig Ekonomi. Stockholm: Fritzes.

Department Report, 1994: 35: "Agenda 2000: Kunskap och Kompetens för Nästa Århundrade." Stockholm: Utbildningsdepartement.

Department Report, 1991: 60: "Småföretag Ger Tillväxt: En Skrift från Industridepar-tement om Regeringens Småföretagspolitik." Stockholm: Industriedepartement.

Government Bills (Regeringens Propositioner)

Government Bill, 2005/06: 100: "Års Ekonomiska Vårproposition." Accessed April 11, 2009. http://www.riksdagen.se/webbnav/index.aspx?nid=37anddok_id=GT03100.

Government Bill, 2004/05: 175: "Från IT-Politik för Samhället till Politik för IT-Samhället." Accessed April 3, 2009. http://www.riksdagen.se/webbnav/index.aspx?nid=37anddok_id=GS03175d2.

Government Bill, 2004/05: 1: "Budgetpropositionen för 2005." Stockholm: Finansdepartement. Accessed March 29, 2009. http://www.regeringen.se/sb/d/108/a/29744.

Government Bill, 2004/5:2. "MaktattBestämma—RätttillVälfärd." AccessedAugust17, 2008. http://www.riksdagen.se/webbnav/index.aspx?nid=37anddok_id=GS032.

Government Bill, 2003/04: 1: "Utbildning och Universitetsforskning." Supple-ment 16. Accessed January 7, 2009. http://www.riksdagen.se/webbnav/index.aspx?nid=37anddok_id=GR031d19.

Government Bill, 2001/02: 100: "2002 Års Ekonomiska Vårproposition." Stock-holm: Finansdepartement. Accessed February 17, 2009. http://www.regeringen.se/sb/d/108.

Government Bill, 2001/02: 7: "Regional Samverkan och Statlig Länsförvaltning." Accessed January 7, 2009. http://www.riksdagen.se/webbnav/index. aspx?nid=37anddok_id=GP037.
Government Bill, 2001/02: 4: "En Politik för Tillväxt och Livskraft i Hela Landet." Accessed October 20, 2008. http://www.riksdagen.se/webbnav/index. aspx?nid=37anddok_id=GP034.
Government Bill, 2001/02: 2: "FoU och Samverkan i Innovationssystemet." Accessed April 2, 2009. http://www.riksdagen.se/webbnav/index. aspx?nid=37anddok_id=GP032.
Government Bill, 2000/01: 72: "Vuxnas Lärande och Utvecklingen av Vuxenutbildningen." Accessed January 8, 2009. http://www.riksdagen.se/webbnav/ index.aspx?nid=37anddok_id=GO0372.
Government Bill, 2000/01: 1: "Utbildning och Universitetsforskning." Supplement 16. Accessed January 8, 2009. http://www.riksdagen.se/webbnav/index. aspx?nid=37anddok_id=GO031D22.
Government Bill, 1999/00: 140: "Konkurrenspolitik för Förnyelse och Mångfald." Accessed January 17, 2009. http://www.riksdagen.se/webbnav/index.aspxsok= &rm=1999%2F2000&doktyp=prop&titel=&bet=&tempbet=&datum=&tom =&nr=140&org=&sort=rel&nid=20019&a=s#sokaaff.
Government Bill, 1999/00: 1: "Budgetpropositionen för 2000." Accessed February 2, 2010. http://www.riksdagen.se/webbnav/index.aspx?nid=37&dok_id=GN031.
Government Bill, 1998/99: 115: "På Ungdomars Villkor Ungdomspolitik för Demokrati, Rättvisa och Framtidstro." Accessed January 10, 2009. http://www. riksdagen.se/webbnav/index.aspx?nid=37&dok_id=GM03115.
Government Bill, 1998/99: 1: "Budgetpropositionen för 1999." Accessed December 12, 2008. http://www.riksdagen.se/webbnav/index.aspx?nid=37anddok_id=GM031D18.
Government Bill, 1997/98: 62: "Regional Tillväxt- För Arbete och Välfärd." Accessed January 10, 2009. http://www.riksdagen.se/webbnav/index. aspx?nid=37&dok_id=GL0362.
Government Bill, 1997/98: 16: "Sverige, Framtiden och Mångfalden: Från Invandrarpolitik till Integrationspolitik." Accessed December 3, 2008. http://www. riksdagen.se/webbnav/index.aspx?nid=37&dok_id=GL0316.
Government Bill, 1997/98: 1: "Budgetpropositionen för 1998." Accessed January 10, 2009. http://www.riksdagen.se/webbnav/index. aspx?nid=37&dok_id=GL031D19.
Government Bill, 1996/97: 150: "1997 Års Ekonomiska Vårproposition." Accessed November 27, 2008. http://www.riksdagen.se/webbnav/index. aspx?nid=37&dok_id=GK03150.
Government Bill, 1996/97: 45: "Lättnad i Ägarbeskattningen i Små och Medelstora Företag." Accessed December 6, 2008. http://www.riksdagen.se/webbnav/index.aspx?nid=37&dok_id=GK0345.
Government Bill, 1996/97: 36: "Den Regionala Samhällsorganisationen." Accessed November 18, 2008. http://www.riksdagen.se/webbnav/index. aspx?nid=37&dok_id=GK0336.
Government Bill, 1995/96: 222: "Vissa Åtgärder för att Halvera Arbetslösheten till År 2000." Accessed March 11, 2009. http://www.riksdagen.se/webbnav/index. aspx?nid=37&dok_id=GJ03222.
Government Bill, 1995/96: 207: "En Ekonomisk Politik för att Halvera den Öppna Arbetslösheten till År 2000." Accessed March 11, 2009. http://www.riksdagen. se/webbnav/index.aspx?nid=37&dok_id=GJ03207.
Government Bill, 1995/96: 206: "Vissa Skolfrågor m.m." Accessed March 10, 2009. http://www.riksdagen.se/webbnav/index.aspx?nid=37&dok_id=GJ03206.
Government Bill, 1995/96: 145: "Kvalificerad Yrkesutbildning m.m." Accessed January 13, 2009. http://www.riksdagen.se/webbnav/index. aspx?nid=37&dok_id=GJ03145.

Government Bill, 1995/96: 25: "En politik för Arbete, Trygghet och Utveckling." Accessed November 16, 2008. http://www.riksdagen.se/webbnav/index. aspx?nid=37&dok_id=GJ0325.

Government Bill, 1994/95: 218: "En Effektivare Arbetsmarknadspolitik m.m." Accessed November 6, 2008. http://www.riksdagen.se/webbnav/index. aspx?nid=37&dok_id=GI03218.

Government Bill, 1994/95: 161: "Regionalpolitik." Accessed October 28, 2008. http://www.riksdagen.se/webbnav/index.aspx?nid=37&dok_id=GI03161.

Government Bill, 1994/95: 150: "Förslag till Slutlig Reglering av Statsbudgeten för Budgetåret 1995/96, m.m." Accessed October 20, 2008. http://www.riksdagen. se/webbnav/index.aspx?nid=37&dok_id=GI03150.

Government Bill, 1994/95: 100: "Förslag till statsbudget för budgetåret 1995/96." Accessed October 20, 2008. http://www.riksdagen.se/webbnav/index. aspx?nid=37&dok_id=GI03100.

Government Bill, 1994/95: 16: "Den Framtida Konsumentpolitiken." Accessed October 20, 2008. http://www.riksdagen.se/webbnav/index.aspx?nid=37&dok_id=GI0316.

Government Bill, 1993/94: 147: "Jämställdhetspolitiken: Delad makt—Delat Ansvar." Accessed October 22, 2008. http://www.riksdagen.se/webbnav/index. aspx?nid=37&dok_id=GH03147.

Government Bill, 1993/94: 140: "Bygder och Regioner i Utveckling." Accessed October 22, 2008. http://www.riksdagen.se/webbnav/index.aspx?nid=37&dok_id=GH03140.

Government Bill, 1993/94: 40: "Småföretagsutveckling." Accessed October 22, 2008. http://www.riksdagen.se/webbnav/index.aspx?nid=37&dok_id=GH0340.

Government Bill, 1992/93: 82: "Kapital för Nya Företag m.m." Accessed October 22, 2008. http://www.riksdagen.se/webbnav/index.aspx?nid=37&dok_id=GG0382.

Government Bill, 1992/93: 56: "Ny Konkurrenslagstiftning." Accessed October 21, 2008. http://www.riksdagen.se/webbnav/index.aspx?nid=37&dok_id=GG0356.

Government Bill, 1991/92: 60: "Om Skattepolitik för Tillväxt." Accessed October 23, 2008. http://www.riksdagen.se/webbnav/index.aspx?nid=37&dok_id=GF0360.

Government Bill, 1991/92: 51: "Om en Ny Småföretagspolitik." Accessed October 23, 2008. http://www.riksdagen.se/webbnav/index.aspx?nid=37&dok_id=GF0351.

Government Bill, 1991/92: 38: "Inriktningen av den Ekonomiska Politiken." Accessed October 23, 2008. http://www.riksdagen.se/webbnav/index. aspx?nid=37&dok_id=GF0338.

Government Bill, 1990/91: 150: "Med Förslag till Slutlig Reglering av Statsbudgeten för Budgetåret 1991/92, m.m. (Kompletteringsproposition)." Accessed October 23, 2008. http://www.riksdagen.se/webbnav/index.aspx?nid=37&dok_id=GE03150.

Government Bill, 1990/91: 100: "Med Förslag till Statsbudget för Budgetåret 1991/92." Accessed October 23, 2008. http://www.riksdagen.se/webbnav/index. aspx?nid=37&dok_id=GE03100.

Government Bill, 1990/91: 87: "Om Näringspolitik för Tillväxt." Accessed October 23, 2008. http://www.riksdagen.se/debatt/visadok. aspx?spec=visa_stort_dokument&dokid=GE0387.

Government Bill, 1989/90: 88: "Om Vissa Näringspolitiska Frågor." Accessed October 23, 2008. http://www.riksdagen.se/debatt/visadok. aspx?spec=visa_stort_dokument&dokid=GD0388.

Government Communications (Regeringens Skrivelse)

Government Communication, 2004/05: 48: "Regeringens Handlingsprogram för Minskad Administration för Företagen m.m." Accessed March 11, 2009. http:// www.riksdagen.se/webbnav/index.aspx?nid=37&dok_id=GS0348.

Government Communication, 2003/04: 129: "En Svensk Strategi för Hållbar Utveckling." Accessed March 11, 2009. http://www.riksdagen.se/webbnav/index.aspx?nid=37&dok_id=GR03129.

Government Communication, 2002/03: 8: "Regeringens Redogörelse för Regelförenklingsarbetet med Särskild Inriktning på Små Företag." Accessed, March 4, 2009. http://www.riksdagen.se/webbnav/index.aspx?nid=37&dok_id=GQ038.

Government Communication, 2001/02: 188: "Utbildning för Kunskap och Jämlikhet." Accessed March 4, 2009. http://www.riksdagen.se/webbnav/index.aspx?nid=37&dok_id=GP03188.

Government Communication, 2001/02: 172: "Nationell Strategi för Hållbar Utveckling." Accessed April 10, 2009. http://www.riksdagen.se/webbnav/index.aspx?nid=37&dok_id=GI0322.

Government Communication, 1996/97: 112: "Utvecklingsplan för Förskola, Skola och Vuxenutbildning Kvalitet och Likvärdighet." Accessed January 16, 2009. http://www.riksdagen.se/webbnav/index.aspx?nid=37&dok_id=GK03112.

Government Communication, 1996/97: 83: "Sverige och den Inre Marknaden." Accessed January 8, 2009. http://www.riksdagen.se/webbnav/index.aspx?nid=37&dok_id=GK0383.

Government Communication, 1996/97: 41: "Jämställdhetspolitiken." Accessed January 13, 2009. http://www.riksdagen.se/webbnav/index.aspx?nid=37&dok_id=GK0341.

Government Communication, 1994/95: 22: "Redogörelse för Regeringens Avregleringsarbete under Period September 1991-September 1994." Accessed October 28, 2008. http://www.riksdagen.se/webbnav/index.aspx?nid=37&dok_id=GI0322.

Government Communication, 1990/91: 50: "Om Åtgärder för att Stabilisera Ekonomin och Begränsa Tillväxten av de Offentliga Utgifterna." Accessed October 28, 2008. http://www.riksdagen.se/webbnav/index.aspx?nid=37&dok_id=GE0350.

Memorandum (Betänkande):

Memorandum, 2002/3: NU7: "Vissa Näringspolitiska Frågor." Accessed March 11, 2009. http://www.riksdagen.se/webbnav/index.aspx?nid=3322&dok_id=GQ01NU7.

Memorandum, 2002/03: FiU20: "Riktlinjer för den Ekonomiska Politiken och Budgetpolitiken." Accessed March 11, 2009. http://www.riksdagen.se/webbnav/index.aspx?nid=3322&dok_id=GQ01FIU20.

Memorandum, 2001/2: NU4: "En Politik för Tillväxt och Livskraft i Hela Landet." Accessed March 11, 2009. http://www.riksdagen.se/webbnav/index.aspx?nid=3322&dok_id=GP01NU4.

Memorandum, 2000/01: NU2: "Utgiftsområde 19 Regional Utjämning och Utveckling." Accessed March 11, 2009. http://www.riksdagen.se/webbnav/index.aspx?nid=3322&dok_id=GO01NU2.

Memorandum, 1996/97: NU1: "Anslag inom Utgiftsområde 24 Näringsliv." Accessed December 6, 2008. http://www.riksdagen.se/webbnav/index.aspx?nid=3322&dok_id=GK01NU1.

Memorandum, 1994/95: FiU20: "Den Ekonomiska Politiken och Slutlig Budgetreglering för Budgetåret 1995/96." Accessed October 21, 2008. http://www.riksdagen.se/webbnav/index.aspx?nid=3322&dok_id=GI01FiU20.

Memorandum, 1992/93: BoU17: "Länsstyrelserna. m.m." Accessed October 19, 2008. http://www.riksdagen.se/webbnav/index.aspx?nid=3322&dok_id=GG01BoU17.

Memorandum, 1991/92: FiU30: "Den Ekonomiska Politiken och Slutlig Budge-tréglering för Budgetåret 1992/93." Accessed October 19, 2008. http://www.riksdagen.se/webbnav/index.aspx?nid=3322&dok_id=GF01FiU30.

Documents from the Swedish Parliament:

Answers to Written Questions:

Answer to Written Question, 2003/04: 1037: "Av Anne Ludvigsson (S) till Näringsminister Leif Pagrotsky om Kvinnors Forskning och Innovationer." Accessed April 6, 2009. http://www.riksdagen.se/webbnav/index.aspx?nid=67&dok_id=GR111037.
Answer to Written Question, 2001/02: 1259: "Margareta Cederfelt (M) till Näringsminister Björn Rosengren om Nyföretagandet." Accessed April 6, 2009. http://www.riksdagen.se/webbnav/index.aspx?nid=67&dok_id=GP111259.

Motion (Riksdagens Motioner):

Motion, 2002/03: Fi17: Fi17: "Med Anledning av Prop.2002/03:100, 2003 Års Ekonomiska Vårproposition." Maud Olofsson, Centre Party. Accessed April 4, 2009. http://www.riksdagen.se/webbnav/index.aspx?nid=410&dok_id=GQ02Fi17.
Motion, 2002/03: Fi15: "Med Anledning av Prop.2002/03:100, 2003 Års Ekonomiska Vårproposition." Lars Leijonborg m.fl., Liberal Party. Accessed April 6, 2009. http://www.riksdagen.se/webbnav/index.aspx?nid=410&dok_id=GQ02Fi15.
Motion, 2001/02: N369: "Kompetensutveckling av Ensamföretagare." Hans Stenberg and Agneta Lundberg. Social Democratic Party. Accessed April 6, 2009. http://www.riksdagen.se/webbnav/index.aspx?nid=410&dok_id=GQ02N369.
Motion, 2000/1: Ub260: "En Kunskapsnation i Världsklass." Bo Lundgren. Conservative Party. Accessed April 1, 2009. http://www.riksdagen.se/webbnav/index.aspx?nid=410&dok_id=GO02Ub260.
Motion, 2000/01: N385: "Landsbygdens Möjligheter." Bo Lundgren. Conservative Party. Accessed April 1, 2009. http://www.riksdagen.se/webbnav/index.aspx?nid=410&dok_id=GO02N385.
Motion, 1999/2000: N340: "Den Framtida Regionalpolitiken." Per Westerberg. Conservative Party. Accessed April 1, 2009. http://www.riksdagen.se/webbnav/index.aspx?nid=410&dok_id=GN02N340.
Motion, 1996/97: N242: "Innovationsklimatet." Ola Rask et al. Social Democratic, Liberal, Conservative, and Christ Democratic Party. Accessed December 12, 2008. http://www.riksdagen.se/webbnav/index.aspx?nid=410&dok_id=GK02N242.
Motion, 1994/95: A52: "Med Anledning av Prop.1994/95:218, En effektivare arbetsmarknadspolitik m.m." Carl Bildt et al. Conservative Party. Accessed November 28, 2008." http://www.riksdagen.se/webbnav/index.aspx?nid=410&dok_id=GI02A52.
Motion, 1993/94: Fi208: "Framtid för Sverige." Invar Carlsson et al. Social Democratic Party. Accessed December 10, 2008. http://www.riksdagen.se/webbnav/index.aspx?nid=410&dok_id=GH02Fi208.
Motion, 1993/94: A254: "Full Sysselsättning." Invar Carlsson et al. Social Democratic Party. Accessed December 10, 2008. http://www.riksdagen.se/webbnav/index.aspx?nid=410&dok_id=GH02A254.
Motion, 1993/94: A56. "Med Anledning av Prop.1993/94:140, Bygder och Regioner i Utveckling." Invar Carlsson et al. Social Democratic Party.

Accessed December 10, 2008. http://www.riksdagen.se/webbnav/index. aspx?nid=410&dok_id=GH02A56.

Motion, 1991/92: A805. "Kvinnors Livssituation." Karin Starrin and Ingbritt Irhammar Centre Party. Accessed November 16, 2008. http://www.riksdagen. se/webbnav/index.aspx?nid=410&dok_id=GF02A805.

Motion, 1991/92: A435. "Kvinnornas Framtid i Skogslänen." Inger Hestvik et al. Social Democratic Party. Accessed November 16, 2008. http://www.riksdagen. se/webbnav/index.aspx?nid=410&dok_id=GF02A435.

Motion, 1990/91: N355. "De Regionala utvecklingsfonderna m.m." Börje Hörnlund et al. Centre Party. Accessed November 17, 2008. http://www.riksdagen. se/webbnav/index.aspx?nid=410&dok_id=GE02N355.

Parliamentary Minutes (Riksdagens Protokoll):

Parliamentary Minutes, 2004/05: 79: "Riksdagens Protokoll." Friday, February 18, 2005. Accessed April 3, 2009. http://www.riksdagen.se/webbnav/index. aspx?nid=101&bet=2004/05:79.

Parliamentary Minutes, 2003/04: 121: "Riksdagens Protokoll." Tuesday, May 25, 2004. Accessed April 3, 2009. http://www.riksdagen.se/webbnav/index. aspx?nid=101&bet=2003/04:121.

Parliamentary Minutes, 2003/04: 96: "Riksdagens Protokoll." Thursday, April 15, 2004. Accessed April 5, 2009. http://www.riksdagen.se/webbnav/index. aspx?nid=101&bet=2003/04:96.

Parliamentary Minutes, 2003/04: 51: "Riksdagens Protokoll." Wednesday, December 17, 2003. Accessed April 3, 2009. http://www.riksdagen.se/webbnav/index. aspx?nid=101&bet=2003/04:51.

Parliamentary Minutes, 2003/04: 14: "Riksdagens Protokoll." Thursday, October 16, 2003. Accessed April 3, 2009. http://www.riksdagen.se/webbnav/index. aspx?nid=101&bet=2003/04:14.

Parliamentary Minutes, 2003/04: 13: "Riksdagens Protokoll." Wednesday, October 15, 2003. Accessed April 3, 2009. http://www.riksdagen.se/webbnav/index. aspx?nid=101&bet=2003/04:13.

Parliamentary Minutes, 2003/04: 12: "Riksdagens Protokoll." Tuesday, October 14, 2003. Accessed April 10, 2009. http://www.riksdagen.se/webbnav/index. aspx?nid=101&bet=2003/04:12.

Parliamentary Minutes, 2003/04: 2: "Riksdagens Protokoll." Tuesday, October 14, 2003. Accessed April 3, 2009. 12http://www.riksdagen.se/webbnav/index. aspx?nid=101&bet=2003/04:12.

Parliamentary Minutes, 2001/02: 103: "Riksdagens Protokoll." Friday, April 26, 2002. Accessed April 2, 2009. http://www.riksdagen.se/webbnav/index. aspx?nid=101&bet=2001/02:103.

Parliamentary Minutes, 2000/1: 45: "Riksdagens Protokoll." Tuesday, December 12, 2000. Accessed April 2, 2009. http://www.riksdagen.se/webbnav/index. aspx?nid=101&bet=2000/01:45.

Parliamentary Minutes, 1999/00: 92: "Riksdagens Protokoll." Wednesday, April 5, 2000. Accessed April 2, 2009. http://www.riksdagen.se/webbnav/index. aspx?nid=101&bet=1999/2000:92.

Parliamentary Minutes, 1997/98: 74: "Riksdagens Protokoll." Wednesday, March 4, 1998. Accessed April 2, 2009. http://www.riksdagen.se/webbnav/index. aspx?nid=101&bet=1997/98:74.

Parliamentary Minutes, 1997/98: 62: "Riksdagens Protokoll." Thursday, February 5, 1998. Accessed April 2, 2009. http://www.riksdagen.se/webbnav/index. aspx?nid=101&bet=1997/98:62.

Parliamentary Minutes, 1995/96: 74: "Riksdagens Protokoll." Friday, March 22, 1996. Accessed April 18, 2009. http://www.riksdagen.se/webbnav/index.aspx?nid=101&bet=1995/96:74.
Parliamentary Minutes, 1994/95: 120: "Riksdagens Protokoll." Wednesday, June 14, 1995. Accessed April 18, 2009. http://www.riksdagen.se/webbnav/index. aspx?nid=101&bet=1994/95:120.
Parliamentary Minutes, 1994/95: 106: "Riksdagens Protokoll." Tuesday, May 16, 1995. Accessed April 18, 2009. http://www.riksdagen.se/webbnav/index. aspx?nid=101&bet=1994/95:106.
Parliamentary Minutes, 1991/92: 6: "Riksdagens Protokoll." Friday, October 4, 1991. Accessed October 18, 2008. http://www.riksdagen.se/webbnav/index. aspx?nid=101&bet=1991/92:6.

Reports from Parliamentary Commitees (SOU):

SOU, 2003: 123: *Utvecklingskraft för Hållbar Välfärd.* Stockholm: Fritzes. (http://www.regeringen.se/sb/d/108/a/1535).
SOU, 2001: 44: *Jämställdhet—Transporter och IT.* Stockholm: Fritzes. (http://naring.regeringen.se/propositioner_mm/sou/pdf/sou2001_44.pdf).
SOU, 2000: 87: *Regionalpolitiska Utredningens Slutbetänkande.* Stockholm: Fritzes. (http://www.regeringen.se/sb/d/108/a/2324).
SOU, 2000: 28: *Kunskapsbygget 2000—Det Livslånga Lärandet. En Sammanfattning av Kunskapslyftskommitténs Slutbetänkande.* Stockholm: Fritzes. (http://www.regeringen.se/content/1/c4/12/41/e1599e2b.pdf).
SOU, 2000: 19: *Från Dubbla Spår till Elevhälsa.* Stockholm: Fritzes. (http://www. regeringen.se/sb/d/108).
SOU, 1999: 141: *Från Kunskapslyftet till en Strategi för Livslångt Lärande.* Stockholm: Fritzes. (http://www.regeringen.se/sb/d/108).
SOU, 1999: 93: Det *Unga Folkstyret. Demokratiutredningens Forskarvolym VI.* Stockholm: Fritzes. (http://www.regeringen.se/sb/d/108).
SOU, 1999: 49: *Invandrare som Företagare—För lika Möjligheter och Ökad Tillväxt.* Stockholm: Fritzes. (http://www.regeringen.se/sb/d/108).
SOU, 1998: 51: Vuxenutbildning och Livslångt Lärande—Inför och Under det Första Året med *Kunskapslyftet.* Stockholm: Fritzes. (http://www.regeringen.se/sb/d/108).
SOU, 1998: 6: *Ty Makten Är Din.* . . . Stockholm: Fritzes. (http://www.regeringen. se/sb/d/108).
SOU, 1997: 186: *Bättre och Enklare Regler.* Stockholm: Fritzes. (http://www. regeringen.se/sb/d/108).
SOU, 1997: 121: *Skolfrågor—Om Skola i en Ny Tid.* Stockholm: Fritzes. (http:// www.regeringen.se/sb/d/108).
SOU, 1997: 87: *Kvinnor, Män och Inkomster—Jämställdhet och Oberoende.* Stockholm: Fritzes. (http://www.regeringen.se/sb/d/108).
SOU, 1997: 40: *Unga och Arbete.* Stockholm: Fritzes. (http://www.regeringen.se/sb/d/108).
SOU, 1996: 55: *Vägar in i Sverige. Invandrarpolitiska Kommittens Slutbetänkande:* Sverige, Framtiden och Mångfalden. Stockholm: Fritzes.
SOU, 1996: 34: *Aktiv Arbetsmarknadspolitik.* Stockholm: Fritzes.
SOU, 1996: 27: *En Strategi för Kunskapslyft och Livslångt Lärande. Delbetänkande från Kommittén om ett Nationellt Kunskapslyft för Vuxna.* Stockholm: Fritzes.
SOU, 1996: 4: *Vem Bestämmer Vad?: EU:s Interna Spelregler inför Regeringskonferensen 1996: En Rapport.* Stockholm: Fritzes.

SOU, 1995: 27: *Regional Framtid: Slutbetänkande av Regionberedningen.* Stockholm: Fritzes.

SOU, 1993: 70: *Strategi för Småföretagsutveckling.* Stockholm: Allmänna Förlaget.

SOU, 1993: 16: *Nya Villkor för Ekonomi och Politik: Ekonomikommissionens Förslag.* Stockholm: Allmänna Förlaget.

SOU, 1991: 104: *Konkurrensen inom den Kommulana Sektorn.* Stockholm: Allmänna Förlaget.

SOU, 1991: 82: *Arbetsorganisation och Produktivitet.* Stockholm: Allmänna Förlaget.

SOU, 1991: 59: *Konkurrens för Ökad Välfärd: Huvudbetänkande.* Stockholm: Allmänna Förlaget.

SOU, 1991: 28: *Konkurrensen i Sverige. en Kartläggning av Konkurrensförhållandena i 61 Branscher: En Rapport till Konkurrenskommittén.* Stockholm: Allmänna Förlaget.

Reports from Political Parties and Organizations:

Conservative Party and Liberal Party, 1991: *Ny Start för Sverige.* Stockholm: Moderata Samlingspartiet and Folkpartiet Liberalerna.

Conservative Party, 1994: *Handlingsprogram Moderaterna.* Stockholm: Moderata Samlingspartiet.

Green Party, 2002: *Partiprogram Miljöpartiet de Gröna.* Stockholm: Miljöpartiet de Gröna.

Green Party, 2000: "Framtidens Bygdebalans för Regionalpolitik och Landsbygdsutveckling." *Report*, No. 1/2000. Stockholm: Miljöpartiet de Gröna.

Social Democratic Party (SDP), 2002: *Partiprogram för Socialdemokraterna: Antaget vid Partikongressen 2001.* Stockholm: Sveriges Socialdemokratiska Arbetareparti.

Social Democratic Party (SDP), 1994: "Näringspolitik för Tillväxt." In *Vårt Alternativ*, No.5. Stockholm: Sveriges Socialdemokratiska Arbetareparti.

Social Democratic Party (SDP), 1992: *Analysgruppens Rapport.* Sveriges Socialdemokratiska Arbetareparti.

Index